The Irrational Executive
Psychoanalytic Explorations in Management

THE IRRATIONAL EXECUTIVE

PSYCHOANALYTIC EXPLORATIONS IN MANAGEMENT

Edited by

Manfred F. R. Kets de Vries

INTERNATIONAL UNIVERSITIES PRESS, INC.

Madison   Connecticut

Library of Congress Cataloging in Publication Data
   Main entry under title:

The Irrational executive.

   Bibliography: p.
   Includes index.
   1. Executives—Psychology—Addresses, essays,
lectures. 2. Organizational behavior—Addresses,
essays, lectures. 3. Psychology, Industrial—
Addresses, essays, lectures. 4. Psychoanalysis—
Addresses, essays, lectures. I. Kets de Vries,
Manfred F. R. [DNLM: 1. Psychoanalytic theory.
2. Organization and administration. 3. Leadership.
WM 460.5.M2 I71]
HF5500.2.I73   1982   658.4′094′019   83-229
ISBN 0-8236-2925-2

Third Printing, 1986

Manufactured in the United States of America

TO: M.D.

Contents

Acknowledgments

I gratefully acknowledge the permission of the authors to reprint their work. I would also like to thank Ted and Eva Lazarus, Murray Palevsky, and Jill de Villafranca for their editorial assistance, and to express my special appreciation to Dr. Sidney Perzow of the Argyle Institute for his many invaluable comments. My gratitude goes to Martin Azarian, President of International Universities Press, for supporting this most unusual venture for his publishing house. Olga Boroweckyj was most helpful not only in deciphering my handwritten material, but also in having the patience to keep on retyping the manuscript. Finally, I would like to thank my wife Elisabet not only for her editorial assistance, but also for her cheerful encouragement of my efforts.

Contributors

TOBIAS BROCHER, M.D., is Director of the Center for Applied Behavioral Sciences, The Menninger Foundation, Topeka, Kansas, and a practicing psychoanalyst.

WILLIAM E. HENRY, PH.D., is Emeritus Professor of Psychology and Human Development, University of Chicago.

ELLIOTT JAQUES, M.D., PH.D., is Head of the School of Social Sciences, Brunel University, England, and a practicing psychoanalyst.

MANFRED F. R. KETS DE VRIES, Econ. Drs., D.B.A., is Professor of Organizational Behavior and Management Policy, McGill University, Montreal, Canada, and a practicing psychoanalyst.

OTTO KERNBERG, M.D., is Medical Director of the New York Hospital-Cornell Medical Center, Professor of Psychiatry, Cornell Medical College, and a practicing psychoanalyst.

LAWRENCE S. KUBIE, M.D. (deceased), was Director of Training of the Sheppard and Enoch Pratt Hospital, Maryland, and a practicing psychoanalyst.

DOUGLAS LABIER, PH.D., is Senior Fellow of the Project on Technology, Work and Character, Washington, D.C., faculty member of the Washington School of Psychiatry, and a practicing psychoanalyst.

JEAN-PAUL LARÇON, Doctorat (3ᵉ cycle), is Associate Professor, Management Policy Centre d'Enseignement Supérieur des Affaires, Jouy-en-Josas, France, and Director of the Centre d'Enseignement et de Recherches Appliquées de Management at CERAM.

HARRY LEVINSON, PH.D., is President of the Levinson Institute, Cambridge, Massachusetts.

MICHAEL MACCOBY, PH.D., is Director of the Program on Technology, Public Policy and Human Development of the Kennedy School of Government, Harvard University, Director of the Project on Technology, Work and Character, Washington, D.C., and a practicing psychoanalyst.

ISABEL E. P. MENZIES, M.A., is a senior staff member at the Tavistock Institute of Human Relations, London, England, and a practicing psychoanalyst.

ROLAND REITTER, D.B.A., is Associate Professor of Management Policy and Director of the Doctoral Program at the Centre d'Enseignement Supérieur des Affaires, Jouy-en-Josas, France.

LOUIS WEINBAUM, ED.D., is a clinical psychologist in private practice.

ABRAHAM ZALEZNIK, D.C.S., is Cahners-Rabb Professor of Social Psychology of Management, Harvard University, Graduate School of Business Administration, Cambridge, Massachusetts, and a practicing psychoanalyst.

Introduction

At present there exists a wide range of systems and theories aimed at explaining the interactions of individuals and groups within organizations, and the functioning of organizations themselves. The contingency models and middle-range theories that have emerged in increasing number in recent years can be seen as predictable reactions to the inadequacies of the universalistic model of organizational rationality that has for so long dominated the field. But even these more modest and probably more realistic attempts at explaining organizational phenomena have left undiminished the pervasive sense of dissatisfaction and impotence that practitioners of management theory feel in their desire to understand and affect organizational functioning.

One way of explaining this persistent situation of discontent is by pointing out the continuing importance of the notion of rationality in management theory. The term occurs over and over again in the literature on the subject. The presumption is that organizational actions are logical and sensible, that the organization effectively and efficiently allocates its resources and pursues its goals. Thus it appears that, in spite of Herbert Simon's popularization[1] of the concept of "bounded" rationality as characterizing administrative behavior—implying that there are limits to individuals' perceptual and information processes—economic man continues to survive in management literature. The notion of the idealized, completely rational decision maker, comparable to the classical *homo economicus* of economic theory, living in a world of optimal choices, has never really been abandoned. It appears

---

[1]Simon, H. A. (1945), *Administrative Behavior*. New York: Free Press.

that most management theorists, like the economists before them, have been reluctant to go beyond the directly observable and pay attention to the determining effects of intrapsychic processes on individual motivation. Instead, for the sake of simplicity, they have assumed man's rationality as implicit in their models. And by taking man, in all his complexity, out of their conceptual frameworks, they have created a one-dimensional view of man.

As a result, behavioristic models and idealized, oversimplified conceptions of human nature predominate in these theories. Findings from the clinical encounter in psychoanalysis, psychiatry, and family therapy have been relatively neglected, viewed as appropriate only to the mentally ill and therefore as inapplicable to individuals functioning in organizations. Not surprisingly, the price for conceptual elegance has been a decline in realism, contributing to the often striking discrepancies in organizational functioning between planned action and actual outcome. Happily, some recent changes in orientation can be observed. The current surge of publications on organizational stress marks a shift from the image of organizational man as rational decision maker.

Organizations are not directed by a *deus ex machina* preoccupied with mere performance quotas. On the contrary, organizations are made up of individuals each of whom brings his own unique personality to bear on decision-making processes. Inevitably, the framing of decisions by individuals, given the complexity of individual personalities and the intricacies of group interaction, causes distortions. These distortions can only be explained by focusing on intrapsychic phenomena—by studying the internal workings of the mind. In short, the myth of organizational rationality needs to be reexamined in the context of what is known about the role of the unconscious in human motivation and its impact on decision making. The comprehension of a level of functioning beyond observable reality becomes the connecting link in our understanding of otherwise puzzling organizational phenomena. And if, from what is known about unconscious processes, deviations from rational action are inevitable, *explanations* of them can be given in terms of our knowledge of precisely these unconscious processes. Such understanding not only has diagnostic advantages, it also sets the stage for more effective implementation, making the need for a psychodynamic paradigm in organizational studies even more evident.[2]

The current volume brings together articles by both leading, analytically oriented management theorists and clinicians interested in organizations. The impetus for this book came from a conference on applied psychoanalysis in organizations held in Austria in the summer of 1980. During the course of the meeting it became apparent that although important work was being done in various parts of the world bringing a more clinical orientation to organizational analysis, much of the work was scattered throughout the literature, published in highly diverse journals aimed at dissimilar audiences. This situation of fragmentation suggested the need for a synthesis of existing work.

The book is divided into three sections. Section I, "The Irrational Executive," demonstrates the extent to which irrational action is common in organizational life and discusses the forces that bring it about. In Section II, "Theoretical Considerations," the issues discussed in Section I are systematically elaborated in theoretical terms. The emphasis is on the interface of the individual with the organization, with the focus shifting from one element of that relationship to the other and finally to the reciprocal influence of each on the other. Section III, "Effecting Change," provides examples of organizational diagnosis and the change process, highlighted by a number of extensive case analyses.

Section I begins with an article by LaBier describing the relationship between irrational processes and career development in the federal government, behavior patterns which would apply to many business organizations as well. He explores degrees of congruence between individual and organization, paying particular attention to the conditions leading to symptom formation.

---

[2]For an elaboration of this point of view see Manfred F. R. Kets de Vries and Danny Miller, *The Invisible Hand: Hidden Forces in Organizations* (In press).

The author emphasizes that the absence of symptoms does not necessarily reflect an absence of pathology. He gives as an example the "irrational adaptives," individuals whose deeply irrational passions are adaptive for their work roles. He then suggests that organizations have a primary responsibility in encouraging and strengthening the development of these pathological wishes.

The question of pathological character structure and irrational behavior in organizations is further developed in Kernberg's study of hospital administration in Chapter 2. A number of diagnostic recommendations concerning the origin of organizational conflict are presented, after which Kernberg describes the schizoid, obsessive, paranoid, and narcissistic leadership styles and explores their impact on the organization. In his examination of leadership, Kernberg pays particular attention to the regressive pressures on the administrator, suggesting that the ideal administrator reflects the regressive fantasies of groups and individuals. The question of pathology at work is further elaborated in Chapter 3, where I present a typology of various work disorders. In the analysis of work behavior, specific attention is paid to the management of aggression and to the role of narcissism. The influence of inner- or outer-directed aggression on work patterns is suggested.

In contrast to the previous chapters, with their emphasis on organizational and individual psychopathology, Chapter 4 by Henry presents the characteristic traits of successful managers. This theme is then taken up by Maccoby in Chapter 5 and Zaleznik in Chapter 6, with the former developing a typology of managers found in the corporation, and the latter presenting two contrasting leadership styles. Maccoby expresses concern that the demands of corporate life may lead to the development of qualities of the "head" and not of the "heart," with emotional impoverishment the result. He views the rise of the "gamesman" type of executive in corporate life as an ominous sign to the extent that, for this type of executive, winning is all that counts; attributes such as courage, compassion, generosity, and idealism are discouraged.

Zaleznik continues in a similar vein in Chapter 6, placing in juxtaposition the charismatic and consensus leader. He views the latter as the prevailing leadership style in both the large corporation and in politics. In his comparison, he is apprehensive about the consensus leader's lack of commitment to deeply held convictions, which results in a style characterized by indirection and manipulation. In explaining the differences between these two styles, Zaleznik contrasts the shadowy, unstable, incompletely integrated introjects of the consensus leader to the strong benevolent ones of the charismatic leader. In his view, the charismatic leader combines a capacity for delay with the ability to act and move assertively, and possesses a strong commitment to ideals.

Levinson in Chapter 7 develops the theme of irrationality in executive behavior, but shifts the discussion from leadership style to a focus on a specific executive problem, the role of anger and guilt in organizational life. He demonstrates how much difficulty executives have in dealing with their own anger and that of others. He indicates how efforts to appease the superego and the denial of anger can lead to irrational decision making. These irrational interaction patterns come even more to the fore in Chapter 8 where I explore the disastrous consequences of excessive dependency of superiors and subordinates on each other. The dynamics of folie à deux are clarified, and a number of case vignettes demonstrate how executives can lose touch with the immediate reality of the organization's environment to the detriment of organizational functioning. The article ends with a number of suggestions about the identification and prevention of this dysfunctional interaction process.

In the last three papers of this section, the focus is on the career conflicts of organization members. In Chapter 9, Kubie discusses the unconscious forces which determine choice of career, indicating how these forces can distort the creative process and lead to irrational action. Jaques (Chapter 10) reviews the human life cycle, using a Kleinian perspective that focuses on the midlife crisis. The author draws attention to a sudden jump in the death rate between the ages of thirty-five and thirty-nine among creative individuals. He describes the transformations which take place in the mode of work at that time, which necessitate a re-working at midlife of the depressive position. In his opinion, this process is set in motion with the realization of the imminence of one's own death. In the concluding article of this section, Zaleznik (Chapter 11) examines the manner in which political leaders and managers deal with disappointment in their careers, using a number of case vignettes to support his suggestions about ways of coping with this crisis.

Section II begins with an article by Levinson and Weinbaum (Chapter 12) on individual adaptation to the organization. The authors suggest that maladaptation arises from three kinds of anxiety: ego anxiety, id anxiety, and superego anxiety. After exploring these various forms of anxiety, Levinson and Weinbaum discuss their view of the ego ideal as the determining agent in organizational identification, which is itself a factor contributing to the psychological equilibrium of the individual. In Chapter 13 Levinson further explores the individual-environment relationship, introducing transference in an organizational context. He argues that transference reactions are not only directed to individuals but also to organizations. Individuals, in his opinion, will attribute to organizations human qualities which will subsequently affect their own behavior. He then continues with a discussion of the dynamics of reciprocation, referring to the psychological contract between individual and organization, a contract that is crucial for the maintenance of psychological equilibrium, growth, and mastery.

Zaleznik and Kets de Vries in Chapter 14 shift the emphasis from the influence of the organization on its members to the individual's effect on the organization. They focus on distribution of authority, management control, and executive action, using as an illustration a study of management succession at Sears Roebuck. A psychopolitical approach to executive action is provided, resulting in the postulation of a number of organizational strategies. A view of the reciprocal influence of individual and organization on each other is provided by Zaleznik in Chapter 15. Taking the exercise of power as the central factor in his model,

Zaleznik looks at organizations as political structures preoccupied with the economics of scarcity and propelled by the organizational participants' drive for power. His problem-solving approach to organizational structure suggests that structure is an instrument rather than an end, that it expresses a working coalition attached to the chief executive officer, and that it is a product of negotiation and compromise among executives with different power bases.

Using a somewhat similar reciprocal influence point of view, Larçon and Reitter in Chapter 16 introduce the concepts of corporate imagery and corporate identity, discussing management theory's preoccupation with organizations as value-coordinated systems and dealing with the question of organizational mythology. They postulate the existence of a corporate identity comparable to individual personality, and suggest how this identity influences corporate development. They describe how the image of the organization is the result of the individual employee's previous history and his working life in the company, the latter largely influenced by political power in the organizational context. The interaction between individual and organization is a continuously evolving process. From these images of the organizational participants, a collective corporate identity emerges, manifested in myth, rituals, and taboos. Using as an example the development of a furniture company in France, the authors suggest that an organization's adaptive capability is to a large extent determined by its identity and by its employees' image of the organization.

The final section of the book, "Effecting Change," begins with an article by Levinson (Chapter 17) discussing organizational development and organizational diagnosis. He is strongly in favor of diagnosis and warns—giving a number of case examples—of the potentially destructive consequences of organizational development programs which rely too heavily on ad hoc problem-solving efforts and expedient techniques. He offers instead a five-step diagnostic frame of reference, emphasizing that an effective consultant needs training both in clinical as well as in organizational dimensions. The theme of the diagnosis of organizations is continued by Brocher in Chapter 18. He deplores the extent to which psychoanalysis and psychiatry have concentrated on individual treatment without paying sufficient attention to societal problems; his particular concern here is with the effects of organizations on individuals. In his opinion, diagnostic advances can only be made using a multidisciplinary approach. As an aid in organizational diagnosis, the author provides a frame of reference describing four identifiable functions in organizations (i.e., formal group leadership, the critical opponent, the majority of followers, and the weakest part of the organization) and describes the nature of the relationships of each with the others.

In Chapter 19 Menzies presents a thorough example of organizational diagnosis. Using a Kleinian frame of reference, she analyzes the nursing service of a general hospital, concentrating on the causes and effects of anxiety in social systems. She illustrates defensive techniques such as splitting, depersonalization, and denial as they are used in organizations to diffuse emerging anxiety feelings. She then discusses the consequences of such action, both for the individual and the organization. A bridge from diagnosis to the actual effort to effect change is provided by Maccoby in Chapter 20. He views psychoanalysis as a form of participant study. Just as in psychoanalysis, effective change in organizations can only take place through the analysis of resistances made possible by a willingness to engage in self-exploration. Continuing this theme in Chapter 21, Maccoby illustrates the socio-psychoanalytic approach with a work-change effort at an automobile mirror factory where the objective was to create an American model of industrial democracy. He explains the program's emphasis on individuation, the stimulation of the fullest possible development of each individual's creative potential in the organization. The study shows how the identification of six character types made it possible to explain key differences in attitudes and reactions to work and its goals. The author suggests that this typology was of great help in reducing potential conflict between management and workers, in improving the work environment, and in leading to the development of different kinds of educational programs tailored to the needs of the various groups, thereby stimulating human development.

The book ends with a classic case description of change from the management literature of the early fifties. Jaques again adopts a Kleinian point of view to describe the changes which took place in the relationships between management and worker in the Glacier Metal Company, an engineering factory in England. He highlights how unconscious systems of defense against depressive and paranoid anxiety caused resistances to social change, and, in commenting on the social change process in general, argues that to make change possible readjustments are needed at the level of fantasy.

The Irrational Executive is designed to be a reference source for management theorists, clinicians, consultants, and management practitioners interested in more realistic ways of diagnosing organizations and more effective ways of instituting change. It should also serve as a catalyst for the further development of the clinical orientation in management theory, thereby helping to restore man to his proper role in our understanding of human organizations.

Manfred F. R. Kets de Vries

Section I
The Irrational Executive

In this clinical study of employees of the federal government, LaBier tests the hypothesis that some work organizations may force people into irrational and pathological behavior. He describes how various human passions may interact with work in the bureaucracy to produce either congruence (no symptoms) or incongruence (symptoms), and he explores the conditions that lead to symptom formation. He cites case vignettes to illustrate four types of symptoms. His formulations should provide a basis for further exploration of the relationship between bureaucratic work and irrational passions in private firms as well as in government organizations, and lead to increased understanding of such concepts as job stress and job satisfaction for people who work in large organizations.

1

Irrational Behavior in Bureaucracy

D O U G L A S   L A B I E R

Can work and career development in the federal government interact with the forces of human character in ways which stimulate psychopathology? What are the implications of this interaction, both for the organization and the management of work, and for the treatment of disturbed individuals who work within the federal government or in similar bureaucracies? This paper reports some findings from an exploratory socio-psychoanalytic study of the above questions, and suggests some areas for further investigation.

A central question addressed in this study is how irrational, unconscious, and pathological passions may be aroused by, interact with, and strengthened by work within the federal gov-

This chapter is a shortened version of an article to appear in *Administration and Society*. By permission of the author.

ernment. It is hypothesized that some work organizations may push people into psychopathology. Symptoms of psychopathology, however, are not necessarily visible in some work environments. Moreover, symptoms that do appear in the context of work do not necessarily reflect pathological passions and attitudes.

The present research was developed to test these hypotheses through clinical study of patients and non-patients who work for departments and agencies of the U.S. Government in the Washington, D.C. area.

METHODOLOGY

The theoretical basis of the research is the socio-psychoanalytic formulations about social and individual character developed over the past forty years by Erich Fromm. It employs some of the principles of socio-psychoanalytic research methodology developed by Fromm and Maccoby (1970) and Maccoby (1976, 1981).

Such methodology involves intensive study of individual and social character in relation to organizational adaptation. The study is based upon (1) intensive interviews which explore attitudes and views about past and present work and career, political and religious beliefs, and personal philosophy; (2) the analysis of dreams, particularly those relating to work; (3) thematic interpretation of Rorschach Tests; and (4) other clinical material obtained through interviews or psychiatric treatment.

Since the research was exploratory, clinical study of individuals was relied on to a greater extent than the more usual combination of both clinical study of individuals and sociological study of work roles and structure. This latter would have constituted the more comprehensive socio-psychoanalytic project of the kind undertaken by Fromm and Maccoby (1970) and Maccoby (1976, 1981). That is, part of the socio-psychoanalytic method involves study of the requirements of different kinds of work and roles, in relation to the types of character found within the roles. Ideally, one determines what character traits and attitudes are required by key roles in the organization. Not all of the people occupying key roles were studied in the present research, but, rather, a sample of both key roles and relevant clinical material.

Themes were interpreted from all of the material obtained from the various parts of the methodology. Consistent with the principle of participant research (see Maccoby, Chapter 20), these themes were discussed with the individuals whenever possible. In some cases, themes were confirmed and further clarified through such dialogue. In other cases, discussion occurred in the context of clinical evaluation or treatment of the individual, in which particular themes were verified by clinical evidence.

Mention should be made here of the use of the Rorschach Test in this research, since elements of Rorschach methodology and interpretation are controversial. The Rorschach was employed in this research as a means of helping to understand and illuminate unconscious attitudes, passions, and dynamic forces of character. The method used was that developed by Maccoby (Fromm and Maccoby, 1970; Maccoby, 1976) as a supplement to the interpretive questionnaire/interview in order to aid in the interpretation and diagnosis of character. This methodology combines the traditional formal analysis of Rorschach responses with interpretation of their symbolic content.

Traditional interpretation of the Rorschach is based upon analysis of localizations, the form, color, shape, shading, and movement determinants of responses, and the perceptual accuracy of responses. These are used for the diagnosis of pathology (Rorschach, 1942; Klopfer et al., 1954; Beck et al., 1961). Others, however, particularly Schafer (1954) and Schachtel (1966), have worked upon the development of character interpretation from the Rorschach in terms of psychoanalytic theory.

Based upon these various contributions, Maccoby developed a method of character interpretation which combines analysis of formal aspects of responses with symbolic analysis of content, movement, and color. This allows an uncovering of unconscious impulses, needs, dynamic character traits, modes of relatedness, etc. In addition, the methodology includes analysis of sequence of perceptions with respect to how certain attitudes or wishes may provoke anxiety, guilt, rage, etc.

This method is experiential, in that it requires seeing things through the eyes of the individual; feeling what determines his or her response. Responses are viewed as projections of the individual's own character attitudes. A detailed description of the development and utilization of this methodology is presented in Fromm and Maccoby (1970). In addition, Fromm (1951) has discussed the experiential method of understanding with reference to dreams and symbolism.

It should also be pointed out that this exploratory study was not limited just to a study of psychotherapy patients who work within the federal government bureaucracy. Such a sample would have been biased and unrepresentative of government employees as a whole, most of whom, one assumes, are not patients in psychotherapy or psychoanalysis. Thus, the individuals studied include people who have been patients as well as those who have not.

They are from lower, middle, and upper levels of work and management of ten organizations of the federal government. They include managers and non-managers; men and women. They consist of people both with and without professional training, and their work covers a range of responsibilities: administrative, scientific, technical, legal, policy-making, legislative, regulatory, etc.

DEVELOPMENT OF THE RESEARCH

The research began with a case study of my own patients in relation to the hypotheses described above. The hypotheses were explored through systematic examination of clinical material in relation to the potential role of the patients' work and career in the development or maintenance of their emotional problems.

Since I work in Washington, D.C., a large number of my patients work within the federal bureaucracy. This is the case for most practitioners in the Washington area. In Washington, the government—Cabinet-level departments, other agencies, the Senate, House of Representatives, and Executive Office of the

President, as well as the various international organizations such as the World Bank—constitute the largest "industry" of the metropolitan area. Whether for reasons of sheer number, or because government work contributes to emotional disturbance, a large number of consumers of therapy in Washington work for government organizations.

An opportunity then arose to study federal workers who were not patients when I was called in as a consultant to one large federal department on the problem of how to understand and respond to employees who seemed to be suffering from a wide range of emotional disturbance on the job. This department was extremely diverse in its scope of activities, and thus presented a cross section of types of work performed in government, such as described above. I was asked to explore possible sources of the apparent emotional disturbance, both in terms of the individuals and in terms of work and management.

The U.S. Government is of particular interest to one who wishes to study the relationship between psychopathology and work. It is the most developed and massive bureaucratic structure in our society, and thus provides an opportunity for investigating the relationship between psychopathology and bureaucracy on a fully developed scale. Also, there is growing public concern about the efficiency of, and the problems within, the work and leadership of the federal bureaucracy. Since the government formulates public policy and carries out programs which affect the full range of our society, such concern is well founded. Questions have been raised, for example, as to whether there is something inherent to the federal system that creates apathy, alienation, and ineffective appraisal/reward systems for its employees. Such questions as these added to the relevance of an exploration of how bureaucratic work interacts with character in ways which generate psychopathology.

The first objective was to understand the symptoms of all the disturbed individuals in terms of both the person's overall character, as interpreted from the material obtained, and the nature of his or her work in the bureaucracy. A study of (1) the individuals employed by the federal department to which I was consultant (conducted with their consent); (2) a study of my own patients; and (3) an initial study of the psychostructure of the work organizations revealed three types of situations in which people showed specific symptoms of emotional disturbance:

1. A small number showed evidence of major, long-standing disturbance, which had developed, in most cases, prior to their entry into government employment. These people, though deeply disturbed, somehow maintained their employment. Often this was achieved with the help of managers who routinely reassigned their work to others and/or shunted them from one supervisor to another.

2. A larger number of people showed symptoms of neurotic conflict in their work situation, and yet had achieved at least moderate success in their careers to date. For many, success in work stood in contrast to disturbance, frustration, and unhappiness in their intimate relations or in their judgments of themselves. These people, one might say, were reasonably successful in matters of the head, but were troubled in matters of the heart, which showed itself at work.[1]

3. A third group of people who showed symptoms of emotional disturbance on the job were those whose emotional attitudes were found to be within the normal range of character. While they showed some pathological tendencies, these were relatively mild, and did not account for the overt signs of disturbance that occurred in the work setting.

It became immediately apparent that the three situations in which people showed symptoms at work presented a complicated and paradoxical picture. To help clarify this, and to balance the picture created by the fact that both the patients and the troubled employees would be considered disturbed individuals, I decided to compare them with a group of people who showed no disturbance at work. These people were successful in their work and career development, and appeared quite well-adjusted. They had never shown signs of emotional disturbance at work.

---

[1]Editor's note: For more on the role of the "head" and the "heart" in career success, see Maccoby (Chapter 5).

Study of such people was expected to help clarify what the differences are between those who develop psychiatric symptoms and those who do not, and why bureaucracy affects different kinds of people in ways that lead to disturbance for some, but successful adaptation for others. This comparison group of "normals" constituted about 25 percent of the total sample studied.

Based upon the Fromm-Maccoby thesis, one would not necessarily expect to find differences between those who develop overt psychiatric symptoms on the job, and those who do not. One would, according to this thesis, have to analyze the situation in relation to the dynamic character forces of the individuals in order to explain one's observations.

Study of these people, who were both symptom-free and successful in their careers, revealed that a number of them were dominated by such irrational attitudes as extreme destructiveness, pursuit of power and glory, insatiable greed, and desire to return to the womb—all of which one would expect to find in people who were *overtly* troubled. Yet they did not show symptoms of their pathological passions in their daily work. This finding is consistent with the Fromm-Maccoby thesis. It raises the question of whether there is something about their work which feeds pathological attitudes and makes them adaptive to the requirements of their work and career success.

The data supported Maccoby's (1980) contention that one must look beyond the presence or absence of symptoms per se, and toward understanding the meaning of symptoms in relation to the forces of human character and the experience of bureaucratic work situations. It became necessary to analyze how work within the government bureaucracy interacts with pathological passions to result in overt symptoms for some people but not others, *regardless* of whether or not the person is truly disturbed.

CONGRUENCE AND INCONGRUENCE BETWEEN WORK AND CHARACTER

Previous research has shown that individuals with certain character traits or tendencies are often attracted to certain kinds of work or organizational structures to which these traits are suited (Maccoby, 1976). Once the person is within the organization, the latter begins to selectively reinforce certain qualities of head and heart which best fit the needs and roles required by the position and the organization.

The findings of the present research lead to the interpretation that specific irrational attitudes, combined with certain intellectual talents, are adaptive to the requirements of particular roles within the federal bureaucracy. This constitutes one major category of individuals studied.

Here, one finds an absence of symptoms, whether the person's passions are predominantly pathological or within the normal range of character. Within this latter group, healthy tendencies predominate, although, like most successful careerists, the individuals lack developed hearts. The former group is dominated by pathological tendencies, but show no symptoms of emotional disorder at work, though some, of course, may show symptoms in their intimate relations, outside of work.

One also finds, in contrast, a second major category of individuals: those who are non-adaptive. The passions and overall character of these people are not adaptive to the role requirements of the organization, whether their passions are irrational or within the normal range. In such circumstances, symptoms of emotional disturbance appear at work.

This formulation of how various human passions may interact with work in the federal bureaucracy to produce either congruence (no symptoms) or incongruence (symptoms) is described more fully below in brief case illustrations.

SITUATIONS OF CONGRUENCE

There are two types of individuals who are congruent with work: the Irrational Adaptives and the Normal Positives. Both groups are adaptive, although the former is predominantly pathological, and the latter predominantly normal. One might raise the question of how both pathological and normal people can be adaptive to the requirements of work. The answer lies in the observation that some roles call more for irrational attitudes than other roles. For example, some roles require more interdependence and particular technical skills, such as auditing. One tends to find people within the normal range of character within and adaptive to such roles.

On the other hand, certain roles are more likely to select out and support the development of irrational passions. These include various "power positions" found throughout government, such as policy formulation and administrative positions, or positions of assistant to Presidentially appointed administrators. Since the goal in such roles is often to dominate, scare, or intimidate subordinates and push programs through quickly, one finds the more pathological people adaptive to such roles.

The Irrational Adaptives

These people show deeply irrational attitudes of two types: (1) lust for power and glory, desire to subjugate and/or destroy others, and greed for personal gain; or (2) passive dependency, desire to return to the womb, and submission to masochistic humiliation.

These attitudes have been systematically rewarded, strengthened, and supported by career advancement and increasing influence within the organization. Although the passions of these individuals are pathological, they are nevertheless adaptive. They have contributed to the person's success at work, particularly if the person is bright and competent.

These people are largely found among those who have arrived at, or are clearly moving into, the middle and upper levels of their organizations. One observes, for the first type, that entry into and success within the highest levels of management, work, and policy-making requires, in many cases, a more pathological extreme of the kind of character described by Maccoby (1976) as the jungle fighter.

Psychologically, the jungle fighter seeks power and domina-

tion over others. He may employ seduction, betrayal, or manipulation to reach the top. Jungle fighters usually show exploitative,
narcissistic, sadistic, and authoritarian tendencies, although they
differ in their degree of emotional maturity.

A recent study of work and management in a major federal
department (Maccoby et al., 1980) shows that such people are
often selected as top-level managers by Presidential appointees
of federal departments and agencies. This is because the appointees, even those who accept appointments with good intentions
and a sense of public service, serve for a relatively brief period
of time, and are under significant political pressure. This leads
them to select jungle fighter types as their top managers, because
of the need to get something done quickly.

An environment which requires the more extreme traits of
the jungle fighter for success feeds the development of deeply
irrational passions, and may push the person "over the edge." As
pointed out above, such passions might be masked by their adap-
tiveness to the work.

For the sample studied, it appears that at the highest levels
of the bureaucracy what is valued most is the ability to appear
and act tough; to put others down and humiliate them; to constantly test others; and to produce a flurry of activity upon demand—a memo, decisive talk at meetings, "firefighting," etc. All
of this appears to be supported and fed, to a great extent, by the
need of the appointed officials immediately above them to create
and push through programs within a short period of time. As one
Presidential appointee stated, "What I look for in a top manager
is someone who knows how to kick ass."

The atmosphere created is one in which the aim is to create
the appearance that something important and powerful is being
done.[2] But one finds, in some settings, that there is little substance
or consequence to all the activity; that is, in many of these higher
levels of management and administration one finds a very busy,

[2]In an interview in *Fortune* (Jan. 29, 1979), former U.S. Treasury Secretary Michael
Blumenthal pointed out that the bottom line in government is not profit, but appearance
and prestige.

demanding, highly charged environment of doing, talking, analyzing, and report writing. Of course, some of this action does affect many employees; for example, a directive to eliminate a certain number of positions in one part of an agency, or to reorganize the agency.

However, this atmosphere may also result in activity which has little, if any, substantive meaning. In such cases, it simply provides an opportunity for the blossoming of passions for power and glory-seeking to a pathological degree. For people in whom such passions are fed, job success may actually deepen their pathological attitudes by allowing them to believe, more and more, in their own image of importance and power, and by encouraging them to lose touch with a more realistic perspective of themselves and their situation.

Since the psychostructure of the upper levels of some departments and agencies seems to support such passions and attitudes, the relationship of character to work is congruent, and one does not necessarily observe symptoms in the work setting. One lawyer, who worked within such a setting for three years, observed that:

> The place is very seductive, because they appeal to your desire to be professional and competent and all that. They tell you that you are going to have an important "impact" on things if you stick with it; that you will be well recognized, and, at the same time, you will be doing good, professional work. This is all very enticing, and the next thing you know you're working twenty hours a day, feeling very important, that you're a "rising star." But when you take a good look at things, you see that the work is really not all that important, and that what you're really after is power, exciting power. And it's all crazy, but nobody seems to recognize it.

Thus, these people possess strong pathological tendencies which gradually become dominant within their character, because the tendencies fit, in many cases, what is supported or perhaps required by the work. These tendencies compete with, and gradually overwhelm, other, healthier, tendencies. These people are often very bright and talented in matters of the head, such as strategic thinking, planning, and plotting options. But their talents, which are necessary to the role, are put in the service of getting power and glory.

One finds that their healthier side gradually withers away from disuse. The work does not stimulate or call forth more positive attitudes, such as a sense of public service, genuine caring about people, or interest in creating rational and useful programs, all of which might have been important in bringing them into government in the first place. Instead, the work at this level of the bureaucracy, for the sample studied, starves the good motives and feeds those of sadism and grandiosity.

It should be pointed out here that a majority of the individuals who are described as Irrational Adaptives worked within one federal department. It is possible that one would find a different picture elsewhere in government. On the other hand, as pointed out above, this particular department represents a cross section of the federal bureaucracy as a whole. In addition, some of the individuals from this group did work in other agencies and departments. Thus, some evidence exists to suggest that one would find, with further study, similar individuals throughout much of the federal bureaucracy.

These individuals do not necessarily experience conscious conflict, at least not in the work setting. Often, however, they sense that something is wrong. Analysis of interviews and unconscious material suggests the presence of not only eroticized pursuit of power and narcissistic attitudes, but also feelings of fraudulence, inner emptiness, terror, and self-betrayal.

One example of a person who could be described as an Irrational Adaptive is Ms. A., a thirty-year-old woman who entered the government after dropping out of college. She quickly worked her way into administrative work, and, over the next ten years, rose rapidly through the hierarchy of several agencies. Ms. A. has most recently worked as a special assistant to high-level administrators who wield great power. She is perceived as an aggressive, competent person who is good at "firefighting." She is also viewed as someone who can be alternately seductive and sexy, or hardened and tough.

Her consciously expressed attitudes are that she enjoys power and being in the "inner circle" because it helps in solving administrative problems, and that she prefers working for strong managers who are not afraid of taking decisive action. Deeper exploration of her attitudes and character reveals tremendous lust for power, and hatred of male authority. One interprets themes of inner fury and pursuit of power as a magical solution to vulnerability and helplessness. She uses her emotional sensitivity, which is considerable, to further her acquisition of power over others.

In conflict with these passions, one finds a sense of destroyed femininity (she recently had herself sterilized and divorced her husband), a feeling of being damned and in purgatory. Around the office, she has begun to call herself, jokingly, a "power groupie." She reported a recurring dream of walking down a long, empty corridor in her agency building, and into her office, which is also empty. All she hears is the sound of her footsteps. As she enters her empty office, she feels a combination of satisfaction and vague terror. One may interpret this dream as illustrating the inner sense of emptiness and isolation that has become the emotional and spiritual price for her lust for power.

Another person is Mr. B., a brilliant young social scientist who had been active in the student protest movement in the late 1960's, and who is now a "rising star" in his job for a Committee on Capitol Hill. He reports that he feels, sometimes, like a little boy in a man's world, who may be hit at any moment for being where he shouldn't be. But he dismisses such feelings with a joke, and reports that, usually, he feels tremendously self-confident about his abilities, competency, and importance to the legislative process.

Although he was initially unconfident about his intellectual talents, Mr. B. has become increasingly attracted to the pursuit of glamour and power afforded by his position and work environment. Success and recognition of his work quickly fanned the flames of his narcissistic passions, and, before long, he found himself plotting his way to the top and planning the demise of those who stood in his path. For example, he successfully undermined the work and reputation of his superior, which contributed to the superior's departure. This cleared the way for Mr. B.'s successful pursuit of the position, which gave him more recognition and "visibility."

Inwardly, Mr. B. feels a deep need to be loved and appreciated. Driven in childhood by a demanding and possessive mother, he has developed considerable intellectual powers, with which he has achieved outward success. But this has been at the expense of feeling, unconsciously, that he must do other people's bidding, that he must perform to win applause, and that he has no freedom. These themes may be interpreted from some of his dreams. For example, in one, he presents a memo he has written to an important Senator, and hopes that the Senator won't notice that it is filled with blank pages.

In addition to the people described above, there is the second subtype of Irrational Adaptive, whose emotional attitudes also seem to be adaptive to their work. Cases of this type are found more within the middle levels of the bureaucracy. They are individuals who are pathologically dependent and submissive, rather than grandiose and power-hungry.

How typical this group is of the middle levels of the bureaucracy cannot be determined without further study. From the cases observed, however, one may hypothesize that their pathological tendencies have contributed to success within their middle levels of management. It is possible that, at least in some of these circumstances, the work and relationships with superiors may require submission to irrational authority. Because of their loyalty and adaptability to the middle rungs of the hierarchy, they are sometimes called, within their organizations, successful "ass kissers," as opposed to the "ass kickers" at the higher levels. While their pathological tendencies and overall character differ from the first group of Irrational Adaptives, they, too, show no symptoms at work. Both groups are enamored with power, but in different ways.

For example, one man who illustrates this type, Mr. C., is lonely, anxious, and depressed in his personal life. However, at work he has received rapid promotion and awards for his work as an attorney for a regulatory agency of the government. Now in his mid-thirties, he reports that he works best when he has "good leadership," which, he states, means someone who can guide and direct what is to be done.

However, one may interpret feelings of deep dependency and mother fixation within Mr. C., which lead him to submit himself to humiliation in hopes of obtaining love and support. Despite his considerable emotional sensitivity and compassion, Mr. C. has sought out the protective umbrella of his agency, as well as bosses who willingly tell him what to do and how to do it. Unconsciously, he is resentful and hostile toward rational authority when he experiences it, and seeks attachment to irrational control and domination. One sees evidence for unconscious hostility in, for example, a dream which occurred during psychotherapy, which he had sought because of unhappiness in his intimate relations with women. During a period of treatment in which Mr. C. was analyzing his relationship with his father, towards whom he reported he had always felt "great respect," he reported a dream in which he sees his father floating down a river in a casket, which is loaded with explosives. He awakens, in a cold sweat, at the moment he realizes that he has the detonator device in his hands.

Another dream illustrates Mr. C.'s unconscious awareness of desires which pull him away from health and independence. In this dream he is riding around and around on a ferris wheel. It finally deposits him on the ground, next to a long, dark tunnel. He finds himself drawn into the tunnel by a mysterious force. As he walks along, he hears the sound of the ocean at the other end, beckoning him. At this point he awakens, terrified. Mr. C. said that he thought the ferris wheel represented his deep feelings about work, because it often consists of a lot of activity which goes nowhere. He said that the rest of the dream was frightening, because it meant that there might be something about his career that was sucking him in towards some terrible end. One may interpret here a desire to return to the womb, which Mr. C. knows, unconsciously, is regressive and destructive, yet supported by his work.

One interesting question raised by these cases of Irrational Adaptives is how numerous are such people in the upper and middle levels of government? Are such people found only within particular parts of the bureaucracy, which are, perhaps, not typical of the whole? With regard to those people already studied, it is remarkable that some of them could be so disturbed and yet function as well as they do in an organization.

The Normal Positives

The research indicates a second category of congruence between characterological forces and work, which is found among people who are within the normal range of adaptation. They are, by traditional psychiatric criteria, "normal"; they are without significant pathological tendencies. Although they, like most people, are within the normal, adaptive, range of character they are not "healthy" from the standpoint of full human development. Yet most of them show real inner capacity for development of such qualities of heart as love of life, concern for others, affirmation of truth, etc. But these have not been stimulated or developed by career experiences or daily work; they remain dormant.

The Normal Positives pursue and accept as normal and well-adjusted a desire for a reasonable degree of success, recognition, and security. While they possess some irrational, repressed attitudes, like most people, these are minor. Healthy, adaptive tendencies predominate within their character. Work does not appear to have fed or stimulated their minor unconscious conflicts, though it might, of course, if the work became severely stressful or developed pathological features.

A useful way of understanding the dominant motivations and attitudes of these people is provided by Fromm's (1947) description of the differences between the productive and the unproductive character orientations. The Normal Positives are people in whom the productive orientation is more dominant.

Fromm described productiveness as an attitude or mode of relatedness, rather than as the capacity for material production or outward success. It refers to the use of human powers such as reason, imagination, love, and the ability to understand the sense of things. It is related to Aristotle's description of the "good man" as one who, by activeness and reason, brings to life the potentials of man, and to Spinoza's concept of "virtue" as equivalent to the use of human powers.

The relative weight of the productive and unproductive orientations varies, of course, in each person's character. The person in whom the productive orientation is dominant experiences himself as the "actor"; not alienated from his or her human powers. The productive orientation requires freedom and independence, guided by reason. Since, of course, most people are a mixture of productive and unproductive orientations, one sees the more positive or more negative aspects of the unproductive orientation according to the degree of productiveness in the total character structure.

For example, within the hoarding orientation one may see a range from practicality to unimaginativeness; within the marketing orientation, from open-mindedness to lack of principles. The more positive sides of these orientations would be seen within people whose dominant orientations are more productive.

Such is the case with the Normal Positives. As a group, they have relatively productive attitudes about work and a wide range of intellectual talents. They are stimulated and "turned on" by their work, often more so than by their intimate relations. Certain positive traits, mostly concerning the head, have been rewarded and strengthened by success and career development within their bureaucratic settings. The part of the bureaucracy in which they work appears to fit their character. They seek out stimulation from their work, and are not afraid to leave a job which becomes deadening.

Thus the work environment has stimulated their development,

but within the limits of a system which does not support the development of qualities of the heart. Capacities for development of the heart remain locked up, or have become deadened, by the conditions for success within the bureaucracy. As a consequence, their own personal development, as well as their potential contributions to improving the bureaucracy, are clearly limited.

One example of a Normal Positive is Mr. D., a fifty-year-old man who has risen to the position of director of a major unit of a large agency. Throughout his career he has constantly looked for new opportunities, and seized them, whenever he felt his existing job had become deadening or no longer held possibilities for further career development. Mr. D. radiates a high level of energy, activity, and enthusiasm. He clearly enjoys challenging work, which he approaches with strategic, systems-like thinking. He is open to new ideas of work organization and leadership, particularly those that contribute to team-building and participation, which he values.

Mr. D. shows cooperative working attitudes, and demonstrates a desire to do well. This has required, to a degree, the repression of some negativistic attitudes. Also, he tends to be initially resistant to demands that he perceives are being placed on him. Outwardly, one observes a tendency toward anxious worry and a capacity to become, in a flash, emotionally cool.

One can interpret from the Rorschach that Mr. D. sees himself, unconsciously, as somewhat of an underling—down on his back, looking up at authority. He seeks love and affection, and does not want to be too adversarial in his work relations, perhaps because this might open up some frightening, unresolved conflicts from childhood, such as autonomy vs. guilt, or rebelling vs. performing.

Within Mr. D.'s character are real, but underdeveloped, capacities for love of life, and creative, intellectual, and spiritual development. Yet he keeps his distance, and does not allow himself to become too emotionally aroused. One sees that work has stimulated the productive side of his character. But his heart remains underdeveloped, partly because of his unresolved emotional issues, and partly because his work environment has not supported such development.

In this respect, he is typical of the Normal Positives studied. As a group, they have probably developed as much as they can, given the limited stimulation of the bureaucracy. If more stimulation were to occur, then more development might be possible. In fact, recent experiments to improve work and management in the federal bureaucracy suggest that it is possible, under certain circumstances, for the bureaucracy to provide more opportunities for development of its employees than now exist (Maccoby et al., 1980).

Another Normal Positive is Mr. E. Now in his mid-forties, he originally studied for the ministry, but left when offered a position with a small manufacturing company. He enjoyed business, but eventually entered the federal government, attracted, he says, by the greater security it offered.

Mr. E. worked in various administrative and management capacities for a variety of federal departments and agencies until reaching a second-ranking position in a major unit of a medium-sized agency. He is viewed as a hardworking, productive person, who is particularly competent with detailed kinds of work, and who enjoys facilitating the career development of younger subordinates.

He views himself, consciously, as a man of contrasts: hardworking, but secretly lazy; outgoing, but also a loner; a pragmatic compromiser, yet a man with principles. These consciously felt contrasts reflect a deeper sense of being two people: the outer person, who is hardened to organizational and career realities—an adaptive achiever within the system—and the inner person, who is soft, compassionate, somewhat dependent, and seeking, perhaps, mother's all-accepting love. One can interpret from the Rorschach, for example, that he unconsciously symbolizes himself as a crustacean—hard on the outside, but soft and vulnerable on the inside; and as a body in search of a backbone. One sees some conflict, though not major, between outward aggressiveness and inward subservience and dependency.

Mr. E. is a man with real abilities, who has always been active and productive in his work and career. But he has now come close to giving up. His desire for comfort and for minimizing risks are gradually overtaking his productive capacities for deep conviction, for service to others, and for spontaneity. Career advancement within the federal bureaucracy has required, for him, a gradual hardening of his exterior and a softening of his heart.

SITUATIONAL CHANGE AS A TRIGGER OF SYMPTOMS

The cases presented so far, of Irrational Adaptives and Normal Positives, illustrate the importance of understanding both the character forces of the individual and the requirements of the role and work environment. All these cases illustrate congruence between character and work, which results in the appearance of "normal adjustment," despite the fact that some of the individuals are pathological, while others are within the normal range.

Such congruence or adaptation exists, however, only as long as a balance is maintained between dynamic character forces and the work. An individual who is adaptive to one work situation is not necessarily adaptive to other work situations or roles. In fact, if the situation undergoes either positive or negative change, the resulting incongruence may trigger symptoms where, before, there were none.

The case of Mr. F. illustrates this. Now in his late forties, Mr. F. once had a flourishing, rapidly rising career as a "hatchet man" under a sadistic, self-centered manager who was particularly close with the agency head and who served under appointment of then-President Nixon. With gradual change of leadership in the agency, and, eventually, the development of a more participative and cooperative organizational structure within his part of the agency, Mr. F. began to openly undermine his new superiors, place obstacles in the path of cooperative work efforts, and increasingly demanded recognition for his "vast experience and knowledge." He began to disrupt meetings and to avoid carrying out directives requested by his superiors.

Study of his attitudes and character reveals strong sadomas-ochistic passions, previously adaptive, which have now, in a sense, broken loose. Unconsciously, he seeks a "Godfather" to control and protect him. He had achieved this, in fact, during the earlier, more successful, part of his career. During that time he had sought out a sadistic, vindictive, but protective boss, and thus Mr. F. had been able to function successfully within the organization.

Internally, Mr. F. experiences resentment and rebellion cou-pled with a need to obtain affection through submission. One observes that his sadomasochistic relationship with his father mirrored his later relationships with superiors at work. Infantile and narcissistic attitudes are interpreted from the Rorschach. He is therefore limited in his ability to deal with work that stimulates emotional aliveness or that requires independence of thought. Mr. F. professes deep moral concerns and is quite active in some political issues within his community. But one finds that these concerns are not rooted in any particular principles; rather, they appear motivated by his unconscious resentment of authority and the need to rebel against it. Since Mr. F. works best doing de-tailed, colorless work under a benign Godfather-type boss, his irrational passions have "erupted" under the recent change of leadership and work structure. He now appears openly troubled at work.

Mr. F. is an example of an Irrational Adaptive individual whose passions became incongruent with the new work environment. Because Irrational Adaptives are dominated by pathological ten-dencies which are adaptive to pathological work environments, they begin to show overt symptoms of their underlying pathology when they experience a healthy improvement in the work situ-ation or role requirements.

SITUATIONS OF INCONGRUENCE

The case of Mr. F. indicates that an individual whose irrational passions and attitudes are not congruent with the requirements of work will show psychiatric symptoms in the work setting. Similarly, people who are within the normal range may also develop symptoms at work. However, such people are incongruent with the work and role requirements not because of underlying pathology, but because of their characterological response to an unhealthy work environment, or severe stress within it. These two situations of incongruence, both of which result in the appearance of symptoms at work, are described and illustrated below.

The Irrational Non-Adaptives

By traditional psychiatric criteria, these people are emotionally disturbed, and show symptoms of their disturbance at work. Their passions interact with aspects of the bureaucratic psychostructure in ways which result in the manifestation of psychiatric symptoms in the work setting. The Irrational Non-Adaptives can be divided into two types, depending on the severity of disturbance.

The first type consists of people who show evidence of significant emotional disturbance, which has interfered with their basic relationships and ability to work throughout most of their lives. Relatively few in number, members of this group have typically been hospitalized on one or more occasions, and have long-standing diagnoses of psychotic disturbance. Manifestations of their disturbance at work include gross distortions of reality, inability to comprehend or execute work responsibilities, or severely impaired relations with co-workers.

Understandably, most of these individuals do not rise very high on the career ladder (though some do, which is, itself, an interesting phenomena to study). In some cases, the demands of work, the behavior of superiors, and other external factors combine to trigger new psychotic episodes or to reinforce the depth of existing pathology.

One possible reason for this is that many managers are frightened by these people and avoid confrontation with the reality of the individual's sickness. In such cases, management's action often consists of ignoring the problem completely, while reassigning the person's work to others, and allowing the disturbed individual to continue drawing his or her paycheck. Or, management might continuously reassign the individual to other supervisors, or to other parts of the organization. Some of these people become known as "floaters," who have serious difficulties in whichever setting, or for whomever, they work.

Ms. G., in her late fifties, had worked for the same federal agency for thirty years, in clerical/secretarial positions. She had been diagnosed paranoid schizophrenic many years earlier, and has been hospitalized numerous times over the years. In the course of working for her most recent supervisor, Ms. G. gradually showed increasing outbursts and accusations towards people in her office. Her supervisor later explained that he was fearful that she might attack someone or try to kill herself. Thus, when she became more overtly paranoid about an alleged conspiracy to deny her a deserved promotion to a supergrade level, management responded by shifting her assignment from one supervisor to another, while humoring her about her prospects for promotion. Discussion with management indicated that they undertook this action in the belief that she would soon "settle down." Unfortunately, however, Ms. G. became increasingly disturbed on the job, and eventually had to be hospitalized.

Obviously, a person as disturbed as Ms. G. would probably experience significant difficulties in any job setting. However, one may raise the question of whether her emotional disturbance may have been fed, or intensified, by a work and management environment which virtually ignored and denied her disturbance. Perhaps further deterioration could have been prevented if management had confronted the problem and assisted her in obtaining professional help.

There is a second group of Irrational Non-Adaptives, much larger in number than people like Ms. G., who also show evidence of prior pathology—unconscious conflict rooted in early relationships—but which is not of psychotic proportions. This group shows clear neurotic conflict and symptoms in the job setting.

Their pathological passions, unlike those of the Irrational Adaptives, are not congruent with the work or role requirements, and
therefore one may observe symptoms of their disturbance in the
job setting. Many of them have developed talents of the head,
which have probably contributed to their having achieved reasonable career success in their organizations. But they suffer,
consciously, from anxiety, depression, alienation, destructive desires, etc. This group of people probably forms the bulk of those
federal government employees in Washington who seek psychotherapy and psychoanalysis.

In contrast to the Irrational Adaptives, these people are often
limited by their conflicts from rising to the highest levels of the
bureaucracy. One reason for this difference may be adaptation.
That is, the Non-Adaptives studied show more passive-aggressive,
independently obstinate, and obsessive tendencies, in contrast
to the Adaptives, who show strong sadomasochistic attraction to
power. In effect, the pathological passions of the Irrational Non-
Adaptives may be less adaptive to the work requirements of the
top levels of the bureaucracy. How widespread this situation is
throughout the federal bureaucracy cannot be determined, however, without further study.

One finds that some of the Irrational Non-Adaptives studied,
once they are under the government's umbrella of bureaucratic
vastness, security, and protection, are able to find some niche
within their organization which actually supports or allows an
acting out of their pathology in the work setting. Within the niche,
they experience few demands for productive work or activity that
might threaten their neurotic "balance."

Thus, some find settings in which their internal conflicts can
be acted out with little consequence, either to themselves or to
the organization. This, of course, contributes to keeping the person immobilized with respect to consciously experiencing his or
her problem.

An example of this is seen in the case of Mr. H. Following
graduate school, Mr. H. sought and obtained a position in an
agency with a reputation for inefficiency and for harboring a lot

of "dead wood" among its employees. He is an only child of a harsh, demanding and ambitious mother and a weak father. Consciously, he experiences the narcissistic duality of extreme, grandiose self-evaluation together with feelings of deep inferiority.

Finding reality disappointing and painful, Mr. H. has developed a Walter Mitty-like fantasy world, in which he imagines himself to be an internationally famous writer, a sought-after Romeo, or a popular rock star. In reality his love life is chronically disappointing, largely because he seeks total devotion and instant love from whomever he dates.

At work, he has managed to find a situation in which little work is assigned to, or expected from, him. He spends the bulk of his day talking, reading the paper, and fantasizing. At home, he frequently listens to live recordings of rock singers, and pretends that he is the star receiving the applause. Mr. H. also spends long hours sleeping and masturbating.

Consciously, Mr. H. desires to work more productively and to develop more realistic expectations and mutuality in his relationships. Unconsciously, however, he is filled with rage toward his mother, against whom he rebels by being passive-aggressive, withholding, and inactive in his work. This, he knows, infuriates her. Yet, he seeks her love and domination of him, and feels empty and frightened inside, without any real powers of his own. Themes of rage, impotency, and magical escape are revealed in his dreams, such as one in which he screams at his mother, feels terror, and then finds himself floating in the air, above everyone, and flying away.

Interestingly, Mr. H. shows a more developed heart than many people who are less troubled. He is compassionate and cooperative with others, within the limits of his illness, and he possesses a well-developed sense of humor. He shows enough sense of reality that, if a particular work assignment is important, he responds to the task and performs competently. One may speculate whether Mr. H. might become more motivated to change if his work were more meaningful and stimulating.

Mr. H.'s inner conflicts and work situation seem to have combined to make it very difficult for him to struggle against his pathological passions and develop himself. Many such people struggle for years in analysis or therapy without noticeable progress, because the role of their work in supporting their neuroses is never analyzed. This was the case with Mr. H. In fact, his case suggests that it may be virtually impossible to begin serious struggle to overcome deep problems until the patient develops the courage, with the help of the therapist, to face the truth about work or career as it relates to his pathology. Such truth might include the need for radical change of work if there is to be any hope for healthy development.

The cases of Irrational Non-Adaptive individuals presented thus far include those with psychotic and neurotic disturbances. Of the latter, one observes that some, like Mr. H., show symptoms of their disturbance in the work setting. Perhaps such people have been unable, for reasons of circumstance or of character, to find a work setting to which their pathology would be adaptive, and thus produce no symptoms. Others, like Mr. F., are people whose irrational passions were once adaptive, but had become non-adaptive because of a change in the work situation. One also observes individuals who, at one time, were Irrational Adaptives, but who have become Irrational Non-Adaptives, not because of a change in the work situation, but because of deepening pathology within themselves.

That is, in some cases, the person's irrational passions and attitudes are fed to such an extent that they "overflow" and become noticeable within the very environment which strengthened and masked them to begin with. For example, one man, Mr. I., was driven by intense lust for power and glory. Quite brilliant in his professional work, he had achieved a senior position at a relatively young age in a part of the government that engaged in work related to legislation. Inflated by his success, recognition, and proximity to power and glamour, Mr. I. became increasingly arrogant, frequently humiliated co-workers, and began to voice wildly exaggerated ideas about the importance of his work to national policy. His irrational passions grew to such proportions that, when challenged one day by a colleague about a minor disagreement over something in a report under preparation, Mr. I. physically attacked his colleague, and had to be forcibly subdued. He was removed from the office literally kicking and screaming, and, shortly thereafter, admitted himself to a mental hospital.

Of course, one may say that such a person already possessed pathological tendencies, and that what happened to him may have been the result of some serious stress or problems in his intimate relations, away from work. These factors should, of course, be explored when attempting to understand or help a person like Mr. I. Nevertheless, the case also indicates the potential contribution to emotional disturbance by a work environment which emphasizes and rewards excessive pursuit of power and grandiosity.

The Normal Negatives

This group shows psychiatric symptoms at work, but without any significant underlying pathology. These people are within the normal range of character, like their counterparts, the Normal Positives, described above. However, the Normal Negatives develop symptoms, sometimes in response to situational stress, or to pathological aspects of their career and work environment which, for them, have stimulated the "negative" and unproductive sides of their character.

That is, the Normal Negatives show the more negative aspects of the unproductive orientation (Fromm, 1947), which is more dominant within their character. For example, such traits as loyalty, fairness, authority, and assertiveness in a predominantly productive person turn into submission, dominance, withdrawal and destructiveness in an unproductive person. These latter tendencies are found within the Normal Negatives.

At work they may show a sometimes gradual, sometimes sudden, development or sharpening of whatever irrational passions or unresolved conflicts exist within their character. But they do not show evidence of major pathological tendencies. What one finds are people of a predominantly unproductive orientation, but within the normal range of adaptation.

Like most workers in the bureaucracy, the Normal Negatives have come to expect increasing influence, security, and recognition for their work. But given their overall character, together with, in some cases, deficiencies in training or competence, many have experienced career frustration, lack of recognition, demotion resulting from agency reorganization, or some situational stress. Such experiences appear to have stimulated the negative sides of their character, as well as, for some, their latent, though relatively minor, irrational passions.

So what appears to be serious pathology can be interpreted, within this formulation, as more of a character reaction to stress, frustration, or a pathological work environment. This, in turn, intensifies desire for the goals and values which they have come to accept as normal, such as equating personal worth with one's salary level and position, or expecting automatic recognition for their work. In cases where the work environment improves or the stress is removed, the symptoms fade.

One could describe these people as *troubled*, but not really *sick*. Their work experience has stimulated in them such responses as rebellious attitudes towards authority, holding out for love and affection from management, paranoid attitudes, hostile or non-cooperative attitudes, etc.

Certain tendencies may be strengthened over others, depending on the bureaucratic requirements. For example, in certain parts of the federal bureaucracy workers experience a situation which causes them to "top out" at a high salary and position level by the time they are around thirty years old. They cannot go further up the career ladder in their forseeable future. The bureaucracy fosters, in this setting, an attitude of paranoid competitiveness for "good" assignments among people who really need to be cooperative, given the nature of the tasks. Those people who choose to remain in such settings often develop destructive, suspicious, or undermining attitudes, alcoholic problems, or passive laziness, all to the dismay of upper management.

As one worker stated:

> The problem is not so much the work itself, but the situation, in which we are forced to claw like animals to get the goodies, the choice assignments, instead of working together, as we should be doing. It's either that, or you become burned out, collect your fat pay check, and drink a lot at lunch. So either way, this situation makes us all act a little nuts.

Whether such situations are common, or found only in isolated circumstances, requires further study. But the fact that they exist at all shows how the organizational environment can stimulate extremely unproductive and negative attitudes among people who were not that way to begin with.

It can also stimulate, in some cases, conditions of stress which results in what looks like symptoms of emotional disturbance. An example of such a Normal Negative is observed in the case of a young woman, Ms. J. She had originally planned to become a school teacher, but had, instead, entered the government after completing a master's degree because of more opportunities for career advancement and better pay. After working at two different agencies over a period of three years, Ms. J. entered a management-oriented path at a different agency. She was bright and outgoing, and was viewed by management as having good potential.

Because of various circumstances, including the sudden death of the office supervisor, she was appointed to the supervisory position on an acting basis, even though the work was classified at three position grades above her own. The person to whom she now reported was known as a hostile, cold, and demanding manager, who was unsupportive of his subordinates. Although Ms. J. recognized her lack of training and experience, she attempted to view the assignment as a challenge.

Soon, however, Ms. J.'s supervisor began to severely criticize her work. At the same time, it was noticed that she was becoming increasingly irritable in her daily interactions with co-workers. Before long, she began to accuse others of stealing papers from her desk and conspiring to get her fired. She was observed, on occasion, to be singing and talking to herself in the bathroom. In addition, her appearance became increasingly disheveled. Finally, Ms. J. was told that she would be returned to her old duties and transferred to a different office, but that disciplinary action would be taken if she didn't "control" herself. Within a short time, her symptoms began to disappear.

How disturbed is Ms. J.? Are her symptoms those of underlying pathology, or of stress imposed upon a relatively normal person?

During an interview about a month later, Ms. J. said that she had felt that she was "going crazy" because her work environment had suddenly become very unfriendly and hostile, just at the time when she felt she needed increased support because of the pressures of her new responsibilities. "It was very different from college and my earlier jobs, where people seemed so much more friendly and helpful." Ms. J. indicated that when she saw the "handwriting on the wall" she was able to get control of herself and start figuring out how to find a better situation.

One may say that, had Ms. J. been really disturbed, she would have been unable to cease her symptoms, no matter what the situation. Analysis of her character supports the view that Ms. J. is a person within the normal range of adaptation, despite her symptoms. One finds that Ms. J. possesses considerable intellectual capacity and the ability to work cooperatively. However, one interprets from the Rorschach a theme of helplessness, and a tendency to become angry, rebellious, and paranoid when her helplessness is aroused, or when she feels pressured to perform without support. This, of course, is exactly what happened in her work situation.

Ms. J. said that she learned from her experience to avoid situations of stress, whenever possible, and to keep her ambitions "realistic" with respect to her experience and training. Unfortunately, perhaps, she did not choose to consult with anyone during this period regarding the stress she was experiencing. If she had talked with a therapist who could understand the relationship between work and character, Ms. J. might have been able to explore the role of the situation in generating her emotional difficulties, including the possibility that management made her situation more difficult for her because she was a woman. Without such exploration of both herself and the situation, it would be premature to conclude that her ambitions should be kept "realistic," i.e., limited.

Several months later, Ms. J. was reported to have gotten married and had taken a position with a different agency.

The next case, that of Mr. K., looks, outwardly, like a person with a clear-cut neurotic symptom. It is vivid, he knows it is irrational, but cannot stop himself from doing it. So one must analyze such a case very carefully, with respect to the role of the situation vs. irrational passions, in the development of his symptom.

Mr. K., in his mid-fifties, had a moderately successful career in journalism, until he joined a small federal agency in a public relations capacity at the age of forty. He states that his decision to join the government was based, primarily, on the extra security provided by government employment.

After a series of steady promotions, Mr. K. was passed over for the position of head of his unit, and talk began circulating that a proposed reorganization of his agency would eliminate many jobs, including his own. During this period, Mr. K. divorced his wife of twenty years and began a series of affairs, including one with a woman whom he later married.

Shortly thereafter, Mr. K.'s superiors learned that he had been writing pornographic notes to women from outside the agency, with whom he conducted business as part of his duties. When confronted about this, Mr. K. acknowledged his indiscretions and bad judgment, and said that it would not recur.

Over the next year, however, he did the same thing with two more women, who reported the incidents to the top officials of the agency. This time, management officially reprimanded him; again, Mr. K. affirmed his intention to control himself. It was later learned, however, that even while this was occurring, he had been making suggestive invitations to a secretary in the next office. Finally, when this, too, was reported, Mr. K. stated that he needed professional help, and sought consultation (this had never been suggested to him by management). He voiced fear that his career and new marriage might be ruined if he could not stop himself from engaging in these actions. He stated that he knew his actions were inappropriate, troubling, and irrational; yet he could not understand why he kept doing them.

Study of Mr. K.'s character indicates that Mr. K. has real capacities of the heart—love of life, cooperativeness, attraction to beauty. But this side of himself does not seem to have ever been developed or stimulated by his work, either in journalism or government service. His description of the work environments of both settings suggested sadomasochistic overtones, which might have been the features of those environments, or which he may have sought out.

One interprets from the Rorschach that Mr. K. feels increasingly dependent, and seeks security through position and power. He seems to worship power and potency, which has probably led him into masochistic relationships in the hopes of receiving it. One sees this, for example, in his relationship with his father, who was stern, distant, and unaffectionate; and with Mr. K.'s first wife, with whom he felt deadened and humiliated during nearly all the years of their marriage. Yet Mr. K. said that he felt too guilty to leave her until the children were grown up. Now, after his remarriage, he continues to give three-fourths of his income to his first wife, even though she has told him that she is willing to accept considerably less. One may interpret from this a tendency toward masochistic submission.

At work, Mr. K. has sought to be loyal and cooperative, but is feeling increasingly angry, powerless, and impotent over his circumstances. It is possible that his loss of opportunity for increased recognition, and threats to his job security, combined to trigger his symptoms at work. His capacity for being a good institutional loyalist was undermined by the work environment, which drew out the negative, unproductive side of his character.

His symptom reflects an unconscious rebellion, through which he is able to affirm love for life—through sexuality—though in an unproductive way.

One may argue, based on all the material, that Mr. K. is within the normal range of character despite his symptom, though certainly he is close to the borderline of pathology. His irrational passions are not that significant, and he has shown outwardly normal adjustment throughout all of his life, until now. He now finds himself seeking a kind of magical refuge as a solution to his inner sense of increasing disintegration. So one may conclude that his symptoms are not the product of serious unconscious, irrational passions. Rather, they can best be interpreted as the response of a relatively normal character to a work situation which has stimulated feelings of impotency and insecurity about his future, and has thus brought out negative and unproductive tendencies of character.

Would a better work environment have stimulated the more positive and productive side of Mr. K.'s character? One can only speculate, but it is interesting to consider what might have been possible with respect to Mr. K.'s development, in a work environment which was designed to bring out the best in people.

There are a number of additional examples of people who have developed symptoms of disturbance without significant underlying pathology. The Normal Negatives show a range of symptomatology in a variety of settings in which the organization and/or management has stimulated their negative tendencies of character.

There is, for example, the case of a middle-aged man, Mr. L., who had achieved regular promotion over the years and who had received numerous awards and citation for his performance. He personified much of the loyalty and dependency of the Company Man (Maccoby, 1976) which, incidentally, one finds in many of the best civil servants, together with a desire to serve the public well and efficiently.

Mr. L. was suddenly downgraded two levels because of agency reorganization. He became severely depressed, considered suicide, and felt humiliated and betrayed. He stated that his entire life and self-worth were synonymous with his career and position level—without it, he was nothing. Mr. L. became immobilized by what had happened to him, and could not bring himself to do anything on his own behalf. So he suffered.

It is important to note that most Normal Negatives show capacity for further development. In effect, the bureaucracy has not only failed to develop their hearts, but has, for many, brought out the worst in them. This, despite legislation designed to reform and improve the civil service system and its working environment (LaBier, 1980).

The four formulations described here—the Irrational Adaptives, the Normal Positives, the Irrational Non-Adaptives, and the Normal Negatives—are based upon my testing of the hypotheses raised at the beginning of this chapter. Since the research was exploratory, the findings should not be considered definitive. It is hoped, however, that the formulations will provide a basis for further exploration of the relationship between bureaucratic work and irrational passions, including possible differences between the public and private sector. Also, they may lead to increased understanding of such concepts as job stress and job satisfaction/dissatisfaction, by shedding light on the relationship between character and work as a determinant of satisfaction or stress. In addition, the formulations may contribute to further study of ways in which to improve diagnosis and treatment of people who work within large bureaucracies and who seek psychotherapy or psychoanalysis.

REFERENCES

Beck, S. J., et al. (1961), *Rorschach's Test*. New York: Grune & Stratton.
Fromm, E. (1947), *Man for Himself*. New York: Holt, Rinehart & Winston.
——— (1951), *The Forgotten Language*. New York: Holt, Rinehart & Winston.
——— & Maccoby, M. (1970), *Social Character in a Mexican Village*. Englewood Cliffs, N.J.: Prentice-Hall.
Klopfer, B., et al. (1954), *Developments in the Rorschach Technique*. New York: Harcourt, Brace & World.
LaBier, D. (1980), Uncle Sam's Working Wounded. *The Washington Post Magazine*, February 17, 6-14.

Maccoby, M. (1976), *The Gamesman*. New York: Simon & Schuster.
——— (1980), Work and Human Development. *Professional Psychology*, 11:509-519.
——— (1981), *The Leader*. New York: Simon & Schuster.
——— et al. (1980), *Bringing out the Best: Final Report of the Project to Improve Work and Management in the Department of Commerce, 1977-79*. The Project on Technology, Work and Character, Harvard University. Discussion Paper No. 91D, Kennedy School of Government, June.
Rorschach, H. (1942), *Psychodiagnostics*. New York: Grune & Stratton.
Schachtel, E. (1966), *Experiential Foundations of Rorschach's Test*. New York: Basic Books.
Schafer, R. (1954), *Psychoanalytic Interpretation in Rorschach Testing*. New York: Grune & Stratton.

Offering a classification of irrational management behavior somewhat more psychoanalytic than LaBier's, and certainly drawn from a narrower context, Kernberg focuses at length on the narcissistic type of executive. (For more on narcissism, see Kets de Vries, Chapter 3.) Maccoby (Chapter 20) takes up some of the same problems of the consultant's role in his paper "Participant Study at Work."

2

Regression in Organizational Leadership

OTTO F. KERNBERG

In an earlier study (1978) I described the effects of regressive pressures in psychiatric institutions on the administrators of those institutions. There I pointed out that while crises in organizations often appear at first to be caused by personality problems of the leader, further analysis reveals a more complex situation. Quite frequently, a breakdown in work effectiveness stemming from various internal organizational factors and relationships between the organization and the environment induces regressive group processes first, and regression in the functioning of the leadership later. If these group processes remain undiagnosed, only their end product may be visible, in what appears to be primitive, inadequate leadership and, more specifically, negative effects of the leader's personality on the organization. Thus, leadership problems are not always the real cause of the crisis. In what

This chapter originally appeared in *Psychiatry*, 42:24-39, 1979. Copyright © 1979, by The William Alanson White Psychiatric Foundation, Inc. Reprinted by special permission of the author and The William Alanson White Psychiatric Foundation, Inc.

follows, I turn to the consideration of regressive pressures stemming from within the administrators themselves. At every step I will emphasize the importance of distinguishing between regressive organizational components and regression in the leader.

My approach is intermediate between two positions: (1) the traditional approach, according to which leadership is "inborn"—particularly "charismatic" leadership; (2) the opposite, more recent theoretical thinking, which considers leadership as derived mostly or exclusively from learned skills and understanding. My approach is based on the findings of various authors (Bion, 1959; Dalton et al., 1968; Emery and Trist, 1973; Hodgson et al., 1965; Levinson, 1968; Main, 1957; Miller and Rice, 1967; Rice, 1963, 1964, 1965; Rioch, 1970a, 1970b; Sanford, 1956; and Stanton and Schwartz, 1954). This approach combines (1) a psychoanalytic focus on the personality features of the leader, (2) a psychoanalytic focus on the functions of regressive group processes in organizations, and (3) an open-systems-theory approach to organizational management. All three aspects interact dynamically, and the origin of failure or breakdown of functioning of individuals, groups, or the organization at large may lie in any one or several of these areas.

The Psychoanalytically Trained Consultant to Organizations

Consultants are usually called in at times of crisis, but the nature of their task is not always clear: an organization may use a consultant to escape from full awareness and resolution of a problem as much as to realistically diagnose the problem and its potential solutions (Rogers, 1973). The consultant's first task is to clarify the nature of his contract, and to assure himself that the resources to carry it out are adequate. This means not only sufficient time and financial support, but the necessary authority to examine problems at all levels of the organizational strcture.

It goes almost without saying that support from the top leader of the organization is essential. The consultant needs to be sufficiently independent from the organization to be able to reach his conclusions without excessive fears of antagonizing the leader; therefore, he must not be too dependent on any one particular client.

One main question that needs to be formulated is whether a certain conflict within the organization represents a problem stemming from (1) "personality issues," (2) the nature of the task of the organization and its constraints, or (3) "morale"—that is, group processes within the organization. The nature of the problem is often described in such confused and confusing terms that a translation into these three domains is difficult.

It is helpful to focus first on the nature of the organizational tasks and their constraints, for only after tasks have been defined, their respective constraints outlined, and priorities have been set up regarding primary and secondary tasks and constraints, is it possible to evaluate whether the administrative structure does, indeed, fit with the nature of the tasks, and if not, how it should be modified. This analysis requires the clarification of the organization's real tasks in contrast to its apparent ones. In one psychiatric hospital, the apparent task was to treat patients and to carry out research, but the real task seemed to be to provide the owners of the institution with an adequate return on their investment. In actuality, the interest in research represented wishes to obtain funding from external sources with which to cover part of staff salaries, and the treatment of patients constituted a constraint on the real task.

Once tasks and constraints have been defined, the administrative structure required for task performance can be examined. Does the organization have effective control over its boundaries, and if not, what administrative compensating mechanisms can be established to restore boundary control? One psychiatric organization depended on one institution for its administrative support funding, and on another for its funding for professional staffing. Chronic fights between administrators and professionals throughout the entire organization reflected the lack of boundary control at the top. The consultant's recommendation—that all funding be channeled into a central hospital administration directed by a professional with administrative expertise—was acceptable to both funding institutions and to the staff at large, and provided the organizational solution to the "morale" problem that had prompted the request for consultation in the first place.

Once boundary control seems adequate, the nature of delegation of authority in the institution and each task system can be studied. Inadequate, fluctuating, ambiguous, or nonexistent delegation on the one hand, and excessive, chaotic delegation on the other, are problems that have to be solved as part of the redefinition of the administrative structure in terms of task requirements.

Having diagnosed the institution's overall task and its constraints, and, it is hoped, corrected the respective administrative structures, it is possible to focus on the nature of the leadership, and more concretely, on the qualities of the leader himself. The consultant should attempt to diagnose the personality qualities of the administrator that influence organizational functioning (these will be elaborated in the third section of this paper), the regressive pulls that the leader is subjected to from group processes in the organization, and his own contributions to such regressive group processes. What kind of intermediate management has the leader assembled? How much understanding in depth does he have for people, their assets and liabilities? How much tolerance of criticism, strength and yet warmth, flexibility and yet firmness and clarity, does he have in his relationships to staff? The accuracy and quality of the leader's judgment of those around him is a crucial indicator, not only of his administrative skills, but of his personality as a whole. What are his reactions under stress? In which direction does his personality regress under critical conditions? The strength of his convictions, the presence or absence of envy of staff, the extent of his moral integrity and courage—these are usually surprisingly well known throughout the organization.

The psychoanalytic exploration of group processes in the organization may become a crucial instrument for the evaluation of problems in both the administrative structure and the personality of the leader. The regressive nature of group processes in psychiatric organizations—"morale"—may reflect conflicts in the organizational structure, the impact of the leader's personality, the regressive pull exerted by patients' conflicts, or combinations of these factors. The more the observed group actually works with patients, the more the patients' conflicts will directly influence the development of regressive group processes within staff and the staff/patient community generally. The closer the observed staff groups are to final decision-making authority, the more the conflicts of top leadership and of organizational structure will dominate. Still, it is impressive how conflicts affecting the total organization are reflected in group processes at *all* levels. Thus, the careful observation of group processes at various administrative levels constitutes a kind of "organizational projective-test battery," which may give the direct information needed to clarify problems at the levels of task definition and constraints, work with patients, administrative structure, and leadership, all in one stroke.

The accuracy of the diagnosis arrived at by the consultant can then be measured in terms of the eventual success or failure of the steps taken to restore a functional administrative structure for the organization. Thus, the shift in functioning of administrative leadership following a redefinition of primary tasks and constraints should improve morale throughout the organization in a relatively short period of time. The restoration of a functional structure—in contrast to an authoritarian structure brought about by distortions of the hierarchical network of power—may effect almost immediate positive changes.

For practical purposes, the consultant usually obtains most helpful information from the active participation of senior and intermediate management in a free and open discussion of issues, in a group atmosphere that permits some exploration of group processes as well as of the content of the administrative problems under examination. The consultant's diagnosis of the problems of top leadership and intermediate management should include an evaluation of the human resources in the organization. Because human resources are the primary potential assets of organizations, the degree of psychological intactness of senior leadership has an important prognostic implication.

When the organization's difficulties can be traced to the leader's personality problems or his general incompetence (lack of technical knowledge, conceptual limitations, or administrative incompetence), the question arises as to whether he can be helped to change, or whether he should be asked to leave his job. There are no obvious answers to this question. Improved functioning may result from reducing the regressive pulls on leaders stemming from group processes in the organization. Improvement in task definition, task performance, boundary controls, and the administrative structure as a whole may all bring out the leader's assets and reduce the negative impact of his personality characteristics. Increase in gratification of his emotional needs outside of the organizational structure may sometimes help. At other times, the best solution seems to be to encourage him to step down by recommending either that his professional functions be changed or that he move within the organization—if such alternatives are available.

Although the recommendation that he resign is always a serious narcissistic blow, if often happens that deep down the administrator knows that he has not been able to do his job well, and may feel relieved when someone from the outside confronts him with that reality. On the other hand, when the consultant arrives at the conclusion that the organization has a bad leader at the top, the consultant might discreetly withdraw (or be discreetly asked to withdraw).

The situation is different, of course, when the problem involves an administrator at a lower hierarchical level. When this is the case, top leadership needs to be helped to understand that firmness in eliminating bad situations is indispensable for the health of the organization at large. To ask a man who cannot do his job to leave may seem aggressive or even sadistic to his superior; but it is usually more sadistic to leave a bad leader in charge of an organizational structure than to ask him to change his functions. The suffering of staff at the hands of a bad leader should be a primary concern of the top leader. Optimal leadership sometimes requires hard decisions, and at times, unfortunately, the leader must be very firm and decisive with somebody who may be a close personal friend.

There are times when the problem can be diagnosed but, for some reason, cannot be resolved. Some organizations function as if they were geared to self-destruction, unable and unwilling to accept positive change. This is a dramatic situation for a consultant and, of course, much more dramatic for the staff of the organization. One important use of an understanding of organizational structure and conflict may be to enable staff, particularly senior staff who are able to obtain an overview of the situation, to diagnose the organizational conflicts and even their sources, and reach realistic conclusions about the prognosis for the organization and, therefore, about their own personal futures.

There are certain situations so bad that the only solution for self-respecting staff is to leave; in other words, there is such a thing as a "poisonous" organizational environment bad for everyone in it. It is impressive how often staff within such a destructive environment deny to themselves the insoluble nature of the problems of the organization and obtain gratification of pathological dependency needs by such denial and failure to admit the need to move on. Understanding organizations in depth can be painful; at times, such awareness does not improve the effectiveness of staff members; but understanding always makes it possible to gain a more realistic, even if painful, grasp of what the future probably will be. The parallel to the painful learning about aspects of one's unconscious in the psychoanalytic situation is implicit: there are similar pathological defenses against becoming aware of reality in the place where one works. At some point the individual has a responsibility to himself which transcends that to the organization. And knowledge of organizational conflicts may permit him to reach more quickly an understanding of what that point is and where his personal boundaries are threatened by an organization from which he should withdraw.

Under less extreme circumstances, there is much that an educated, task-oriented staff can do to help its leadership correct or undo distorted administrative structures and reduce the effects of pathology of top leadership. Intermediate management staff may be of particular help to the organization and the top administrator in preserving functional administrative relationships by openly communicating their analysis of the situation. In this regard, the responsibility of followers not to perpetuate and exacerbate the problems of the leader cannot be overemphasized.

Disruption of functional administration always brings about regression to "basic group assumptions." I refer here to Bion's (1959) "basic assumptions" groups: "dependency," "fight-flight," and "pairing," which are activated when groups—and organizations—do not function adequately. When such regressive phenomena in groups involve intermediate leadership and staff at large, they may reinforce the personality difficulties of individual staff members and reduce their awareness of the need for change or their willingness to fight for it. If individual staff members courageously spell out what the situation is, it may have a positive therapeutic effect in increasing rational behavior throughout the organization; in such instances, the positive effect results from criticism based not upon "fight-flight" assumptions, but upon a genuine interest in helping the leader and staff improve their understanding of and functioning in the organization. Open communication among the intermediate management group may also help reduce their mutual suspicion and distrust and their fear of speaking up. An alliance for the sake of the functional needs of the organization is a good example of political struggle in terms of the task, rather than in terms of perpetuating distortions in the distribution of authority and power.

For the top administrator, particularly at a time of crisis when uncertainty is increased for him and everyone else, the availability of senior staff willing to speak up openly and responsibly, without excessive distortion by fear or anger, can be very reassuring. A mutual reinforcement of staff able and willing to provide new information to the leader and a leader who encourages such staff action may strengthen the group throughout.

"Participatory management" as a general principle is an important protection against the regressive effects of the leader's personality on the administrative structure. The degree of participatory management, or the degree of centralized decision making, depends on a variety of factors. When administrative structure has been distorted by regressive pulls on top leadership, from whatever source, increasing participatory management is indicated. Such an emphasis on participatory decision making does not mean a replacement of a functional by a "democratic" structure. Flexibility is necessary regarding the extent to which the organization shifts back and forth from centralized to participatory management; at periods of rapid environmental change, of crisis or turbulence in the external environment, there may be a need for increased centralized decision making. At times of external stability, increased decentralization and participatory management may be helpful. Internal change often requires participatory management, especially in the preparatory or early stages of change. A centralized, simplified administrative structure may become functional in times of internal consolidation or stability.

AUTHORITARIAN PERSONALITY AND AUTHORITARIAN ORGANIZATIONAL STRUCTURE

Adorno and his co-workers (1950) have described the "authoritarian personality" as tending to be overconventional, rigidly adhering to middle-class values, and oversensitive to external social pressures; he is inappropriately submissive to conventional authority, and at the same time, extremely punitive to those who oppose such authority and to those under him; he is generally opposed to feelings, fantasies, and introspection, and tends to shift responsibility from the individual onto outside forces; his thinking is stereotyped, rigid, and simplistic; he tends to exercise power for its own sake and admires power in others; he is destructive and cynical, rationalizing his aggression toward others; he tends to project onto others—particularly "out groups"—his own unacceptable impulses; and finally, he is rigid with regard to sexual morality.

While Adorno and his co-workers applied psychoanalytic concepts to study the metapsychological determinants of such a personality structure, in their methods and clinical analyses they combined both personality and sociological criteria: their authoritarian personality structure seems to me a composite formation, which reflects various types of character pathology exacerbated by authoritarian pressures exerted by social, political, and cultural systems. In my view, within the restricted frame of reference of the study of leadership of psychiatric institutions, the social, cultural, and political issues may be relatively less important than the mutual reinforcement of authoritarian pressures by the institutional structure and by various types of character pathology that contribute to authoritarian leadership behavior. In what follows, I explore the pathological contributions of specific personality characteristics of the leader to the development of authoritarian pressures throughout the organizational structure. I wish to emphasize again, however, that a leader's authoritarian behavior may stem from features of the organizational structure, and not necessarily from his personality.

Sanford (1956) has pointed out the necessity to distinguish between authoritarian behavior in leadership roles and authoritarianism in the personality, and that the two do not necessarily go together. An authoritarian administrative structure is one that is invested with more power than is necessary to carry out its functions, whereas a functional structure is one in which persons and groups in position of authority are invested with adequate—but not excessive—power.

The adequate power invested in the leadership in a functional structure usually receives reinforcement from social and/or legal sanctions. *Authoritarian* behavior that exceeds functional needs must be differentiated from *authoritative* behavior that represents functionally adequate or necessary exercise of authority. In practice, authority—the right and capacity to carry out task leadership—stems from various sources (Rogers, 1973). Managerial authority refers to that part of the leader's authority which has been delegated to him by the institution he works in. Leadership authority refers to that aspect of his authority derived from the recognition of his followers of his capacity to carry out the task. Managerial and leadership authority reinforce each other; both are, in turn, dependent upon other sources of authority, such as the leader's technical knowledge, his personality characteristics, his human skills, and the social tasks and responsibilities he assumes outside the institution. The administrator is responsible not only to his institution but also to his staff, to his professional and ethical values, to the community, and to society at large: responsibility and accountability represent the reciprocal function of the administrator to the sources of his delegated authority. In addition, because of his personality characteristics, or because he belongs to special groups or to political structures that invest him with power unrelated to his strictly technical functions, the leader may accumulate power beyond that required by his functional authority—the excessive power that constitutes the basis for an authoritarian structure.

In contrasting an authoritarian administrative structure with a functional administrative structure, I am emphasizing the opposition between authoritarian and functional structure, and not that between authoritarian and democratic structure. This point is important from both theoretical and practical viewpoints. A tendency exists in some professional institutions—and psychiatric institutions are no exception—to attempt to modify, correct, or resolve by means of democratic political processes problems created by an authoritarian structure, that is, to arrive at corrective decisions in a participatory or representative decision-making process. Insofar as those involved in actual tasks should, indeed, participate in the decision-making process, such "democratization" is helpful; but where decision making veers toward being determined on a political rather than on a task-oriented basis, distortions of the task structure and of the entire administrative structure may occur. These are extremely detrimental to the work being carried out, and eventually may even reinforce the authoritarian structure they are intended to correct. In addition, the attempt to correct authoritarian distortions by political means leads to the neglect of a functional analysis of the problem. This is certainly a temptation for top leadership: by means of political management or manipulation, they may be able to dominate the negotiations across task boundaries. If so, they may come to rely more and more on the exercise of political power, eventually focusing almost exclusively on the increment or protection of their power base and neglecting the functional interests of the institution.

SOME FREQUENT PATHOLOGICAL CHARACTER STRUCTURES IN THE ADMINISTRATOR

Schizoid Personality Features

Schizoid personality features may, in themselves, protect the leader against excessive regression; his emotional isolation makes him less pervious to regressive group processes. But the proliferation of distorted fantasies about him is hard to correct because of his distance and unavailability. An excessively schizoid leader may also frustrate the appropriate dependency needs of his staff; usually, however, schizoid leadership at the top tends to be compensated for by the warmth and extroversion of managerial figures at the intermediate level.

A very schizoid head of one department of psychiatry conveyed the impression that "no one was running the place"; most authority for daily operations had been delegated to the director of clinical services, who was seen as the actual leader of staff and who, because of his excellent capacity for carrying out functions at the boundary between the department head and the staff, did indeed fulfill important leadership functions. But the needs of the senior staff for mutual support, warmth, and understanding were not met, and the atmosphere of each being on his own was transmitted throughout the entire institution. Although this department was considered a place with ample room for independent, autonomous growth of staff "if one had it within oneself," a considerable number of staff members were not able to work in this relative human isolation and decided to leave.

In another institution, a markedly schizoid hospital director was insufficiently explicit and direct in the decision-making process as to create ambiguity with regard to delegation of authority. No one knew for sure how much authority was vested in any particular person, and no one cared to commit himself to anything without repeated consultations with the director. This produced excessive cautiousness and hypersensitivity about, and politicization of, decision making throughout the organization. Eventually, the message was conveyed that one had to become a very skilled and tactful manipulator to get ahead in the department, and that direct emotional expression was risky. Thus, the leader's personality characteristics, through group interactions, filtered down and became characteristic of the entire organization.

Obsessive Personality Features

Obsessive personality features in top leadership are found quite frequently. On the positive side, the focus on orderliness, precision, clarity, and control may foster stable delegation of authority and clarity in the decision-making process. Contrary to what one would expect, there is usually very little doubtfulness in obsessive personalities in leadership positions; severely obsessive personalities, characterized by excessive doubt and hesitation, usually don't reach top positions. Thus, while chronic indecisiveness in the administrator may have obsessive origins, it is most frequently a consequence of the leader's narcissistic problems. Obsessive personalities, then, usually function rather efficiently from an organizational viewpoint. Their clear stand on issues and their commitment to values have important creative functions for the institution at large.

On the negative side, some dangers are the leader's excessive need for order and precision, his need to be in control, and the expression of the sadistic components that often go with an obsessive personality. An inordinate need for orderliness and control may reinforce the bureaucratic components of the organization—that is, encourage decision making on the basis of rules and regulations and rather mechanized practices, all of which may interfere with the creativeness of staff and with appropriate autonomy in the decision-making process at points of rapid change or crisis. Excessive bureaucratization may at times protect the organization from political struggle, but it also reinforces passive resistance in the negotiations across boundaries and fosters misuse of resources.

Because the leader's pathological defensive mechanisms and particularly his pathological character traits tend to be activated in times of stress, an increase in obsessive perfectionism and pedantic style may characterize the obsessive leader at critical moments. This may create additional stress for the organization at a time when rapid and effective decision making is required. An educated awareness on the part of the staff that under such conditions it is necessary to protect the security system of the leader in order to get the work done may be very helpful. This, of course, is true for the effects of pathological character features of any kind in the leader, and to know how to help him in times of crises is a basic skill demanded of intermediate management.

A major problem created by some obsessive personalities in leadership positions is that of severe, unresolved sadism. The need sadistically to control subordinates may have devastating effects on the functional structure of the organization. Whenever there is strong opposition among staff to a certain move by the administrator, he may become obstinate and controlling, vengefully "rubbing the message in," and forcing his "opponents" again and again into submission. Such behavior reinforces irrational fears of authority and the distortion of role perception in the staff; it also fosters a submissiveness to hierarchical superiors, which reduces effective feedback from and creative participation by the entire staff.

The end result may be the development of chronic passivity, a pseudodependency derived from fear of authority rather than from an authentic "dependent" group, and the spread of authoritarian, dictatorial ways of dealing with staff and patients throughout the institution. In one department of psychiatry, the appointment of an obsessive and sadistic director drove the most creative members of the senior professional leadership away from the institution within a year and brought about consolidation around the leader of a group of rather weak, inhibited, or mediocre professionals willing to pay the price of sacrificing their autonomous professional development for the security and stability afforded them by submission to the leader. The repetition of these conflicts approximately a year later at the next lower level of organizational hierarchy, however, created such a combination of general "fight-flight" grouping and overall breakdown in carrying out organizational tasks that the administrator was finally removed by the combined efforts of staff at large.

Paranoid Personalities

Paranoid personalities always present a serious potential danger for the functional relationships that administrators must establish with their staff. The development of "fight-flight" conditions in the group processes throughout the organization—a development that may occur even in the most efficiently functioning organization from time to time—may propel into the foreground a "leader of the opposition." With the silent tolerance or unconscious collusion of the majority of staff, a violent attack on the administration by this opposition leader may induce the top leader to regress into paranoid attitudes, even if he does not have any particularly paranoid traits. In other words, there is always a potential—particularly in large organizations with several levels of hierarchy—for suspiciousness, for efforts to exert sadistic control, and for projection of the administrator's rage onto staff. When the administrator also has strong paranoid character features, the danger of paranoid reactions to "fight-flight" conditions is intensified, and he may perceive even ordinary discussions or minor opposition as dangerous rebelliousness or hidden attacks. The need to suppress and control the opposition, which we saw in the obsessive leader with sadistic trends, becomes paramount in the paranoid leader. Because of the ease with which the leader may interpret what "they" say as lack of respect, mistreatment, and hidden hostility toward him, staff may now become afraid of speaking up. Staff's fearfulness, in turn, may increase the administrator's suspiciousness, thus generating a vicious circle.

Because paranoid personalities are particularly suitable to take on the leadership of basic assumptions groups in a "fight-flight" position, the "leader of the opposition" is often a person with strong paranoid tendencies. This does not mean that all leaders of revolutions are paranoid personalities, but that because of the nature of their psychopathology, paranoid personalities may function much more appropriately under such revolutionary conditions. The fighting "in-group" that they represent becomes "all good," and the external group or the general environment they fight becomes "all bad." The successful projection of all aggression outside the boundaries of the group he controls permits the paranoid oppositional leader to function more effectively within the boundaries of his group, even though at the cost of an important degree of distortion of external reality. But when such a paranoid leader succeeds in occupying power and takes over control of the organization, the very characteristics that helped him gain leadership of the "fight-flight" group may become very damaging to the institution. The tendency to project all hostility outside—that is, to see the inside of the institution as good and the environment as bad—may temporarily help to protect the good relations between the leader and his followers; in the long run, however, the price paid for this is institutionalization of paranoid distortions of external reality, distortions in the boundary negotiations between the institution and its environment, and the possibility that the leader's capacity to carry out his organizational tasks will break down. Within the organization, the vengeful persecution of those the paranoid leader suspects of being potential enemies may eliminate creative criticism to a much larger extent than in the case of obsessive personalities with sadistic features.

The director of one psychiatric institution that functioned closely with several other psychiatric institutions felt chronically endangered by what he saw as power plays directed against him by the leaders of the other institutions. At first he appealed to his own staff for help and support, and morale temporarily improved; they felt united against an external enemy. Eventually, however, by constantly antagonizing leaders and representatives of the other institutions, the director became less able to carry out his functions in representing his own institution, and started to blame subordinates within his own system for his difficulties in obtaining the necessary space, staff, funding, and community influence. He began to suspect some of the members of the intermediate management of his institution of having "sold out to the enemy," further reducing the effectiveness of his institution vis-à-vis its professional environment. The situation reached a final equilibrium by virtue of a protective transformation of the boundaries of the institution into a true barrier, behind which it isolated itself from the local community and redefined its task in terms of a regional chain of institutions to which it belonged.

The following example, in contrast, illustrates the resolution of paranoid regression induced by "fight-flight" conditions in an organizational leader without paranoid personality characteristics. In this case, the director of a hospital was very suspicious and upset over a senior member of his staff, Dr. B., who seemed to challenge him at all professional meetings. The director saw Dr. B. as a severely paranoid character whose group behavior was splitting staff and potentially damaging the organization, and who perhaps should not continue on the staff. He nevertheless accepted other staff members' judgment that Dr. B. was a good clinician and was providing valuable services to the hospital. A consultant recommended to the director that he meet privately with Dr. B. and discuss his group behavior. The director did so and discovered that Dr. B was much more open and flexible in individual meetings than in group situations. But the challenging behavior continued in groups and the director now concluded that regardless of the personality characteristics of the "leader of the opposition," a group process must be fostering his contentious behavior and that a study of this particular organizational area was indicated. In the course of the ensuing study, it became apparent that there were serious conflicts within the institution that had reduced the effectiveness of the professional group to which Dr. B. belonged, so that "fight-flight" assumptions chronically predominated among them and induced Dr. B. to take the role of their leader. Analysis of the organizational problem led to resolution of the conflicts concerning the entire professional group; Dr. B., finding himself no longer supported by the "silent consensus," and actively discouraged by the group itself, finally stopped dominating group discussions.

Narcissistic Personality Features

Of the dangers to institutions stemming from the leader's character pathology, those derived from narcissistic personality features are perhaps the most serious of all. I must stress that I am using the concept of narcissistic personality in a restrictive sense, referring to persons whose interpersonal relations are characterized by excessive self-reference and self-centeredness, whose grandiosity and overvaluation of themselves exist together with feelings of inferiority, who are overdependent on external admiration, emotionally shallow, intensely envious, and both depreciatory and exploitative in their relations with others (Kernberg, 1970, 1974).

The inordinate self-centeredness and grandiosity of these persons stands in dramatic contrast to their ever-present potential for envy of others. Their inability to evaluate themselves and others in depth brings about a lack of capacity for empathy and for sophisticated discrimination of other people, all of which may become very damaging when they occupy leadership positions. In addition, when external gratification is not forthcoming, or under conditions of severe frustration or failure, they may develop paranoid trends, rather than depression and a sense of personal failure. Such paranoid tendencies reinforce even further the damaging impact on the organization of the leader's narcissistic character structure.

Because narcissistic personalities are often driven to assume positions of authority and leadership by intense needs for power and prestige, individuals with such characteristics are found rather frequently in top leadership positions. They are often men of high intelligence, hardworking and eminently talented or capable in their field, but with narcissistic needs that dramatically neutralize or destroy their creative potential for the organization.

Pathologically narcissistic people aspire to positions of leadership more for their power and prestige—as a source of admiration and narcissistic gratification from staff and from the external environment—than because of commitment to a task or ideal represented by the functions carried out by the institution. As a consequence, they may neglect the functional requirements of leadership, the human needs and constraints involved in the work, and the value systems against which administrative and technical responsibilities have to be measured. Leaders with narcissistic personalities are unaware of the variety of pathological human relations they foster around them and throughout the entire organization as their personalities affect administrative structures and functions at large.

In contrast to leaders with pathological obsessive and paranoid features, the narcissistic leader not only requires submission from staff, but also wants to be loved by them. He fosters and artificially increases the staff's normal tendency to depend on and idealize the leader: as staff become aware how important it is for the administrator to receive their unconditional, repetitive expressions of love and admiration, adulation and flattery become constant features of the process of communicating with him.

Before proceeding further, it must be emphasized that the negative manifestations of pathological narcissism have to be differentiated from the normal narcissistic manifestations that are part of the gratifications of any position of responsibility and leadership, gratifications that may be the source of increased effectiveness in leadership as well as compensation for administrative frustrations. I have examined the differences between normal and pathological narcissism in earlier works (Kernberg, 1970, 1974) and will limit myself to outlining some of these differences as they apply to the person in the leadership position.

Administrative and leadership positions in general provide many sources of gratification for narcissistic needs for success, power, prestige, and admiration. Under optimal circumstances these needs have been integrated with mature ego goals and the need to live up to a mature ego ideal and superego standards. Normal narcissistic gratifications have mature qualities; for example, normal self-love is enlightened and deep, in contrast to childlike and shallow self-aggrandizement; normal self-love goes hand in hand with commitments to ideals and values and the capacity for love of and investment in others.

Under optimal circumstances, the leader of a psychiatric institution may obtain normal narcissistic gratification from being able to develop an ideal department or hospital, opportunities for professional growth and development of staff, scientific progress, organizational and administrative effectiveness, and above all, the best possible treatment for the patients in the institution's care. Narcissistic gratifications also come from the administrator's awareness that he can help to provide work gratification for his staff, which fosters their self-respect and can contribute to broad goals representing social and cultural value systems. In other words, striving for a position of leadership may involve idealism and altruism intimately linked with normal narcissism.

With pathological narcissism, in contrast, the narcissistic leader's aspirations center around primitive power over others, inordinate wishes to be held in awe by them, and wishes to be admired for personal attractiveness, charm, and brilliance rather than for mature human qualities, moral integrity, and creativity in providing task-oriented professional and administrative leadership. Under conditions of pathological narcissism, the leader's tolerance for the normal, unavoidable frustrations that go with his position is low, and a number of pathological developments take place within him, in his interactions with staff, and throughout the entire organizational structure.

Above all, the preeminence of unconscious and conscious envy has very detrimental consequences for his relationships with staff. Insofar as he cannot tolerate the success and gratification that others obtain from their work, and sees the professional success of others as overshadowing or threatening his own and therefore unacceptable to him, the narcissistic administrator may become very resentful of the most creative members of his staff. Narcissistic personalities may often be very helpful to trainees or junior members of the staff, whose development they foster because they unconsciously represent extensions of the leader's own grandiose self. When these younger colleagues reach a point in their development in which they become autonomous and independent, however, the leader's previous support may shift to devaluation and relentless undermining of their work.

For example, a narcissistic mental health professional who assumes administrative functions that interfere with his clinical or research interests may envy those of his colleagues who continue developing their clinical identity. One solution in such instances—instances which are fairly common—is for the senior administrator to obtain his narcissistic gratification from taking administration as the field of his theoretical or practical specialized expertise, or to have some professional area other than his administrative work in which he can continue doing creative work on his own.

It is part of normal narcissism to be able to enjoy the happiness and triumph of those one has helped to develop; enjoyment of the work and success of others—a general characteristic of the normal overcoming of infantile envy and jealousy—is missing in the narcissistic personality. The narcissistic administrator may also envy some of his staff for the strength of their professional convictions; it is one of the tragedies of narcissistic personalities that their very lack of deeply felt human values brings about a chronic deterioration of those value systems and convictions they do have.

The encouragement of staff submissiveness is another consequence of pathological narcissism. Since narcissistic leaders tend to surround themselves with "yes men" and shrewd manipulators who play up to their narcissistic needs, more honest and therefore occasionally critical members of the staff are pushed onto the periphery and eventually may constitute a relatively silent, but dissatisfied and critical opposition. The dependent group of admirers further beclouds the administrator's self-awareness and fosters in him additional narcissistic deterioration.

The narcissistic leader might depreciate those he perceives as admiring him, but he cannot do without them; and his respect for the integrity of those who criticize him gradually erodes into paranoid fears. In terms of internalized object relations, it is as if the narcissistic leader induces in the human network of the organization a replication of his internal world of objects, a world populated only by devalued, shadowy images of others and by images of dangerous potential enemies.

The narcissistic leader's inability to judge people in depth is a consequence of his pathology of internalized object relations. It stems both from the narcissistic personality's tendencies to achieve "part object" rather than "total object" relations (Kernberg, 1967, 1970) and from his lack of commitment to professional values and to value systems in general. The narcissistic administrator therefore tends to judge people by superficial impressions of their behavior in terms of their past "prestige" or in terms of political considerations, rather than by a mature judgment of the nature of the task, the nature of the person required to carry it out, and the personality and knowledge of the one involved. The inability to judge people in depth and the reliance on people who play up to the administrator's needs for admiration reinforce each other and bring about the danger that eventually the narcissistic leader will be surrounded by people similar to himself, people suffering from serious behavior disorders, or people cynically exploiting their awareness of his psychological needs.

Paradoxically, in large institutions the more the administrative structure is distorted by the leader's narcissistic pathology, the more compensating mechanisms may develop in the form of breakdown of boundary control and boundary negotiations, so that some institutional functions may actually go "underground," or in more general terms, become split off from the rest of the organization. It is as if a parallel existed here to what happens in some cases of severe psychopathology, wherein generalized splitting or primitive dissociation of the ego permits the patient to maintain some semblance of adaptation to external reality at the price of fragmentation of his ego identity. But, the general thesis still stands that the overall creativity of the organization suffers severely under such excessively narcissistic leadership. Although in the short run the grandiosity and expansiveness of the narcissistic leader may transmit itself throughout the organization as a pressure to work or as "charismatic" excitement and bring about a spurt of productivity, in the long run the deteriorating effects of pathological narcissism predominate. They tend to drown creativity in sweeping dependency or in the cynicism that develops among those in the organization with the greatest knowledge and strongest convictions.

When the institution directed by a narcissistic leader is small, the negative effects may be overwhelming from the beginning, for everybody is directly affected by the leader's problems. The development of understanding is hampered by the leader's constant doubts and uncertainty about everything—doubts derived from unconscious envy, devaluation, and lack of conviction—and by his need constantly to change his interests as he loses enthusiasm for what is no longer new and exciting. The narcissistic leader's incapacity to gratify realistic dependency needs of staff—in the simplest terms, his incapacity really to listen—frustrates staff's basic emotional needs and at the same time strengthens the negative consequences of the distortions in group processes: the submissive and dependent in-group and the depressed and angry out-group mentioned before.

The severely narcissistic leader whose ambition is frustrated by the external reality of the organization may require so much additional support from his staff that most of their energy is spent in attempts to restore his emotional equilibrium. In one department of psychiatry, the chairman had reached his position at an early stage of his career, when he was still one of the promising members of his generation; however, he had progressively lost his professional leadership functions and had become chronically embittered and depressed. After a number of years, those senior staff members who remained saw it as their principal organizational task to protect the leader from unnecessary stress and narcissistic lesions, and to stimulate his capacities by ongoing applause and rewards. As a result, the general productivity of the department decreased noticeably.

At times, it is amazing and encouraging to observe how staff members of institutions directed by a narcissistic leader may maintain their personal integrity, autonomy, and independence in spite of the corrupting influence of their immediate environment. These isolated members may provide an outside consultant with the most meaningful information about the organization's "hidden agendas" and preserve the hope for change in the midst of general despondency. It is as if the social situation of the institution reflected the intrapsychic life of the narcissistic personality—with fragments of healthy ego floating in the midst of a sea of deteriorated internalized object relations.

Although narcissistic leaders often radiate charismatic qualities, and have the capacity to stimulate the group's identification with the leader's confidence in himself, not all narcissistic leaders are charismatic and not all charismatic leaders are narcissistic. Personal charisma may stem from a combination of various personality traits and may be embedded in strength of technical, moral, and human convictions. Sometimes staff accuse a strong and committed leader of being "narcissistic" when in reality they are projecting onto him their own frustrated narcissistic aims and expressing envy of the successful man. The "consensus" leader—whom Zaleznik (see Chapter 6) has contrasted with the "charismatic" one—may also present either severe narcissistic or normal personality characteristics. One has to differentiate the mature "consensus" leader, who has the capacity to explore the thinking of his staff and to use creatively the understanding and skills of his administrative group for carrying out the task, from the power-oriented, smoothly functioning, politically opportunistic, narcissistic "consensus" leader, who shrewdly exploits group phenomena for his narcissistic aims.

There is a special kind of narcissistic leader whose gratifications come mostly from keeping himself in the center of everybody's love, and at the same time in the center of the decision-making process, while he coolly sacrifices any considerations regarding value systems or the organization's functional needs to what is politically expedient. The typical example is the leader who is a "nice guy" with no enemies, who seems slightly insecure and easily changeable, and who at the same time is extremely expert in turning all conflicts among his staff into fights that do not involve himself. The general narcissistic qualities of shallowness, inability to judge people sensitively, inability to commit oneself to any values, are dramatically evident in this case, but what seems to be missing is the direct expression of grandiosity and the need to obtain immediate gratification from other people's admiration. At times this kind of leader obtains gratification from his position by using it as a source of power and prestige beyond the organization itself. He may let the organization run its own course, trying to keep things smooth, so long as his power base is stable.

A somewhat similar outcome may stem from a different type of personality structure—that of individuals with strong reaction formations against primitive sadistic trends. In this case, the direct friendliness of the leader in his relations with his immediate subordinates stands in contrast to violent conflicts within the level below that of his immediate administrative group. Still another type of consensus leader has achieved his position on the basis of his technical or professional skills, and has been willing to accept the position without ever fully assuming the responsibilities it entails. This is one of the conditions contributing to an essentially leaderless organization: the man at the top is really more interested in a particular work of his own than in developing authentic leadership, and for that reason stays away from the painful process of making hard decisions. In summary, both charismatic and consensus leadership may stem from various normal and pathological sources.

One major question that can be affected by pathological narcissism is the perennial one of when to compromise and when to stick to one's convictions in a conflict. At one extreme, the rigid, self-righteous person who has to have his own way and cannot accept any compromise may reflect pathological narcissism; at the other extreme, the person willing to sell his convictions—and his staff—down the river for any opportunistic reason may equally reflect severe pathological narcissism. Somewhere in between are the realistic compromises in which the leader's essential convictions are respected and effective boundary negotiation is carried out to achieve a creative balance among conflicting priorities, tasks, and constraints. In other words, intelligent political maneuvering may distinguish between what is essential to the task and what is not. Sometimes it takes very long-range vision indeed to separate the immediate political implications of a certain move from its value in terms of the overall, long-range organizational tasks and goals. Pathological narcissism dramatically interferes with the leadership function that differentiates the expedient from the constructive.

THE CHOICE OF A NEW LEADER

When choosing a leader for an organization, it is necessary to explore intensively the broad area of human or interpersonal skills; these skills, in other words, should not be inferred from what may be only surface adaptability and social charm. As we have seen, skill in judging immediate situations, skill in negotiating conflicts on a short-term basis, the fact of "not ever having had any enemies," and driving ambition are not necessarily good indicators for high-quality leadership. The following are typical of the questions that should be formulated in the selection of leadership.

How much creativity has the candidate shown in his area in the past? How much investment does he have in a professional source of gratification that will continue to be available to him even while he undertakes his administrative functions? How much gratification will he obtain from actual creativity as an administrator, and how much from the satisfaction of his needs for applause and admiration? Implied here is the depth of identification of the prospective administrator with professional values and with value systems in administrative theory, and his capacity to identify with the goals of the organization. As a general rule, if the future administrator is judged capable of giving up his new administrative functions without a major loss of his professional self-esteem, if, in other words, he has alternative sources of gratification, these sources of gratification and the sense of security they bring will be an important asset for the leader in his new position.

A major issue is the extent to which the administrator is aware of and invested in basic professional values, in contrast to being opportunistically involved with fashionable issues in order to bring about short-term gains. Particularly during times of rapid change, a number of basically uncreative and even mediocre professionals rise to the fore because they quickly shift to work in newly fashionable areas.

Another question is to what extent the candidate has shown the courage to fight openly for his convictions, rather than manipulating conflicts in the interests of power and prestige. The courage to stand up for his beliefs, to fight for his staff, to challenge the established powers—obviously in terms of the task, rather than in terms of immature emotional rebelliousness—is an important asset. One has to differentiate here the courage that stems from strength of conviction from that which represents paranoid querulousness, obsessive stubbornness, or narcissistic ruthlessness, but in practice it is not difficult to make that distinction. Strength and decisiveness are of course crucial for the painful decision-making process that is the main task of the administrator.

The extent to which the candidate obtains authentic enjoyment from the growth and development of other people is yet another important consideration in the selection of leadership. The creativity and success of those who work under him should not be threatened by his own excessive conflicts around envy.

Those in charge of evaluating potential leaders are usually aware of the importance of the leader's moral integrity as well as his purely professional skills and assets; my stress has been on the further importance of the leader's attitudes toward values—including professional values—and his relations with internal as well as external objects.

I mentioned earlier that there are normal narcissistic gratifications in leadership functions which, realistically viewed, should contribute to the prevention of pathological regressions in the administrator's personality and help to compensate for the regressive pulls that may be coming from group processes throughout the organization. In addition, an adequate resolution of his oedipal conflicts may permit the leader to protect himself from regressive group processes and may contribute to his ability to take the position of leadership, to enjoy success, to triumph over rivals, and to combine assertiveness with tolerance and humanity—all important aspects of administrative work. Similarly, sufficient gratification of his sexual and dependent needs outside the organizational structure will also help the leader to resist regressive group pressures. I am not saying, of course, that these issues are practical considerations that should enter the selection process. Regardless of its important role in his functioning, the administrator's personal and intrapsychic life, in contrast to his behavior, should remain private. His character structure and moral integrity, however, are part of the public domain.

Finally, under the best of circumstances there will be certain built-in organizational constraints related to the "human condition" of social organizations—to the limitations of the personalities of all the individuals involved; some battles need to be fought over and over again, even endlessly. The "ideal" administrator, like the "ideal" organization or the "ideal" group, will still reflect regressive group and individual fantasies.

REFERENCES

Adorno, T. W., et al. (1950), *The Authoritarian Personality*. New York: Harper.
Bion, W. R. (1959), *Experiences in Groups*. New York: Basic Books.
Dalton, G. W., et al. (1968), *The Distribution of Authority in Formal Organizations*. Cambridge, Mass.: Harvard University Press.
Emery, F. E., & Trist, E. L. (1973), *Towards a Social Ecology*. New York: Plenum.
Hodgson, R. C., Levinson, D. J., & Zaleznik, A. (1965), *The Executive Role Constellation:*

An Analysis of Personality and Role-Relations in Management. Cambridge, Mass.: Harvard University Press.

Kernberg, O. F. (1967), Borderline Personality Organization. *J. Amer. Psychoanal. Assn.*, 15:641-685.

———— (1970), Factors in the Psychoanalytic Treatment of Narcissistic Personalities. *J. Amer. Psychoanal. Assn.*, 18:51-85.

———— (1974), Further Contribution to the Treatment of Narcissistic Personalities. *Internat. J. of Psycho-Anal.*, 55:215-240.

———— (1978), Leadership and Organizational Functioning: Organizational Regression. *Internat. J. Group Psychother.*, 28:3-25.

Levinson, H. (1968), *The Exceptional Executive: A Psychological Conception*. Cambridge, Mass.: Harvard University Press.

———— (1971), *Organizational Diagnosis*. Cambridge, Mass.: Harvard University Press.

Main, T. F. (1957), The Ailment. *Brit. J. Med. Psychol.*, 30: 129-145.

Miller, E. J., & Rice, A. K. (1967), *Systems of Organization*. London: Tavistock.

Rice, A. K. (1963), *The Enterprise and Its Environment*. London: Tavistock.

———— (1964), Individual, Group and Intergroup Processes. *Human Relations*, 22:565-584.

———— (1965), *Learning for Leadership*. London: Tavistock.

Rioch, M. J. (1970a), The Work of Wilfred Bion on Groups. *Psychiatry*, 33:56-66.

———— (1970b), Group Relations: Rationale and Techniques. *Internat. J. Group Psychother.*, 10:340-355.

Rogers, K. (1973), Notes on Organizational Consulting to Mental Hospitals. *Bull. Menn. Clin.*, 37:211-231.

Sanford, N. (1956), The Approach of the Authoritarian Personality. In: *Psychology of Personality*, ed. J. L. McCary. New York: Logos Press.

Stanton, A. M., & Schwartz, M. (1954), *The Mental Hospital*. New York: Basic Books.

Zaleznik, A. (1974), Charismatic and Consensus Leaders: A Psychological Comparison. *Bull. Menn. Clin.*, 38:222-238.

In this chapter Kets de Vries elaborates further on work pathology by ex-
amining the causes and consequences of defective adaptation to the work en-
vironment, paying particular attention to the role of aggression and narcissism
in the manifestation of these various irrational behavior patterns.

3

Defective Adaptation to Work:
An Approach to Conceptualization

MANFRED F. R. KETS DE VRIES

> My view of life is utterly meaningless. I suppose an evil
> spirit has set a pair of spectacles on my nose, of which
> one lens is a tremendous magnifying glass, the other an
> equally powerful reducing glass.
>
> —*Søren Kierkegaard*

Working has been one of man's most constructive expressions
of living. Not only material needs but psychological needs as well
are served by it, including the maintenance of psychosocial equilibrium. The view of work as man's "link to reality" was understood
by Freud early on, and studies concerned with the detrimental
effects of unemployment (Bakke 1960; Singield 1968) have confirmed his view. In transforming existing ideas about work, Freud
complemented Marx's conceptions about economic determinism
with evidence that work transcended the mere focus on material
needs. Freud tied work to the individual's emotional state, viewing it as a way an individual develops and confirms his sense of
self-esteem. Menninger (1942) expanded Freud's ideas, mention-
ing that "in work, as contrasted with purposeless destruction, the

This chapter originally appeared in the *Bulletin of the Menninger Clinic*, 42:35-49, 1978.

aggressive impulses are molded and guided in a constructive direction by the influence of the creative (erotic) instinct" (p. 136). Others (e.g., Hendrick, 1943) have postulated an "instinct of workmanship" as an innate drive in man. White (1959, 1963), from a more developmental point of view, introduced the idea of "effectance motivation"—an individual develops a sense of effectiveness as a result of his ability to influence and master his environment by way of work.

But the ability to work is not an automatic process. Most people at some point in their lives experience impasses in their work capacity, usually of a temporary nature. Such experiences emphasize the importance of work for an individual's emotional and physical well-being. Incidences of work impairment and work inhibition also indicate the ambivalent nature of man's attitudes toward work: work which is associated by some with pleasure will be regarded by others as a necessary and material evil, a drudgery, and will be intensely resented. Moreover, the various forms of work alienation, with its overtones of powerlessness, meaninglessness, isolation, and self-estrangement, have become commonplace. Concepts such as job enrichment or enlargement, work restructuring, and organization development—all endeavors to make work more challenging and less monotonous—illustrate industry's concern about work alienation. Difficulties in coping with the work environment can lead not only to problems in production of a quantitative or qualitative nature but also to phenomena such as accident proneness, strikes, sickness, or industrial fatigue, and labor turnover. All these problems can be considered as the consequences of defective adaptation to the work environment.

A SENSE OF INADEQUACY

Freud, in his role as a theorist, made a pioneering effort to deal with the problem of work inhibition. In his study "Inhibitions, Symptoms and Anxiety" (1926), he tried to discern patterns in work impairment:

In inhibition in work—a thing which we so often have to

deal with as an isolated symptom in our therapeutic work—the subject feels a decrease in his pleasure in it or becomes less able to do it well; or he has certain reactions to it, like fatigue, giddiness or sickness, if he is obliged to go on with it. If he is a hysteric he will have to give up his work owing to the appearance of organic and functional paralyses which make it impossible for him to carry it on. If he is an obsessional neurotic he will be perpetually being distracted from his work or losing time over it through the introduction of delays and repetitions [p. 89].

In describing the reactions of various psychiatric stereotypes to work, Freud laid the foundation for a better understanding of the problem of work impairment.

Erikson (1963) continued Freud's endeavors, but placed greater emphasis on the social context and introduced as one of his "eight stages of man" the polarity of industry versus inferiority. He views this stage, which others have described as latency or as a period of "entrance into life," as crucial in the development of attitudes toward work. For Erikson, a sense of "industry involves doing things beside and with others [and implies] a first sense of division of labor and of differential opportunity" (p. 260). It is the period during which play becomes a guiding force and a building block for adaptive behavior. But adaptation to the world of work is not enough to establish the sense of effectiveness. A sense of inadequacy and inferiority may prevent the child from being at ease in any interpersonal encounter, or "a child's development . . . [may be] disrupted when family life has failed to prepare him for school life, or when school life fails to sustain promises of earlier stages" (p. 260). The final results of these developmental impairments are frustrations and disappointments in dealing with the work environment, which in turn contribute to job dissatisfaction and career stagnation.

AGGRESSION AS A DOUBLE BIND

Such incidents as accident proneness, impaired work performance, and absenteeism are merely the symptoms of a more deeply rooted psychological conflict centered around an individual's inner wishes, emotions, and motives. An individual's ability to cope with his immediate surroundings, to deal with the hazards and uncertainties of working life while fulfilling his aspirations, places high demands on those defenses needed for self-preservation. One derivative of the preservation of the self is the management and control of aggression which is closely tied to the enhancement or impairment of self-esteem; moreover, an individual's particular way of coping with aggression in the process of human development becomes an important factor in his attitudes toward work.

But the management and control of aggression resembles a two-edged sword—aggression can be directed inward or outward. The daily politics of organizational life with its built-in competitiveness gives ample evidence of projecting and directing aggressiveness toward others. However, the self-destructive aspects of inner-directed aggression remain puzzling because of the apparent contradiction with man's need for self-preservation.

Freud (1917) discussed the psychodynamics of the relationship between self-destruction or inner-directed aggression and self-preservation in his classic work, "Mourning and Melancholia." He explained the self-destructive elements present in grief as a reaction to narcissistic identification. This identification process implies that an individual views others as mirrors of the self; the attractive aspects of others will be incorporated with feelings of love and affection, while unattractive aspects will be expelled. With the loss of a loved person, a depletion of the self occurs; and due to the emotional attachments developed in the original identification process, remorse and self-reproach about the loss follow.

The notion that inner-directed aggression is linked with man's narcissism—an archaic love of self which provides the underpinning of self-preservation and is experienced gradually during the course of human development as a sense of self-esteem—has been furthered by Rochlin (1973), who supports the contention that an injury to narcissism always provokes aggression. The loss of self-esteem may be caused by an individual's self-doubts and demands, or by devaluation and abuse of others. Rochlin argues that the outlet may be twofold: Aggression may be projected onto others, or an individual may turn it upon himself, causing both social and inner conflicts.

Survival and adaptation to organizational life seem to be determined by the balance between inner-directed and outer-directed aggression. If aggression is too much inhibited and inner-directed, the result may be immobilization and incapacity to engage in any form of self-assertion. The organizational consequences of uncontrollable, outward-directed aggression are obvious. Disequilibrium in the balance between assertiveness and self-control may cause work adaptation problems.

With this brief overview as background, I shall delineate patterns of work adaptation problems in which man's management of aggression has a central role. That the various forms of work problems are highly interdependent, are not mutually exclusive, and can occur concurrently is self-evident; but in the effort to discern patterns, I may occasionally oversimplify or create artificial boundaries.

THE NARCISSISTIC POSITION

Early in the process of human development narcissism can be considered a necessary ingredient for self-preservation; however, extended, unmodified narcissism at a later stage of life may cause serious work disorders.

The Role of the Ego Ideal

The "narcissistic position" is probably the most complex cause of work problems because its manifestations can be so diverse. But threatened narcissism remains at the core. When threatened narcissism results in unrealistic incorporation and identification with reference figures who undermine self-esteem, fantasies centered around power and omnipotence gain in importance and even take over to counteract the experience of helplessness and loss. These fantasies can eventually replace reality. A consequence may be an unrealistic development of the ego ideal—that part of the powerful agency of inner surveillance, the conscience, which serves as a guide for the development of one's identity and one's aspirations. Unrealistic demands from the ego ideal make omnipotence and omniscience the only acceptable state of existence, and hence lead inevitably to disappointment. The individual is caught between the need to strive for perfection to placate his ego ideal, and his inner doubts about his ability to accomplish these goals.

The wish to be exceptional and the impossibility of achieving perfection turns any work effort a priori into a meaningless endeavor. Disturbed work capacity frequently evolves as a consequence of an emotional overinvestment in the grandiose self. Tartakoff (1966) noticed in her therapeutic work the wish to aggrandize, and she introduced the notion of a "Nobel Prize complex," exemplified by individuals with highly ambitious goals. She believed that the recurring problems around productive work were a consequence of the "all-or-nothing" attitude which characterizes these persons' aspirations. In her comments about this narcissistic form of work inhibition, she stated:

> The "Dream of Glory" which these patients entertain has been reinforced by goals in our social structure. It is, in fact, the personal expression of the American Dream—a narcissistic fantasy which has become institutionalized. The unconscious determinants of the Dream have remained repressed; therefore, feelings of depletion, precipitated by a realistic or fantasied disappointment, be it on the level of love or work, lead quickly to a sense of failure, often accompanied by depression and psychosomatic symptoms . . . [p. 238].

She later said that

> one is reminded of an addiction which is characterized by an insatiable desire to recover an infantile state of gratification which can never be fulfilled in reality. Disillusionment in such instances may not occur until middle age, when recognition

and reward on an ascending scale are no longer forthcoming [pp. 246-247].

The main theme in the "narcissistic position" seems to be the predominance of inner-directed aggression which, as I have indicated, can be viewed as a defensive means of coping with injured narcissism. Feelings of self-depreciation and inadequacy are the usual outcomes. Due to the "all-or-nothing" attitude surrounding this type of person's aspirations, the relationship with the work environment becomes fragile. Any disturbance of this individual's fantasies from within the organization may break "the spell" and lead to states of apathy, passivity, work inhibition, and recurring stress reactions. Moreover, a sense of depersonalization sets in. I am reminded of Camus's "stranger" for whom there was no feeling, no emotion, only a sense of numbness. The death of his mother, a girl's love for him, a terrible murder, all did not really matter to him; these events just passed by, like a movie, and he was an uninterested spectator.

The Installment Plan Approach

Since the desired perfection of living up to an exalted self-image becomes an impossible state to achieve, the individual begins to fear criticism, ostracism, and punishment; this fear, in turn, results in social anxiety. Such individuals seem to live in a continuous state of preparedness; they express uneasiness about the future and have a sense of impending doom, emotions which become particularly prominent in social situations. Around these individuals exists an aura of tension, a sense of anxiety and guilt due to an unforgiving, harsh conscience.

Freud (1916), in an article about people whom he called "the exceptions," mentions those who are "criminals out of a sense of guilt"—individuals who paradoxically seem to be in search of punishment. This concept may be applied to the work situation. The mere fact of being at work is perceived as a form of exposure, which makes one vulnerable and could turn into a danger. Good illustrations are stage fright and fear of examinations. Failure becomes identified with a loss of love and the accompanying danger of humiliation. The threat and fear of punishment may become so overwhelming that the conscience in a symbolic sense requires a sacrifice as a way of expiating feelings of guilt. For such individuals, regular, self-induced punishment to release tension—like paying off in installments—seems preferable to the continuous, threatening alternative of a sudden, much less controllable request for complete redemption. These individuals engage in unacceptable practices in the work situation and thereby continuously provoke criticism. This narcissistic form of work inhibition characterizes people who are unable to finish their organizational tasks and seem incapable or unwilling to live up to their promises.

Closely linked to this form of work inhibition is the need some individuals demonstrate to engage in incessant, frantic work activity (sometimes described as "Sunday neurosis" in people who become upset when they do not work). Although this behavior pattern seems far removed from the previous one, it is merely another way of expressing inner-directed aggression. These individuals go through robotlike movements, substituting means for ends, form for substance, and resemble the mythological figure Sisyphus who engaged in endless, impossible tasks without any real purpose. This pattern is not only a form of self-punishment but can also be considered a way of coping with and warding off a sense of self-fragmentation, which implies a lack of congruency in self-images. Inasmuch as inactivity may cause depressive reactions stemming from anxiety about adequacy, self-worth, and general fragmentation of the self, hyperactivity becomes a way of warding off this danger by placating the conscience through the "sacrifice" of work without concern for its meaningfulness.

The symptoms of disturbed work capacity are a manifestation of an excessive emotional investment by the grandiose self. Overwork and other forms of frantic activity turn into a means of preventing an emerging emotional breakdown and a dangerously increasing fragmentation of the self. These symptom patterns demonstrate that the ability to work necessitates an integration and moderation of existing grandiose fantasies with realistic ambitions and action patterns.

The Rivalrous Position

The problem of rivalry in the work setting has probably evolved out of the "narcissistic position." Again the role of inner-directed aggression is central, in this case as one of the possible strategies for dealing with the problem of rivalry.

In his review of the human life cycle, Erikson (1963) discussed the polarity of "initiative versus guilt," a dilemma which occurs during the oedipal stage of development:

> The danger of this stage is a sense of guilt over the goals contemplated and the acts initiated in one's exuberant enjoyment of new locomotor and mental power: acts of aggressive manipulation and coercion which soon go far beyond the executive capacity of organism and mind and therefore call for an energetic halt on one's contemplated initiative. While autonomy concentrates on keeping potential rivals out, and therefore can lead to jealous rage most often directed against encroachments by younger siblings, initiative brings with it anticipatory rivalry with those who have been there first and may, therefore, occupy with their superior equipment the field toward which one's initiative is directed. Infantile jealousy and rivalry, those often embittered and yet essentially futile attempts at demarcating a sphere of unquestioned privilege, now come to a climax in a final contest for a favored position with the mother; the usual failure leads to resignation, guilt, and anxiety [pp. 255-256].

The continuation of conflict around rivalry, the persistence in adult life of ghosts from the past, the interminable competition to be the "favored one" can lead to inhibited aggression, anxiety, and guilt over self-assertion and can cause problems in the work situation. These developments may have been induced by an originally precocious, premature specialization of talents that preempted the initiative to experiment. The threat of not living up to these originally excessive promises may result in work inhibition.

The simultaneous fear of failure and success is closely related to the issue of rivalry. The fear of failure, evoking memories of humiliation and defeat, does not need much explanation, but the same cannot be said about fear of success. Freud (1916) wrote about "those wrecked by success" who became sick when a deeply rooted and long-cherished wish was fulfilled. He gave the example of a professor who cherished the wish of receiving his former teacher's position at the university. When this wish came true, a depressive reaction soon followed; he engaged in accusations of a self-depreciatory nature and was unable to work. Shakespeare's Lady Macbeth is another individual who had an emotional breakdown after obtaining what she desperately wanted.

The fixation on success, limitless achievement, and societal acclaim arouses primitive emotions centered around annihilation and loss of self, since success may be unconsciously equated with the need to undergo a personality transformation, i.e., to lose one's original identity. Success is also associated with the fear of retaliation from those with whom one is in competition. That success and competitiveness evoke the envy of others and make an individual stand out led Maslow (1968) to introduce the idea of the "Jonah complex," the fear of one's own greatness. The Prometheus myth and the Don Juan legend moralize about the dangers of incurring the wrath of the gods. The goddess Nemesis, who symbolizes envy and is the enemy of too much success and happiness, represents the universal fear that too much success and happiness causes *koros* (self-satisfaction), and too much *koros* leads to *hubris* or excessive pride, which cannot be tolerated and will provoke punishment. The story of Polycrates, tyrant of Sumos, provides illustration. Terrified by his unheard-of luck and hoping to forestall the envy of the gods, he threw a priceless ring into the sea. But the ring returned in the belly of a fish, and Polycrates knew that Nemesis had refused his sacrifice and that misfortune would come his way.

People in the grip of the "rivalrous position" see the potential competition with work associates as having an impact far beyond the reality of the situation. Superiors and subordinates arouse strong aggressive feelings which become inner-directed and contribute to a state of work paralysis. The legacy of memories about conflicted competitiveness in the early family environment prevents a conflict-free attitude toward present reality.

THE DEPENDENT POSITION

Work adaptation problems can also be attributed to the "dependent position" in which inner-directed aggression is coupled with dependent reactions. Again I must refer to the process of human development—to identification, the internalization of values, and the various ways an individual deals with frustration and dissatisfaction in his interactions—to find explanations. Crises in early interpersonal human encounters are frequent and may cause emotional disruptions and perceptual distortions. It is only under optimal conditions of "good enough" care that disappointment with idealized figures or role models will occur gradually, without traumatic incident. Consistency in childrearing contributes to a sense of realism in the internalization of values, and reduces excessive discrepancies between a person's fantasies and reality.

When excessive disruption of relationships with parental figures occurs (e.g., traumatic loss), severe (as opposed to gradual) disappointment sets in and disrupts the desired internalization process, so that what in ordinary circumstances should lead to an increasing sense of mastery and control over the environment and to feelings of independence now changes into something which might be described as a "search for the lost object." An undefined sense of loss, of longing, continues to dominate the psychic structure, leading to feelings of dependency. Even though the excessive use of shame as a controlling device leads to a pervasive sense of doubt, the heightening of conscience may give rise to a deep and lasting sense of guilt in interpersonal relationships. Dependent behavior with the purpose of alleviating these feelings and finding support for one's actions becomes a way of life.

Various studies on childhood (Bowlby 1969, 1973; White 1972) indicate that impaired development of this type may lead the adult to be apathetic, to have difficulties in taking initiative, and to experience problems in personal control and human relations.

Apathy becomes a way of withdrawing from stimuli when other efforts to reduce tension are chronically frustrated. Helplessness and dependency seem to result from a state of chronic tension between highly charged narcissistic aspirations and the sense of impotence encountered in attempting to live up to these expectations.

White (1952), in his perceptive longitudinal study of three lives, illustrates this process with a description of a temporary crisis of dependency and work inhibition in one of his subjects. Joseph Kidd, a businessman, experienced a precocious early development that stressed appearances—he was a "beautiful child"—and that predisposed him to both helplessness and self-consciousness. His childhood was devastated by conflicting demands and feelings of inferiority which led to a serious emotional crisis during his student years. Highly dependent on the esteem of others to maintain his psychological equilibrium, Kidd manifested all the symptoms of the "dependent position":

> I often think about how I look and what impression I am making upon others; my feelings are easily hurt by ridicule or by the slighting remarks of others; when I enter a room I often become self-conscious and feel that the eyes of others are upon me; I often interpret the remarks of others in a personal way; I pay a good deal of attention to my appearance: clothes, hats, shoes, neckties. . . .
> I had lost all ability to concentrate, remember, think and concentrate. I just couldn't study because when I did I became all nerved up and jumpy [pp. 171-172].

Joseph Kidd eventually managed to work himself out of this psychological impasse; but for others who do not have sufficient emotional resources, the "dependent position" becomes a chronic problem.

The "dependent position" is not only characterized by a sense of longing but by another factor as well. In a symbolic sense the notion of work becomes equated with a sense of independence and being in control—perceptions and feelings that cause a fear of becoming a target and being victimized. My earlier comments about the "installment plan approach" to psychological punishment apply here as well. Working, when it is perceived as a form of independence, becomes a threat since it may arouse the attention of others, and with attention may come disapproval. The issue is reminiscent of the fear of success associated with the "rivalrous position." Therefore, the way of avoiding disapproval is through self-recrimination which, in turn, serves both as an invitation for positive reassurance and as a means of warding off imagined dangers. A combination of the fear of victimization and disapproval causes postponement or avoidance of responsibility. The individual, not wanting to be taken seriously, takes refuge in helplessness, ignorance, idleness, and irresponsible, seemingly playful acts. Work problems such as accident proneness, alcoholism, drug addiction, and hypochondria may all be expressions of the "dependent position."

People in the "dependent position" make excessive demands on others and tend to become angry and anxious when their demands are not met. Such reactions may not cause concern unless they lead to a state of depression. Naturally, the other end of the spectrum, excessively independent behavior, has its own problems, such as inability to establish close relationships, with consequent negative implications for collaboration and teamwork. However, given the work environment's emphasis on activity, decision making, and assertiveness, excessive dependency is the more serious problem.

THE REBELLIOUS POSITION

As I have pointed out, inner-directed aggression is usually at the core of work problems. But one form of work problem can be linked to outer-directed aggression, which, combined with a sense of independence, may cause work problems that take the form of rebellion.

Camus (1951) summarized the problem of rebelliousness by saying, "I rebel—therefore we exist" (p. 22) and added that "the rebel . . . from his very first step, refuses to allow anyone to touch what he is. He is fighting for the integrity of one part of his being. He does not try primarily to conquer, but simply to impose" (p. 18). For those in the "rebellious position," complete work paralysis is uncommon; the individual will usually retain his ability to function. Unfortunately, it is precisely his way of functioning that becomes the problem. The provocative manner that characterizes his work behavior becomes a cause of irritation and annoyance and may result in discharge or demotion. The "rebellious position" is often typical of "job hoppers"—those individuals who seem incapable of holding onto a job for a prolonged period of time. These people manage continuously to get in trouble with their superiors and seem caught in an endless cycle of being hired and fired. Their life in organizations has all the characteristics of a self-fulfilling prophecy where the worst is expected and therefore occurs.

For individuals prone to the "rebellious position," work resembles a duty, a demand imposed by authority figures, and therefore the opposite of pleasure. Although not necessarily a conscious process, work turns into a symbolic struggle for obedience and control.

Again the origins of this condition can be found in childhood development. Generally, these individuals portray a lack of identification with parental authority, a possible outcome of excessive frustration with parents, resulting from their seeming rejection. A combination of rejection and insufficient parental control weakens one's motivation for compliance by undermining the development of internal constraints, foresight, and an appreciation of the consequences of one's actions. Parents are perceived as confusing and inconsistent; there is no making sense of them; they are obstacles that must be overcome. These patterns of family interactions are transferred to other authority figures and will eventually determine the nature of interpersonal relationships. Lack of identification with parental authority may turn into a compensatory reaction as reflected in rebelliousness. The final outcome resembles a kind of masochistic transference reaction to authority figures which has strong destructive overtones, implying that for those in the "rebellious position," aggression is not only outer-directed but has, in addition, an inner-directed component.

Although this pattern of provocative behavior occasionally may be viewed as a sign of real independence, in most instances the term "pseudoindependence" is probably more accurate, because of the highly charged emotions centering around the desire to rebel. What is missing in these individuals' human relationships is the sense of playfulness which prevents defensive rigidity and which is one of the building stones for adaptive behavior.

The classical entrepreneur, the individual who jumps from one new undertaking to another, has some characteristics of the "rebellious position." However, the entrepreneur circumvents the destructive "roller coaster ride" of disappointments and frustrations in work relationships that characterize the "rebellious position" by his decision to become his own man, and thus the entrepreneur eventually masters his conflicts about control by being in control of his own structured situation. But most people who fall into the "rebellious position" do not show the entrepreneur's foresight of making a career choice which excludes dealing with superiors. Instead, these individuals usually drift through organizational life troubled by frustrations and disappointments.

HOMO FABER AND HOMO LUDENS

An individual's failure to function in an organizational setting seems to a large extent to be the legacy of frustrating interpersonal experiences at earlier stages of life. The symptoms that individuals exhibit in organizations are basically the outcomes of defensive reactions. The avoidance of feelings of self-fragmentation, a sense of nothingness, only leads to rigidity and prevents adaptive behavior. Adaptability, with its implicit playfulness, acceptance of the unexpected, and ease of action, is too risky. The individual controls his inner-directed and outer-directed aggression and ensures selected outlets for his aggression with ritualistic behavior. Based on his ethological studies Lorenz (1966) comments,

for a living being lacking insight into the relation between causes and effects it must be extremely useful to cling to a behavior pattern which has once or many times proved to achieve its aim, and to have done so without danger. If one does not know which details of the whole performance are essential for its success as well as for its safety, it is best to cling to them all with slavish exactitude [p. 72].

Man prefers known dangers to the unknown, even if the former means illness. Insight is feared; it deviates from established patterns, disturbs the homeostatic state, and causes uneasiness. Defensive strategies are devised to deal with these unknown situations; but these defenses are certainly not impregnable. Symptoms become indications that all is not well. Unfortunately, to put an end to self-fulfilling prophecies, to reevaluate, and more importantly to break repetitive patterns are difficult endeavors, painful journeys of personal insight. But although man clings to the known with incredible tenacity, he also will "search for a cure," given sufficient pain and discomfort. And although it may take time to disrupt a sense of wish fulfillment—to realize that there are no "instant solutions" but, instead, only arduous roads to change—change is possible. If childhood did not provide security and a base for developing adaptive behavior, adulthood can, but with much greater effort and discomfort. It necessitates a journey of critical reevaluation, a reexamination and redefinition of behavior, an effort which ultimately may increase self-awareness and insight and prevent defective adaptation to work. It may even make work pleasurable.

Karl Menninger (1942) understood this process well and argued that for work to be pleasurable the following conditions have to be met:

Externally there must be a minimum of compulsion, an opportunity for comfortable group feeling with fellow-workers, absence of intense discomfort or fatigue in the performance of the work, proper provision for interspersed rest and recreation periods, a realization of pride in the product and a conviction that the work is useful and appreciated. *Internally*, there must be relative freedom from guilt feelings connected with pleasure and from neurotic compulsions either to work or not to work [p. 166].

These conditions are extremely demanding, particularly the intrapersonal and interpersonal ones. They imply a direct confrontation with the self, an integration of feeling and thinking, and a determination of one's role in the organization. Direct confrontation with the self also involves honesty about one's feelings and belief systems.

While physiological changes mark the predictable, natural points for psychological growth in childhood, adulthood provides less dramatic opportunities for change but does not exclude change, including adaptation to organizational life. A weakening of the personality's defensive structures is only one step and, by itself, would leave a person wide open to emotional disarray. More is needed to eliminate anxiety about change and to replace rigidity in behavior with greater adaptability, an implicit acceptance of confrontation, and self-evaluation. What might be needed is a form of "regression in the service of the ego," implying the reintroduction in adulthood of the play element so important in childhood. Play once made for a sense of efficacy, added to feelings of security, and helped to prevent rigidity in behavior.

The culture historian Huizinga's (1944) advocacy of the need for a play element in culture, the reunion of *homo faber* with *homo ludens*, has not lost its significance. The combination of play and work aids in preventing repetition compulsion and will strengthen those external and internal forces needed for effective functioning. Awareness that work needs a play element may help an individual avoid being "stuck" in dysfunctional behavior patterns in organizations. It is adaptability in behavior which, in the final analysis, makes for relaxed, more open interpersonal relations, prevents symptom formation, forestalls work problems, and makes work pleasurable.

REFERENCES

Bakke, E. W. (1960), The Cycle of Adjustment to Unemployment. In: *A Modern Introduction to the Family*, ed. N. W. Bell & E. F. Vogel. Glencoe, Ill.: Free Press.

Bowlby, J. (1969), *Attachment and Loss. Vol. 1: Attachment.* New York: Basic Books.
——— (1973), *Attachment and Loss. Vol. 2: Separation, Anxiety and Anger.* New York: Basic Books.
Camus, A. (1951), *The Rebel.* New York: Vintage.
Erikson, E. H. (1963), *Childhood and Society.* New York: Norton.
Freud, S. (1916), Some Character-Types Met with in Psycho-Analytic Work. *Standard Edition,* 14:309-333. London: Hogarth Press, 1957.
——— (1917), Mourning and Melancholia. *Standard Edition,* 14:237-258. London: Hogarth Press, 1957.
——— (1926), Inhibitions, Symptoms and Anxiety. *Standard Edition,* 20:75-174. London: Hogarth Press, 1959.
Hendrick, I. (1943), Work and the Pleasure Principle. *Psychoanal. Quart.,* 12(3):311-29.
Huizinga, J. (1944), *Homo Ludens: A Study of the Play-Element in Culture.* Boston: Beacon Press.
Lorenz, K. (1966), *On Aggression.* New York: Harcourt, Brace & World.
Maslow, A. H. (1968), The Jonah Complex. In: *Interpersonal Dynamics: Essays and Readings on Human Interaction,* Rev. Ed., ed. W. G. Bennis et. al. Homewood, Ill.: Dorsey.
Menninger, K. A. (1942), *Love Against Hate.* New York: Harcourt, Brace & World.
Rochlin, G. (1973), *Man's Aggression: The Defense of the Self.* Boston: Gambit.
Singield, A. (1968), *The Long-Term Unemployed.* Paris: Organization for Economic Co-operation & Development.
Tartakoff, H. H. (1966), The Normal Personality in Our Culture and the Nobel Prize Complex. In: *Psychoanalysis—A General Psychology: Essays in Honor of Heinz Hartmann,* ed. R. M. Loewenstein et al. New York: International Universities Press.
White, R. W. (1952), *Lives in Progress: A Study of the Natural Growth of Personality.* New York: Dryden Press.
——— (1959), Motivation Reconsidered: The Concept of Competence. *Psychol. Rev.,* 66:297-333.
——— (1963), *Ego and Reality in Psychoanalytic Theory.* [*Psychological Issues,* Monogr. 11.] New York: International Universities Press.
——— (1972), *The Enterprise of Living: Growth and Organization in Personality.* New York: Holt, Rinehart & Winston.

In this chapter Henry addresses the problem of clarifying and predicting executive functioning. Since the clue to the failure of many highly competent persons to be effective in management positions lies in their social relationships, this paper explores the importance of the personality structure in the selection of executives by examining the personality traits held in common by a group of successful business executives. Maccoby in Chapter 5 and Zaleznik in Chapter 6 take up the same issue. The effect of the cost of being "successful" is also explored.

4

The Business Executive: The Psychodynamics of a Social Role

WILLIAM E. HENRY

The business executive is a central figure in the economic and social life of the United States. His direction of business enterprise and his participation in informal social groupings give him a significant place in community life. In both its economic and its social aspects the role of the business executive is sociologically a highly visible one. It has clearly definable limits and characteristics known to the general public. These characteristics indicate the function of the business executive in the social structure, define the behavior expected of the individual executive, and serve as a guide to the selection of the novice.

Social pressure plus the constant demands of the business organization of which he is a part direct the behavior of the ex-

---

This chapter originally appeared in *The American Journal of Sociology*, 54:286-291, 1949, by permission of the author and the University of Chicago Press. Copyright © 1949, the University of Chicago Press.

ecutive into the mold appropriate to the defined role. "Success" is the name applied to the whole-hearted adoption of the role. The individual behaves in the manner dictated by the society, and society rewards the individual with "success" if his behavior conforms to the role. It would punish him with "failure" should he deviate from it.

Participation in this role, however, is not a thing apart from the personality of the individual. It is not a game that the person is playing; it is the way of behaving and thinking that he knows best, that he finds rewarding, and in which he believes. Thus the role as socially defined has its counterpart in personality structure. To some extent, too, the personality structure is reshaped to be in harmony with the social role. The extent to which such re-shaping of the adult personality is possible, however, seems limited. An initial selection process occurs which reduces the amount of time involved in teaching the appropriate behavior. Persons whose personality structure is most readily adaptable to this particular role tend to be selected, whereas those whose personality is not already partially akin are rejected.

This paper describes the personality commonalities of a group of successful business executives. The research upon which it is based explored the general importance of personality structure in the selection of executive personnel. Many aptitude tests have been employed in industry to decrease the risk involved in the hiring of untried personnel and to assist in their placement. These tests have been far less effective in the selection of high-level executive personnel than in the selection of clerical and other non-administrating persons. Many business executives have found that persons of unquestioned high intelligence often turn out to be ineffective when placed in positions of increased responsibility. The reasons for their failure lie in their social relationships. No really effective means has yet been found to clarify and predict this area of executive functioning. It is to this problem that our research[1] was directed.

From the research it became clear that the "successful"[2] business executives studied had many personality characteristics in common. (It was equally clear that an absence of these characteristics was coincident with "failure" within the organization.) This personality constellation might be thought of as the minimal requirement for "success" within our present business system and as the psychodynamic motivation of persons in this occupation. Individual uniqueness in personality was clearly present; but, despite these unique aspects, all executives had in common this personality pattern.

ACHIEVEMENT DESIRES

Successful executives show high drive and achievement desire. They conceive of themselves as hardworking and achieving persons who must accomplish in order to be happy. The areas in which they do their work are clearly different, but each feels this

---

[1]The research undertaken will be described in its entirety in a subsequent report. In summary, it involved the study of over one hundred business executives in various types of business houses. The techniques employed were the Thematic Apperception test, a short undirected interview, and a projective analysis of a number of traditional personality tests. The validity of our analyses, which are done "blind", rested upon the coincidence of the identical conclusions from separately analyzed instruments, upon surveys of past job performance, and upon the anecdotal summary of present job behavior by the executive's superiors and associates.

[2]Success and failure as here used refer to the combined societal and business definitions. All our "successful" executives have a history of continuous promotion, are thought to be still "promotable" within the organization, are now in positions of major administrative responsibility, and are earning salaries within the upper ranges of current business salaries. Men in lower supervisory positions, men who are considered "failures" in executive positions, and men in clerical and laboring jobs show clear deviations from this pattern. This suggests, of course, that this pattern is specific for the successful business executive and that it serves to differentiate him from other groupings in industry.

The majority of these executives come from distributive (rather than manufacturing) businesses of moderately loose organizational structure in which cooperation and team work are valued and in which relative independence of action is stressed within the framework of a clearly defined overall company policy. In organizations in which far greater rigidity of structure is present or in which outstanding independence of action is required, it is possible that there will be significant variations from the personality pattern presented here. We are currently extending our data in these directions.

drive for accomplishment. This should be distinguished from a type of pseudoachievement drive in which the glory of the end product alone is stressed. The person with this latter type of drive, seldom found in the successful executives, looks to the future in terms of the glory it will provide him and of the projects that he will have completed—as opposed to the achievement drive of the successful executive, which looks more toward the sheer accomplishment of the work itself. The successful business leader gets much satisfaction from doing rather than from merely contemplating the completed product. To some extent this is the difference between the dreamer and the doer. It is not that the successful executives do not have an overall goal in mind or that they do not derive satisfaction from the contemplation of future ease or that they do not gain pleasure from prestige. Far more real to them, however, is the continual stimulation that derives from the pleasure of immediate accomplishment.

MOBILITY DRIVE

All successful executives have strong mobility drives. They feel the necessity of moving continually upward and of accumulating the rewards of increased accomplishment. For some the sense of successful mobility comes through the achievement of competence on the job. These men struggle for increased responsibility and derive a strong feeling of satisfaction from the completion of a task. Finished work and newly gained competence provide them with their sense of continued mobility.

A second group relies more upon the social prestige of increased status in their home communities or within the organizational hierarchy. Competence in work is of value and at times crucial. But the satisfactions of the second group come from the social reputation, not from the personal feeling that necessary work has been well done. Both types of mobility drive are highly motivating. The zeal and energy put into the job is equal in both instances. The distinction appears in the kinds of work which the men find interesting. For the first group the primary factor is the nature of the work itself—it is challenging, is it necessary, is it interesting? For the second group the crucial factor is its relation to their goals of status mobility—is it a step in the direction of increased prestige, is it appropriate to their present position, what would other people think of them if they did it?

THE IDEA OF AUTHORITY

The successful executive posits authority as a controlling but helpful relationship to superiors. He looks to his superiors as persons of more advanced training and experience, whom he can consult on special problems and who issue to him certain guiding directives. He does not see the authorities in his environment as destructive or prohibiting forces.

Those executives who view authority as a prohibiting and destructive force have difficulty relating themselves to superiors and resent their authority over them. They are either unable to work smoothly with superiors or indirectly and unconsciously do things to obstruct the work of their bosses or to assert their independence unnecessarily.

It is of interest that to these men the dominant crystallization of attitudes about authority is toward superior and toward subordinates, rather than toward self. This implies that most crucial in their concept of authority is the view of being a part of a wider and more final authority system. In contrast, a few executives of the "self-made," driving type characteristic of the past of business enterprise maintain a specific concept of authority with regard to self. They are the men who almost always forge their own frontiers, who are unable to operate within anyone else's framework, and to whom cooperation and team work are foreign concepts. To these men the ultimate authority is in themselves, and their image does not include the surrounding area of shared or delegated power.

ORGANIZATION AND ITS IMPLICATIONS

While executives who are successful vary considerably in their intelligence-test ratings, all of them have a high degree of ability to organize unstructured situations and to see the implications of their organization. This implies that they have the ability to take several seemingly isolated events or facts and to see relationships that exist between them. Further, they are interested in looking into the future and are concerned with predicting the outcome of their decisions and actions.

This ability to organize often results in a forced organization, however. Even though some situations arise with which they feel unfamiliar and are unable to cope, they still force an organization upon it. Thus they bring it into the sphere of familiarity. This tendency operates partially as a mold, as a pattern into which new or unfamiliar experiences are fit. This means, of course, that there is a strong tendency to rely upon techniques that they know will work and to resist situations which do not readily fit this mold.

DECISIVENESS

Decisiveness is a further trait of this group. This does not imply the popular idea of the executive making quick and final decisions in rapid-fire succession, although this seems to be true of some of the executives. More crucial, however, is an ability to come to a decision among several alternative courses of action—whether it be done on the spot or after detailed consideration. Very seldom does this ability fail. While less competent and well-organized individuals may become flustered and operate inefficiently in certain spots, most of these men force their way to a conclusion. Nothing is too difficult for them to tackle and at least try to solve. When poorly directed and not modified by proper judgment, this attitude may be more a handicap than a help. That is to say, this trait remains in operation and results in decision-making action regardless of the reasonableness of the decision or its reality in terms of related facts. The loss of this trait (usually found only in cases in which some more profound personality change has also occurred) is one of the most disastrous for the executive: his superiors become apprehensive about him. This suggests an interesting relationship to the total executive constellation. The role demands conviction and certainty. Whenever a junior executive loses this quality of decisiveness, he seems to pass out of the socially defined role. The weakening of other aspects of the ideal executive constellation can be readily reintegrated into the total constellation. The questioning of the individual's certainty and decisiveness, however, results in a weakening of the entire constellation and tends to be punished by superiors.

Strong Self-Structure

One way of differentiating between people is in the relative strength or weakness of their notions of self-identity, their self-structure. Some persons lack definiteness and are easily influenced by outside pressures. Some, such as these executives, are firm and well-defined in their sense of self-identity. They know what they are and what they want and have well-developed techniques for getting what they want. The things they want and the techniques for getting them are, of course, quite different for each individual, but this strength and firmness is a common and necessary characteristic. It is, of course, true that too great a sense of self-identity leads to rigidity and inflexibility; and, while some of these executives could genuinely be accused of this, in general they maintain considerable flexibility and adaptability within the framework of their desires and within the often rather narrow possibilities of their own business organization.

Activity and Aggression

The executive is essentially an active, striving, aggressive person. His underlying motivations are active and aggressive, although he is not necessarily overtly aggressive and hostile in his dealings with other people. This activity and aggressiveness are always well channeled into work or struggles for status and prestige—which implies a constant need to keep moving, to do something, to be active. This does not mean that they are always in bodily movement and moving physically from place to place (though this is often true) but rather that they are mentally and emotionally alert and active. This constant motivator unfortunately cannot be shut off. It may be part of the reason why so many executives find themselves unable to take vacations at leisure or to stop worrying about already solved problems.

APPREHENSION AND THE FEAR OF FAILURE

If one is continually active and always trying to solve problems and arrive at decisions, any inability to do so successfully may well result in feelings of frustration. This seems to be true of the executives. In spite of their firmness of character and their drive to activity, they also harbor a rather pervasive feeling that they may not really succeed and be able to do the things they want to do. It is not implied that this sense of frustration comes only from their immediate business experience. It seems far more likely to be a feeling of long standing within them and to be only accentuated and reinforced by their present business experience.

This sense of the perpetually unattained is an integral part of this constellation and is part of its dilemma. It means that there is always some place to go, but no defined point at which to stop. The executive is "self-propelled" and needs to keep moving always and to see another goal ever ahead, which also suggests that cessation of mobility and of struggling for new achievements will be accompanied by an inversion of this constant energy. The person whose mobility is blocked, either by his own limitations or by those of the social system, finds this energy diverted into other channels. Psychosomatic symptoms, the enlargement of interpersonal dissatisfactions, and the development of rationalized compulsive and/or paranoid-like defenses may reflect the redirection of this potent energy demand.

STRONG REALITY ORIENTATION

Successful executives are strongly oriented to immediate realities and their implications. They are directly interested in the practical, the immediate, and the direct. This is, of course, generally good for the immediate business situation, though the executive with an overdeveloped sense of reality may cease to be a man of vision; for a man of vision must get above reality to plan and even dream about future possibilities. In addition, a too strong sense of reality, when the realities are not in tune with ambitions, may well lead to a conviction that reality is frustrating and unpleasant. This happens to many executives who find progress and promotion too slow for their drives. The result is often a restlessness rather than an activity, a fidgetiness rather than a well-channeled aggression, and a lack of ease that may well disrupt many of their usual interpersonal relations.

The Nature of Their Interpersonal Relations

In general the mobile and successful executive looks to his superiors with a feeling of personal attachment and tends to identify himself with them. His superior represents for him a symbol of his own achievement and desires, and he tends to identify himself with these traits in those who have achieved more. He is very responsive to his superiors—the nature of this responsiveness, of course, depends on his other feelings, his idea of authority, and the extent to which he feels frustrated.

On the other hand, he looks on his subordinates in a detached and impersonal way, seeing them as "doers of work" rather than as people. He treats them impersonally, with no real feeling of being akin to them or of having deep interest in them as persons. It is as though he viewed his subordinates as representatives of things he has left behind, both factually and emotionally. Still uncertain of his next forward step, he cannot afford to become personally identified or emotionally involved with the past. The only direction of his emotional energy that is real to him is upward and toward the symbols of that upward interest, his superiors.

This does not mean that he is cold and that he treats all subordinates casually. In fact he tends to be generally sympathetic with many of them. This element of sympathy with subordinates is most apparent when the subordinate shows personality traits that are most like those of the superior. Thus the superior is able to take pride in certain successful young persons without at the same time feeling an equal interest in all subordinates.

The Attitude Toward His Own Parents

In a sense the successful executive is a "man who has left home." He feels and acts as though he were on his own, as though his emotional ties and obligations to his parents were severed. It seems to be most crucial that he has not retained resentment of his parents, but has rather simply broken their emotional hold on him and been left psychologically free to make his own decisions. We have found those who have not broken this tie to be either too dependent upon their superiors in the work situation or to be resentful of their supervision (depending, of course, upon whether they are still bound to their parents or are still actively fighting against them).

In general we find the relationship to the mother to have been the most clearly broken tie. The tie to the father remains positive in the sense that he views the father as a helpful but not restraining figure. Those men who still feel a strong emotional tie to the mother have systematically had difficulty in the business situation. This residual emotional tie seems contradictory to the necessary attitude of activity, progress, and channeled aggression. The tie to the father, however, must remain positive—as the emotional counterpart of the admired and more successful male figure. Without this image, struggle for success seems difficult.

The Nature of Dependency Feelings and Concentration upon Self

A special problem in differentiating the type of generally successful executive is the nature of his dependency feelings. It was pointed out above that the dependency upon the mother image must be eliminated. For those executives who work within the framework of a large organization in which cooperation and group-and-company loyalty are necessities, there must remain feelings of dependency upon the father image and a need to operate within an established framework. This does not mean that the activity-aggression need cannot operate or that the individual is not decisive and self-directional. It means only that he is so within the framework of an already established set of overall goals. For most executives this overall framework provides a needed guidance and allows them to concentrate upon their achievement and work demands with only minimal concern for the policy-making of the entire organization. For those executives who prefer complete independence and who are unable to work within a framework established by somebody else, the element of narcissism is much higher and their feelings of loyalty are only to themselves rather than to a father image or its impersonal counterpart in company policy. These feelings differentiate the executives who can co-operate with others and who can promote the overall policy of a company from those who must be the whole show themselves. Clearly there are situations in which the person highly concentrated upon self and with little feeling of dependency loyalty is of great value. But he should be distinguished in advance and be placed only in situations in which these traits are useful.

The successful executive represents a crystallization of many of the attitudes and values generally accepted by middle-class American society. The value of accumulation and achievement, of self-directedness and independent thought and their rewards in prestige and status and property, are found in this group. But they also pay the price of holding these values and of profiting from them. Uncertainty, constant activity, the continual fear of losing ground, the inability to be introspectively leisurely, the ever present fear of failure, and the artificial limitations put upon their emotionalized interpersonal relations—these are some of the costs of this role.

The problem facing the new type of industrial leader—the gamesman—is the fact that his work develops his head, but not his heart. Maccoby reaches these conclusions on the basis of interviews with 250 managers in twelve well-known corporations, concentrating on healthy companies. He discusses the four basically different character types of leaders: the craftsman, the jungle fighter, the company man, and the gamesman. He also examines the manifestation of stress symptoms, the way managers view intellectual and emotional qualities, and the balance between love and work.

5

The Corporate Climber Has to Find His Heart

MICHAEL MACCOBY

A new type of man is taking over the leadership of the most technically advanced large companies in America. In contrast to the jungle-fighter industrialists commonly associated with the turn of the century, the new leader is driven not to build or preside over empires, but to organize winning teams. Unlike the security-seeking organization man who became the stereotype of the Fifties, he is excited by the chance to cut deals and to gamble.

The new industrial leader is not as hardhearted as the autocratic empire builder, nor is he as dependent on the company as the organization man. But he is more detached and emotionally inaccessible than either. And he is troubled by that fact: he recognizes that his work develops his head but not his heart.

As a practicing psychoanalyst, I reached these conclusions on

This chapter originally appeared in *Fortune*, December, 1976, pp. 98-108. By permission of the author.

the basis of interviews with 250 managers, ranging from chief executives down to lower-level professional employees in twelve well-known corporations.[1] In some cases we returned to particular managers several times to talk about how their work was influencing the development of their characters. We spent at least three hours with most, as long as twenty hours with some. In a few cases we also interviewed their wives and children, and seventy-five executives took Rorschach tests.

In contrast to psychoanalysts who study the emotionally disturbed, we concentrated on healthy people in healthy companies. Most of the companies have sales exceeding $1 billion a year, and all are highly technological, the creators of some of the most advanced products of our age. They practice, and some invented, managerial techniques and business strategies that others admire and copy. Their top managers tend to speak out on major public issues, and a few have held high government positions. No one has accused these companies of trying to overthrow governments, bribe officials, or beg Washington to bail them out of their mistakes.

CREATURES IN A CORPORATE CULTURE

I wanted to find out what motivates the managers of these corporations—what mix of ambition, greed, scientific interest, security seeking, or idealism. How are managers molded by their work? What is the quality of their lives? What type of person reaches the top (and which falls by the wayside)?

Once we had studied the interviews and the Rorschach tests, it became clear that the corporation is populated by four basically different character types. These are "ideal" types in the sense that few people fit any one of them exactly. Most executives are mixtures of two or more, but in practically every case we were

[1]The study was sponsored by the Harvard Seminar on Science, Technology, and Public Policy, and supported by the Andrew W. Mellon Foundation. With the help of Douglass Carmichael, Rolando Weissmann, Dennis M. Greene, Cynthia Elliott, and Katherine A. Terzi, I conducted the interviews over six years.

able to agree on which type best described a person. And the individual and his colleagues almost always agreed with our assessment.

The Craftsman, as the name implies, holds traditional values, including the work ethic, respect for people, concern for quality, and thrift. When he talks about his work, he shows an interest in the *process* of making something; he enjoys building. He sees others, co-workers as well as superiors, in terms of whether they help or hinder him in doing a craftsmanlike job.

Many of the managers in the great corporate laboratories, such as Du Pont and Bell Labs, are craftsmen by character. Their virtues are admired by almost everyone. Yet they are so absorbed in perfecting their own creations—even to the exclusion of broader corporate goals—that they are unable to lead complex and changing organizations.

The Jungle Fighter lusts for power. He experiences life and work as a jungle where it is eat or be eaten, and the winners destroy the losers. A major part of his psychic resources are budgeted for his internal department of defense. Jungle fighters tend to see their peers as either accomplices or enemies, and their subordinates as objects to be used.

There are two types of jungle fighters, lions and foxes. The lions are the conquerors who, when successful, may build an empire. In large industry, the day of the lions—the Carnegies and the Fords—seems virtually ended. The foxes make their nests in the corporate hierarchy and move ahead by stealth and politicking. The most gifted foxes we encountered rose rapidly by making use of their entrepreneurial skills. But in each case they were eventually destroyed by those they had used or betrayed.

The Company Man bases his sense of identity on being part of the protective organization. At his weakest, he is fearful and submissive, seeking security even more than success. At his strongest, he is concerned with the human side of the company, interested in the feelings of the people around him, and committed to maintaining corporate integrity. The most creative company men sustain an atmosphere of cooperation and stimulation, but they tend to lack the daring to lead highly competitive and innovative organizations.

The Gamesman sees business life in general, and his career in particular, in terms of options and possibilities, as if he were playing a game. He likes to take calculated risks and is fascinated by techniques and new methods. The contest hypes him up and he communicates his enthusiasm, energizing his peers and subordinates like the quarterback on a football team. Unlike the jungle fighter, the gamesman competes not to build an empire or to pile up riches, but to gain fame, glory, the exhilaration of victory. His main goal is to be known as a winner, his deepest fear to be labeled a loser.

MOLDED BY THE PSYCHOSTRUCTURE

The higher our interviews took us in the corporation, the more frequently we encountered the gamesman—he is the new corporate leader. Again, it must be emphasized that the top-level executive is not a pure type, but rather a mixture. He most often combines many of the traits of the gamesman with some attributes of the company man. He is a team player who identifies closely with the corporation.

The gamesman reaches the top in a process of social (in contrast to natural) selection. The companies that excel tend to be run by people who are well adapted to fulfill the requirements of the market and the technology, and who create an atmosphere that encourages productive work. These executives in turn stimulate traits in their subordinates that are useful to the work, while discouraging those that are unnecessary or impede it. As an executive moves to the top, therefore, his character is refined.

Any organization of work—industrial, service, blue or white collar—can be described as a "psychostructure" that selects and molds character. One difference between the psychostructure of the modern corporate hierarchy and that of the factory is the fineness of fit required between work and character. Managers must have characters closely attuned to the "brain work" they perform. Only a minimal fit is required to perform simplified, repetitive tasks in a factory.

The gamesman's character, which might seem to be a collection of near paradoxes, can best be understood in terms of its adaptation to the requirements of the organization. The gamesman is cooperative but competitive, detached and playful but compulsively driven to succeed, a team player but a would-be superstar, a team leader but often a rebel against bureaucratic hierarchy, fair and unprejudiced but contemptuous of weakness, tough and dominating but not destructive. Competition and innovation in modern business require these gamelike attitudes, and of all the character types, only the gamesman is emotionally attuned to the environment.

As the manager adapts to the requirements of the corporation, something else happens to his character. The work stimulates and reinforces attitudes essential for intellectual innovation and team-work—what I call qualities of the head. But it does not stimulate the qualities of the heart.

The True Seat of Courage

Most people conceive of the heart as being the opposite of the head: they think it means softness, while the head means tough-minded, realistic thought. But this view is of relatively recent conception, having emerged during the last couple of centuries, and it does not adequately describe the way I use the terms. I think of the head and heart in the older Judeo-Christian and Islamic traditions, which consider the heart to be not only the home of compassion, generosity, and idealism, but also the true seat of consciousness and courage.

As the instrument of calculation, the brain can decipher codes, solve technical problems, and keep accounts. But a person must have a strong heart to resolve deep emotional doubts or to summon up the courage needed to act out of moral conviction. Only a well-developed heart can invest information with spiritual weight. It takes a well-developed heart to make difficult judgments in terms of the human values involved.

The managers we interviewed recognized that their work developed their heads but not their hearts. In answering questionnaires, they consistently identified intellectual qualities as more "important for your work" than emotional qualities. They also indicated that their jobs "stimulated or reinforced" qualities of the head more than those of the heart (see Table 1).

THEY NEVER FIRE ANYBODY

Many executives believe that developing such qualities as compassion and empathy would bring them into conflict with

Table 1
CHARACTER TRAITS IMPORTANT TO WORK AND STIMULATED BY WORK

Qualities of the Head	Very Important for Work (Percent)	Stimulated by Work (Percent)
Ability to take the initiative	91	58
Satisfaction in creating something new	74	51
Self-confidence	86	50
Coolness under stress	71	40
Cooperativeness	74	37
Pleasure in learning something new	68	35
Pride in performance	88	35
Flexibility	76	33
Open-mindedness	81	30

Qualities of the Heart	Very Important for Work (Percent)	Stimulated by Work (Percent)
Independence	45	21
Loyalty to fellow workers	47	18
Critical attitude to authority	21	17
Friendliness	35	16
Sense of humor	53	14
Openness, spontaneity	46	14
Honesty	72	12
Compassion	18	4
Generosity	13	2
Idealism	9	1

corporate goals. One was flabbergasted by the very idea of sensing his subordinates' feelings, of developing a heart that listens. "If I let myself feel their problems," he said, "I'd never get anything done. It would be impossible to deal with people."

Other managers have told me that if they were not emotionally detached they could not make decisions to build new factories or change technology in ways that would put people out of work. In the long run, they claim, these decisions will be socially beneficial, but to carry them out they have to avoid dwelling on the immediate suffering caused.

Those arguments are made by executives who are weak-hearted—indeed, one would say flabby-hearted. They cannot bear to look at suffering, for to do so is to become paralyzed. They must detach themselves emotionally and put the adverse consequences out of their minds. Most executives we interviewed had never personally fired anyone. Weak-hearted, they virtually blanched at the prospect.

A strong-hearted person weighs the suffering involved in a decision, has empathy for those who will be hurt by it but he does not shrink from the decision if he is convinced that it is right. The difference is that his decision bears greater weight, having been made with compassion, and a searching look at all the facts. If the strong-hearted executive can find ways of alleviating the suffering, he will. That is true leadership.

It Can Start at Age Five

The executive's emotional detachment stems largely from careerism. Obsessed with winning, the gamesman views all of his actions in terms of whether they will help him succeed in his career. But careerism does not begin in the corporation—it can begin at age five. Parents start the ball rolling by evaluating their child's behavior in terms of its market value. Is he smart enough? Is her personality right? Can he sell himself? The parents, themselves careerists, threaten the child not with punishment, but with failure in the career market of school and workplace.

Overly concerned with protecting his career, the gamesman constantly betrays himself, since he must ignore idealistic, compassionate, and courageous impulses that might jeopardize his future. As a result, he never fully develops a strong, independent sense of self, and he eventually loses touch with his deepest strivings. It is symptomatic of an undeveloped heart that many managers told us they give in too easily to others and don't know what they want (see Table 2). To stand up to others requires courage, and to know what you want implies the sense of volition that comes from a strong heart.

Erich Fromm, the psychoanalyst and social philosopher, has described careerism in terms of the "marketing orientation," pointing out that the individual's sense of identity, integrity, and self-determination is lost when he treats himself as an object whose worth is determined by its fluctuating market value. As he sells himself, the marketing individual experiences, or more likely represses, a deep sense of shame, self-contempt, and guilt. The fact that half the managers we interviewed said they blame themselves too much may reflect the authoritarian consciences of some, but many feel guilty because they have sacrificed self-respect. Their self-blame is not an irrational feeling, but grows out of a nagging sense of self-betrayal: they have chosen career over the higher needs of self, family, and society.

Careerism demands detachment. To succeed in school, the child needs to detach himself from a crippling fear of failure. To sell himself, he detaches himself from feelings of shame and humiliation. To compete and win, he detaches himself from compassion for the losers. To devote himself to success at work, he detaches himself from family.

"THERE IS A SHELL AROUND MY HEART"

As a result, high-ranking corporate managers exercise and develop many positive intellectual characteristics, while their

Table 2
DIFFICULTIES REPORTED BY CORPORATE MANAGERS

Category	Percent
Fear	
Often restless	58
Anxious	48
Have unwarranted fears	28
Detachment	
Keep your feelings to yourself	61
Difficulty saying what you mean	59
Avoid people	35
Lack of Self-Determination	
Give in too easily to others	59
Don't know what you want	46
Other Related Symptoms	
Tend to blame yourself too much	50
Depression	44
Overeat	32
Lack sufficient energy to do what you want	36
Sleep badly	30
Obsessive thoughts	19
Gastrointestinal symptoms	18
Have thoughts of acting destructively	12
Sexual difficulties	12
Thoughts of suicide	5

emotional qualities tend to atrophy. They lack passion and com-passion. They are cool or lukewarm. They are emotionally cautious and protected against intense experience. The process of bending one's will to corporate goals and moving up the hierarchy leads to meanness and emotional stinginess.

Without a developed heart, an executive lacks some of the qualities that would be most helpful in managing creative people and complex tasks. A hard-hearted jungle fighter, even if he is brilliant, cannot hold onto creative people because he lacks the sensitivity to work with them. At the opposite extreme, a creative person with a weak or underdeveloped heart does not possess the inner strength to make tough decisions.

I encountered an executive who, out of softheartedness, left a subordinate in a job the man wanted but did not have the ability to perform. As things turned out, the job was botched, and the subordinate was given a negative evaluation. This could have been avoided if the executive had either summoned up the courage to reassign the man earlier or, better yet, had been interested in helping him develop his talents.

Only a person with a strong heart will fight for the welfare of an organization when doing so might endanger his career. For example, I ran across a gamesman who had been assigned to a project he sensed was bound to fail. Thinking only of his career, he would not risk alienating his boss by urging that the whole idea be abandoned. Rather, he got himself transferred to avoid being personally tarnished.

The gamesman cannot be a careerist at work and a loving, full-hearted person in his private life. Based on interviews, I rated managers on their productiveness in work and love—the latter being defined as interest in other people. As Table 3 indicates, 80 percent expressed at least moderate interest in work, while only 45 percent showed that much interest in and concern for others. Like King Midas, who could not touch his own daughter without turning her to gold, the manager can no longer choose when to be intimately related and when to be detached. One president told me that despite his attempts to be a good father, his children resented him bitterly. "I don't blame them," he said. "Even though I appear frank and open, they know there is a shell around my heart, that they can't really touch me."

If his wife does not share his careerist drive, the gamesman finds he cannot respond to her on an emotional level—and so he "runs away" from her, becoming a workaholic. But most games-men who make it to the top have wives who are very much like themselves. These women typically spend a lot of their time on committees, performing civic duties that enhance their image and

Table 3
PRODUCTIVENESS IN LOVE AND WORK

Work Scale	Percent
Deep scientific interest in understanding, dynamic sense of the work, animated	0
Centered, enlivening, craftsmanlike, but lacks deeper scientific interest in the nature of things	22
The work itself stimulates interest, which is not self-sustained	58
Moderate productive, not centered; interest in work is essentially instrumental, to ensure security, income	18
Passive unproductive, diffused	2
Rejecting of work, rejects the real world	0
	100

Love Scale	Percent
Loving, affirmative, creatively stimulating	0
Responsible, warm, affectionate but not deeply loving	5
Moderate interest in another person with more loving possibilities	40
Conventional concern, decent, role-oriented	41
Passive, unloving, uninterested	13
Rejecting of life, hardened heart	1
	100

that of the corporation. In bringing up children, they encourage those traits that will best prepare them to be winners like the parents. One gamesman's wife told me that her "number one goal is to have a happy home so my husband and children have a springboard for success."

Most managers described a good friend as a person who would support them in their careers. Their definitions ran as follows: "Someone I can depend on when the going gets rough." "I can count on him for support." "I can confide in him. He will help me no matter what." Fewer than 10 percent identified a friend as a person who shared their spiritual goals or, as an exceptional manager put it, "a person who would be open enough to tell me what I need to do for growing and progressing in life."

Although the executives wanted help from their friends, not even one in ten said that helping others was one of his goals in life. In contrast, more than half the workers we studied in a Tennessee factory mentioned helping others as one of their aims. When asked her goals in life, a black woman working in the paint shop answered: "Sure, I want a house and financial security, but I can't walk down the street with money in my pocket and not heed the cries of those who are in need. If I did that, I'd be nothing."

In their deepest recesses, a good many managers seem to be wondering whether *they* really amount to much of anything. A highly successful executive, in charge of product development in a large company at the age of forty, already feels himself a failure: "I am considering whether all this is worth it," he said. "I started thinking about this four or five years ago. I feel a lack of joy. I don't see where all this is leading to."

I asked him whether he felt his life lacked meaning. "Yes," he replied, "it is running full tilt without direction. This environment is continually in a crisis mode. It's all high speed. You can't talk about trivia. It turns me off when my wife wants to chatter. It's stupid when you think about it; what else can you do but listen?"

Some successful executives who are not consciously critical of corporate life reveal a contradictory reaction in their dreams. A gameswoman who has risen close to the top of a large multinational company told us that her job was an interesting challenge, one that gave her the opportunity for a great deal of independence and self-development. "I really enjoy my work," she said. "I moan and groan, but I've had some fantastic opportunities and challenges."

A Telephone in Her Casket

What were the challenges she enjoyed so much? The major one turned out to be the competition with other executives for top positions in the corporation. What she claimed to value—challenge and independence—appeared really to be anxious struggle and lonely careerism. As she said, "The main thing is the ability to survive in this environment."

Despite her conscious enthusiasm, this woman's recurring dream seems to express a very different *unconscious* experience. She dreams that she is buried alive and all she wants is a telephone in her casket. It sounds like a joke, but such a dream is all too serious: it symbolizes the experience of emotional deadness in the corporate womb, and her acceptance of her fate (as long as she can stay in the executive competition). Rather than rebelling at being buried alive and fighting to become free, she only asks for a telephone to communicate with others.

A gifted scientist-executive who has begun to feel disillusioned with his work dreamed that he entered a large hotel on a beach (perhaps looking for an easy protected life). The lower story is missing (everything is up in the head). There was a ladder inside and he climbed up (successful career). The place was mushy with bat droppings and spiders (crazy intrigues at the top). He finished the dream with a vision of horror: "I look out the window, but the beach is no longer there. There is a stockyard. I feel death around me. I fly out of the building through the air. It is a great feeling to get out."

One of the most compassionate and idealistic managers we interviewed experienced an internal conflict with his own gamesmanlike wish to win. "I need love and need to give it," he said, "but I tend to cover it up in my work." This man worked in a company where the spirit is friendlier than in most. After visiting another corporation where the atmosphere was one of cutthroat competition, he had a dream. "I went into a city of buildings," he recalled. "They were gleaming and slimy, all hotels. It was really a cemetery. Everybody in the rooms was dead and embalmed. Yet they were sitting, posed as if alive. It was in the

Southwest, where I had gone on business. A brilliant blue day and sunshine outside. The corpses were looking out of the windows."

Like the woman executive, the unconscious symbol he chose for corporate life was death, meaning the killing of one's own feelings, the molding of the self into a waxen pose within ultramodern glass coffins. When our research group discussed the man's dream and interview, the conflict seemed so great that I felt he was headed for illness. In fact, he developed an ulcer soon afterward and took a leave of absence.

"I DON'T FEAR DEATH NOW, BUT. . ."

An old and tiring gamesman is a pathetic figure, especially after he has lost a few contests and, with them, his confidence. Once his youth, vigor, and even the thrill in winning is lost, he becomes depressed and goal-less, questioning the purpose of his life.

No longer energized by the team struggle and unable to dedicate himself to something he believes in beyond himself, he feels starkly alone. His attitude has kept him from deep friendship and intimacy. He is not like the aging craftsman, whose goal in life has not been winning but making something better. The craftsman can retire from the corporation and still be energetic and interested in new ideas. The gamesman has not sufficiently developed the self to appreciate science or art for their own sakes. Without the thrill of the contest, there is nothing.

A gamesman who had once been on the way to the top said, "I never wanted security—I felt we were all good racehorses and we'd be allowed to run. I wanted to be part of the winning team. The corporation had begun to take off. It was wide open." Now, two of his projects have failed in succession, and he has been given a staff position with vague responsibilities. His superiors worry about what to do with him. He has become an alcoholic. His conversation was depressed. "I don't fear death now," he said, "but I fear discomfort. Hard knocks grind your ego down. There is a lot of pain there, too."

PROFESSORS AREN'T ANY BETTER

Is this grim picture much different from what one sees in other careerist workers outside industry? Lacking comparable data, I can only speculate. But when I discussed the matter with top government bureaucrats, they recognized the four psychological types and responded to the issues of the head and the heart. And comparing my own experience in universities, I would say that although academics consider themselves more "humane" than businessmen, the managers we interviewed are no more competitive, and a lot more cooperative with one another, than most professors.

If corporate managers engaged in the nit-picking and downputting common in universities, little would be created and produced. If they treated their subordinates with the neglect and contempt common in the attitude of professors toward graduate students, no one would work for them. These days, the talented jungle fighter probably has a much better chance for advancement in the university than he would in the corporate psychostructure.

Nevertheless, the fact that other careerists may exhibit similar symptoms is not a reason to dismiss the problem in the corporation. For one thing, as I have pointed out, strong-hearted executives make better managers than weak-hearted ones. Yet the strong-hearted are not socially selected by the corporation. I have encountered a few, but they are exceptions. Our meritocratic society measures performance from childhood on almost solely by ability in intellectual problem solving—but we have no measures for a strong heart. And those who sparkle in business school may or may not possess courage and compassion.

When I reported our findings to top managers at one company we studied, the executives were touched and worried. Many managers consider themselves religious people or humanists. The contradiction between the effects of corporate life and their values troubled them. Typically, they looked for a managerial solution. How could they change their work or institute new programs to develop the heart? The question took me by surprise, but since then it has made me think about how the heart might be developed within the corporate system. I have not yet found an answer.

WHERE WILL THE LEADERS COME FROM?

The emotional and spiritual underdevelopment of corporate executives is a problem not only for the individual careerist, but also for society as a whole. Acting through the market, managers serve society's material needs out of their own greedy self-interest. If they meet those needs successfully, they will in turn be rewarded. The system has given us what we asked from it: unprecedented wealth and material comfort.

In the process, executives must use their heads—to analyze demand, to design products, to fashion effective advertising, and so on. And at this, they are extremely adept. The trouble is that, in rising to the top, they sacrifice the capacity to develop values that go beyond winning the game. And the larger society, of which business is but a subsystem, depends for its greatness not only on the head but on the heart—the qualities of courage, compassion, generosity, idealism. If the most dynamic sector of society continues to select out these qualities, where will we find future leaders who possess the moral strength to know right from wrong, and the courage to act on those convictions?

Zaleznik continues the study of leadership styles, contrasting the charismatic leader with the consensus leader. He finds that the consensus form of leadership, which has deep roots in the American character, is the prevailing style, both in business and in politics. Citing many examples, he follows the developmental issues which play a role in the genesis of these styles, and he discusses the relationship of leader-audience, comparing role-playing with dramatization. Like Maccoby (Chapter 5), who expresses concern about the rise of the gamesman in organizations, Zaleznik comments on the price of consensus leadership.

6

Charismatic and Consensus Leaders: A Psychological Comparison

ABRAHAM ZALEZNIK

One of the outgrowths of industrialization and the development of bureaucracy is the consensus leader. Unlike his opposite, the charismatic leader who generates strong feelings and appears as a distinctive personality, the consensus leader is difficult to distinguish clearly as a person.

The consensus leader would seem to fit the outlines of the antihero who, while a "common man" figuratively speaking, does have the distinction of being able to survive the rigors of insti-tutional politics. The questions for psychoanalysts, historians, and political scientists interested in the relationship between personality and politics center on understanding the character structure of the survivor who becomes leader through the control of consensus mechanisms. What manner of man is the consensus leader?

This chapter originally appeared in the *Bulletin of the Menninger Clinic*, 38:222-238, 1974.

How do charismatic and consensus leaders differ in personality structure and dynamics? To what types of pathology are charismatic and consensus leaders vulnerable; and, if these pathologies differ, how can the underlying patterns of conflict and defense be explained? How do pathological manifestations affect the pattern of leadership, and do these manifestations have consequences for the decisions made by these two types of leaders?

Sociologist David Riesman and his collaborators, in *The Lonely Crowd: A Study of the Changing American Character* (1950) found two types of national character which they called the "inner-directed" and the "other-directed." Briefly, the inner-directed person relies on his own beliefs and ideas to guide his thoughts and actions, while the other-directed personality depends on the views of others to determine his response. This distinction can be taken as a point of departure for examining and comparing charismatic and consensus leaders in an effort to answer the questions I have posed.

THE CHARISMATIC LEADER

The psychoanalytic study of charismatic leadership began with Freud's (Breuer and Freud, 1893-1895) early work on hysteria and the nature of the influence one person can have on another, especially when deep emotional attachments are unilateral. At the root of hysterical symptoms is the unconscious love an individual feels for another—a love that can progress from fantasy to idealization of the object. All children pass through such phases in their love of their parents in which fantasy compels the child to center his emotional ties on the loved parent. These ties are the basis for influence on thoughts and feelings, intimately affecting character through the mechanisms of incorporation, identification, and imitation. If one cannot have the loved object, one will try to be like him, to gain his approval, and in all respects meet his standards and expectations. To be sure, maturation modifies and transforms an individual's attachments; therefore, both the leader and the led experience many different types of relationships, ranging from the deep and sometimes pathological to the purely objective and rational.

The concept of charisma and its applications to leadership and authority were originated by the German sociologist Max Weber (1947). He used charisma in the religious sense as a spiritual quality, an inner light, which resulted from divine revelation and conversion. As applied to leadership, "it is the charismatically qualified leader as such who is obeyed by virtue of personal trust in him and his revelation, his heroism or his exemplary qualities so far as they fall within the scope of the individual's belief in his charisma" (p. 328). In its more general application, charisma refers to any combination of unusual qualities in an individual which are attractive to others and result in special attachments, if not devotion, to his leadership. John F. Kennedy had such qualities, as illustrated by his ability to attract crowds during his Presidential campaign, and as especially evidenced in the "jumping" phenomenon demonstrated by young girls in the crowd who would jump up and down and squeal with delight over his appearance, much like the crowd response to a "teen-age rock idol." Certainly, Kennedy's appeal grew substantially as a result of his performance in the famous debates with Nixon. The legend grew into the imagery of Camelot, with the brave and fearless band of brothers kept together by the youthful leader, ready to take on all challengers and overcome all obstacles in "getting America moving again."

A somewhat different quality of charisma was exhibited by Charles de Gaulle (Hoffman and Hoffman, 1968). France in defeat was an aberration awaiting a leader to restore her to her proper place in the constellation of nations. Aloof and distant, de Gaulle was nevertheless heroic in the depth of his conviction that France must not only be served but must also follow the path of greatness.

Franklin D. Roosevelt presented still another type of charismatic leader. Instead of aloofness and elitism, this patrician conveyed a sense of pragmatism in overcoming economic paralysis at home and a new kind of tyranny abroad. Speaking to the hearts of the people, Franklin Roosevelt forged a new coalition in American politics, drawing together the liberal/intellectual, the blue-collar worker, the farmer, and the ethnic minorities. Studies of his Presidency have yet to discern how he elicited loyalty from such diverse groups and from whence came the wellspring within his personality which fed his talent for communication.

The list of charismatic leaders could easily be expanded to include individuals with other types of personalities; all of whom had the capacity to secure the emotional ties of others to themselves. Gandhi, for example, embodied both the earlier conception of charisma as a spiritual quality and the modern preoccupation with the revolutionary personality. The study of developing nations suggests, as in the case of India, that the transition from tribal feelings and orientation to village and clan on the one hand, to attitudes of nationhood on the other, frequently turns on the presence of a charismatic individual. The list of such personalities is long and includes Sukarno in Indonesia, Nkrumah in Ghana, Nasser in Egypt, and, of course, Mao Tse-tung in China.

To discover what makes for the successful emergence of such charismatic leaders, one must look at the interface of psychology and history. Erik Erikson (1958, 1969) is pioneering in the new field of psychohistory with his inquiry into Martin Luther's late adolescent identity crisis, and with his more recent study of the emergence of Gandhi's *satayagraha*, or passive resistance, in leading the workers of the Ahmadabad textile mills out on strike.

Generalizations that can be made from the psychohistorical study of these great leaders seem to center on the fusion of great personal and historical conflicts. For Martin Luther, the personal issue was loyalty to his father and obedience to authority. His father wanted his gifted son to study law and take advantage of the new secular careers which offered possibilities for upward mobility. Yet, because of deep oedipal conflicts, young Luther could neither accede to his father's wishes nor rebel in an outright way. Rebellion against his father became possible when he entered a monastery to follow the priesthood, for he could then submit to the overriding code of obedience of another authority figure. However, such a compromise could not stabilize the conflict for long, and the issue of rebellion or submission escalated from the authorities in the monastery to the Pope, and ultimately to God. Erikson says this crisis resulted in a series of transformations in Luther which cannot be easily explained by sublimation or the neutralization of energy. Instead, such transformations can only be understood by a close look at the individual's endowments, the demands of narcissism, and, above all, the nature of historical change, where personal conflicts provide the means of communication between leader and led. Luther was not alone in his doubts about obedience, particularly on the issue of accepting intermediaries in man's relationship to God. The emergence of strong princes and the resulting conflict between secular and religious authority gave Luther some powerful allies in his struggle, to which he attracted the masses through his personal eloquence and the message that good works are a sign of predestined salvation.

As mentioned earlier, the study of charismatic leadership must start with the origins of influence and the forms of psychic disequilibria which arise in early object ties. Here Riesman's (1950) designation of the "inner-directed" personality may be applied to the charismatic leader. Such a leader has a highly developed and well-populated inner life as a result of introjecting early objects and later identifying with objects, symbols, and ideals which have some connection to the introjects. The imagos, or internal audience, exert a powerful influence on the leader and form the basis for the ties he establishes with the masses.

The study of Charles de Gaulle illustrates how introjects work in the development of a charismatic leadership style. Stanley and Inge Hoffman in their paper "The Will to Grandeur: de Gaulle as Political Artist" (1968) correlate de Gaulle's majestic sense with the quality of his internal audience which he projected upon France. De Gaulle's introjects established the sense of independence he manifested in school and later in his career; but this independence did not involve rebellion against his parents. As the Hoffmanns show, de Gaulle remained deeply attached to his parents; even so, he was able to transform this attachment into an idealized relationship with France. To de Gaulle, authority transcended men and ordinary human relationships so that when an individual submitted, it was to ideals. Therefore, he avoided conventional compliance, as demonstrated in his dealings with Pétain, and later with Churchill and Roosevelt. For these latter two, de Gaulle remained a perplexing and vexing figure, seemingly without power but enormously absorbed in the effort to attain one overriding goal—restoring France to her rightful place in the constellation of nations. De Gaulle was able to bide his time in England during the war, personifying France in waiting. He was also able to withdraw, accept defeat, and sustain himself through his imagos, awaiting the call to power in 1958. Once in power, he acted decisively to extricate France from Algeria without waiting to test for consensus and acceptance.

This capacity to wait and accept passivity, then to act and move assertively would seem to depend upon the sustaining effects of benevolent introjects, for such self-assurance must come from being at one with these inner images. From this integration, the charismatic leader secures his sense of being special, and here the relationship to mother appears significant. In Freud's words, "A man who has been the indisputable favorite of his mother keeps for life the feeling of a conqueror, that confidence of success that often induces real success" (quoted by Jones, 1953, p. 5). However, this statement does not completely explain how introjects function for creative individuals in all fields. Some transformations take place in which the sense of being special and the attachment to early objects as introjects are related to social and historical reality with both a past and a future.

To understand this transformation requires a look at the types of psychopathology manifested in the lives and works of charismatic leaders. The psychopathology of the charismatic leader is straight out of Shakespeare: megalomania, paranoia, all the massive psychic upheavals of a King Lear are still valid indicators of how great men fall ill. Although examples abound, there are still too few good analytic studies.

Studies of Adolf Hitler (Erikson, 1950; Langer, 1972) serve as counterpoints to studies of charismatic leaders who secure and communicate visions of the future—visions which mobilize and focus the forces of change in society. In contrast, Hitler's life and work exemplify the return to primitive modes of thinking and acting. Only a charismatic leader of this kind could link his own primitive fantasies to a nation's potential for regression, with history as witness to the almost unbelievable outcome. For a partial explanation, we must again look at the nature of the introjects and their origins in personal history and development.

Hitler was possessed by an internalized audience which mirrored unsettled, yet intense attachments to his parents. To begin with, Hitler had doubts about his own origin and legitimacy, and there was also some question about whether his father was born of an illegitimate relationship—both of which found expression in his obsession with a pure race. Hitler's father, who died when the boy was thirteen years old, was twenty-three years older than his mother. Hitler had either witnessed or was obsessed by fantasies that his father beat his mother. In any case, Hitler's relationship to his father was distant, which left him not only with a hatred for his father but with an insecure feeling about what it means to be a man. This hatred became the basis for his hatred of the Jews; he projected upon the Jews what he hated in himself, and he set out to destroy them.

Hitler's incestuous love for his mother, who also died during his adolescence, provided the emotional reservoir which fed his desire for a "pure" reconstructed and unravished German nation. This love of mother and nation remained deeply erotic—untransformed sexuality and aggression—and became the motive power for his sadism. However, Hitler retained a two-sided view of his mother—the earthly, warm, seductive side and the powerful "iron virgin" side (to use Erikson's term)—the latter becoming his, and ultimately Germany's, ideal for the nation. The quality of these introjects and his inability to fuse the contrasting images of his parents led to his intense, hysterical love affair with the German people—an affair conducted at the expense of humanity and perpetuated by an inability to tame impulses which, once unleashed, only destroyed.

Although it is seemingly a long journey from the nature of influence in the parent-child relationship to the structure of power relations in political life, the conceptual links—love and sexuality on the one hand and aggression on the other—are reasonably clear as illustrated in the foregoing examples. In the cohesive political structure, the direction of love toward a leader or some representation, such as an ideology or a totem, serves to bind members to each other (Freud, 1921). If, at the same time, the group's aggression is dampened or is directed toward some external object (e.g., toward tasks to be achieved or toward the representation of some common enemy who in real or mythological terms threatens the group's survival), then the structure is preserved. This classic model of group cohesion may also describe a condition of object surrender, where the followers hand over their egos to the leader and remain susceptible to his commands and directives. They submit in order to preserve their love of the leader, and whatever esteem they experience comes from the sense of devotion to the ideals and causes established in the leader's image.

The study of charismatic leaders invariably is a study of change, specifically the relationship between personal and historical change. Undoubtedly in all generations there are potential charismatic figures who never appear on the stage of history. Individual conflicts and attempts at their resolution remain purely personal events until great historical crises call forth new definitions of self-interest. When established authority structures begin to crumble, seldom is only one segment of society affected; the effects are visible in the family, community, religious institutions, universities, and, of course, government. Therefore, more than one charismatic leader appears at one time. The Great Depression of the 1930's and World War II pushed many great men forward both to generate and resolve crises. Similarly, the demise of these great men brought about a new era. There has been no genuinely charismatic leader in the United States since Franklin Roosevelt (although John Kennedy had some attributes of such a leader). Likewise, in Great Britain after Winston Churchill, the succession of leaders has been a product of close political infighting, reflecting the problems of alliance (rather than crisis) politics. Even in the great dictatorships, the mantle has not been passed to another individual as often as to a coalitional or bipartite leadership structure. When the last of the charismatic leaders of World War II, Charles de Gaulle, relinquished power, his successor, Georges Pompidou, exemplified the type of leader who rises from the anonymity of bureaucratic function to the top position as a result of consensus politics.

The Consensus Leader

The consensus form of leadership has deep roots in the American national character, for Americans seem to have a basic distrust of charismatic leaders. The nation which began with the overthrow of authority had to establish a legacy in which authority of all kinds (not the least of which is paternal) was suspect. In addition, the experience of subduing nature with technology has produced a sense of optimism peculiarly American—an optimism that produced a system in which a man is judged by *what* he does rather than by *who* he is. Status by achievement rather than ascription, furthermore, supports a peer-group culture built on the dual images of pragmatism and egalitarianism.

With this foundation, which rejects the paternal image and charisma, the question of leadership is ambiguous. The types of leaders (political as well as institutional) who have gained power in the United States present a new personality configuration in which the idealized image, as well as the problematic image, is that of brother and peer rather than of father. The philosophical basis for this new personality configuration can be found in the works of George Herbert Mead (1934) and Charles Horton Cooley (1956). In their theory and philosophy, these writers based the formation of the American character on the conscious assessments and acceptances of others: in other words, character is defined by an individual's memberships and roles. Noting that group formations occur within the fabric of society and that there is an interrelationship between groups and institutions, these theorists were led to conclude that the American ego belongs to society. Since control of aggression is central to the types of constraints that groups exert upon individuals, the taming of destructive impulses is assured by the individual's unwillingness to risk the impoverishment and possible ostracism which would be his lot if he violated group codes. Libido is less troublesome since group relationships have absorbed and ritualized unconscious homosexual impulses; yet, overt aggression, such as competitiveness, status striving, and outright attempts to secure dominance and control, runs counter to the ideology of primary group ties among brothers.

On the whole, our understanding of the psychology of the concensus leader is limited. Such leaders do not generate much interest among psychobiographers; besides, anonymity is a characterological trait of consensus leaders and accounts in no small measure for their successful rise to power. The consensus leader's classical tactic is to establish his position in the center of the political spectrum and gradually to widen the power base, isolating the opposition outside the consensus structure. Centrists tend to be followers rather than leaders of opinion. They avoid substantive positions for as long as possible and, instead, concentrate their energies on procedure.

One of the striking characteristics of consensus leadership is the relative absence of strong emotional bonds between leader and follower. The leader is the first among equals; and calculated self- and group-interests are the ties that bind men to the structure. However, men are willing to compromise in order to reach some satisfactory consensus in which interest groups neither win nor lose. Therefore, in a sense, dependency in consensus structures is masked, for the polity is mutually dependent; and the leader, if anything, is more dependent on his followers than they on him. This reversal of the usual dependency pattern is especially marked in complex bureaucracies where the leader knows less about any particular issue than selected subordinates. What a chief executive brings to policy making is more a sense of timing then expertise.

As a case example, let us look at Lyndon Baines Johnson as Senate majority leader and as President of the United States (Geyelin, 1966). Although there is little doubt that history will judge him brilliant as majority leader and more equivocally as President, Johnson exemplified the consensus style of leadership in his ability to bring together diverse points of view and personalities in the Senate even (or perhaps especially) under a President from the opposing party. Johnson liked to quote the prophet Isaiah, "Come, let us reason together," condensing the complex of calculated interests of senators and their constituencies. He could reason, mediate, and persuade more adroitly when his own position was either unformed or genuinely neutral. He also functioned for consensus when he brought forth the political IOUs which he amassed by doing things for others. Given the tradition of compromise and the avoidance of win-lose tactics in the Senate, many senators found Johnson's actions in keeping with their own desires to avoid polarization and exaggerated contentions.

Johnson's brilliant performance as majority leader suggests that he experienced the self-enhancement which occurs when the demands of a job and the psychological dynamics of the individual are in almost perfect harmony. In his early years as President, Johnson turned the grief of the nation into a national sentiment to fulfill a program in civil rights and domestic reform which the fallen hero had been unable to accomplish. However, Johnson's decisive victory in the 1964 election gave him power in his own name, providing a mandate for his style of leadership while, at the same time, signifying rejection of his opponent, who seemed to evoke extremist images (particularly on issues of war and peace). Yet, what occurred over the next four years prompts a number of questions: Did Johnson's personality change, and did he abandon the consensus style for an arbitrary and autocratic position which was out of keeping with national sentiment? Or, did his problems as President reflect the limitations of the consensus style of leadership?

The Vietnam War was a product of consensus politics and does not reflect a change either in Johnson's style of leadership or his personality (Halberstam, 1972). The choices were to stay out and let the fate of the Indochina peninsula go its way, or to launch an all-out military operation to secure the existence of South Vietnam. Although the American people were not prepared for the second course, the first course of action, to stay out, aroused fears about the domino effect in Southeast Asia. The Washington bureaucracy and the power structure were fearful about the public reaction to the fall of a new territory to a Communist government, for they were still sensitized by public reaction to the events in China in 1949. Therefore, the compromise, or the consensus position, was to respond with enough force to tip the balance in favor of South Vietnam while, at the same time, avoiding not only the classical economic argument of guns versus butter but also the decisions accompanying mobilization for warfare. Events largely have indicated that these decisions reached through consensus were unwise; and the military operations of 1972 suggest that our government under President Nixon was still entrapped by the consensus approach. Therefore, one of the limitations of the consensus approach to leadership is that the accumulation of individual compromises in decision making can and often does result in a rigid, extremist position.

In its most highly developed form, consensus leadership is a product of large-scale corporations and works especially well when goals are explicit and measurement of outcomes is equally clear-cut. To a striking degree, policy initiatives come from below and are debated and modified long before they reach the attention of or become identified with the consensus leader.

An extreme example of consensus as a mechanism and style of leadership is the Japanese system of *ringisei*. Policy proposals are debated at lower levels of management and only move to higher levels of authority when a consensus has been reached with each participant signifying his agreement by initialing the policy documents. When the policy initiatives finally reach the Chief Executive, his role is purely symbolic—attesting to the consensus. The consensus leader in Japan, a position usually reserved for elder statesmen, is like a grandfather (to use the analogy of kinship structures); in less extreme cases, the consensus leader functions as an older brother, in contrast to the charismatic leader as a parental figure.

The particular strengths of the consensus style are in the individual's capacity to form alliances initially with a small number of individuals and then progressively to gain wider participation in decision making by distributing power throughout the hierarchy and by encouraging initiatives from below. Such alliances and participative structures would be impossible to sustain without the consensus leader's orientation to peers and his sensitivity to their motives and interests. These characteristics were outstanding features in the personality of one of American industry's great corporate innovators.

A recent history of Pierre Du Pont's corporate leadership (Chandler and Salisbury, 1971) traces the evolution of the Du Pont Corporation and General Motors as a product of consensus leadership. Pierre Du Pont came to power along with two cousins, Coleman and Alfred, who collectively succeeded the older generation of Du Ponts. When Coleman, the elder cousin, lost interest in the corporation, Pierre and Alfred became contenders for leadership. Pierre's strategic position in dealing with the financial affairs of the corporation placed him in the best spot for assuming leadership, in contrast to Alfred's narrow specialization in the manufacture of gunpowder. Given his position and personality, Pierre found it congenial to encourage initiative from below and to solidify a coalition with subordinates by appealing to their interests and motives. Alfred, on the other hand, experienced his isolation as somewhat consistent with his defenses and could not put together a workable coalition to counter Pierre.

Among the personality attributes which suited Pierre for consensus leadership were a sense of attachment and responsibility to subordinates. This trait he developed early in life, perhaps as a result of his father's premature death. Pierre became a surrogate father to his younger siblings; in fact, they called him "Dad." However, as surrogate, he avoided the emotional and behavioral characteristics of the strong and even autocratic father. He was truly an older brother. His attachment to peers both in his family and in the Du Pont Corporation probably accounts for the fact that he did not marry until late in life and that he never had children.

To maintain a consistent attitude of caring, responsibility, and attachment to peers, the consensus leader must moderate both libido and aggression. If the libidinal charge is too intense or insufficiently disguised, excessive anxiety would be aroused in others and would result in the dissolution of group formations.[1] Perhaps more significant in understanding the consensus leader's character structure is the role of aggression, which must be low-key, directed outside the group (if manifested at all), and, in general, limited in the degree to which it is actually experienced by both the consensus leader and his group. An understanding of the vicissitudes of aggression suggests that the consensus leader apparently experiences excessive guilt in containing, if not resolving, the oedipus complex, and therefore he must maintain reaction formation as an ego defense. Although both guilt and reaction formation sustain the consensus leader's intense sense of responsibility toward his group, these affective repressors account for the frequency with which such leaders appear bland, opaque, and gray in demeanor and personality. However, those individuals for whom reaction formation and guilt are such prominent aspects of their psychic experience occasionally lose control and often react with anger that is disproportionate to the provocation. On the other hand, when anger may be genuinely used in the service of action, it seems to them that such an expression is beyond the range of permissible behavior.

All of these formulations concerning the consensus leader are familiar in relation to the outcomes of the infantile oedipus complex. However, although these formulations are valid, I believe they are somehow incomplete. Therefore, a more specific look at the nature of psychopathology in consensus leaders must be taken.

[1]Bion's (1961) work on the psychodynamics of group formations offers interesting observations and interpretations on the manifestations of anxiety in groups.

Those who opt for corporate and political leadership are very bright people, ambitious, upwardly mobile; yet, with all their intellectual gifts, they persist in magical beliefs about performance and accomplishment. These fantasies begin with the person's sense of having *been* special, of winning the oedipal struggle. As long as one maintains the sense of being special, he will not fall into the predepressive, or detached and affectively isolated state so aptly presented in Albert Camus' *The Stranger* (1946). The loss of the sense of being special occurs when a setback causes a leak in the narcissistic reservoir. The disruptions in self-esteem may also occur in what Elliott Jaques (1965) described as the "mid-life crisis," when individuals who have achieved substantial success are beset with disappointments associated with the failure of reality to live up to expectations; this condition leads to regressive longings and the wish to return to the idyllic states encapsulated in preoedipal fantasies. Defense against these longings is built into adaptation to reality, whereby individuals establish a fit with some social reality and, in this sense, function through hyperadaptation and excessive activity.

Consensus leaders seem to lack stable, benevolent, and well-integrated introjects. The explanation for this inner impoverishment in personality is that in early development the individual experienced disruption in object ties, particularly in separation from mother and in his reactions to the birth of younger siblings. When such disruptions occur, there may be a precipitous and premature reach for new objects, bypassing the mental process of turning inward to fantasy and recovering the object through internalization and identification. The consequences of such a pattern of development can be found in cognitive and affective modes—the "radar effect" of turning outward, or field dependency.

Subject and Audience: the Theater of Leadership

I want to engage in one further comparison of charismatic and consensus leaders—one that is particularly appropriate during a season of political campaigning. During a campaign, we become exquisitely attuned to and consequently manipulated by the stage-craft of politics. Both the consensus and the charismatic leader employ a form of theatrics in the way they present themselves to an audience and in evoking the actions and reactions they seek. However, this similarity is superficial and misleading. The consensus leader's performance tends to utilize role playing as a form of acting, while the charismatic leader's performance is a renewed dramatization, merging (if only momentarily) the internalized audience and the real audience.

The charismatic leader has a continuous dialogue with his internal images which are joined episodically with the external audience. For this reason, the observer in initially observing charismatic figures has the experience of standing outside a dramatization. The appeal is voyeuristic; the fascination is being a witness to the unfolding of a personality which occurs as though the actor were performing unobserved. This feeling of watching from the outside permits both the performer and the audience to relax their defenses, to "suspend disbelief," and to allow their emotions to surge and to join with those of others. Once joined, this distance between performer and audience suddenly disappears. The audience is on the inside, having lost the separation of self and objects which characterizes rational thought in which intellect and emotion are split off. Within the audience, the images of parents as protectors and love objects surface in a collapse of time—a merging of past and present. The orator now has a hold on his audience. If he is a demagogue, he can seduce them into ignoring reality; and, instead of creating a future, he recreates a past in a mythological form in which scapegoats are presented to focus hatred and to mislead. If the charismatic leader is in communication with benevolent images, he appeals to a future—a new reality that is an unexpected combination of intellect and emotion which transcends the limits of narrow rationality. (After all, it was narrow rationality that led the United States into Vietnam and then later sought to extricate us with our original purpose intact and the rules of power unchanged.)

The Hoffmans (1968) further explain the charismatic leader's dramatizations in terms of the warmth the leader seeks. For the charismatic leader, as in the case of de Gaulle:

> The warmth he needs is not the intimacy of equals, but the support and sympathy of the led. The "melancholy" that is the accepted price of domination, that willing sacrifice of ordinary human relations, becomes intolerable and leads to "ill-explained retreats" only when the *leader's* soul becomes engulfed by what Clemenceau . . . called its worst pain: cold—the indifference or hostility of the led. The warmth he needs is public [p. 854].

For the consensus leader, the mass audience provides little warmth and, in fact, is an object of mistrust, a feeling which parallels his reaction to his internal audience. His inner images are vague, illusory, and contradictory. Consequently, they provide little warmth and support for the consensus leader's sense of self-esteem, and even less substance for projecting a collective belief or idea onto the public. The consensus leader in politics, therefore, uses a type of role playing rather than dramatization.

Role playing is a very calculating method of communicating ideas to an audience and requires a structure made up of three parts: a stereotyped image, an audience of one, and the player. The stereotype must be easily recognized and simply presented, e.g., Mr. Nixon's famous "Checkers" speech in which he evoked the stereotype of the naive but honest son who is the victim of oppression at the hands of a powerful aggressor. The audience of one and the player both accept the stereotype but maintain it as an object outside of themselves. They avoid close identification with the stereotype, since otherwise it would arouse too much emotion which is unacceptable both in the psychology of consensus and in role playing. The emotional level can also be kept down by preventing the audience of one from merging with a collective audience—"playing it cool" is the key.

Of course, television is ideally suited for role playing. Besides being a "cool medium," it prevents the audience from forming bonds with one another or directly with the player. Technically, television maintains distance between the stereotype, the audience of one, and the player.

When this structure is established with a low-keyed emotional tone, the role play can be brought to its conclusion. Here the player tries to present himself as a peacemaker, a preserver of law and order, a reformer, a protector of property, a friend of the disadvantaged, or any of the other political images. It is even possible in concluding the role play to disguise a policy or decision by presenting the opposite image. If the President is about to undertake a major air bombardment in Indochina, then the conclusion of the role play is to present himself as a peacemaker and negotiator, which may have been the purpose behind Mr. Nixon's decision to "blow the cover" on Dr. Kissinger's secret negotiations with the North Vietnamese. If he is about to take action which will probably displease the right wing of his consensus position, then predictably it is timely for a role play to evoke recognizable stereotypes and self-presentations in line with conservative choices.

The consensus leader through indirectness and the capacity to manipulate through role playing seeks to enlarge and control the center of the political spectrum and to prevent it from fragmenting into many interest groups. While this capacity may be successful in being elected to office, the cost for the consensus leader and consequently his constituents is potentially high. He seldom experiences the peace of mind which comes from the security of purpose, the commitment to deeply held convictions, and the realization that he is master of his own house. For too long he has sought to control the insecurities of the sibling and the competition of peer relationships through maneuvering and adjustment to the outside world.

CONCLUSION

The personality traits of both charismatic and consensus leaders have been too often disregarded. It has been argued that a leader's role is defined by the situation. However, this argument ignores the significance of personality characteristics which determine how an individual will respond. Any leader will act or react in ways consistent with his personal style and will resort to his habitual modes of managing internal and external conflict. I cannot offer a definitive answer to the relative weight of situational and personal factors in determining decisions. However, I believe the personality factors have been underestimated in their capacity to determine how a chief executive acts upon the constraints and opportunities available to him. In fact, many leaders discover themselves in trouble when shifting events place a burden on their defensive apparatus because these events demand modes of action which lie beyond the leader's personal style.

For example, many of the problems Woodrow Wilson experienced in his relationship with the Senate after the negotiation of the peace treaty resulted from a shift in group psychology—from attachment to the strong leader to the urge to equalize power consistent with peer-group attitudes. Had Wilson been able to adapt to the requirements of this consensus psychology, he might have salvaged the treaty and the League of Nations. But Wilson reacted like the father under attack from rebellious sons. Under these conditions of stress he resorted to his appeal to the masses, his favored coalition, and bypassed leaders in the Senate for whom consultation was both necessary and desirable in their quest for a new distribution of power. The appeal to the masses failed, and Wilson was unable to shift his Presidential style, a fact that contributed (at least in part) to his subsequent stroke and incapacitation (George and George, 1956).

In the various phases of a lifetime, the progression from infancy to old age, the decisive event in adulthood, for which the early years are preparation, is the change from being the son and peer to being the father and leader (at least in the family, if not in organizational or elective politics). However, this progression seems to have been interrupted culturally as well as politically. The emergence of the fraternal ideal as the substitute for the heroic father has created a standard which only adds to the anxieties under which the transition from son to father takes place.

But there is a limit to how effective cleverness, adroitness, and flexibility can be in circumventing reality and anxiety. When this limit is reached in the cyclical currents of group psychology ,the turn may well be toward the leadership of a charismatic man who knows how to wait.

REFERENCES

Bion, W. R. (1961), *Experiences in Groups and Other Papers*. New York: Basic Books.

Breuer, J., & Freud, S. (1893-1895), Studies on Hysteria. *Standard Edition*, 2. London: Hogarth Press, 1955.

Camus, A. (1946), *The Stranger*. New York: Knopf.

Chandler, A. D., Jr., & Salisbury, S. (1971), *Pierre S. Du Pont and the Making of the Modern Corporation*. New York: Harper & Row.

Cooley, C. W. (1956), *Social Organization*. Glencoe, Ill.: Free Press.

Erikson, E. H. (1950), *Childhood and Society*. New York: Norton.

——— (1958), *Young Man Luther: A Study in Psychoanalysis and History*. New York: Norton.

——— (1969), *Gandhi's Truth: On the Origins of Militant Non-violence*. New York: Norton.

Freud, S. (1921), Group Psychology and the Analysis of the Ego, *Standard Edition*, 18:65-143. London: Hogarth Press, 1955.

George, A., & George, J. (1956), *Woodrow Wilson and Colonel House: A Personality Study*. New York: Day.

Geyelin, P. (1966), *Lyndon B. Johnson and the World*. New York: Praeger.

Halberstam, D. (1972), *The Best and the Brightest*. New York: Random House.

Hoffman, S., & Hoffman, I. (1968), The Will to Grandeur: de Gaulle as Political Artist. *Daedalus*, 97:829-887.

Jaques, E. (1965), Death and the Mid-Life Crisis. *Internat. J. Psycho-Anal.*, 46:502-514.

Jones, E. (1953), *The Life and Work of Sigmund Freud*, Vol. 1. New York: Basic Books.

Langer, W. C. (1972), *The Mind of Adolf Hitler: The Secret Wartime Report*. New York: Basic Books.

Mead, G. H. (1934), *Mind, Self and Society from the Standpoint of a Social Behaviorist*, ed. C. W. Morris. Chicago: University of Chicago Press.

Riesman, D. et al. (1950), *The Lonely Crowd: A Study of the Changing American Character*. New Haven: Yale University Press.

Weber, M. (1947), *The Theory of Social and Economic Organization*, ed. T. Parsons. New York: Oxford University Press.

Levinson's study of irrational behavior in executives centers on the fact that anger and guilt are significant factors of executive action that generally go unrecognized in management planning, organizing, and decision making. He points out that executives frequently make decisions in a way that enables them to deny their anger to themselves and to appease their superiors: in short, management by guilt. He discusses guilt-producing problems, how they arise, and their cost to the organization. Like Kets de Vries in Chapter 3, he pays heed to aggression as a problem of personality.

7

Management by Guilt

HARRY LEVINSON

Ever since the pre-World War I days of industrial engineering, many people have sought to make management a highly defined process built around some basic assumption about how that task can best be organized. We therefore have such conceptions as management by task force, management by system, management by goals, management by control, and management by coordination. In each of these, the basic assumption is the primary determinant for organizing the executive's perception of his task. Each is a purposive concept.

These structural efforts, which have made significant contributions to management efficiency over the years, are intended to counteract behavior that might be irrational in terms of the task to be done. They usually require a statement of goals and projected targets, together with logically deduced programmatic

This chapter originally appeared in *Emotional Health in the World of Work*, Harper and Row, 1969. By permission of the author.

statements derived from these goals. Organization charts describe who is responsible to whom for what. Job descriptions tell in detail what the jobholder is supposed to do. Appraisal systems provide for periodic evaluations of how the job is done. Personnel policies and procedures state the rules that govern employees from hiring to retirement.

This proposition assumes that people, for the most part, are rational. Therefore the more clear, specific, and comprehensive the organizational structure can be, presumably the more people will respond rationally within it. Generally speaking, these assumptions are valid. However, the appeal to rationality is frequently likely to be unsuccessful. Unless the effort to counteract irrationality also recognizes the sources of that irrationality and focuses attention on them, then it may be ineffective.

Sociologists have pointed out that in addition to the formal structure of an organization, there is an informal structure. The latter has more effect on the nature of its operations. Informal structure is created when formal structure fails to do its job. Formal structure often can be reorganized to include informal structure and thereby to adapt to organizational realities.

Much that passes for rational decision making, based on objective criteria, is also likely to be a product of a person's efforts to maintain his psychological equilibrium. Specifically, much of the irrational in management practices arises because of people's efforts to cope with their own anger and to avoid the anger of others. Executives go to great lengths to avoid conflict because of their discomfort with feelings of anger. But the very fact that they have angry feelings, when they often feel it is wrong to be angry, leaves them feeling guilty. With these two feelings to contend with, executives frequently make decisions in such a way that they can deny their anger to themselves and appease their superegos. In short, we speak of management by guilt.

The fact of anger and guilt as significant determinants of executive action goes unrecognized in management organizing, planning, and decision making. The problem, however, cannot be dealt with simply by changing organization structure.

GUILT-INDUCING PROBLEMS

Failure to Produce

Here is a typical case, as reported by the executive who had to make the final decision about the man involved. Included are all the elements found repeatedly in management by guilt: disappointment in the man; failure to confront him realistically about his job behavior; procrastination in reaching a decision about him; coverup compliments to ease the guilt of managerial anger; transfer to another position; finally, discharge.

Ewell Sturdy was in the new products division of a food products manufacturer. He was generally acknowledged in the company to be brilliant but lazy. He could develop information about a new market or a new field quickly, but he seemed unable to follow through to the point of action.

At the time of writing, he had been in the company more than fifteen years, the last year and a half in the same assignment. During his tenure in his present assignment, he had produced no innovations in product or market. As a result, he was not given a salary increase. Sturdy angrily protested, saying that he had rendered valuable service. In his view, he was being shortchanged again by a company that had never fully recognized or utilized his talents. Though he had been complimented by superiors many times during his employment, he had never been adequately paid. He cited chapter and verse about his contributions. He attributed the company's failure to recognize him to the jealousy of his supervisors and political undercurrents in the company.

Sturdy thereupon talked with the comptroller, who was not his immediate superior. In addition to complaining to the comptroller about his own lot, he accused his superiors of criticizing the comptroller. When the comptroller investigated the alleged criticism, he found it to be wholly imaginary on Sturdy's part. This finding led the comptroller to talk with Sturdy's immediate superior, who investigated further.

The superior's investigation disclosed that Sturdy's past supervisors reaffirmed the present judgment that he was highly intelligent but never completed a job. None would have him back. Many said he should have been fired shortly after he was hired. They alluded to "high-level influence" or his "family situation" as reasons for not doing so.

When his superior discussed these findings with him, Sturdy replied that he had indeed been moved many times, as a result of which he had no opportunity to show what he really could do. Some of the areas to which he had been assigned were new and risky. Others had simply folded up. He quoted supervisor after supervisor, each of whom in one way or another had complimented him for good work or special accomplishment. A double check with the supervisors Sturdy had mentioned produced the same reply: They did not want him back.

Again the superior told Sturdy what he had found. Sturdy was at a loss to explain the feelings of his former supervisors. Nevertheless, he still felt misjudged, poorly treated, and misunderstood. At first he wanted to prove himself anew to his present superior, but when he learned that he could have three months to find another job, he promptly set about looking for one.

But the story did not end with Sturdy's departure. The manager who had to discharge him was angry not only at Sturdy for failing to do his job, but also, more importantly, at his colleagues and superiors. The latter had passed the buck from year to year and thereby had allowed for denial and projection on Sturdy's part. With each transfer, they gave Sturdy a "Northeast promotion." They could not, of course, promote him. But they felt so guilty about their own anger toward him and their feeling that perhaps they, too, were at fault, that they compensated for their feelings with compliments and a "promotion." Not a real promotion, mind you; but an almost-promotion, a small raise and fancier title.

Sturdy's superior felt he had been made the goat for everyone else's procrastination. He had to carry the responsibility—and the blame—for terminating a man of fifteen years' service.

Sturdy himself had been clearly victimized. Though his superiors repeatedly rationalized their behavior by saying they were trying to be fair, as a matter of fact their behavior was destructive. It was apparent early in his career with the company that he was not doing well. If, after a reasonable time, he had been terminated, he still would have been young enough to try other jobs in other companies. Conceivably in one or another he might have found himself. As it turned out, he did not find himself, and worse still, he lost fifteen precious years. During all that time, he must have known he really was not doing well. He said he thought he had not been given adequate raises. Despite his accusations against others, he must have had some feeling that there was dissatisfaction with his performance. Yet when those who were dissatisfied covered over their dissatisfaction, he had no way of knowing his real situation. In effect, his superiors, out of their guilt feelings, killed his occupational chances with kindness. In the process they hurt each other because each supervisor managed to transfer him to another. No doubt each felt guilty about unloading him on the other. They also hurt the company because the man drew his salary for years without producing.

The most sound, most effective behavior is based on reality. A person must have adequate reaction to his behavior if he is to govern it according to the realities he must deal with. Without adequate information about himself, he is operating in the psychological dark. When he discovers that he has had inadequate or incorrect information, usually after many years, he is then justified in saying that he has been treated unfairly. He has. Every man has a right to know in unmistakable terms how he is performing in his job. He is, after all, spending days and years of his life out of which he has a right to expect a reasonably satisfying return.

Such management by guilt is extremely costly to the organization in another way, as indicated by this conclusion that lay behind a recent arbitration award:

> . . . In particular, and notwithstanding the grievant's unhappy record, the arbitrator must take notice of the fact that the grievant was allowed to invest all of his working life with this (organization). This appears to have resulted from an ov-

erindulgent attitude on the part of those in charge and it must be regarded as condonation of the grievant's misconduct. It must be assumed that the long-continued unrewarding policy of appeasement and of condonement to some degree must have lulled the grievant into a false sense of security and resulted in his periodic contemptuous attitude toward those in authority. . . .

CONCERN FOR LONG-SERVICE EMPLOYEES

Often management by guilt arises out of misdirected concern for employees with long service. I do not mean to imply that long service should not be recognized and rewarded. I insist, however, that failure to tell them about their performance is a poor reward for such service. For example:

An accountant was responsible for all phases of accounting, including projected costs of alternative decisions. He was in his mid-fifties, had spent thirty-five years with his company, the last fifteen as comptroller. He was not a college graduate, but had had specialized training. His many years in the business stood him in good stead. He was energetic, loyal, and was noted among his superiors for running a well-disciplined department, but he rarely originated anything new.

In the ordinary course of events, his superior was replaced. His new superior, a vice-president faced with many other problems, left the comptroller pretty much to his own devices. They consulted on special occasions. As more and well-trained younger people entered the business, problems began to appear. People from other departments complained to the vice-president that the comptroller was intruding into their work. The comptroller complained that the company's standards were slipping. He was dissatisfied with prospective candidates for his job. He became increasingly critical of others and finally of the vice-president. He blamed his vice-president for not doing anything about the problems, and the vice-president in charge of operations for causing them.

More and more vice-presidential conference time was devoted

to the controller's problems. The controller, for his part, became more indiscreet in his complaints and more uncontrolled in meetings.

In a company reorganization, the controller's new superior turned out to be the much criticized vice-president of operations. The latter decided that it would be necessary to have a brutally frank discussion with the controller. The controller was shocked to be told straightforwardly about his behavior. He demanded to know why he had not been told by his previous superior, with specific examples of his behavior. Without such information, he had concluded that his performance was acceptable. In effect, he had been permitted to be irresponsible.

The confrontation brought about noticeable change. The controller's problems and behavior had been characteristic of him for a long time, so he was not going to be a new man. But he did have enough ego strength to be capable of making a conscious effort to improve his performance, and he did so. He could have done so long before.

An important function of the organizational structure in any business is to control impulsive behavior. The structure ideally facilitates productive behavior; ideally it also prohibits behavior destructive to the organization. The failure of the first vice-president to supervise pulled the structural rug from under the controller. He became increasingly uncontrolled in an almost desperate bid for controls. The cost over some years was: failure to train a successor; little initiative and innovation; impairment of team effort because of frictions with others; plus endless hours of vice-presidential worry and conference time.

OBLIGATION TO ANOTHER

A frequent problem that leads an executive to management by guilt is his anger toward someone to whom he feels obligated. He feels, therefore, quite consciously, that he has no right to be angry with the person who has been so loyal or helpful. He suppresses his disappointment. Moreover, he continues to feel guilty for his hostility to his faithful subordinate. Inasmuch as he cannot express his anger directly, he unconsciously displaces his anger. It comes out in subtle critical ways and in assignments on which the target of his anger is bound to fail. Here is such an example:

A young executive took over the management of a small organization which had recently experienced a split among its owners. Two long-term, middle-management employees, Del and Mac, remained with the organization when the split occurred. They had a wealth of information about the company's operations. As a result, for several years both men were invaluable to the new executive. He felt further obligated to them because he was a relative of the family that owned the business, and in effect they had been loyal to that family.

The senior of the two loyal employees, Del, was particularly helpful in orienting the new executive. The executive came to lean on him, seeing him as a knowledgeable and competent man in an elder statesman role. However, as time passed, it became apparent to the new executive that the company was not moving ahead as it should. The executive formulated plans for a larger and more profitable operation. He talked these over with Del. Despite his college education and his business experience, Del did not seem to understand what the executive had in mind. He protested about the likelihood of increased overhead and saw no need for additional management help. He seemed to learn nothing from attending trade association meetings or contacts with others in the same business.

Despite his lack of business imagination, Del was well liked. He spoke easily, met others freely, and impressed them. He was an excellent storyteller and the life of any party he attended. He used these talents to help maintain employee loyalty. The executive, though recognizing that Del was no businessman, appreciated Del's support and tried to keep Del close to him, both in organizational structure and in personal contact. The executive was not altogether content with this arrangement, but he excused it by saying he enjoyed Del's company.

After a couple of years of putting up with what he perceived

as Del's roadblock point of view, the executive discovered that
the junior of the two loyal employees, Mac, was doing Del's
thinking for him. Despite his loyalty to Del, the executive became
angry enough to create a new assignment for Del, which was a
combination of makework and trivial duties. Del created further
problems by talking too much about company business. Still,
there was no open discussion of these problems. Instead, the
executive, talking to others, would depreciate Del's family. In-
directly he was blaming Del for the alleged shortcomings of his
children.

The executive continued to protest his loyalty to Del, saying
that no one in the organization was more loyal to him or more
dependable. The relationship continued for more than fourteen
years, relatively unchanged. During this period, Del had many
health problems. The executive believed them to be due to tension. He was unaware that he himself might have helped increase
the tension, although he was painfully aware that somehow he
had failed Del.

As the executive himself pointed out, Del was essentially a
public relations man. He could have been, and in many ways was,
highly successful at that job. But the executive, because of the
operation of the mechanism of idealization, felt obligated to make
something else of him, something he was not and could not be.
When Del failed to meet these unrealistic expectations, after
being pushed and prodded to greater heights, the executive saw
him as an obstructionist. He punished him by putting him on the
shelf and criticizing his family. For years Del lived with his boss's
thinly veiled hostility and his own feelings of failure. He paid a
high psychological price, as did the executive, because the latter
was guided by his guilt feelings instead of rational judgment.

A similar situation often occurs with spinster secretaries who
in effect have married the business and who have served a major
executive during a good part of their careers. With age and increased loneliness, they tend to become more isolated, frustrated,
and rejected. This experience, in turn, often leads them to be
irritable, discourteous, and sometimes openly hostile to younger

employees. Most of the time, executives are reluctant to confront such a woman with her behavior, particularly if she cried when they first tried to do so. Yet, unless the woman is aware of the results of her behavior, she has little reason for changing it. More important to her, she may well need professional help. The executive's failure to confront her deprives her of the leverage to get help. One important way for a person to learn that she needs help is to realize that, despite her best efforts, she is not performing adequately on that job.

Of course confrontation is no panacea, and it does not replace the empty loneliness such people live with constantly. If you and others in the organization make special efforts to help relieve the loneliness, you can thereby diminish the intensity of the anger. Usually when others try to befriend the lonely person, they are helpless without his cooperation. Sometimes it takes confrontation to bring about that cooperation.

THE URGE TO REFORM

Many people outside of managerial ranks have a picture of management as harsh, autocratic, and exploitative—and some executives are. However, management more often is destructive to people by procrastination and overkindness in a mistaken and inappropriate effort to make people better. This example is a clear demonstration:

When, after he had been in the company for several years, Ed Allen's supervisors appraised him, they described him as an incompetent office manager. According to his superiors, he was limited in his ability; he had a poor personality; he was unable to handle help; he was unwilling to suggest, adopt, or agree to new ideas. His thinking was muddled and his decisions were never definitive. After this evaluation had been arrived at, he was transferred to another smaller office, which he also managed. There, shortly after his arrival, he acquired a new manager.

Allen presented a challenge to the new manager, so much a challenge that the manager tried for ten years to "develop" him.

First, the new manager tried praise and encouragement. Allen's reaction was, "It's about time my work was appreciated and my expertness was recognized." There was no improvement in his work.

Next the manager tried toughness. This disturbed Allen for a while and he tried a little harder. But then he apparently decided his manager was basically intolerant and he would just have to live with intolerance.

The manager tried group pressure. He reviewed policies and procedures with all his immediate subordinates together. Allen changed some of his forms and managed to cut down on some paper work, but his cost-cutting efforts were sporadic and desultory at best.

Allen and his manager then talked at length and repeatedly, particularly about Allen's staff. Allen complained that he had not had enough help and that the help he did have was not good enough. Despite help offered him through the addition of automated equipment and the reduction of reports, the size of Allen's staff remained constant.

When all this effort failed, when ten years had passed, and when there continued to be complaints from higher management, someone else took over Ed Allen's work, and Ed was given early retirement.

The company prided itself on its lenient attitude to employees with long service. The price of its lenience can only be imagined. How much rejection and hostility did Allen experience from his superiors? With how much anger did his subordinates have to live over the years? By what stretch of the imagination could Allen possibly experience his work life as successful when all he knew was failure? No one knew the answers to these questions. No one had ever asked Allen about his feelings.

The guilt feelings of the company management were reflected in the impulsive way they got rid of him. When they decided to terminate him, among themselves they set a termination date. Six months before that date, they notified him that he would be terminated, paid him for the next six months, and had a man ready to step into his job the moment he was informed what would happen to him. In one day he was notified, fired, and paid off.

THE YOUNG VS. THE OLD

The movement of a younger man into a position of authority over older men usually seems to result in conflicting feelings in both parties. The younger man's feelings usually include some feelings of guilt that he has vanquished his older competitors. It is hard for him not to feel that he has taken away from them an opportunity for them to move up, and they may privately agree. His pleasure with his success is often tempered by an underlying disquiet. His guilt feelings make it difficult for him to make rational decisions, for so many of his decisions are tinged with the effort to appease the older men—without success. He seems to be chagrined, too, that nobody warned him of these feelings and the problems they produce. One young president put it this way:

> I am many years junior to the other executives in our organization who report to me. Unfortunately, the fact of age differences is seldom faced, and the difficulties of variations in energy levels are responsible for the lack of rapport. They accuse me of by-passing my older, more experienced associates for the younger, more compatible ones. This is just an excuse for their own incompetence or inability. They criticize me for impatience, aggressiveness, and poor judgment. The last occurs whenever I make a decision without consulting them. But they are extremely cautious, they lack aggressiveness, and their judgment is markedly conservative. Of course, this conflict confuses the subordinates of these executives and leads to some choosing of sides. Can some method be devised that recognizes the possibility of this conflict immediately on the appointment of a younger man to an important managerial position with older subordinates? Might it not be beneficial to have frank discussions with the parties involved about the possibility of such problems developing? Would a committee method of decision making give some relief to me in my relationship with them?

The guilt here is most evident in the new president's inability to take charge. He sees only differences in orientation and style of administration. He does not see that the older men will continue to hang back and fight him until they are certain he is stronger than they. He is unconsciously afraid to be stronger, and therefore unrealistically feels guilty because he had surpassed older men. He would rather turn to a committee, in effect abdicate leadership, in an effort to appease them and his superego.

Conflict with Direction of Policy

Probably the most painful situation involving management by guilt takes place when an executive feels that he is being forced to take action that he feels is unfair or unwarranted. Without an adequate basis in his own mind for taking the action, he seizes upon some minor incident, which he then magnifies out of proportion. His anger becomes equally exaggerated as he reacts to his own guilt. But when the subordinate mounts his own attack, the superior finds himself even more on the defensive because he cannot cope with both the subordinate's anger and his own guilt feelings simultaneously. The following case illustrates this point.

Rusk was the manager of local operations of a large manufacturing company. He had been in this position about five months when two of the company's more prominent directors visited his location. They had no criticism of his management, but they had plenty to say about his lack of social grace. He served them too much liquor, they complained, and he picked up the check for drinks in a local bar when one of them was officially the host. Not that Rusk drank too much—just that he lacked some of the social amenities. In their view, therefore, he should not be the local manager. Taking his cue from the directors, the president began to voice the feeling to the vice-president who was Rusk's superior that he should begin looking for a new manager.

The vice-president felt Rusk was honest and diligent. He did not try to hide bad news, he had reasonably good knowledge of his operations, and he had recently completed a building program within his budget. He apparently had the cooperation of his subordinates. True, he tended to be a little slow in making decisions, he was not particularly astute, and he used too many words. On the whole, however, he was doing well where he was.

The pressure mounted from above, but there seemed to be no adequate managerial reason to discharge the man. The personality factors seemed not to be that important to the vice-president. Yet there was no question that the pressure was almost a direct demand that Rusk be fired. The vice-president kept a constant alert for an obvious managerial failure to serve as a cause for dismissal, or for an obvious demonstration of managerial success to support his contention that Rusk could manage satisfactorily.

Unfortunately, Rusk provided an opening for criticism just at this time. Not only was his budget proposal late in getting to the vice-president, but also his requests seemed unusually high. The vice-president attacked sharply. He said he would not tolerate a late budget, and that the high requests could have been avoided by advance planning.

This provoked counterattack by Rusk. He pointed out that his subordinates were permitted to authorize certain expenditures, though he was not. Several of his subordinates were officers of subsidiary corporations, but he was not—a direct slap as he saw it. He had been promised stock options and a bonus, but neither had materialized. In short, he complained, higher management demonstrated no confidence in him.

The vice-president did not argue with Rusk. He knew that Rusk's complaints were valid, and furthermore, that Rusk's observations were also valid. Higher management did not have confidence in him. He told Rusk what he should have told him in the first place, but his own guilt feelings had not let him; namely, that regardless of why he did not have top management support, since he did not have it, he might just as well find another job because he could never be successful in this company.

AGGRESSION AS A PROBLEM OF PERSONALITY

In previous examples, guilt has arisen with respect to aggression stimulated in a specific managerial situation. Some people have chronic difficulty with their aggressions. These people have problems managing others. Thus people who ordinarily are non-autocratic become autocratic and perfectionistic as supervisors when influenced by guilt. What is evident in these situations is the executive's inability to satisfy his own superego, despite his constant striving for perfection, nor is anyone else able to satisfy his standards. The results are devastating to the growth of subordinates, though often they maintain a high level of performance as long as the supervisor is in control. The problem tends to grow worse as the supervisor grows older and his capacities begin to decline. As he is less and less able to meet his own ideal performance, he tends to become more irritable, angry, and depressed. Here is a case in point:

A high-level executive has been with his company thirty years. Off the job he is relaxed, congenial, and popular. He is dedicated to whatever he may be doing at the moment—from bridge to fishing. He does not drink, but he is tolerant of others' drinking. He is active in church and charitable affairs. He is solicitous of his friends and he is generally a soft touch for charity.

His many talents led to his rise in the company. Supervision, however, is not one of his talents, except with those who are as talented as he. He is impatient with the average. He is excessively dominant to the point of arrogance. He is a poor teacher because he has the answers and is too impatient to let his group work out the solutions. He has a timid group of subordinates. He does not have time to provide all the answers, so he pays close attention to those projects in which he has an interest at the expense of the others and of his responsibility in general. Promising young men have left the organization as a result of his inadequate supervision. Among them was a man of long experience who should have been his logical successor.

Repeated discussions about his overconscientiousness and overdedication have gotten nowhere, nor have "Dutch uncle" talks about delegating work, patience in teaching, or about giving his subordinates a chance to make mistakes. Moreover, he is becoming more pessimistic and moody as competition increases and new products are developed which are outside of his experience.

This man's "moods" will increase to the point where his underlying depression is obvious and he will ultimately require treatment. As a matter of fact, he actually needs treatment now, but neither he nor his superior can accept that fact.

In this situation the managerial problem is that the guilt-ridden man is in a supervisory position. In the following case, the boss is unwilling to recognize that such a person, despite his obvious talents, cannot supervise:

A fifty-year-old man has fifteen years of experience in the business. He is intelligent, well educated, and imaginative. He is pleasant, courteous, extremely considerate of others, and has a high sense of ethics. He is a good salesman. His physical appearance impresses others. He is essentially a very wholesome and somewhat naive individual. He is extremely anxious to avoid hurting another person's feelings, and has a great distaste for any unpleasantness in his relationships with other people. He is very trusting of people. He is somewhat indecisive and tends to look at a person's virtues rather than his performance.

His boss asks

How can this man be made an effective manager over 150 people and get results? His leadership tends to waiver and his indirect approach leaves people not fully recognizing the problem or what he wants to accomplish.

How can this man be helped to become effective within the framework of his own personality? He obviously has the capacity to do the job, but the effective leadership of the organization appears to be lacking. His reliance on gentle persuasion is insufficient.

This man's superego will not let him tolerate his own aggressive feelings or the hostility of others. He contains his own feelings and denies the anger of others. Short of extended treatment (unlikely at his age and because he does not regard himself as being

maladjusted or sick), he cannot change his superego. His boss
would do both himself and the man a service by not making him
a supervisor.

A more subtle and therefore more difficult situation involves
the executive who in repeated small ways puts himself in a bad
light. His errors in judgment are not in themselves significant;
that they occur, however, raises doubts about his judgment in the
eyes of his supervisors. He leads when he should wait for support,
and he waits for support when he should lead. Throughout all
this, he is the picture of agreeableness. Apparently he hears the
criticisms of his performance, but his behavior does not change.
His superiors become angry with him, and then disappointed.
Then some trivial event occurs, and they fire him. "Not qualified
for higher responsibilities," they say. The man himself is dis-
mayed. "But they never told me they were dissatisfied," he says.
"I asked them to tell me why, but they can't. I did a good job.
It must be strictly political."

The executive is partly right. His superiors cannot cite chapter
and verse. When they try, the reasons are so trivial that they
cannot specify the reasons to themselves. They just do not know,
and though they are uneasy for not knowing, they are certain they
have made the right decision. Each trivial incident has aroused
their anger. But it is not appropriate to have much anger for trivial
incidents, so the anger is repressed. The executive is such a fine
fellow and works so hard that his bosses feel guilty for their mo-
mentary anger. Guilt increases as each incident provokes more
anger and more repression. Finally they build up enough residual
anger, enough guilt for feeling angry, and then more anger for
feeling guilty, that they strike out against their subtle tormentor,
even to the point of feeling like fools because they do not have
a significant objective reason for firing him.

Though neither the executive nor his superiors nor others
familiar with the situation can understand what happened, a second careful look usually tells the story. Much of the time, what
appears to be precipitous and unwarranted firing results from
those guilt feelings in a person that motivate him to seek punish-

ment and rejection from others. In other words, he manages to put his worst foot forward and to be punished by being fired, to assuage his own guilt feelings. At the height of success, he manages to defeat himself, but is never able to see the seeds of his defeat in his own behavior. This is the unrecognized pattern: guilt, self-punishment by provoking others; guilt in others for having aggressive feelings toward him; buildup of aggression and guilt; impulsive firing, to be relieved of the guilt and the provocation to aggression.

A SECOND LOOK

These examples are only a few of the instances in which anger, and guilt for anger become significant determinants of executive action. These behaviors occur when the aggressive drive is stimulated beyond the ego's capacity to deal with it more constructively, and the superego reacts to the rising aggression.

Many times it is difficult to recognize subtle forms of your own anger or that of others. Often you have fairly evident cues in your own behavior: a feeling of uneasiness and self-criticism after a decision about another person; feeling less comfortable with the other person than before; avoiding the other person, seeing him less, having difficulty conversing with him; criticizing him more to others repeatedly or justifying your own actions repeatedly; giving him the dirty jobs; or bending over backwards to be nice to him, as if he were something special.

As you review problem situations with this idea in mind, you should ask yourself what were the conditions under which your own or someone else's anger and guilt might have been stimulated. They may include one or more of these:
1. Real or imagined attack by someone else
2. Threat to self-esteem, violating the ego ideal, values, or rules of living
3. Feeling of being manipulated, overcontrolled, exploited or imposed upon, or otherwise made to feel inadequate
4. Feeling of being disappointed or let down, reflecting the frustration of dependency needs, expectations or support

5. Lack of clear structure, making it difficult to know what one is supposed to do and not do
6. Stimulation of rivalry with someone else, whether subordinate, colleague, or superior
7. Failure to provide adequate controls for people who need structure to help them control their anger

If you recognize that you or someone else is angry and that you are trying to avoid saying so, then the sooner you can put an end to the game of make-believe, the better for both parties. This does not mean open warfare or a verbal slugging match. Rather, it requires that, recognizing your anger, you control it sufficiently to sit down with the other person and state the problem, together with your feelings about it. Then you have the often difficult task of hearing the other person out.

What was particularly threatening to the other man? What made him so afraid (often unconsciously) that he had to defend himself in this way? You cannot ask him these questions, nor could he give you adequate answers if he wanted to, but you can sense some of the feelings the subordinate might have had in the situation. Your awareness of such feelings, however vaguely he understands them, will help him gain another perspective.

If the problem has to do with job performance, it is important to reassess whether he can do what is expected of him. Too often people are expected to make drastic changes in their personalities, which is impossible. Are you asking too much? What kind of help will he, with his particular assets and shortcomings, need to get the job done?

In fact, does he belong in this organization? Regardless of whether he has not been able to grow, or should not have been hired in the first place, or does not fit with the new management, or some other reason, is this really for him? If the man really does not have a reasonable opportunity to satisfy himself and the organization, then he might be better off in another organization where he can savor success. It is a fairly common experience that many men were boosted along in their careers by being fired, an action that required them to find some more rewarding work.

This is not to be used as a rationalization for wielding the axe of discharge. Irresponsible treatment of human beings is nothing less than sadistic behavior, which no rationalization will ever justify.

A more responsible way of facing this problem is to spell out the pros and cons and weigh the alternatives. A clear statement of fact as you see it is an important part of his reality. You may not be completely right, but you must act on your own judgment, and that in itself is fact for the other person.

If you and the subordinate together decide the subordinate must go, or if you decide it yourself (assuming that the man is not being fired for cause), then you can give him invaluable help finding another job. Probably you know companies other than your own, and one may well have a place where the subordinate can make a contribution. You do not have to pass him off on someone else. You have only the reasonable responsibility for reporting his abilities and the conditions under which they thrive. If you can also indicate the conditions under which the subordinate does not do well, your honesty will command the respect of the other organization and make it more willing to employ the subordinate. Some executives do this themselves, some use their personnel departments, and some use the same executive recruitment agencies that are finding a replacement to place the man who is departing. Whatever is done along these lines, you will feel that you have done your best by the subordinate, and the latter will probably feel that he was treated fairly and with consideration for his dignity as a human being.

A fundamental guideline in this, as in any other human relations situation, is the question, "What are the equities in this situation?" What is fair to the man and to the organization? Decision by equity is a high-sounding phrase. It is not easy to define. It neither punishes the man nor overcompensates him. Punishment is thinly disguised anger. Overcompensation results from not too thinly disguised guilt. Either behavior leaves both parties feeling angry, for when one "bends over backwards," he leaves the other person with the feeling that he does so to make up for a wrong or that he is patronizing the other.

Folie à deux—the irrational pattern of interaction resulting from excessive dependency between executives and subordinates—is discussed in this chapter. Kets de Vries illustrates in a series of case vignettes situations where both superiors and subordinates have lost touch with the immediate reality of the organization's environment, and he suggests various ways to prevent, or at least limit, the emergence of folie à deux.

8

Managers Can Drive Their Subordinates Mad

MANFRED F. R. KETS DE VRIES

Managers, no less than other people, have personality quirks. Little things they do on occasion can drive their subordinates "up the wall." In the main, however, subordinates tolerate their manager's quirks because for the most part the manager's style is acceptable, and for many subordinates it is much more than that. But what happens to subordinates when a manager seems to be all quirks, when there is no in-between? To take an example:

As an administrator, J. Edgar Hoover struck many as an erratic autocrat, banishing agents to Siberian posts for the most whimsical reasons and terrorizing them with so many rules and regulations that it was impossible to adhere to all of them (*Time*, Dec. 22, 1975). Hoover viewed his directorship as infallible; subordinates soon learned that dissent equaled disloyalty, and that no whim of his, however insignificant could safely be ignored. For example, refusal to participate in a weight-reducing program was likely to incur his wrath, and rumor had it that chauffeurs had to avoid making left turns while driving him (apparently his car had once been struck by another car when he was making a left turn).

If it originated from Hoover, a trivial and unimportant order changed in meaning. Even if the directive was unclear, subordinates would have to take some form of calculated action and, it was said, could only expect trouble if they did not take the directive seriously. In such an atmosphere, these directives often assumed a life of their own. Slavish obedience to the rules was all that counted, along with the annual tally of the number of fines, convictions, or apprehended fugitives credited to his agency's efforts. And problems arose if the figures did not increase each year.

Naturally, those agents who embraced the concept of the director's omnipotence were more likely to succeed. To ensure compliance, inspectors would be sent out to field offices in search of violations (the breaking of some obscure rule or instruction). If a "contract was out" on the special agent in charge of the office, a "violation" would inevitably be found since, apparently, the inspector's own future at the FBI was at stake if no violations were discovered, in which case, a "contract" might be issued on him. If one wanted to survive in the organization, participation in many of these absurdities was often unavoidable. Moreover, many of these bizarre activities seem to have been treated as quite normal aspects of organizational life and were carried out with great conviction.

While Hoover at the FBI, Hitler before the collapse of the Third Reich, and, even more recently, Jim Jones at the mass suicide in Guyana, are newsworthy examples of what leaders can do to subordinates when they lose touch with reality, the effects of dependence also occur in less heralded tales.

The president of a faltering company in the apparel industry seemed increasingly unwilling to face the facts of his company's declining profits. Two months before the banks eventually took control, the president was still holding meetings during which nonexistent orders, the development of revolutionary new machinery, and the introduction of innovative products were discussed. These new developments were supposed to turn the company around and dramatically change its position in the industry. The president ignored the dismal profit-and-loss picture, inefficiencies in production, and poor sales performance, attributing them to unfair industry practices by competitors, or even to sabotage, and assured his managers that change was imminent and that the company would be out of the red shortly.

Sadly enough, these glorious ideas were far removed from reality. While the president seemed to originate most of these fantasies, his close associates not only participated in them, but also encouraged his irrational thoughts and actions. The rare subordinate who expressed his disbelief found himself ostracized and threatened with dismissal, while among the small but increasingly isolated group of managers the belief persisted that everything was not lost, and that miraculous developments were just around the corner. Only when the banks took control was the spell finally broken.

What is striking about both these anecdotes is the shift of delusions and unusual behavior patterns from the originator of these activities to one or more others who are closely associated with him or her. These associates not only take an active part but also frequently enhance and elaborate on these delusions. The delusions seem to escalate in intensity when the people involved try to solve problems concerned with an already deteriorating situation. They inevitably aggravate the situation, and become correspondingly more and more reluctant to face external reality. Comfortable in their own chosen, closed environment, they do not welcome the opinion of outsiders, seeing them as threatening the status quo and disturbing their tunnel vision.

Also noticeable in these two examples is just how contagious the behavior of a senior executive can be, and how devastating its effect on his subordinates and his organization. In Hoover's case, his subordinates' reaction further encouraged him to continue in his dysfunctional behavior. Perhaps the special nature of Hoover's organization may have contributed to the fact that very few subordinates were willing to refuse to participate in some of these bizarre activities. In any case, many conformed to his wishes, and some may actually have believed in the appropriateness and importance of his actions. In the second example, again the process of mental contagion is central.

In psychiatric literature, mental contagion is a recurring theme. This particular process of influence, which usually goes together with some form of break with reality occurring among groups of individuals, is generally known as *folie à deux*—that is, shared madness. Although folie à deux as a way of interaction has been limited to seriously disturbed relationships between two people, a broader definition of this particular psychological process may be helpful in understanding the interactions between leaders and followers in organizations.

One may gain insight into what is frequently described as an "eccentric" leadership style if one studies emotionally charged, superior-subordinate relationships characterized by an impaired ability to see things realistically within the context of folie à deux. One may discover that this phenomenon, with various degrees of intensity, is a regular occurrence in organizations, and can be considered one of the risks of leadership.

A senior executive should not underestimate the degree of influence he wields in his organization. Recognizing dependency—need for direction—as one of man's most universal characteristics, a manager should be aware that many of his subordinates will sacrifice reality for its sake, participating in even irrational decisions without mustering a critical stand and challenging what is happening.

To preserve dependency, both subordinates and superiors create closed communities, thereby losing touch with the immediate reality of the organization's environment to the detriment of organizational functioning. When reality is not totally abandoned, however, this phenomenon is often difficult to recognize. Still, in view of its damaging consequences, even in a limited form, it deserves serious attention. I will explore this aspect of leadership, hoping to help managers diagnose and prevent the incidence of its potentially disastrous effects.

THE PARADOX OF DEPENDENCY

Two French psychiatrists were the first to coin the term folie à deux. Other names given to this phenomenon have been double insanity, mental catagion, collective insanity, or psychosis of association. Folie à deux essentially involves the sharing of a delusional system by two or more individuals.[1] This phenomenon has frequently been observed among family members living an isolated existence.

To better understand this psychological process, let us look for a moment at the early childhood development of a person who instigates this form of mental contagion. A central theme in the origin of this disorder appears to be difficulty in establishing feelings of basic trust with people (originally with the parents). Lack of basic trust due to the absence of sustained interpersonal care, accompanied by anxiety because of frustrating, humiliating, and disappointing experiences will contribute to a lack of cohesive sense of self, a sense of betrayal, and a perception of the environment as hostile and dangerous. The individual's personality will develop accordingly.

In his dealings with others, such a person will continually take precautions and be on his guard for any confirmation of his suspicions. In situations of power, as a reactive way of dealing with what he sees as a hostile environment, he will be highly susceptible to grandiose fantasies and prone to delusions.

Apart from suffering the emerging paranoid disposition, a person who lacks trust also suffers an absence of closeness and, consequently, has frustrated dependency needs. For such a person, the world becomes a dangerous place where only a few individuals can be trusted. If an opportunity arises to satisfy these dependency needs, the attachment he makes to others can become extremely

---

[1]For an elaboration of the idea of folie à deux, see Kets de Vries (1980) and Kets de Vries and Miller (in Press).

intense, frequently overpowering all other behavior patterns. Because this attachment is so important, he will do anything—even sacrifice reality—to preserve it.

The individual to whom this attachment is directed, and who is not without his own dependency needs (though perhaps not of such an intense nature) may enjoy the way the other person is taking care of him and giving him some form of direction and guidance in life. One outcome may be that he will strongly identify with those things for which the other person stands. However, the price for these feelings of closeness becomes acceptance of the behavior and actions of the domineering person, often without much concern for their base in reality.

This identification process appears to be of a special nature, and contains elements of the defense mechanism sometimes called *identification with the aggressor*—an unconscious process whereby a person takes for his own the image of a person who represents a source of frustration for him. Paradoxically enough, the process is gratifying because it becomes a way of overcoming a sense of inner weakness. Through identifying with the aggressor, the susceptible person neutralizes his own hostile and destructive wishes (which can be viewed as a reaction to feelings of helplessness and dependency on the dominant partner), and fear of retaliation about these wishes. At the same time he gains through the alliance, since the symbolic merger with the aggressor rescues him from becoming the victim.

DYNAMICS OF FOLIE À DEUX

We have seen that folie à deux is marked by contagious irrational behavior patterns, but how does it occur in organizations?

Suppose a senior executive, under the strain of leadership, trying to cope with often disconcerting imagery around power and control in addition to the general pressures of the business environment, gradually loses touch with the organization's reality. Also, this individual's charismatic personality may once have attracted executives with highly ungratified dependency needs to the organization, or it may have been the organizational climate itself which was conducive to a reawakening of these executives' dependency needs.

Whatever the reason, these managers may have become dependent on the senior executive. Although strong, these needs do not at first completely overpower all other behavior patterns. What does change dependency needs into folie à deux? The change occurs when both senior executive and subordinates become dependent on each other in a situation which offers few outside sources of gratification; their complete commitment to each other can thus be taken as symptomatic.

At some point, triggered by an event usually associated with a depriving experience of the past, the senior executive may become preoccupied with delusionary ideas (and this is not necessarily a conscious process), one of which is that his subordinates are taking unfair advantage of him. As a result, he develops a certain amount of hostility. But, at the same time, since the subordinates' expressions of attachment to him finally fulfill his own need for attention, so long ungratified, he experiences guilt about his feeling of hostility.

In spite of his lingering resentment, therefore, the senior executive is extremely reluctant to give up his relationships with his subordinates. They may be among the few close relationships he has been able to establish. Consequently, in order to defend himself against his own emerging hostility toward his subordinates, he externalizes it and attributes the hostility to others.

The senior executive absolves the closely associated executives of responsibility for these feelings; it is "the others" who are to blame. This blame can take many forms, eventually encapsulating everything that may be going wrong with the company. The senior executive, who has been the originator of this process, now needs his subordinates to support his delusionary ideas and actions—not only because these ideas are his defense against hostility, but also because he may lose his feelings of closeness with his subordinates if he does not get their support. There seems to be only one option—namely, to induce his subordinates to participate.

If a subordinate resists, the senior executive will become overtly hostile, including him in his vision of "the other camp"—the enemy. Naturally, the subordinate's level of anxiety will rise as a double-bind situation develops for him; he will have to choose between the loss of gratification of his dependency needs and exposure to the senior executive's wrath on the one hand, or the loss of reality on the other.

In many instances, the subordinate will solve this intrapsychic conflict by giving in to the psychological ultimatum, "identify with the aggressor," thus satisfying his own dependency needs and deflecting the hostility of the senior executive. Separation from the person who started this process is viewed as much more of a direct, tangible loss than the loss of reality.

Identifying with the aggressor usually implies participating in his or her persecutory fantasies. The shared delusions are usually kept well within the realm of possibility, being based on actual past events or certain common expectations, and because they do contain a bit of reality, the process is difficult to discern. Through participation in these fantasies, the subordinates maintain their source of gratification, lower their anxiety and guilt level, and express their anger in a deflected form by directing it toward others. The process is mirrorlike; the actions of the initiator of the process become reflected in those of the subordinates, and vice versa, and can be viewed as the outcome of an effort to save the alliance from breaking up.

Now let us look at some of these dynamics in greater detail.

Getting Trapped

In organizations, folie à deux can be one of the pitfalls of leadership. Often, however, this dimension of leadership is not seen for what it is, and contagious behavior patterns are more often than not accepted and rationalized as being merely side products of an eccentric or autocratic leadership style.

Take, for example, the behavior and actions of the first Henry Ford, who had been acclaimed not only a mechanical genius but

also, after the announcement of the five-dollar day, as a philan-
thropist. Because of the darker sides of his actions, however, this
image eventually changed. While the public merely ridiculed his
escapades, for the employees of the Ford Motor Company the
situation was not a laughing matter. His despotic one-man rule
and his continuous search for enemies increasingly had repercussions in every function of the company. He began to view Wall
Street bankers, labor unions, and Jews as his enemies, seeing
each group as supposedly endangering his complete control over
the company and obstructing him in his grandiose plans (e.g., the
Peace Ship mission to stop the First World War, or his senatorial
campaign).

At one point there may have been an element of reality to
some of Ford's notions (i.e., the labor union movement), but over
time what there was got lost. One can regard the relationship
between the senior Henry Ford and his lieutenants Liebold, So-
rensen, and, particularly, Bennett, in the context of folie à deux.
Using a system of intimidation, helped by a large number of
Detroit underworld characters, Bennett spread terror in the organization, a process originally instigated by Henry Ford but
perfected by Bennett and his henchmen.

Executives who did not participate in the idiosyncracies of
Henry Ford and his close associates were fired. The Model T,
which carried the company to its original success, eventually became a burden. Reinforced in his behavior by his close subordinates, Henry Ford refused even to consider the possibility of
changes or modifications in his original model of a cheap car for
the masses. Only in 1927, after the Model T had been in production for nineteen years, and only after an incredible loss of
market share to General Motors, was Henry Ford willing to make
a model change.

This example illustrates how contagious a senior executive's
behavior can be, and how originally functional behavior can become increasingly damaging to the organization and even bring
the company close to bankruptcy. Henry Ford's subordinates only
encouraged his views, although it remains open to question which

subordinates were only conforming and which ones truly believed in their actions.

A more contemporary example involves the behavior of a manager of an isolated plant in a mining community who had developed the belief that the head office wanted to close down the production facility. The recent introduction by the head office of a new factory control system started him in his belief, and regular visits by head office staff to implement the new control system only reinforced these ideas, which he communicated to his subordinates and which were widely accepted. Although the production figures were more than adequate, a collusion began to develop among plant personnel, including the manager, to falsify information in order to show the plant in an even more favorable light. Only a spot check by the internal auditor of the head office brought these malpractices to light.

In many of these instances, however, a major question remains. How much of the behavior of the subordinates can be accurately described in the context of folie à deux, and how much is mere compliance to the eccentric leadership style of a senior executive? The latter situation is illustrated by this example:

The division head of a company that manufactured machinery equipment would habitually mention the advanced product technology used in his plants to each visitor and at talks at trade association meetings. On promotion trips abroad, he was always trying to obtain license arrangements for his technology. And occasionally he would be successful. But, in spite of the fact that the company was turning out a high-quality product, there was nothing unique about the technology. As a matter of fact, most competitors were using comparable or even more advanced technological processes. Although most of his subordinates were aware of the actual state of affairs, they were unwilling to confront the division head with the facts. Compliance seemed easier than confrontation.

It is worth noting that mere compliance, if continued long enough, can evolve into stronger alliances, possibly resulting in active participation in these irrational actions. These examples also emphasize some of the characteristics of folie à deux; for example, the relative isolation of the actors, their closeness, the existence of a dominant partner, and the emergence of delusionary ideas.

The Search for Scapegoats

Interaction that contains elements of folie à deux can contribute to collusion among subgroups that fosters organizational myths and fantasies often only remotely related to reality. In such instances, for some cliques, the organization's overall objectives and strategies become of lesser interest than tactical considerations. As concern for the maintenance of various irrational notions consumes more energy, there is less congruence between specific actions and available information.

It appears as if the members of these groups live in a polarized world that no longer includes compromise or the acceptance of differences. Everyone is pressured to choose sides. It is also a world where one continuously has to be on one's guard against being singled out as a target for unfriendly actions. In such an organization, scapegoating becomes a predominant activity directed not only toward individuals within the organization but also toward such groups as the government, labor unions, competitors, suppliers, customers, or consumer organizations. What may have been a well-thought-out program may become distorted. For instance, alertness to the environment, which at one time may have been an organizational strength, can turn into a watch for imminent attack—a caricature of its original purpose.

Because of structural arrangements, subgroups frequently overlap with departments or other units. When this happens territorialism prevails, with people jealously guarding areas of responsibility. The determination of boundaries between departments can lead to disputes, and the seeking or accepting of help from other groups may be considered a weakness, or even a betrayal.

For example, in a large electronics company a vice president of production development began to imagine that two of his colleagues, a vice president of R & D and a vice president of manufacturing, wanted to get rid of him. He perceived that his two colleagues were trying to reorganize his department out of existence and incorporate it into their own functional areas. At every available opportunity, he communicated this concern to his subordinates and expected them to confirm his own suspicions. Disagreement was not tolerated; resistance to his view resulted in either dismissal or transfer to another department. Gradually, many of his executives began to believe in his statements and to develop a siege mentality which led to a strong sense of group cohesion.

Relationships between this group and members of other departments became strained, with once minor interdepartmental skirmishes escalating into open warfare. Committee meetings with members of other departments became public accusation sessions about the withholding of information, inaccurate data, and intrusion into each others' territory. In addition, because of his recurring complaints about poor quality of delivered material and late deliveries, the vice president's contacts with some of his suppliers deteriorated. (A subsequent examination by a new vice president found that most of these accusations were unwarranted.)

Eventually, managers of other departments began to avoid contact with product development people, thereby confirming their suspicions. Over time, the rest of the company built up a number of separate, informal information systems to avoid dealing with the product development group. Finally, after the product development group made a number of budgetary mistakes because of distorted information, the president transferred the vice president and reorganized the department.

In this example one can see how excessive rivalry and suspicion can lead people to adopt a narrow perspective of organizational priorities and become defensive and controlling. Without integrating mechanisms to counterbalance their effect, these attitudes can fractionate an organization, understandably leading participants to take refuge in policies and procedures, collusive activities, and other forms of organizational gamesmanship. Cooperation will disappear and priorities will become distorted.

Where elements of folie à deux seep into organizations, conflict becomes stifling, creativity is discouraged, and distrust becomes the prevailing attitude. Instead of taking realistic action, managers react to emergencies by withdrawing or scapegoating as an undercurrent of fear pervades the overall organizational climate. As ends and means become indistinguishable, the organization will drift along, losing touch with originally defined corporate goals and strategies.

ENTREPRENEURIAL DANGERS

Because of the great intensity and closeness that develop in small isolated groups, entrepreneurial ventures tend to be particularly susceptible to folie à deux behavior patterns. In many instances the venture is undertaken because of the entrepreneur's desire to overcome his feelings of dependency, helplessness, and rejection by adopting the opposite posture of financial and psychological risk-taking. In addition, the entrepreneur may have a strong need for achievement, control, and power, as well as an intense concern for autonomy (Kets de Vries, 1980).

The relationship between entrepreneur and enterprise is usually an involved and conflict-ridden one in which the company has great emotional significance for the individual. Frequently, this type of attachment may lead to growth and succession crises, episodes aggravated by developments of a folie-à-deux nature, as the following example shows:

The president and founder of a medium-size electronics company often expressed concern about the need for more professional management in his company. He liked to state that the entrepreneurial phase had been passed and that the time had come to make organizational changes, prepare to go public, and plan for succession. To that end, he became personally involved in the recruitment of MBAs at various business schools. His charismatic appeal and his strong advocacy of professional management attracted a great number of MBAs. The MBA influx was balanced, however, by a steady exodus of many of the same MBAs who soon realized the difficulties in conforming to the president's demands.

Under the guise of being "a happy family," the founder felt he could intrude in the private family affairs of his subordinates. The responsibility that he had promised to delegate to the newcomers turned out to be poorly defined assignments without much authority, which frequently led to failure. A person's career advancement depended on his or her closeness to the president, compliance with his wishes, and willingness to participate in often irrational behavior patterns. The price of resistance was exile to various obscure sales offices. Eventually, the company had to pay a toll for this leadership, but the president blamed the steady drop in sales and profits on government intervention, union activities, and sabotage by a number of singled-out employees.

Hoarding of information, playing of favorites, inconsistent handling of company policies, and, in general, the creation of ambiguous situations constitute a common phenomenon in entrepreneurial companies. Because the company's survival depends upon the entrepreneur, many subordinates are easily drawn into supporting him even when his actions are irrational. Those unwilling to participate leave, while conformers and those susceptible to folie à deux relationships remain.

This phenomenon may explain why a strong layer of capable middle managers is missing in so many entrepreneurial companies. Those who remain in situations of folie-à-deux-like behavior will spend a great part of their energies on political infighting and in supporting the irrational behavior and beliefs of the entrepreneur. These activities can become even more intense if members of the entrepreneur's family are employed in the company so that family and organizational dynamics become closely intertwined.

MANAGEMENT OF FOLIE À DEUX

If a folie à deux pattern occurs in an organization, what can be done to cope with it? How can managers prevent getting stuck in this peculiar circular process? How can they recognize the symptoms?

Before outlining the steps managers can take, I want to stress that some aspects of what might look like folie à deux are not always organizationally undesirable. As I indicated earlier, in the initial phases interpersonal processes that could lead to folie à deux may be a source of strength contributing to team building, commitment to goals and strategies, or even to the establishment of effective environmental scanning mechanisms. Unfortunately, in the long run, interpersonal relationships that in extreme form typify folie à deux may become a danger to the organization's operations, and even to its survival.

The first steps in the containment of folie à deux are recognizing those individual and organizational symptoms:

Observe your managers. Managers likely to initiate this type of behavior usually show specific personality characteristics. For example, they may appear to possess considerable personal charm and seductiveness, qualities that may have been originally responsible for their attractiveness. A closer look, however, will reveal that this behavior is often a cover-up for attitudes of conceit, arrogance, demonstrative self-sufficiency and self-righteousness. Individuals prone to folie à deux find it extremely difficult to alter their concepts and ideas; their actions often contain a rigid quality.

Because of his need to dominate and control other people, this type of executive usually stands out. He will deeply resent any form of authority by others. He seems to be continually on his guard, prepared to fight suspected, often imagined, dangers. Hyperalertness, hypersensitivity, and suspiciousness of others tend to become ways of life. He is frequently preoccupied with people's hidden motives and searches for confirmation of his suspicions. He evinces a great concern about details, amplifying and elaborating on them. Not surprisingly, a constant state of interpersonal tension in the organization will be one of the effects of such behavior.

Such an executive will easily feel slighted, wronged, or ignored. Lack of trust and confidence in others can make him extremely self-conscious, seclusive, reserved, and moody. Frequently, there is querulousness, insensitivity, and a lack of consideration of others, and he will be deficient in a sense of playfulness and humor. Dramatic mood swings can be observed: If an attitude of friendliness and companionship temporarily prevails, such behavior will be quickly shattered by the slightest provocation, after which the full force of hate, mistrust, and rage may break loose.

When behavior of a folie à deux nature starts to spread, the influenced persons may show similar behavior patterns, although usually not of such an intensive nature. A key problem of all the participants in this form of mental contagion remains the existence of highly ungratified dependency needs, and it is exactly those needs that the instigators of this process fulfill. By being directive, self-assured, and willing to take complete control, these executives attract those followers who need to be treated this way.

Look at their organizations. The danger signals of folie à deux can also be detected by looking at possible peculiarities of the organization's culture and its ways of operation. One symptom is unusual selection and promotion procedures that largely reflect a senior executive's idiosyncracies rather than a concern for a candidate's overall managerial capabilities. Strange, selective, and unsystematic decision-making patterns, erratic information systems, and excessive control and extreme secrecy can also be taken as danger signs.

Other indications may be a department's preoccupation with details at the cost of overall company effectiveness, and excessive manifestation of various stress symptoms in the organization, such as a large turnover of executives and a high degree of absenteeism. Further signs are frequent changes in organizational goals, the existence of grandiose, unrealistic plans, and insistence upon supposed conspiracies, or the actual creation of the latter.

Whatever the exact nature of the disturbing behavior pattern or process one notices, one should keep folie à deux processes in mind as a possible cause. Once symptoms are recognized, managers need to take corrective action, as well as to design procedures that will counteract folie à deux:

Establish a trusting relationship. By the time folie à deux is in full swing the manager involved is beyond helping himself. A

disposition toward delusional thinking can be difficult to overcome. Appeals to the manager's logic and reality do not help; on
the contrary they might evoke uncompromising, hostile, and aggressive reactions. Rather, in these instances, one has to establish
some degree of trust and closeness with the affected manager to
make him willing to entertain the possibility that his assumptions
of the organizational environment are invalid.

This change in attitudes is not going to be arrived at easily,
but without such a change it will not be possible for an affected
manager to make a realistic self-appraisal of inner strengths and
weaknesses. Substituting reality for fantasies is likely to be a slow
and difficult process involving reintegration and adjustment of
many deeply ingrained behavior patterns. Because of the intensity
of the delusions, in many instances these persons may need professional guidance.

The outlook for the affected followers is more positive and
usually less dramatic. Frequently, mere separation from the affected senior executive will be sufficient to break the magic spell.
Some form of disorientation may occur at the beginning, but
proper guidance by other non-affected executives will soon help
to bring the managers back into more normal, reality-oriented
behavior patterns.

Monitor your own susceptibilities. One way to make the occurrence of this behavior less likely is to be aware of your own
susceptibility to it. Most people are to some extent vulnerable.
We like to be taken care of at times and do not seriously object
when others make decisions for us and guide our behavior. Moreover, an activity such as scapegoating has its attractive side, since,
blaming others for things you may be afraid of, but tempted to
do yourself, creates not only a sense of moral righteousness but
also a sense of satisfaction about your own behavior. Furthermore,
as long as the interpersonal interactions retain a firm base in
reality, these behavior patterns are not disturbing or dangerous.
Unfortunately, the slide into irrational action is easy.

To prevent yourself from entering into a folie à deux pattern
you should periodically take a critical appraisal of your own values,

actions, and interpersonal relationships. A certain amount of courage is needed for such confrontations with yourself, and because it is hard to recognize your own "blind spots" and possible irrational behavior patterns, you might consider getting help in this appraisal process from outside the organization.

The ability for self-examination enhances a person's identity, fosters adaptation to change, and limits susceptibility to controlling influences. These qualities, which form the basis for mature working relationships and mutual, reality-oriented problem-solving, provide a deterrent to episodes of folie à deux and make possible a healthy organizational climate. Thus, executives who are willing to test and reevaluate reality will be the ones who in the end will possess real freedom of choice and will be able to act from a sense of inner security.

Solicit the help of interested parties. Awareness of the occurrence of folie à deux is of limited help when the instigator is a powerful senior executive who happens to be a major shareholder. Occasionally, in such instances, the support of a countervailing power such as the government or a union may be necessary to guide the organization away from possible self-destructive adventures. Other possible interested parties who could blow the whistle are customers, suppliers, and bankers.

The situation becomes somewhat less problematic when the chief executive officer is not a major shareholder, for then the board of directors and the shareholders can play a more active monitoring role. One of their responsibilities will be to watch for possible danger signs. Naturally, the possibility always exists that board members will be drawn into the delusionary activities of a senior executive, but such an event is less likely to happen with a board of outside directors.

In any case, because boards traditionally follow the directives of the Chief Executive Officer, the possibility of folie à deux indicates how important the selection of board members is. Important criteria in this selection process will be an independent mind, a sturdy sense of identity, diversity of background among members, and a firm orientation to reality which can neutralize a folie à deux process.

Reorient the work climate and structure. Organizational solutions to folie à deux become more feasible when the instigator is not a senior executive officer. Then confrontation, transfer, or, in serious cases, dismissal will be sufficient to stop the process. Also important, however, are the systems and procedures in an organization. For instance, reward systems that promote irrational behavior also give it implicit approval. Thus it is crucial to foster a healthy climate where irrational processes cannot take root.

The support of those in the organization who manifest individual responsibility and independence of mind, as well as selecting and promoting managers who behave accordingly, can be a buffer against folie à deux. An organizational culture of mutual collaboration, delegation of duties, open conflict resolution, and respect for individuality will expose a process of mental contagion before it can spread. Such organizational patterns will lessen dependency needs and force conflict into the open, thus counteracting the incidence of vicious circles in interpersonal behavior.

Other aids in helping managers focus on reality are objective information systems and the use of many different sources for information gathering and processing. Interdepartmental committees and formal control systems can fulfill a similar function.

Contemporary pressures toward participative management, or work democratization, are other ways of preventing, or at least limiting, the emergence or proliferation of folie à deux. These structural changes can reduce the power of senior executives and restrict the advantage they may take of their subordinates' dependency needs.

References

Kets de Vries, M. F. R. (1980), *Organizational Paradoxes: Clinical Approaches to Management*. London: Tavistock.
———— Miller, Danny (in press) *The Invisible Hand: Hidden Forces in Organizations*.

Kubie discusses the need for studies on the unrecognized neurotic forces which affect both the choice of and the pursuit of a career in scientific research, pointing out that the subtle interplay of reason and emotion and of conscious and unconscious forces are as important in the lives and activities of scientists as in anyone else's. Scientific research, for instance, makes demands upon the young investigator which may exploit his neurotic vulnerability. The author examines a number of other situations where neurotic forces distort the creative drive.

9

Some Unsolved Problems of the Scientific Career

L A W R E N C E   S.   K U B I E

It is my thesis that the life of a young scientist challenges our educational system from top to bottom with a series of unsolved problems which await investigation. Among these are certain subtle problems, arising out of unrecognized neurotic forces, which are basically important both in the choice and in the pursuit of scientific research as a career. It will not be the purpose of this paper to argue that every young scientist should be psychoanalyzed; and the reader is asked to keep this disclaimer in mind. Nevertheless in any multidisciplinary investigation of these complex interrelated problems, I believe that the psychoanalytic study of a random sampling of scientists, both young and old, would be one of the essential instruments.

In this connection it will be argued that Science in the abstract

This chapter originally appeared in *American Scientist*, 41:596-613, 1953.

and Scientists as human beings pay a high price for the fact that
during the preparation of young people for a life of scientific
research their emotional problems are generally overlooked. This
discussion will not attempt to outline a full remedy for this neglect,
for it would be premature to make such an attempt before more
is known about the problem. Here again, however, in exploring
possible remedies, a psychoanalytic study of an adequate sample
of young scientists would provide information which would help
towards an ultimate solution. I hope that this paper will also
contribute to a more general recognition of the fact that many
young scientists require special help in their struggles for emotional maturation.

My own clinical experiences with this group suggest that the
emotional problems which arise early in the careers of young
scientists are more taxing than are those which occur in other
careers. Yet without instruments with which to measure and compare these imponderables, this cannot be proved. Nor can it be
claimed that the problems to be detailed below are peculiar either
to science in general or to any special field of science. In fact,
since the stresses which arise in different careers have never been
systematically compared, it cannot even be determined whether
or to what extent emotional problems vary from one career to
another, either in degree or kind. Therefore, the reader may well
ask why this paper is published before such investigations have
been carried out. Its justification lies in the fact that such studies
will themselves require a large investment of time, money, and
trained personnel, none of which will be made available until
responsible educators become convinced that such studies are
essential enough to justify careful planning, a coordinated multidisciplinary approach, and generous financial support. Before
such studies are made, all that we can do is to indicate fragmentary
observations, which suggest that it would be enlightening to make
socioeconomic studies of the lives of young and old scientists, plus
psychoanalytic studies of a statistically adequate random sample
of them.

These investigations would throw light on such problems as:

(1) the special stresses, both economic and psychological, which occur in the life of the young scientist; (2) the great variety of conscious and unconscious forces whose interplay determines a young man's choice of scientific research as a career; (3) the interplay of conscious and unconscious forces in his subsequent emotional and scientific maturation; (4) how the special stresses which develop later in life react upon the earlier emotional forces which originally turned him towards science; (5) how unconscious stresses influence the young investigator's general approach to scientific research and scientific controversy; (6) how the unconscious symbolic significance of particular scientific problems and theories can distort the logic and the judgment even of men of exceptional ability. This paper will attempt only to illustrate the wide variety of problems which are relevant to these general headings.

As a personal note I should add that my observations, both on myself and on colleagues in various fields of science, have been made at random over a period of nearly thirty years. They began in the Twenties, when I was working in one of the laboratories of the Rockefeller Institute. It soon became known that I had had some previous training in psychiatry. Presently I found that if I were to have any time for my own work I had literally to lock my door for a few hours each day. Otherwise, almost every afternoon, young colleagues and sometimes older ones would drift in to talk, not about scientific issues but about their personal problems. At that time my psychiatric training and experience were limited, and I knew nothing at all about psychoanalysis. Yet these random and unsolicited revelations made it clear not only that, as one would expect, a scientist's ability to endure the prolonged frustration and uncertainties of scientific research depend on neurotic components in his personality (both masked and overt), but also that there are significant relationships between masked neurotic components in the personality of an apparently normal scientist, and such things as (1) the field of work he chooses; (2) the problems within that field which he chooses to investigate; (3) the clarity with which he habitually uses his native capacity for logical thinking; (4) the ways in which he attacks scientific problems; (5) the scientific causes which he espouses; (6) the controversies in which he becomes entangled and how he fights; and (7) the joy or sorrow which is derived from the work itself, and also from his ultimate success or failure. Thus over the intervening years I have seen men of imagination and erudition whose scientific lives were none-theless baffled and unproductive, and also men with lesser gifts who seemed to function freely, creatively, and productively; sci-entists who were happy in spite of failure, and others who became depressed in spite of acknowledged and recognized success. Al-though such facts were new to me twenty-five years ago, they had long been an accepted part of human wisdom. This makes it strange that their deeper sources in human nature and their spe-cial importance to scientific workers have never been systemat-ically explored. I cannot attempt such an exploration here, but it may be possible to make articulate the challenge to all scientists which lurks in these ancient and unexplored caverns of the human spirit.

THE EMOTIONAL EQUIPMENT WHICH THE YOUNG SCIENTIST BRINGS TO HIS CAREER

The young scientist often reaches maturity after a lopsided early development. In this development he resembles many other intellectuals. A typical history is that an intellectually gifted child develops neurotic tendencies which hamper his early aggressive and psychosexual development. If at this point he is intellectually stimulated by one or another of the emotionally significant adults of his life, he is likely to turn away from athletics and the social life which he finds difficult to more bookish activities, thus post-poning indefinitely the facing of earthier challenges. If success rewards his consolatory scholarly efforts during adolescence, he may in later years tend to cultivate intellectual activity exclusively. In this way absorption in the intellectual life will frequently be paralleled by an increasing withdrawal from athletic and social and psychosexual activities. As a result, by the time he reaches adulthood his only triumphs and gratifications will have been won in the intellectual field, his range of skills will have become restricted, and the life of the mind will be almost the only outlet available. Because of the extra drain the laboratory makes on the student's time, the young man who sets out to become a scientist spends adolescence putting every emotional egg in the intellectual basket to a greater extent than is true for most other young intellectuals. By such steps as these, the sense of security and the self-esteem of the young intellectual come to stand on one leg; so that when research is begun he invests in it a lifetime of pent-up cravings. After such a development, it is inevitable that scientific research will be supercharged with many irrelevant and unfulfilled emotional needs; so that the lifework of the young scientist tends to express both the conscious levels of his intellectual aspirations, and his unfulfilled instinctual needs and unconscious conflicts.

Even the most brilliant scientific successes cannot solve unconscious personal problems, nor gratify unrecognized instinctual pressures. Whenever anyone works under the whiplash of unsolved unconscious conflicts, whether he is painting a picture, writing a play, pursuing a scientific discovery, or making a million dollars, the individual is prone to work with desperation. If there is failure, he blames his unhappiness on his failure. But, to his amazement and dismay, he discovers that depression may follow success no less than failure. Basically this is because success also leaves his deeper problems unsolved. If we always bear in mind that the pursuit of unconscious and often unattainable needs plays a determining role in the intellectual career, the familiar phenomena of depression attending success would not perplex us. We should wonder rather at the shortsightedness of a process of scientific education in which self-knowledge is the forgotten man, and in which emotional maturation is left to chance.

THE CHOICE OF A CAREER

The aspects of this vexing problem which are peculiar to a career in science require certain general considerations. I suppose

it is not inaccurate to say that of the many unsolved problems of
human life, two which are of major importance are how to enable
successive generations to learn from the mistakes of their predecessors without repeating them, and how to make it possible
for young people to anticipate the future realistically. Not literature nor the arts nor formal education has solved these two
problems, which are interdependent in every aspect of life. Both
are relevant to the choice of a career. When a youth decides to
become a doctor, a lawyer, a businessman, or an artist, the decision is not made on the basis of a realistic foreknowledge of what
one of these careers would be like as compared to another, nor
out of a deep introspective knowledge of himself and of how he
would fit into the lifework he has chosen. Even if his own father
is a lawyer or a doctor, he will have had an opportunity to observe
only the outer aspects of that life, the dramatization of its activities;
he cannot have felt its joys and sorrows directly. What he will
have experienced vicariously through identification with his parent will depend less upon what that life was really like than upon
how it affected him; and upon the subtle balance of conscious and
unconscious, hostile and loving components in his identification
with the parental figure. Nor do adults know how to communicate
the truth about their own adult lives to their children. Consequently the adolescent's and even the college student's anticipation of the quality of life in any future career is dominated by
fantasies. To a remarkable degree this is true even of more familiar
and humdrum careers. The quality of adult living belongs to the
remote and mysterious future; it is something the flavor of which
the child cannot anticipate. Until this obstacle to communication
between the generations is overcome, successive generations will
continue in the future, as in the past, to make their choice in the
darkness of fantasy and confusion. The child of a wealthy broker
who was "on the Street" took these words literally, as children
do, and looked for his father in every pushcart peddler who
passed. Although the visual misconception of the child was corrected as he matured, an emotional hangover remained which
had an important influence in determining the choice of his life-

work. Usually the less familiar the career a young man chooses, the greater will be the importance of fantasies, both conscious and unconscious, among the forces which determine the initial choice of a career, and also his subsequent adjustment to, and his happiness and effectiveness in the one selected.

One natural conclusion to be drawn from these considerations would seem to constitute an argument for the wider use of aptitude testing in the choice of careers. Actual experience, however, and a hardheaded and realistic skepticism make one cautious about expecting too much help from these devices. The most extensive trials of the value of aptitude testing were the so-called "Stanines," which the USAAF developed during the war for the screening of air cadets and their allocation to training as pilots, bombardiers, and navigators. In terms of its relevance to this problem, I would summarize the results of this experience as follows:

(1) The tests of aptitudes were remarkably accurate as far as they went.

(2) It was possible to sort out those with the automatic speed and motor skills and/or the mathematical precision needed for various tasks.

(3) Men were placed accurately on a point scale as to their relevant psychometric and neuromuscular capacities.

(4) In this way the tests selected accurately a small group at one extreme, most of whom would succeed in training, and another small group at the opposite pole, most of whom would fail. (There were exceptions to the results even at both extremes.)

(5) As was to be expected, however, the vast majority of the men tested fell into the central zone of the normal curve of distribution, while only a relatively small percentage of those tested was placed at the two extremes.

(6) With rare exceptions, the individuals who fell into the extremes knew their own aptitudes and ineptitudes before going through any tests. From their experiences at play, in sports, in school, and on various jobs, they knew already that they were specially adept or specially maladroit with respect to certain types of activity. Indeed, the representatives of the two extreme ends

of the scale were usually able to describe their strong and weak points almost as precisely as these could be measured.

(7) Consequently the tests are of greatest use when jobs are scarce in times of peace, or else in times of war when an individual may want desperately to be accepted by a special branch of the service for some particular position, and may therefore exaggerate his native skill or hide his native ineptitude. But at other times when there is no special incentive to deception (beyond the usual need for self-deception), the men at the end zones need no tests.

(8) The next important lesson of the entire experiment with the "Stanines" was that for the majority, who fall in the great middle zone of the normal curve of distribution, although their minor variations in aptitudes can be measured with considerable precision by various "human engineering" devices, these variations do not determine either success or failure, happiness or unhappiness in a career. By exclusion, therefore, we may conclude from the results of the "Stanines," that for most of us (that is, for the Average Man) a subtle balance of conscious and unconscious forces determines how effectively we use our native aptitudes, whether intellectual, emotional, sensory, neuromuscular, or any combination of these aptitudes. For most of us it is not the minor quantitative differences in the machine itself, but the influence of these conscious and unconscious emotional forces on our use of the human machine which determines our effectiveness. For me this was the ultimate lesson from the experience of the Air Force with the "Stanines," and I believe, furthermore, that this result is what might be expected in any similar effort to predict success and failure in civilian careers by the use of precise aptitude tests alone.

This is the stumbling block against which the aptitude testers always stub their toes, and until they learn how to evaluate with equal precision the influence of unconscious emotional forces, they will continue to mislead young people into thinking that scores on aptitude scales will determine successes and failures, happiness and unhappiness in their lifework.[1]

Although these unconscious, irrational, and symbolic forces are subtle and difficult to describe, they determine how most of us use our equipment, and the fate of our lives under conditions of success as well as failure. We shall attempt to discuss a few of these forces in relation to scientific problems and also to the life of science. To youngsters, the dream of a life of scientific research is charged with complicated and usually unnoticed symbolic con-notations, which alter steadily during growth from youth to man-hood. Therefore, what science "means" consciously to any mature scientist has as many unconscious layers as the stages of his interest in science. No valid generalizations can be made about this con-dition until many scientists have been studied analytically and the data collated.

Some of those who show scientific interest and capacity in their youth subsequently lose these qualities completely, whereas others pursue them throughout life. In only a few instances it has been possible to study the evolving symbolic connotations of a scientist's interest in scientific matters. In these few cases the "scientific" interests of early childhood frequently turn out to have been in part a window-dressing for quite different concerns. I cannot overemphasize the importance of keeping the fact in mind that human behavior is like a centipede, standing on many legs. Nothing that we do has a single determinant, whether conscious, preconscious, or unconscious. In singling out certain neglected unconscious symbolic determinants it may often sound as though I were overlooking all of the others. This is only because I want to emphasize the importance of the unconscious forces, precisely because they have been neglected so consistently, and because,

---

[1]As a sharp contrast to the engineering approach of the aptitude testers, I would cite the studies which Anne Roe (1951a, 1951b, 1951c, 1951d, 1952, 1953) has been making since 1946. She has used various projective techniques, certain aptitude and psychometric devices, personal documents, life histories, and personal interviews to study the person-alities of various kinds of scientists, scholars, and artists. Her results are necessarily still fragmentary but already they offer many suggestive leads, and her bibliographies are essential guides to the scanty literature in this field. The results also indicate how enormous is the amount of work which remains to be done.

as a direct consequence of this neglect, they tend to be destructive.

One of these unconscious forces is the child's fearful and guilt-laden curiosity about the human body, both its tabooed external aspects and its mysterious inner workings. A familiar example of this force may be noted in the physician whose interest in medicine has some of its roots in the child's buried envy of the doctor who could gratify the forbidden bodily curiosities and enter the sickroom from which the child was excluded. How universal this drive would be, and how it would vary with the age of the child and the quality of his relationships to others cannot be decided by guessing. Nor can I document this forcefully without presenting a mass of clinical data for which there is neither time nor space. Somewhat scattered data, gathered during the occasional opportunities to make analytical studies of various kinds of scientists, have shown that even widely varying forms of scientific interest can serve as an acceptable cover for some of the forbidden concerns of childhood. Furthermore, this tendency to utilize various facets of the outer world as a symbolic projection of inner conflicts does not cease when the child becomes adult, but may continue throughout life. This fact is of more than academic interest, since the scientific activities of the adult can be distorted by the same unconscious childhood conflicts out of which his original interest in science may have arisen. Indeed, this must result whenever adult activities continue to represent earlier conflicts, and projections of unconscious personal conflicts can often be recognized even through their adult scientific disguises in the reasoning and experiments of outstanding scientists.

As an example of the role of unconscious residues of childhood's battles, I would cite the gynecologist whose ancient and infantile curiosities were not to be satisfied by the justified activities of his profession, and who was plagued by an insatiable compulsion to visit burlesque shows. One could hardly ask for a better experimental demonstration of the fact that unconscious needs cannot be gratified by conscious fulfillment. A comparable example is found in the X-ray man whose choice of career was determined predominantly by his unconscious curiosity about the internal structure of his mother's body. In all innocence both men dedicated their lives to the service of childhood cravings which were buried in guilt and fear. It should be our goal to learn how to guide gifted young men so that they will not build their entire lives on such psychological quicksands.

Neurotic Distortions of Scientific Research: General Considerations

The first step in any program of scientific research is to observe nature phenomena while taking care not to alter these phenomena by the very process of observing them. In spite of the most meticulous care, however, the ever-present unconscious forces of the observer color in some degree the glasses through which he makes even simple observations. Therefore it is out of such tinted observations that he develops his scientific theories. Initially, these are hypotheses about possible relationships between the observed data. Hypotheses are always more vulnerable to distortion by unconscious processes than are the primary observations themselves. Therefore the next step for the research worker is to test his theories, together with their inevitable distortions, in experiments which either isolate and quantify the original data, or that test the consequences of the derived theories. Without our realizing it, the process of investigation tends in this way to balance the distortions introduced by unconscious bias. Once he has set up his initial experiments, however, the scientist again becomes an observer. Now, however, he no longer observes facts in nature, but rather in a milieu which he has created artificially by means of his experiment.

Each successive step in these scientific processes calls forth a greater investment of conscious and unconscious feeling; yet if the experimenter is to be objective about the outcome of his experiments he must somehow manage to climb out of his own psychic skin so as to be able to criticize his own handiwork. This is as essential to objective scientific work as it is to artistic creativeness, but it is never easy, because it is impossible for an investigator to prevent the intrusion of his unconscious biases into such sequences of experiment and observation.

Furthermore, even these steps constitute merely the foundation for another round of observation, theory, and experiment. From experimentally derived observations come a second order of theories, in which unconscious biases have even greater weight; and these theories in turn must be subjected to new experimental tests which require still further sequences of observation and of theory. Thus the structure of science adds layer on layer, each burdened by more subtle and complex unconscious emotional investments, demanding of the scientist an ever greater clarity about the role of his own unconscious processes in his conscious theories and experiments, and each requiring an ever more rigorous correction for the influence of unconscious preconceptions.

For none of this self-critique in depth does our educational process prepare us. Yet much of it was implicit in Claude Bernard's (1927) *An Introduction to the Study of Experimental Medicine* when he wrote:

> The metaphysician, the scholastic, and the experimenter all work with an *a priori* idea. The difference is that the scholastic imposes his idea as an absolute truth which he has found, and from which he then deduces consequences, by logic alone. The more modest experimenter, on the other hand, states an idea as a question, as an interpretative and more or less probable anticipation of nature, from which he logically deduces consequences which, moment by moment, he confronts with reality by means of experiment [pp. 27-28].

Again in another connection Claude Bernard pointed out that the scientist and the philosopher are subject to the same internal human laws, prey to the same emotions, prejudices, and biases, and that these operate equally in the philosopher and the scientist. The difference is that for the scientist the fact that a theory seems true to him, that it feels true, or even that it is logically or mathematically possible does not make it true. For the scientist, the theory is not true until he has taken it to the laboratory, "leaving his theories in the cloakroom," and subjected it to the ultimate test of the experimental method.

Other observers of the world of science have referred to this fact. Every scientist can read with profit and delight Charles Richet's (1927) spirited and witty *Natural History of a Savant*, and Gregg's (1941) sage volume of lectures on *The Furtherance of Medical Research*, both of which touch on these questions. More recently R. C. Tolman (1943) referred challengingly to the "criteria for selecting diligent and competent scientists, the effects of personal bias on results, the relation between subjective origins and objective outcomes of scientific experiments" (p. 4).

This is a portrait of the ideal scientist, ideally in action. It implies that the subtle interplay of reason and emotion, and of conscious and unconscious forces, are as important in the lives and activities of scientists as of anyone else. If this is true, then nothing could be more important to science than that scientists should know themselves in the neo-Socratic or Freudian sense, that is, in terms of the interplay between their own conscious and unconscious processes. Yet, as we have already stated (Kubie, 1953) in the education of the scientist, as of everyone else, self-knowledge in depth is the forgotten man of our entire educational system (Lombard, 1950).

Since the father of modern physiology, a great immunologist, a senior statesman among medical educators, and a great atomic physicist all have recognized the confusing influence of subtle psychological processes in scientific work, then surely it is time for the problem to be made the central focus of a major investigation, in which psychoanalytic techniques will be one of the essential tools.

THE DISTORTION OF THE CREATIVE DRIVE BY NEUROTIC FORCES

It is rarely recognized that research makes demands upon the young investigator which may exploit his neurotic vulnerabilities. For instance, a drive for "originality" may cloak a difficulty in mastering existing facts and techniques, or it may serve to disguise an unconscious hostility to all existing authority. How often is this drive for originality naively mistaken by teacher and student for creative scientific imagination? How often, therefore, is the young investigator encouraged to penetrate into new territory before he has mastered the terrain from which the expedition must start? It is no answer to these questions to say that the same misinterpretations occur among young artists, writers, and musicians. Fallacious values and goals are destructive whenever they occur, and in many different fields of work. Nor does it lessen the significance of any of the examples which follow to dismiss them as psychopathological. Such pathology is only an exaggeration of what occurs in more subtle and disguised forms in everyone. The wider and more easily recognized deviations of pathology illuminate the "normal" for us, and sensitize us to slighter anomalies which we otherwise would overlook.

For instance, unresolved neurotic anxieties may impel one overanxious young investigator to choose a problem that will take a lifetime or, alternatively, may drive another into easy, get-rich-quick tasks, which yield a yearly paper, a yearly acclaim, the yearly promotion. The former tendency to postpone the day of reckoning indefinitely occurs in the young scientist who deals with his anxieties by pretending that they do not exist. The latter is found in the man who finds it impossible to endure suspense and uncertainty for more than a few months. Neurotic anxiety can take either form; and young scientists frequently walk a tightrope between these two alternatives, that is, between the annual piecework type of productivity and the long-drawn-out tasks which postpone indefinitely any ultimate testing of theories against experimental data and observations of nature.

Then there is the battle with phobic indecision over which tasks to undertake, or how to undertake it: an indecision which may arise not out of an inadequate mastery of specific facts and techniques, but from a general neurotic tendency to obsessional doubting. I have seen this symptom work identical destruction in the careers of a young playwright who could not decide which of two equally good plots to use, and of a young chemist who could not decide which of two equally promising leads to follow.

There was also the scientist who had proved his case, but who was so driven by his anxieties that he had to bolster an already proved theorem by falsifying some quite unnecessary additional statistical data. This was a compulsive act, comparable to a kleptomania by a wealthy man, or to the action of a successful and famous writer who suffered from a compulsion to insert a few words from someone else into everything he wrote.

Again there is the scientist who is always pursuing a new scientific father. This occurs more frequently than is realized. One outstandingly able young scientist ran through five careers, abandoning each one after a brilliant start just as he reached the point of launching his own independent work. When he could no longer postpone accepting a professorship, he broke down and disappeared from the world of science.

But the most ubiquitous tragedy of all is the anxiety-driven scientist who lives on a treadmill—the man who has tasted what it means to gain temporary easement from his anxieties by doing a fine piece of scientific work, but who thereafter is driven not by a quest for further truth but by an insatiable need to repeat the same achievement in an effort to assuage anxieties whose origins were unconscious. This investigator uses scientific research precisely as the man with a handwashing compulsion uses soap and water, or as an addict uses drugs.

I cannot leave this phase of the problem without referring to one highly technical and complex issue. In psychiatry we recognize certain rough parallelisms between types of illness and types of personality. These can have comparable influence in research. During the exploratory phase, while crude data are being gathered, an investigator ought to be free from rigidity. He should be ready to abandon preconceived objectives and anticipated goals, so that any hints that come from unexpected findings can be pursued. He must be psychologically free to follow uncharted courses. Therefore, premature systematization of the data must be avoided. This requires that type of free and imaginative flexibility which is sometimes attributed to the so-called "hysterical" personality. Later, a more rigid process is required, one which has some of the features of the obsessional neurosis, or even some of the tendency of a paranoid patient to organize his delusions into logical systems. Scientific research thus seems to require that, as the work progresses, the investigator should be free to operate now with one type of personality and now with another. It would be profitable to compare analytically the personalities of those scientists who can change in this way and of those who cannot, especially in relation to their scientific productivity. This would seem to be a problem of basic importance for the optimal use of scientific personnel.

Dr. Anne Roe has given me permission to quote a letter of September 13, 1952, in which she summarizes some of her unique studies in this field:

> Any brief summary of these data is necessarily inadequate, and the generalizations require qualifications; but certain differences among these groups of scientists show up, both on the test material and in the life patterns. These are most striking in interpersonal relations, in the handling of anxiety and aggression, in the patterns on intelligence tests, and in the use of imagery.
>
> The typical physicist and biologist grew up with a minimum of group social activity, entered into heterosexual activities rather late and is now not much interested in any social activities. The psychologists and the anthropologists for the most part were early conscious of their own and the family's social status, began dating early and enthusiastically, and are still enormously involved with other persons, one way and another. Both physicists and biologists show an unusual independence of parental ties, without guilt; and present attitudes toward the father are characteristically respectful, but lacking in closeness. Attitudes towards the mother are variable. Many of the psychologists and anthropologists, on the other hand, went through periods of great family dissension, and are still angry with or disparaging of their parents. I am sure it is significant also that in the families of these groups, the mother was most often the dominant character. This was rare in the other groups.
>
> The biologists, as a group, rely strongly and effectively on

rational control. This appears in their lives, in their general unaggressiveness, and in their unproductiveness and intense concern with form on the Rorschach. The physicists have a good deal of free anxiety, shown in their behavior and on the Rorschach, particularly in the large amounts of K and k. This is better controlled among the theoretical than among the experimental physicists. The difference between biologists and physicists is like the difference between compulsive obsessives and anxiety hysterics (I do not imply that all biologists are obsessives and all physicists hysterics). I am quite sure that there are relationships, of a nature still obscure to me, between the preoccupation with space, the type of symbolization that physics uses (which has spatial concomitants) and the choice of physics as a profession; but I suspect that insofar as space symbolizes distance from other persons (as Schilder says) it is more comforting than anxiety-arousing for these men, and I do not believe that their disinterest in persons is always compensatory. The psychologists and anthropologists are enormously productive on the Rorschach, quite unconcerned with rational controls for the most part, and intensely preoccupied with persons. Their handling of anxiety is quite varied; but as a group they are much the most freely aggressive, and this often has strong oral elements.

The level of intelligence of my group is extremely high, but there are interesting differences in patterning: the theoretical physicists surpass the others on both verbal and spatial tests; experimental physicists tend to be low on verbal and high on spatial; anthropologists are high on verbal and low on non-verbal; psychologists are high on both; biologists show all combinations, but generally the geneticists and biochemists are relatively higher on non-verbal and the others reverse this.

Differences in use of imagery during thinking are also fairly sharp. It is not easy to get a good report on this, and I am not happy about my data; yet they are remarkably consistent. In their conscious thinking, biologists are chiefly visualizers; among physicists the experimentalists rely most often on visual imagery, and the theorists on symbolization (usually mathematical and closely allied to verbal symbolization) or imageless thought. Psychologists and anthropologists rely predominantly on auditory verbal thinking. It occurred to me that it was possible that whatever process was most relied upon during the day would be the one to show up in hypnagogic revery. For those who are strongly visualizers or verbalizers, hypnagogic imagery is usually but not always in the same mode; for those whose dominant mode of conscious thought is symbolic or imageless it may be visual or auditory or symbolic, but usually with other twists to it. It would be interesting to find out if there are similar differences in the dream process.

I should add that the one thing which characterizes every one of my groups of eminent scientists is the high degree of ego-involvement in the vocation, both now and earlier. That this is the major factor in their vocational success seems highly probable; but without a comparison group of less successful scientists I can't be certain about this. The ways in which this came about and the situations that made it possible are, of course, extremely varied. In some instances, I can demonstrate quite direct relations between professional activities and specific emotional problems. In others I cannot; and I am not convinced that a genuinely neurotic problem is always involved. But I am convinced that it is the matter of personal involvement that is significant for problems of vocational choice and success.

I have included this long excerpt in spite of the fact that the researches of Dr. Roe in this area are still incomplete and inconclusive—as she herself points out—because even her tentative conclusions are unique, exciting and suggestive, and also because her work gives us an indication of how great an investment of time, effort, personnel, and money an adequate study of this problem would entail (Roe, 1953).

THE INFLUENCE OF UNCONSCIOUS SYMBOLIC PROCESSES ON THE
PRODUCTION OF LOGICAL THOUGHT AND LOGICAL ERROR IN
SCIENTIFIC RESEARCH

It is obvious that conscious emotions which are close to the surface can influence a man's scientific work, especially perhaps those anxious ambitions and pettier jealousies which are bred by certain special economic and professional insecurities which may induce a young scientist to push for quick and showy results. Of far greater importance, however, is the subtler influence of streams of unconscious feelings which may be represented symbolically yet compulsively in the scientific activity of an individual, just as they are represented in neurotic symptoms and in dreams, or in all artistic and literary creativity. At this point, therefore, I must explain what the concept of symbolic representation means in this connection.

The symbols by which we think are multivalent tools, always representing many things simultaneously, some conscious, some preconscious, and some unconscious. In logical thinking, the conscious and preconscious symbolic processes represent external reality without disguises; what we call "logic," therefore, is in essence a coding of relationships which are inherent among such internal and external data as are accessible to our direct perceptual processes. One might almost say that although logic resides in the mind, its roots are in the relations among external facts themselves. It is a neglected consequence of this principle that it is literally impossible to be "illogical" about accessible data, except when one has an unconscious axe to grind. Failures in logic are a measure of man's capacity to deceive himself with unconscious premeditation, by misperceiving observational data, and by misusing conceptual data for his own unconscious purposes. Many years ago William Alanson White warned that when anyone says that two and two are five, he does so because he has to; and that the way to meet this problem is not to teach him to say by rote that two and two are four, but to discover with him why he needs to believe otherwise.

It is an inevitable consequence of these facts that in spite of any degree of intellectual brilliance, individuals whose psychological development has been distorted by unsolved unconscious conflicts will have significant limitations in their capacity to build concepts out of the accessible data of external reality. This, indeed, is the greatest psychological hazard of the young intellectual—the fact that unconscious emotional forces persist in him in the form of unconscious needs and unconscious conflicts over these needs. In some, these forces will be expressed in obvious neurotic symptoms. In others, they cause subtle distortions of patterns of living. Sometimes they are expressed in distortions of artistic or intellectual (in this instance, scientific) activities. Naturally there are varied combinations of these three alternatives; but it is an impressive paradox that among individuals in whom unconscious problems are expressed in obvious neurotic symptoms, their scientific work frequently escapes the distortions which occur in other scientists whose unconscious processes have no outlet through overt neurotic symptoms. This is not always the case; but it is frequently true that the masked influence of unconscious psychological forces can warp the thinking of a brilliant investigator even when he shows no overt neurotic quirks.

Let me give a few brief examples of the operation of unconscious conflicts on scientific work and scientific careers.

I have known scientists of great ability whose work nevertheless always tended to be vague and ambiguous. Some of these men unconsciously designed their laborious experiments so as to prove nothing. For unconscious reasons they could not allow themselves to find out the answers to their own scientific questions. Such an unconscious conflict over seeing and/or knowing with a preponderant unconscious need *not* to see and *not* to know, arises in early years. In adult life it accounts for some tragic failures among scientists of brilliant capabilities. This conflict can also produce nihilistic critics who, however brilliant, may also be essentially destructive. For them it is as though seeing and knowing were transgressions which were endlessly tempting but always forbidden in the end. It is conceivable that adequate psychoanalytic therapy early in their training might have saved at least some of these gifted yet wasted and unhappy lives.

Experiments under hypnosis have demonstrated that unconscious processes can take over the intellectual equipment of a scientist and misuse that equipment for their own unrecognized purposes. Under post-hypnotic suggestion, for instance, highly skilled and experienced mathematicians have been led to attempt to prove theorems which they knew to be absurd or to solve mathematical problems which were known to be insoluble. This is the same type of process by which unconscious conflicts and purposes can lead a neurosurgeon to misapply his technical skills, or by which the subtle reasoning of a chemist or physicist, or the ingenuity of a clinical psychologist in devising or interpreting psychological tests, can be misapplied. Actually this is no more mysterious than is the way in which unconscious processes regularly exploit the need for or the conventional impulse towards cleanliness. One will find in the literature of psychoanalysis many studies of the effects of unconscious processes in disturbances of various normal activities such as eating, washing, dressing, painting, writing, sports, play, sleep, sex, and excretion; but to my knowledge there are no similar studies of the power of unconscious processes to disturb the equally symbolic methods of scientific research. Yet the surreptitious influence of these forces on scientific activities may determine the success or failure of an entire life (Jones, 1931).

That ancient tragedy of human nature, the success which brings no joy with it, occurs at least as frequently in the life of the scientific investigator as in art and business. A life of fruitful scientific exploration may end in a feeling of total defeat, precisely because in spite of scientific success the unconscious goals of the search have eluded the searcher. Sometimes at the end of a career this need to reach some still undefined goal has led a successful scientist to turn to a pseudoscientific investigation of the supernatural. More often it leads to depression and a total arrest of all scientific productivity. Sometimes success breeds panic directly, as was observed in the case of a graduate student in physics, a man of outstanding ability, when the head of the department came up behind him in the laboratory one day, and said, "You handed in the best examination I have ever received." Thereupon the student laid down his apparatus and left the laboratory in a panic, which prevented his returning for several weeks.

When they operate below the level of conscious awareness and therefore are not subject to conscious control and direction, the early patterns of familial loves and hates, of submissions and rebellions, may exercise a profound influence on the later work of a scientific investigator, even to the extent of determining his choice of science as a career, his field of work in science, the problems he chooses, the causes he espouses, and the very experiments which he undertakes. While this fact has long been acknowledged, it has never been appreciated in sufficient detail.

There is, for instance, the force of unconscious imitation, to which all of us are liable, imitation even of those very traits against which we may have rebelled most vigorously in childhood. Manifestations of this, both gross and subtle, occur all around us and in every aspect of life. There is the child of the alcoholic who hated the parent's alcoholism yet becomes an alcoholic. There is the child of a parent with a tyrannical temper, firmly resolved never to raise his voice in anger against his own children, yet who hears his father's voice issue from his own mouth as he yells at his three-year-old son in an automatic imitation of the voice and manner which he had always hated in his own father. A famous professor of biochemistry in one of our leading medical schools was the son of a fundamentalist minister against whose narrow ranting he rebelled. Yet the son spent an entire afternoon ranting, as his father was wont to do, but this time it was against the gentle religiosity of a hapless salesman of scientific apparatus who visted his laboratory. This same professor also used every biochemical controversy as a pulpit from which to expound sarcastic diatribes against his colleagues, quite like the paternal sermons which had offended him during his childhood.

Also in rebellion against a fundamentalist background, a famous professor of psychology showed a missionary zeal in defense of a mechanized concept of human behavior, so narrowly partisan, indeed so "fundamentalist," that in essence the concept destroyed the value of his whole theoretical approach, which could otherwise have been of considerable scientific significance. Again, there was an eminent physiologist whose desiccated approach to certain problems bore the destructive imprint of an early conflict over whether or not to join the priesthood.

Such thought-provoking reactions are not rare. Many more examples could be cited, but they would merely serve to illustrate again the fact that the human beings who do research work are the subtle and complex instruments of their unconscious and conscious processes; and that the very content of a scientist's investigations as well as his vulnerability to the emotional stresses of research will reflect in varying manner the influence of those psychological forces which are unconscious residues from the unresolved neurotic problems of his early childhood. This fact indicates that an essential element is left out of the training of Man the Scientist, namely, an opportunity to free himself from bondage to the unconscious residues of his own childhood.

SUMMARY

Research is a strange and challenging occupation for any young man to contemplate. We still know far too little about the unconscious components of the forces which lead a man or woman to go into research, or about the influence of the unconscious elements in determining the success or failure of his efforts. All of these problems, with their general as well as their special human significance, should be explored. How to do this is a matter for special consideration, since it presents many difficulties. Perhaps the first step would be to subject to psychoanalytic exploration and in selected instances to psychoanalytic therapy a random sampling of: (1) promising young men who hope to make scientific research their life work; (2) men who have already devoted many years to research, including (a) men who in spite of high native endowments have been unproductive, (b) others who have been creative but who have ended up nonetheless in frustration and despair, and (c) finally those who have succeeded and who have enjoyed fully the fruits of their achievements.

Just as psychiatry has had to study elations in order to understand depressions, so in such a study it would be important to keep in mind that it is just as important to study successes as failures. In science as in other fields, success or failure cannot be

accounted for by differences in intellectual capacity alone. Consequently, an analytical study of those who succeed and of those
who fail and of the many gradations between success and failure
would be of value not only to science but also to those foundations
and universities that wish to use men wisely to advance the frontiers of human knowledge.

To uncover in this way some of the unconscious factors which
determine the choice of a career, and to explore the subtler forces
which determine whether or not that career will be externally
productive and internally fulfilling, would be a major contribution
to human wisdom. To the best of my knowledge no such study
has ever been made of any occupational or professional group. A
start must be made somewhere, and in view of the paramount
importance of science in today's world, it might be appropriate
to start with scientists. Such an enterprise would merit the support
of scientific foundations. The sums which are spent on research
are so huge that it would seem to be common sense, business
sense, and scientific sense to study the men who expend these
investments.

References

Bernard, C. (1927), *An Introduction to the Study of Experimental Medicine*. New York: Macmillan.
Gregg, A. (1941), *The Furtherance of Medical Research*. New Haven: Yale University Press.
Jones, E. (1931), The Problem of Paul Morphy—A Contribution to the Psychoanalysis of Chess. *Internat. J. Psycho-Anal.*, 12:1-23. (Reprinted in *Essays in Applied Psychoanalysis*, Vol. I. London: Hogarth Press, pp. 165-196.)
Kubie, L. S. (1953), The Problem of Maturity in Psychiatric Research. *J. Med. Ed.*, 28:10.
Lombard, G. F. F. (1950), Self-Awareness and Scientific Method. *Science*, 112:289-293.
Osler, W. (1923), *The Evolution of Modern Medicine*. New Haven: Yale University Press.
Richet, C. (1927), *Natural History of a Savant*. London: J. M. Dent.
Roe, A. (1951a), Psychological Tests of Research Scientists. *J. Consult. Psychol.*, 15:492-495.
——— (1951b), A Study of Imagery in Research Scientists. *J. Personal.*, 19:459-470.
——— (1951c), A Psychological Study of Eminent Biologists. *Psychol. Mongr.*, No. 331, 65, 14.
——— (1951d), Analysis of Group Rorschachs of Psychologists and Anthropologists. *J. Proj. Tech.*, 16:212-224.
——— (1952), Group Rorschachs of University Faculties. *J. Consult. Psychol.*, 16:18-22.
——— (1953), *The Making of a Scientist*. New York: Dodd, Mead.
Tolman, R. C. (1943), Physical Science and Philosophy. *Scientific Monthly*, 57:166-174.

Coining the term "mid-life crisis," Jaques looks at the transformation in the mode of work which takes place at mid-life. He compares the hot-from-the-fire creativity of one's twenties and early thirties with the sculptured creativity of the later part of the life cycle. The reality of one's own death is the crucial feature of mid-life crisis, he states, and points out that the successful outcome of mature creative work lies in constructive resignation both to the imperfection of men and to the shortcomings of one's own work. This constructive resignation lends serenity to life and work. To illustrate his points he gives examples from the lives of creative people.

10

Death and the Mid-Life Crisis

ELLIOTT JAQUES

In the course of the development of the individual there are critical phases which have the character of change points, or periods of rapid transition. Less familiar perhaps, though nonetheless real, are the crises which occur around the age of thirty-five—which I shall term the mid-life crisis—and at full maturity around the age of sixty-five. It is the mid-life crisis with which I shall deal in this paper.

When I say that the mid-life crisis occurs around the age of thirty-five, I mean that it takes place in the middle thirties, that the process of transition runs on for some years, and that the exact period will vary among individuals. The transition is often obscured in women by the proximity of the onset of changes connected with the menopause. In the case of men, the change has

This chapter originally appeared in the *International Journal of Psycho-Analysis*, 46:502-514, 1965.

from time to time been referred to as the male climacteric, because of the reduction in the intensity of sexual behavior which
often occurs at that time.

CRISIS IN GENIUS

I first became aware of this period as a critical stage in development when I noticed a marked tendency towards crisis in
the creative work of great men in their middle and late thirties.
It is clearly expressed by Richard Church in his autobiography
The Voyage Home:

> There seems to be a biological reason for men and women,
> when they reach the middle thirties, finding themselves beset
> with misgivings, agonizing inquiries, and a loss of zest. Is it
> that state which the medieval schoolmen called *accidie*, the
> cardinal sin of spiritual sloth? I believe it is.

This crisis may express itself in three different ways: the creative career may simply come to an end, either in a drying up of
creative work, or in actual death; the creative capacity may begin
to show and express itself for the first time; or a decisive change
in the quality and content of creativeness may take place.

Perhaps the most striking phenomenon is what happens to
the death rate among creative artists. I had got the impression
that the age of thirty-seven seemed to figure pretty prominently
in the death of individuals of this category. This impression was
upheld by taking a random sample of some 310 painters, composers, poets, writers, and sculptors, of undoubted greatness or
of genius. The death rate shows a sudden jump between thirty-
five and thirty-nine, at which period it is much above the normal
death rate. The group includes Mozart, Raphael, Chopin, Rimbaud, Purcell, Baudelaire, Watteau. There is then a big drop
below the normal death rate between the ages of forty and forty-
four, followed by a return to the normal death rate pattern in the
late forties. The closer one keeps to genius in the sample, the
more striking and clearcut is this spiking of the death rate in mid-
life.

The change in creativity which occurs during this period can be seen in the lives of countless artists. Bach, for example, was mainly an organist until his cantorship at Leipzig at thirty-eight, at which time he began his colossal achievements as a composer. Rossini's life is described in the following terms:

> His comparative silence during the period 1832-1868 [i.e. from forty to his death at seventy-four] makes his biography like the narrative of two lives—swift triumph, and a long life of seclusion.

Racine had thirteen years of continuous success culminating in *Phèdre* at the age of thirty-eight, he then produced nothing for some twelve years. The characteristic work of Goldsmith, Constable, and Goya emerged between the ages of thirty-five and thirty-eight. By the age of forty-three Ben Jonson had produced all the plays worthy of his genius, although he lived to be sixty-four. At thirty-three Gauguin gave up his job in a bank, and by thirty-nine had established himself in his creative career as a painter. Donatello's work after thirty-nine is described by a critic as showing a marked change in style, in which he departed from the statuesque balance of his earlier work and turned to the creation of an almost instantaneous expression of life.

Goethe, between the ages of thirty-seven and thirty-nine, underwent a profound change in outlook, associated with his trip to Italy. As many of his biographers have pointed out, the importance of this journey and this period in his life cannot be exaggerated. He himself regarded it as the climax to his life. Never before had he gained such complete understanding of his genius and mission as a poet. His work then began to reflect the classical spirit of Greek tragedy and of the Renaissance.

Michelangelo carried out a series of masterpieces until he was forty; his "David" was finished at twenty-nine, the decoration of the roof of the Sistine Chapel at thirty-seven, and his "Moses" between thirty-seven and forty. During the next fifteen years little is known of any artistic work. There was a creative lull until, at fifty-five, he began to work on the great Medici monument and then later on "The Last Judgment" and frescoes in the Pauline Chapel.

Let me make it clear that I am not suggesting that the careers of most creative persons either begin or end during the mid-life crisis. There are few creative geniuses who live and work into maturity in whom the quality of greatness cannot be discerned in early adulthood, in the form either of created works or of the potential for creating them: Beethoven, Shakespeare, Goethe, Couperin, Ibsen, Balzac, Voltaire, Verdi, Händel, Goya, Dürer, to name but a very few at random. But there are equally few in whom the effects of their having gone through a mid-life crisis cannot be discerned. The reactions range all the way from severe and dramatic crisis, to a smoother and less troubled transition—just as reactions to the phase of adolescent crisis may range from severe disturbance and breakdown to relatively ordered re-adjustment to mental and sexual adulthood—but the effects of the change are there to be discerned. What then are the main features of this change?

There are two features which seem to me of outstanding importance. One of these has to do with the mode of work; the second has to do with the content of the work. Let me consider each of these in turn. I shall use the phrase "early adulthood" for the pre-mid-life phase and "mature adulthood" for the past-mid-life phase.

CHANGE IN MODE OF WORK

I can best describe the change in mode of work which I have in mind by describing the extreme of its manifestation. The creativity of the twenties and the early thirties tends to be a hot-from-the-fire creativity. It is intense and spontaneous, and comes out ready-made. The spontaneous effusions of Mozart, Keats, Shelley, Rimbaud are the prototype. Most of the work seems to go on unconsciously. The conscious production is rapid, the pace of creation often being dictated by the limits of the artist's capacity physically to record the words or music he is expressing.

A vivid description of early adult type of work is given in Gittings's biography of Keats:

> Keats all this year had been living on spiritual capital. He had used and spent every experience almost as soon as it had come into his possession, every sight, person, book, emotion or thought had been converted spontaneously into poetry. Could he or any other poet have lasted at such a rate? . . . He could write no more by these methods. He realized this himself when he wished to compose as he said 'without fever'. He could not keep this high pulse beating and endure.

By contrast, the creativity of the late thirties and after is a sculpted creativity. The inspiration may be hot and intense. The unconscious work is no less than before. But there is a big step between the first effusion of inspiration and the finished created product. The inspiration itself may come more slowly. Even if there are sudden bursts of inspiration, they are only the beginning of the work process. The initial inspiration must first be externalized in its elemental state. Then begins the process of forming and fashioning the external product, by means of working and reworking the externalized material. I use the term sculpting because the nature of the sculptor's material—it is the sculptor working in stone of whom I am thinking—forces him into this kind of relationship with the product of his creative imagination. There occurs a process of interplay between unconscious intuitive work and inspiration, and the considered perception of the externally emergent creation and the reaction to it.

In her note "A Character Trait of Freud's," Rivière (1958) describes Freud's exhorting her in connection with some psychoanalytic idea which had occurred to her:

> Write it, write it, put it down in black and white. . . . Get it out, produce it, make something of it—*outside you*, that is; give it an existence independently of you [p. 146].

This externalizing process is part of the essence of work in mature adulthood, when, as in the case of Freud, the initially externalized material is not itself the end product, or nearly the end product, but is rather the starting point, the object of further working over, modification, elaboration, sometimes for periods of years.

In distinguishing between the precipitate creativity of early adulthood and the sculpted creativity of mature adulthood, I do not want to give the impression of drawing a hard and fast line between the two phases. There are of course times when a creative person in mature adulthood will be subject to bursts of inspiration and rapidfire creative production. Equally there will be found instances of mature and sculpted creative work done in early adulthood. The "David" of Michelangelo is, I think, the supreme example of the latter.

But the instances where work in early adulthood has the sculpted and worked-over quality are rare. Sometimes, as in scientific work, there may be the appearance of sculpted work. Young physicists in their twenties, for example, may produce startling discoveries, which are the result of continuous hard work and experimentation. But these discoveries result from the application of modern theories about the structure of matter—theories which themselves have been the product of the sculpted work of mature adulthood of such geniuses as Thomson and Einstein.

Equally, genuinely creative work in mature adulthood may sometimes not appear to be externally worked over and sculpted, and yet actually be so. What seems to be rapid and unworked-over creation is commonly the reworking of themes which have been worked upon before, or which may have been slowly emerging over the years in previous works. We need look no farther than the work of Freud for a prime example of this process of books written rapidly, which are nevertheless the coming to fruition of ideas which have been worked upon, fashioned, reformulated, left incomplete and full of loose ends, and then completed through the emergence of new ideas for overcoming previous difficulties.

The reality of the distinction comes out in the fact that certain materials are more readily applicable to the precipitate creativity of early adulthood than are others. Thus, for example, musical composition, lyrical poetry, are much more amenable to rapid creative production than are sculpting in stone or painting in oils. It is noteworthy, therefore, that whereas there are very many poets and composers who achieve greatness in early adulthood—indeed in their early twenties or their late teens—there are very few sculptors or painters in oils who do so. With oil paint and stone, the working relationship to the materials themselves is of importance, and demands that the creative process should go through the stage of initial externalization and working-over of the externalized product. The written word and musical notation do not of necessity have this same plastic external objective quality. They can be sculpted and worked over, but they can also readily be treated merely as a vehicle for the immediate recording of unconsciously articulated products which are brought forward whole and complete—or nearly so.

QUALITY AND CONTENT OF CREATIVITY

The change in mode of work, then, between early and mature adulthood, is a change from precipitate to sculpted creativity. Let me now consider for a moment the change in the quality and content of the creativity. The change I have in mind is the emergence of a tragic and philosophical content which then moves on to serenity in the creativity of mature adulthood, in contrast to a more characteristically lyrical and descriptive content to the work of early adulthood. This distinction is a commonly held one, and may perhaps be considered sufficiently self-evident to require little explication or argument. It is implied, of course, in my choice of the adjectives "early" and "mature" to qualify the two phases of adulthood which I am discussing.

The change may be seen in the more human, tragic, and less fictitious and stage quality of Dickens's writing from *David Copperfield* (which he wrote at thirty-seven) onwards. It may be seen also in the transition in Shakespeare from the historical plays and comedies to the tragedies. When he was about thirty-one, in the midst of writing his lyrical comedies, he produced *Romeo and*

Juliet. The great series of tragedies and Roman plays, however, began to appear a few years later; *Julius Caesar, Hamlet, Othello, King Lear*, and *Macbeth* are believed to have been written most probably between the ages of thirty-five and forty.

There are many familiar features of the change in question. Late adolescent and early adult idealism and optimism, accompanied by split-off and projected hate, are given up and supplanted by a more contemplative pessimism. There is a shift from radical desire and impatience to a more reflective and tolerant conservatism. Beliefs in the inherent goodness of man are replaced by a recognition and acceptance of the fact that inherent goodness is accompanied by hate and destructive forces within, which contribute to man's own misery and tragedy. To the extent that hate, destruction, and death are found explicitly in early adult creativeness, they enter in the form of the satanic or the macabre, as in Poe and in Baudelaire, and not as worked-through and resolved anxieties.

The spirit of early adult creativeness is summed up in Shelley's *Prometheus Unbound*. In her notes on this work, Shelley's wife has written:

> The prominent feature of Shelley's theory of the destiny of the human species is that evil is not inherent in the system of the Creation, but an accident that might be expelled. . . . God made Earth and Man perfect, till he by his fall 'brought death into the world, and all our woe'. Shelley believed that mankind had only to will that there should be no evil in the world and there would be none. . . . He was attached to this idea with fervent enthusiasm.

This early adult idealism is built upon the use of unconscious denial and manic defenses as normal processes of defense against two fundamental features of human life—the inevitability of eventual death, and the existence of hate and destructive impulses inside each person. I shall try to show that the explicit recognition of these two features, and the bringing of them into focus, is the quintessence of successful weathering of the mid-life crisis and the achievement of mature adulthood.

It is when death and human destructiveness—that is to say, both death and the death instinct—are taken into account, that the quality and content of creativity change to the tragic, reflective, and philosophical. The depressive position must be worked through once again, at a qualitatively different level.[1] The misery and despair of suffering and chaos unconsciously brought about by oneself are encountered and must be surmounted if life is to be endured and creativity is to continue. Nemesis is the key, and tragedy the theme, of its recognition.

The successful outcome of mature creative work lies thus in constructive resignation both to the imperfections of men and to shortcomings in one's own work. It is this constructive resignation that then imparts serenity to life and work.

THE DIVINE COMEDY

I have taken these examples from creative genius because I believe the essence of the mid-life crisis is revealed in its most full and rounded form in the lives of the great. It will have become manifest that the crisis is a depressive crisis, in contrast to the adolescent crisis, which tends to be a paranoid-schizoid one. In adolescence, the predominant outcome of serious breakdown is schizophrenic illness; in mid-life the predominant outcome is depression, or the consequences of defense against depressive anxiety as reflected in manic defenses, hypochondriasis, obsessional mechanisms, or superficiality and character deterioration. Working through the mid-life crisis calls for a reworking through of the infantile depression, but with mature insight into death and destructive impulses to be taken into account.

This theme of working through depression is magnificently expressed in *The Divine Comedy*. This masterpiece of all time was begun by Dante following his banishment from Florence at

[1]Editor's note: In the Kleinian view, every individual passes in the normal course of events through phases in which first psychotic (with splitting of "good" and "bad" objects, and persecutory fear), then depressive anxiety mechanisms predominate. These processes will continue in some form in adulthood, and are also operative in organizations.

the age of thirty-seven. In the opening stanzas he creates his setting in words of great power and tremendous psychological depth. He begins:

> In the middle of the journey of our life, I came to myself within a dark wood where the straight way was lost. Ah, how hard it is to tell of that wood, savage and harsh and dense, the thought of which renews my fear. So bitter is it that death is hardly more.

These words have been variously interpreted; for example, as an allegorical reference to the entrance to Hell, or as a reflection of the poet's state of mind on being forced into exile, homeless and hungry for justice. They may, however, be interpreted at a deeper level as the opening scene of a vivid and perfect description of the emotional crisis of the mid-life phase, a crisis which would have gripped the mind and soul of the poet whatever his religious outlook, or however settled or unsettled his external affairs. The evidence for this conclusion exists in the fact that during the years of his early thirties which preceded his exile, he had already begun his transformation from the idyllic outlook of the *Vita Nuova* (ages twenty-seven to twenty-nine) through a conversion to "philosophy" which he allegorized in the *Convivio*, written when he was between thirty-six and thirty-eight years of age.

Even taken quite literally, *The Divine Comedy* is a description of the poet's first full and worked-through conscious encounter with death. He is led through Hell and Purgatory by his master Virgil, eventually to find his own way, guided by his beloved Beatrice, into Paradise. His final rapturous and mystical encounter with the being of God, represented to him in strange and abstract terms, was not mere rapture, not simply a being overwhelmed by a mystical oceanic feeling. It was expressly a vision of supreme love and knowledge, with control of impulse and of will, which promulgates the mature life of greater ease and contemplation which follows upon the working through of primitive anxiety and guilt, and the return to the primal good object.

Dante explicitly connects his experience of greater mental integration, and the overcoming of confusion, with the early infantile relation to the primal good object. As he nears the end of the 33rd Canto of "Paradiso," the climax of his whole grand scheme, he explains:

> Now my speech will come more short even of what I remember than an infant's who yet bathes his tongue at the breast.

But the relationship with the primal good object is one in which reparation has been made, Purgatorio has been traversed, loving impulses have come into the ascendant, and the cruelty and harshness of the superego expressed in the Inferno have been relieved. Bitterness has given way to composure.

In Dante, the result of this deep resolution is not the reinforcing of manic defense and denial which characterizes mystical experience fused with magic omnipotence; but rather the giving up of manic defense, and consequent strengthening of character and resolve, under the dominion of love. As Croce has observed:

> What is not found in the 'Paradiso', for it is foreign to the spirit of Dante, is flight from the world, absolute refuge in God, asceticism. He does not seek to fly from the world, but to instruct it, correct it, and reform it . . . . he knew the world and its doings and passions.

AWARENESS OF PERSONAL DEATH

Although I have thus far taken my examples from the extremes of genius, my main theme is that the mid-life crisis is a reaction which not only occurs in creative genius, but manifests itself in some form in everyone. What then is the psychological nature of this reaction to the mid-life situation, and how is it to be explained?

The simple fact of the situation is the arrival at the mid-point of life. What is simple from the point of view of chronology, however, is not simple psychologically. The individual has stopped growing up, and has begun to grow old. A new set of external circumstances has to be met. The first phase of adult life

has been lived. Family and occupation have become established
(or ought to have become established unless the individual's adjustment has gone seriously awry); parents have grown old, and
children are at the threshold of adulthood. Youth and childhood
are past and gone, and demand to be mourned. The achievement
of mature and independent adulthood presents itself as the main
psychological task. The paradox is that of entering the prime of
life, the stage of fulfillment, but at the same time the prime and
fulfillment are dated. Death lies beyond.

I believe, and shall try to demonstrate, that it is this fact of
the entry upon the psychological scene of the reality and inevitability of one's own eventual personal death, that is the central
and crucial feature of the mid-life phase—the feature which precipitates the critical nature of the period. Death—at the conscious
level—instead of being a general conception, or an event experienced in terms of the loss of someone else, becomes a personal
matter, one's own death, one's own reality and actual mortality.
As Freud (1915) has so accurately described the matter:

> We were of course prepared to maintain that death was
> the necessary outcome of life. . . . In reality, however, we
> were accustomed to behave as if it were otherwise. We showed
> an unmistakable tendency to put death on one side, to elim-
> inate it from life. We tried to hush it up. . . . That is . . . our
> own death, of course. . . . No one believes in his own
> death. . . . In the unconscious, everyone of us is convinced
> of his own immortality [p. 289].

This attitude towards life and death, written by Freud in another context, aptly expresses the situation which we all encounter
in mid-life. The reality of one's own personal death forces itself
upon our attention and can no longer so readily be shelved. A
thirty-six-year-old patient, who had been in analysis for seven
years and was in the course of working through a deep depressive
reaction which heralded the final phase of his analysis some eighteen months later, expressed the matter with great clarity. "Up
till now," he said, "life has seemed an endless upward slope, with
nothing but the distant horizon in view. Now suddenly I seem

to have reached the crest of the hill, and there stretching ahead is the downward slope with the end of the road in sight—far enough away it's true—but there is death observably present at the end."

From that point on this patient's plans and ambitions took on a different hue. For the first time in his life he saw his future as circumscribed. He began his adjustment to the fact that he would not be able to accomplish in the span of a single lifetime everything he had desired to do. He could achieve only a finite amount. Much would have to remain unfinished and unrealized.

This perspective on the finitude of life was accompanied by a greater solidity and robustness in his outlook, and introduced a new quality of earthly resignation. It reflected a diminishing of his unconscious wish for immortality. Such ideas are commonly lived out in terms of denial of mourning and death, or in terms of ideas of immortality, from notions of reincarnation and life after death, to notions of longevity like those expressed by the successful twenty-eight-year-old novelist who writes in his diary, "I shall be the most serious of men, and I shall live longer than any man."

Unconscious Meaning of Death

How each one reacts to the mid-life encounter with the reality of his own eventual death—whether he can face this reality, or whether he denies it—will be markedly influenced by his infantile unconscious relation to death—a relationship which depends upon the stage and nature of the working through of the infantile depressive position, as Melanie Klein discovered and vividly described (1940, 1955). Let me paraphrase her conclusions.

The infant's relation with life and death occurs in the setting of his survival being dependent on his external objects, and on the balance of power of the life and death instincts which qualify his perception of those objects and his capacity to depend upon them and use them. In the depressive position in infancy, under conditions of prevailing love, the good and bad objects can in some measure be synthesized, the ego becomes more integrated, and hope for the reestablishment of the good object is experienced; the accompanying overcoming of grief and regaining of security is the infantile equivalent of the notion of life.

Under conditions of prevailing persecution, however, the working through of the depressive position will be to a greater or lesser extent inhibited; reparation and synthesis fail; and the inner world is unconsciously felt to contain the persecuting and annihilating devoured and destroyed bad breast, the ego itself feeling in bits. The chaotic internal situation thus experienced is the infantile equivalent of the notion of death.

Ideas of immortality arise as a response to these anxieties, and as a defense against them. Unconscious fantasies of immortality are the counterpart of the infantile fantasies of the indestructible and hence immortal aspect of the idealized and bountiful primal object. These fantasies are equally as persecuting as the chaotic internal situation they are calculated to mitigate. They contain omnipotent sadistic triumph, and increase guilt and persecution as a result. They also lead to feelings of intolerable helplessness through dependence upon the perfect object which becomes demanding of an equal perfection in behavior.

Does the unconscious, then, have a conception of death? The views of Melanie Klein and those of Freud may seem not to correspond. Klein assumes an unconscious awareness of death. Freud assumes that the unconscious rejects all such awareness. Neither of these views, taken at face value, is likely to prove correct. Nor would I expect that either of their authors would hold to a literal interpretation of their views. The unconscious is not aware of death per se. But there are unconscious experiences akin to those which later appear in consciousness as notions of death. Let me illustrate such experiences.

A forty-seven-year-old woman patient, suffering from claustrophobia and a variety of severe psychosomatic illnesses, recounted a dream in which she was lying in a coffin. She had been sliced into small chunks, and was dead. But there was a spider's-web-thin thread of nerve running through every chunk and connected to her brain. As a result she could experience everything. She knew she was dead. She could not move or make any sound. She could only lie in the claustrophobic dark and silence of the coffin.

I have selected this particular dream because I think it typifies the unconscious fear and experience of death. It is not in fact death in the sense in which consciously we think about it, but an unconscious fantasy of immobilization and helplessness, in which the self is subject to violent fragmentation, while yet retaining the capacity to experience the persecution and torment to which it is being subjected. When these fantasies of suspended persecution and torture are of pathological intensity, they are characteristic of many mental conditions: catatonic states, stupors, phobias, obsessions, frozen anxiety, simple depression.

A CASE OF DENIAL OF DEATH

In the early adult phase, before the mid-life encounter with death, the full-scale reworking through of the depressive position does not as yet necessarily arise as a part of normal development. It can be postponed. It is not a pressing issue. It can be put to one side, until circumstances demand more forcibly that it be faced.

In the ordinary course of events, life is full and active. Physiologically, full potency has been reached, and activity—social, physical, economic, sexual—is to the fore. It is a time for doing, and the doing is flavored and supported to a greater or lesser degree—depending on the individual's emotional adjustment—by the activity and denial as part of the manic defense.

The early adult phase is one, therefore, in which successful activity can in fact obscure or conceal the operation of strong manic defenses. But the depressive anxiety that is thus warded off will be encountered in due course. The mid-life crisis thrusts it forward with great intensity, and it can no longer be pushed aside if life is not to be impoverished.

This relationship between adjustment based upon activity in

the early adult phase, and its failure in mid-life if the infantile depressive position is not unconsciously (or consciously, in analysis) worked through again, may be illustrated in the case of a patient, Mr. N., who had led a successful life by everyday standards up to the time he came into analysis. He was an active man, a "doer." He had been successful in his career through intelligent application and hard work, was married with three children, had many good friends, and all seemed to be going very well.

The idealized content of this picture had been maintained by an active carrying on of life, without allowing time for reflection. His view was that he had not come to analysis for himself, but rather for a kind of tutorial purpose—he would bring his case history to me and we would have a clinical seminar in which we would conduct a psychoanalytic evaluation of the case material he had presented.

As might be expected, Mr. N. had great difficulty in coping with ambivalence. He was unconsciously frightened of any resentment, envy, jealousy, or other hostile feelings towards me, maintaining an attitude of idealized love for me and tolerant good nature towards every attempt on my part to analyze the impulses of destructiveness and the feelings of persecution which he was counteracting by this idealization.

When we finally did break through this inability to cope with ambivalence—indeed, a pretty complete unfamiliarity with the experience—it emerged that, in all his relationships, his idealization was inevitably followed by disappointment—a disappointment arising out of failure to get the quality of love he was greedily expecting in return, and nursed by envy of those whom he idealized.

It was out of the analysis of material of this kind that we were able to get at the reflection in the analysis of his early adult mode of adjustment. He admitted that he was ill, and that unconscious awareness of his illness undoubtedly was the main reason for his seeking analysis. Being active, and overconcerned for others, were soporifics to which he had become addicted. Indeed, he confessed, he had resented my analysis taking this defensive addiction away from him. He had secretly entertained ideas of stopping his analysis "because all this thinking about myself, instead of doing things, is no good. Now I realize that I have been piling up my rage against you inside myself, like I've done with everyone else."

Thus it was that during the first year of his analysis, the patient lived out many of the techniques which had characterized his early adult adjustment. It was with the onset of the Christmas holiday that the unconscious depressive anxiety, which was the main cause of his disturbance in mid-life, came out in full force. It is this material that illustrates the importance of the depressive position and unconscious feelings about death in relation to the mid-life crisis.

He had shown definite signs before the holiday of feelings of being abandoned, saying that not only would he not see me, but his friends were to be away as well. Three days before the end of the holiday, he telephoned me and, in a depressed and tearful voice, asked if he could come to see me. I arranged a session that same evening.

When he came to see me, he was at first afraid to lie on the couch. He said that he wanted just to talk to me, to be comforted and reassured. He then proceeded to tell me how, from the beginning of the holiday, a black gloom had settled upon him. He yearned for his mother to be alive, so that he could be with her and be held and loved by her. "I just felt completely deserted and lost," he said. "I sat for hour after hour, unable to move or to do any work. I wanted to die. My thoughts were filled with suicide. Then I became terrified of my state of mind. That's why I phoned you. I just had never conceived it as even remotely possible that I could lose my self-control like this." Things were made absolutely unbearable, he then explained, when one of his children had become nearly murderously aggressive towards his wife a few days before. His world seemed to have gone to pieces.

This material, and other associations, suggested that his wife stood for the bad aspect of his mother, and his son for the sadistic murderous part of himself. In his fear of dying, he was reexperiencing his own unconscious fantasies of tearing his mother to pieces, and he then felt abandoned and lost. As I interpreted on these lines, he interjected that the worst thing was the feeling of having gone to pieces himself. "I can't stand it," he said, "I feel as though I'm going to die."

I then recalled to him a dream he had had just before the holiday, which we had not had time to analyze, and which contained material of importance in the understanding of his infantile perception of being dead. In this dream he was a small boy sitting crying on the curb in his home town. He had dropped a bottle of milk. It lay in jagged shattered bits in the gutter. The fresh good milk ran away, dirtied by contact with the muck in the gutter. One of his associations to the dream was that he had broken the bottle by his own ineptness. It was no use moaning and crying over the spilt milk, since it was himself, after all, who had caused the damage.

I related his dream to his feeling of being abandoned by me. I was the bottle of milk—containing good milk—which he destroyed in his murderous rage because I abandoned him and went dry. He unconsciously felt the Christmas holiday as losing me, as he felt he had lost his mother and the good breast, because of his ineptness—his violence and lack of control—and his spoiling me internally with his anal muck. He then felt internally persecuted and torn to pieces by the jagged bits of the bottle, representing the breast, myself, and the analysis; as Klein (1955) has expressed it, "the breast taken in with hatred becomes the representative of the death instinct within" (p. 313).

I would conclude that he had unconsciously attempted to avoid depression by paranoid-schizoid techniques of splitting and deflecting his murderous impulses away from me, through his son against his wife. These techniques had now begun to fail, however, because of previous analytical work with respect to his splitting and denial. Whereas he had been able to deny what in fact turned out to be a pretty bad situation in his home, by perceiving it merely as the product of his own projections, he now became filled with guilt, anxiety, and despair, as he began to appreciate more that in reality the relationships at home were genuinely intolerable and dangerous, and were not just a projection of his own internal chaos and confusion.

During the succeeding months, we were able to elaborate more fully his attitude towards death as an experience of going to pieces.

A connection between his phobic attitude to death, and his escape into activity was manifested, for instance, in his recalling one day a slogan that had always meant so much to him—"Do or die." But now it came to him that he had always used his own personal abbreviation of the slogan—simply "Do." The possibility of dying just did not consciously exist for him.

On one occasion he demonstrated at first hand how his fear of death had caused him always to retreat from mourning. A friend of his died. The patient was the strong and efficient one, who made all the necessary arrangements, while friends and family stood about helplessly, bathed in tears and paralyzed with sorrow. He experienced no feeling—just clear-headedness and a sense of action for the arrangements which had to be made. He had always been the same, had done the same when his father and his mother had died. More than that, however, when I interpreted his warding off of depression by means of denial of feeling and refuge in action, he recalled an event which revealed the unconscious chaos and confusion stirred within him by death. He remembered how, when a cousin of his had suddenly collapsed and died a few years before, he had run back and forth from the body to the telephone to call for a doctor, oblivious of the fact that a small group of people had gathered about the body, and not realizing that everyone but himself was perfectly aware that his cousin was quite dead, and had been for some time before he arrived upon the scene.

The chaos and confusion in the patient in connection with death, I would ascribe to his unconscious infantile fantasies equivalent to death—the fantasies of the destroyed and persecuting breast, and of his ego being cut to pieces.

Mainly, I think, because of the love he got from his father, probably reinforcing his own innate good impulses and what he has had described to him as good breast-feeding in the first five weeks with his mother, he had been able to achieve a partial working through of the infantile depressive position, and to develop his good intellectual capacities. The partial character of his working through was shown in the extent of his manic denial and activity, and his excessive use of splitting, introjection, and projection, and projective and introjective identification.[2]

During the period of early adulthood—the twenties and early thirties—these paranoid-schizoid and manic defense techniques were sufficiently effective. By means of his apparent general success and obsessional generosity, he was able to live out the role of the good mother established within, to nurture the good part of himself projected into others, to deny the real situation of envy and greed and destructiveness expressed by him as his noxiousness, and to deny the real impoverishment of his emotional life, and lack of genuine love and affection in his behavior as both husband and father.

With the onset of mature adulthood in his mid-thirties, his defensive techniques began to lose their potency. He had lost his youth, and the prospect of middle age and of eventual death stimulated a repetition and a reworking through of the infantile depressive position. The unconscious feelings of persecution and annihilation which death represented to him were reawakened.

He had lost his youth. And with both his parents dead, nobody now stood between himself and the grave. On the contrary, he had become the barrier between his children and their perception of death. Acceptance of these facts required constructive resignation and detachment. Unconsciously such an outlook requires the capacity to maintain the internal good object, and to achieve a resigned attitude to shortcomings and destructive impulses in oneself, and imperfections in the internal good object. My patient's unconscious fantasies of intolerable noxiousness, his anx-

[2]Editor's note: Projective identification is a mode of projection in which certain traits of the self or even an overall resemblance of the self are attributed to the other person in order to harm, possess, or control the person. It can be contrasted with introjective identification where the opposite takes place, that is, the traits or overall resemblance of the other is incorporated.

ieties of having polluted and destroyed his good primal object so
that he was lost and abandoned and belonged nowhere, and his
unconscious fantasies of the badness of his internalized mother
as well as his father, precluded such detachment and resignation.
The psychological defenses which had supported his adjustment
in early adult life—an adjustment of a limited kind, of course,
with a great core of emotional impoverishment—failed him at the
mid-life period when, to the persecutory world in which he unconsciously lived, were added his anxieties about impending middle and old age, and death. If he had had a less well-established
good internal object, and had been innately less constructive and
loving, he might have continued his mature and adult life along
lines similar to his early adult type of adjustment; but if he had,
I think his mid-life crisis would have been the beginning of a
deterioration in his character, and bouts of depression and psychosomatic illness, due to the depth and chronicity of his denial
and self-deception, and his distorted view of external reality.

As it has worked out, however, the positive factors in his
personality makeup enabled him to utilize his analysis, for which
he developed a deep sense of value and appreciation. The overcoming of splitting and fragmentation first began to show in a
session in which, as out of nowhere, he saw two jagged-edged,
right-angled triangles. They moved together, and joined to make
a perfect square. I recalled the dream with the broken bits of
bottle to him. He replied, "It's odd you should mention that; I
was just thinking of it. It feels like the bits of glass are coming
together."

EVASION OF AWARENESS OF DEATH

One case history does not of course prove a general thesis. It
can only illustrate a theme, and the theme in this instance is the
notion that the circumstances met by this patient at the mid-life
phase are representative of a general pattern of psychological
change at this stage of life. The extent to which these changes are
tied up with physiological changes is a question I am not able to

tackle. One can readily conjecture, however, that the connection must be an important one—libido, the life-creating impulse, represented in sexual drive—is diminishing, and the death instinct is coming relatively more into the ascendant.

The sense of the agedness of parents, coupled with the maturing of children into adults, contributes strongly to the sense of aging—the sense that it is one's own turn next to grow old and die. This feeling about the age of parents is very strong—even in patients whose parents died years before there is the awareness at the mid-life period that their parents would then have been reaching old age.

In the early adult phase of life, contemplativeness, detachment, and resignation are not essential components of pleasure, enjoyment, and success. Manically determined activity and warding off of depression may therefore—as in the case of Mr. N.—lead to a limited success and pleasure. Splitting and projection techniques can find expression in what are regarded as perfectly normal patterns of passionate support for idealized causes, and equally passionate opposition to whatever may be felt as bad or reactionary.

With the awareness of the onset of the last half of life, unconscious depressive anxieties are aroused, and the repetition and continuation of the working-through of the infantile depressive position are required. Just as in infancy—to quote Klein again (1940)—"satisfactory relations to people depend upon the infant's having succeeded against the chaos inside him (the depressive position) and having securely established his 'good' internal objects" (p. 314), so in mid-life the establishment of a satisfactory adjustment to the conscious contemplation of one's own death depends upon the same process, for otherwise death itself is equated with the depressive chaos, confusion, and persecution, as it was in infancy.

When the prevailing balance between love and hate tends more towards the side of hate, when there is instinctual defusion, there is an overspill of destructiveness in any or all of its various forms—self-destruction, envy, grandiose omnipotence, cruelty, narcissism, greed—and the world is seen as having these persecuting qualities as well. Love and hate are split apart; destruction is no longer mitigated by tenderness. There is little or no protection from catastrophic unconscious fantasies of annihilating one's good objects. Reparation and sublimation, the processes which underly creativeness, are inhibited and fail. And in the deep unconscious world there is a gruesome sense of invasion and habitation by the psychic objects which have been annihilated.

In primitive terms, the process of sculpting is experienced partly as a protective identification, in which the fear of dying is split off and projected into the created object (representing the creative breast). Under the dominance of destructiveness the created object, like the breast, is felt to

> remove the good or valuable element in the fear of dying, and to force the worthless residue back into the infant. The infant who started with a fear that he was dying ends up by containing a nameless dread [Bion, 1962, p. 96].

The conception of death is denuded of its meaning, and the process of sculpted creativity is stopped. It is the experience of a patient who, having created a work of art by spontaneous effusion, found that "it goes dead on me; I don't want to have anything more to do with it; I can never work on it further once it is outside, so I can never refine it; it completely loses its meaning for me—it's like a strange and foreign thing that has nothing to do with me."

The ensuing inner chaos and despair is unconsciously fantasied in terms akin to an inferno: "I came to myself within a dark wood . . . savage and harsh and dense." If this state of mind is not surmounted, hate and death must be denied, pushed aside, warded off, rejected. They are replaced by unconscious fantasies of omnipotence, magic immortality, religious mysticism, the counterpart of infant fantasies of being indestructible and under the protective care of some idealized and bountiful figure.

A person who reaches mid-life, either without having successfully established himself in marital and occupational life, or having established himself by means of manic activity and denial with consequent emotional impoverishment, is badly prepared for meeting the demands of middle age, and getting enjoyment out of his maturity. In such cases, the mid-life crisis, and the adult encounter with the conception of life to be lived in the setting of an approaching personal death, will likely be experienced as a period of psychological disturbance and depressive breakdown. Or breakdown may be avoided by means of a strengthening of manic defenses, with a warding off of depression and persecution about aging and death, but with an accumulation of persecutory anxiety to be faced when the inevitability of aging and death eventually demands recognition.

The compulsive attempts, in many men and women reaching middle age, to remain young, the hypochondriacal concern over health and appearance, the emergence of sexual promiscuity in order to prove youth and potency, the hollowness and lack of genuine enjoyment of life, and the frequency of religious concern, are familiar patterns. They are attempts at a race against time. And in addition to the impoverishment of emotional life contained in the foregoing activities, real character deterioration is always possible. Retreat from psychic reality encourages intellectual dishonesty, and a weakening of moral fibre and of courage. Increase in arrogance, and ruthlessness concealing pangs of envy—or self-effacing humbleness and weakness concealing fantasies of omnipotence—are symptomatic of such change.

These defensive fantasies are equally as persecuting, however, as the chaotic and hopeless internal situation they are meant to mitigate. They lead to attempts at easy success, at a continuation on a false note of the early adult lyricism and precipitate creation—that is, creation which, by avoiding contemplation, now seeks not to express but to avoid contact with the infantile experience of hate and of death. Instead of creative enhancement by the introduction of the genuinely tragic, there is emotional impoverishment—a recoil away from creative development. As Freud (1915) incisively remarked: "Life is impoverished, it loses in interest, when the highest stake in the game of living, life itself, may not be risked" (p. 290). Here is the Achilles heel of much young genius.

WORKING THROUGH THE DEPRESSIVE POSITION

When, by contast, the prevailing balance between love and hate is on the side of love, there is instinctual fusion, in which hate can be mitigated by love, and the mid-life encounter with death and hate takes on a different hue. Revived are the deep unconscious memories of hate, not denied but mitigated by love; of death and destruction mitigated by reparation and the will to life; of good things injured and damaged by hate, revived again and healed by loving grief; of spoiling envy mitigated by admiration and by gratitude; of confidence and hope, not through denial, but through the deep inner sense that the torment of grief and loss, of guilt and persecution, can be endured and overcome if faced by loving reparation.

Under constructive circumstances, the created object in mid-life is experienced unconsciously in terms of the good breast which would in Bion's (1962) terms

> moderate the fear component in the fear of dying that had been projected into it and the infant in due course would re-introject a now tolerable and consequently growth-stimulating part of its personality [p. 96].

In the sculpting mode of work the externally created object, instead of being experienced as having impoverished the personality, is unconsciously reintrojected, and stimulates further unconscious creativeness. The created object is experienced as life-giving. The transformation of the fear component in the fear of dying into a constructive experience is forwarded. The thought of death can be carried in thinking, and not predominantly in projective identification, so that the conception of death can begin to find its conscious realization. The reality testing of death can be carried out in thinking, separated partly from the process of creating an external object. At the same time the continuing partial identification of the creative sculpting with the projection and reintrojection of the fear of dying gives a stimulus to the sculpting process because of its success in forwarding the working through of the infantile projective identification with a good breast.

9

10 ELLIOTT JAQUES

Thus in mid-life we are able to encounter the onset of the tragedy of personal death with the sense of grief appropriate to it. We can live with it, without an overwhelming sense of persecution. The infantile depressive position can be further worked through unconsciously, supported by the greater strength of reality testing available to the nearly mature individual. In so reworking through the depressive position, we unconsciously regain the primitive sense of wholeness—of the goodness of ourselves and of our objects—a goodness which is sufficient but not idealized, not subject to hollow perfection. The consequent feeling of limited but reliable security is the equivalent of the infantile notion of life.

These more balanced conditions do not, however, presuppose an easy passage through the mid-life crisis. It is essentially a period of purgatory—of anguish and depression. So speaks Virgil:

> Down to Avernus the descent is light. But thence thy journey to retrace, there lies the labour, there the mighty toil by few achieved.

Working through again the infantile experience of loss and of grief gives an increase in confidence in one's capacity to love and mourn what has been lost and what is past, rather than to hate and feel persecuted by it. We can begin to mourn our own eventual death. Creativeness takes on new depths and shades of feeling. There is the possibility, however, of furthering the resolution of the depressive position at a much deeper level. Such a working through is possible if the primal object is sufficiently well established in its own right, and neither excessively idealized nor devalued. Under such circumstances there is a minimum of infantile dependence upon the good object, and a detachment which allows confidence and hope to be established, security in the preservation and development of the ego, a capacity to tolerate one's shortcomings and destructiveness, and withal, the possibility of enjoyment of mature adult life and old age.

Given such an internal situation, the last half of life can be lived with conscious knowledge of eventual death, and acceptance of this knowledge, as an integral part of living. Mourning for the dead self can begin, alongside the mourning and reestablishment of the lost objects and the lost childhood and youth. The sense of life's continuity may be strengthened. The gain is in the deepening of awareness, understanding, and self-realization. Genuine values can be cultivated—of wisdom, fortitude and courage, deeper capacity for love and affection and human insight, and hopefulness and enjoyment—qualities whose genuineness stems from integration based upon the more immediate and self-conscious awareness and acceptance not only of one's own shortcomings, but of one's destructive impulses, and from the greater capacity for sublimation which accompanies true resignation and detachment.

SCULPTED CREATIVITY

Out of the working through of the depressive position, there is further strengthening of the capacity to accept and tolerate conflict and ambivalence. One's work need no longer be experienced as perfect. It can be worked and reworked, but it will be accepted as having shortcomings. The sculpting process can be carried on far enough so that the work is good enough. There is no need for obsessional attempts at perfection, because inevitable imperfection is no longer felt as bitter persecuting failure. Out of this mature resignation comes the serenity in the work of genius, true serenity, serenity which transcends imperfection by accepting it.

Because of the greater integration within the internal world, and a deepening of the sense of reality, a freer interaction can occur between the internal and external worlds. Sculpted creativity expresses this freedom with its flow of inspiration from inside to outside and back, constantly repeated, again, and yet again. There is a quality of depth in mature creativity which stems from constructive resignation and detachment. Death is not infantile persecution and chaos. Life and the world go on, and we can live on in our children, our loved objects, our works, if not in immortality.

The sculpting process in creativity is facilitated because the preparation for the final phase in reality testing has begun—the reality testing of the end of life. For everyone, the oncoming years of the forties are the years when new starts are coming to an end. This feeling can be observed to arise in a particularly poignant way by the mid-forties. This sense of there being no more changing is anticipated in the mid-life crisis. What is begun has to be finished. Important things that the individual would have liked to achieve, would have desired to become, would have longed to have, will not be realized. The awareness of oncoming frustration is especially intense. That is why, for example, the issue of resignation is of such importance. It is resignation in the sense of conscious and unconscious acceptance of inevitable frustration on the grand scale of life as a whole.

This reality testing is the more severe the greater is the creative ability of the individual, for the time scale of creative work increases dramatically with ability. Thus the experience is particularly painful in genius, capable of achieving vastly more than it is possible to achieve in the remaining years, and therefore frustrated by the immense vision of things to be done which will not be done. And because the route forward has become a cul de sac, attention begins its Proustian process of turning to the past, working it over consciously in the present, and weaving it into the concretely limited future. This consonance of past and present is a feature of much mature adult sculpting work.

The positive creativeness and the tone of serenity which accompany the successful endurance of this frustration, are characteristic of the mature production of Beethoven, Goethe, Virgil, Dante, and other giants. It is the spirit of the "Paradiso," which ends in words of strong and quiet confidence:

> But now my desire and will, like a wheel that spins with even motion, were revolved by the Love that moves the sun and other stars.

It is this spirit, on a smaller scale, which overcomes the crisis of middle life, and lives through to the enjoyment of mature creativeness and work in full awareness of death which lies beyond—resigned but not defeated. It is a spirit that is one criterion of the successful working through of the depressive position in psychoanalysis.

References

Bion, W. (1962), *Learning from Experience*. New York: Basic Books.
Freud, S. (1915), Thoughts for the Times on War and Death. *Standard Edition*, 14:273-300. London: Hogarth Press, 1957.
Klein, M. (1935), A Contribution to the Psychogenesis of Manic-Depressive States. In: *Contributions to Psycho-Analysis*. London: Hogarth Press, 1948.
——— (1940), Mourning and Its Relation to Manic-Depressive States. In: *Contributions to Psycho-Analysis*. London: Hogarth Press, 1948.
——— (1955), On Identification. In: *New Directions in Psycho-Analysis*. New York: Basic Books.
Rivière, J. (1958), A Character Trait of Freud's. In: *Psycho-Analysis and Contemporary Thought*, ed. J. D. Sutherland. London: Hogarth Press.

Severe disappointment in one's career can either foster or arrest develop-ment. If disappointment is suppressed or denied instead of faced, the individual is likely to founder on the hidden, unresolved conflicts. The process of mastery requires a reorganization of personality based on insight into oneself, which brings about a renewal of energy for work. Taking a number of examples from business and politics Zaleznik discusses psychological dimensions which can influence the coping process. The chapter concludes with the author's sugges-tions for a number of steps which managers can take to make disappointment a catalytic experience for personal growth.

11

Management of Disappointment

ABRAHAM ZALEZNIK

Several years ago *Life* magazine presented some unusually astute reflections on the leadership of President Johnson. These observations, seen in the broadest possible perspective, provoked a new set of questions about the motivation of leaders and, in-directly, offered fresh thinking about organizations, business as well as political.

The editors of *Life* began with the comment that President Johnson was not equally at home in each of the wide range of problems facing him. He would rather act on domestic problems than on international issues; and if events forced him to look beyond our borders, he much preferred to deal with the new nations, the "have nots" in Asia, Africa, and Latin America, than with the "haves" of the established industrial societies in Europe.

In brief, President Johnson identified with the underdog and, left
to his own devices, would have attacked the problems of poverty,
disease, education, and related concerns which seem at their core
to cause human suffering. The thrust of his leadership was aimed
invariably at nurturing those for whom he felt strongly empa-
thetic.

While these observations inevitably involve some oversim-
plification, they appear justified by the record of his Presidency.
The editors of *Life* concluded with these comments:

> It can be argued—and is by many presidential scholars—that
> the man in the White House does not have a great deal of
> choice about the problems he gets or even how to deal with
> them. Perhaps that is so, but the Presidency still is a highly
> personal office. What pleases and placates, what intrigues and
> gratifies, what stimulates and flatters the man in the Oval
> Office subtly regulates the push and the priorities in the affairs
> of state that in the long run shape the era [*Life*, May 12, 1967,
> p. 46b].

Two points strike the reader of these editorial comments. The
first is the tragic sense of leadership implied in the notion that
events outside his control may not permit a man to do those things
which he dearly wishes to do and for which he is eminently suited.
The second is the suggestion, even if only by inference, that we
have here something more than a special situation or the idio-
syncrasies of one man at one time and in one place.

We are not dealing with the problems of political leaders alone,
although in many of the examples to follow I have used public
figures, since their careers are well documented; we are more
concerned here with the problems of the head man of a business.
For him, particularly, there may be some important generalizations about leadership in the idea that a man's inclinations, unknown to himself, channel him in a certain direction. A chief
executive may therefore count himself lucky if he is able to utilize
those tendencies with which he feels most comfortable, and over
which in the end *he may have the least conscious control*. If we
follow these leads, we soon delve into the borderland between
personality and action in organizations.

It is my intention to take an excursion into this borderland, leaving the relatively safe, if somewhat arid, territory of organization theory which chooses to see management in terms divorced from the issues of personality. While, from a purely rational standpoint, a chief executive should be able to adjust the style and substance of his actions to the problems which press for solution, he is above all else a human being. The strategies and policies offered in his name, and the rationalistic terms with which they are advanced, often obscure the personal commitment behind those formal programs. And, in fact, without the conviction drawn from personal commitment, the chief executive's attempts at persuasion and influence often leave others cold. On the other hand, while the conviction may be apparent, the direction of policy may appear so inconsistent and even unreal as to perplex subordinates and arouse wonder at the apparent displacement of personal concerns onto the business of the organization.

In effect, then, a corporate executive may face a paradoxical situation where he must live with himself and be himself while attempting to formulate realistic goals and the means for implementing them.

Personal Equation

Some time ago a young businessman exemplified some of the hazards involved in this paradox. Charles Luckman came to the presidency of Lever Brothers evidently intent on making a personal impact on the company and on the business community. His career ended abruptly when it became clear that his efforts at personal role building had far outstripped the sound development of business strategy and structure (*Fortune*, April, 1950).

The career of John Connor, former president of Merck & Co., Inc., and a Secretary of Commerce, illustrates another aspect of the gap between personal initiatives and the practical opportunities offered by the power structure for expressing them. As *Fortune* commented in "The Paradoxical Predicament of John Connor":

Jack Connor took office with an ebullience he has been hard put to maintain. Within the Commerce Department, Connor is something less than the complete boss: his chief lieutenants are answerable less to him than to the President, who appointed them, has the power to promote, and holds their political loyalties. And despite his resounding Cabinet title, Connor finds he has a lot less influence on policy than he was once accustomed to [*Fortune*, February, 1966, p. 188].

This gap between what a leader wants to do and what he is able to accomplish within the realities of power relationships poses a severe test for the individual. In Connor's case, according to *Fortune*, a sense of optimism helped him endure frustration: "Putting the best possible face on what could have only been a severe disappointment, Connor made no complaint" (*Fortune*, February, 1966, p. 152). But there is a limit to any man's endurance, as indicated in Connor's later decision to resign his post and return to private enterprise.

For some executives, leadership is the conscious effort to subordinate their personal expression while meeting the expectations others set. These executives usually do not provide remarkable case histories of business failure, but neither do they stand out as achievers. More significantly, they, along with a few intimates, measure the costs of unrealized hopes.

Where an individual expects, because of ability, position, or wealth, to exert influence on events, there is no escape from the personal commitment to action. And where such commitment is great, the potential for loss and disappointment is equally great.

In the spring of 1966, Howard Hughes sold his holdings in Trans World Airlines. While he realized enormous monetary gains in this transaction, he endured a high personal cost because he gave up his influence, if not outright control, over one of the major international airlines. His decision to end a battle for corporate control implied a personal reappraisal of the potential gains and losses to him in continuing the effort. That it was no simple outcome of investment logics was reflected in the comments of Charles Tillinghast, President of Trans World, who explained

Hughes's actions this way: "Perhaps he is a proud personality and wanted to divest voluntarily" (*Fortune*, July, 1977, p. 119).

As these illustrations suggest, the executive career turns on the subtle capacity to take personal risks in making decisions and putting them into action. This personal view of the executive career can, by extension, provide ideas for understanding better what actually goes on in organizations and in the exercise of leadership. Someday this personal view may also provide a theory which can be articulated and used in building organizational structures. In the meantime, we need to know considerably more about the many sides of an individual's leadership style.

In studying effective executives, one usually asks: What were the man's experiences with success, and how did he build on them in his career? Psychological studies of creative people, including leaders, suggest that preoccupation with success may be less important than the role of disappointment in the evolution of a career (Rochlin, 1965). Both the great strengths and weaknesses of gifted leaders often hinge on how they manage the disappointments inevitable in life.

The experience of disappointment is a catalytic psychological event that may foster developmental growth or retardation. When the individual faces disappointment, he usually has to pull back his emotional investment in people and activities and reexamine them before reinvesting them in a new outward direction. The key idea, however, is in the *facing* of disappointment. If disappointment and the pains attendant on it are denied or otherwise hidden from view, the chances are great that the individual will founder on the unresolved conflicts at the center of his experience with disappointment.

ROLE OF CONFLICT

To achieve psychological understanding of the motives underlying a leadership style, one must be prepared to deal with the unexpected. In human affairs, relationships seldom persist for the obvious, surface reasons. The central problem in the case of leadership styles is to grasp the meanings of behavior and the multiple causes of action.

The concepts of *meaning* and *cause* when applied to human activities have at least two points of reference. The first is the relation of the leader's acts to some problem in his environment. For example, Alfred Sloan's actions in establishing a rational, formal organization in General Motors can be analyzed in relation to the problem of constructing a balance between centralized and decentralized functions within a company made up of complex marketing, engineering, and production strategies (Chandler, 1962). The second point of reference for behavior is the inner world of the actor. Here, we are concerned not only with the individual's goals, but also with the nature of the stimuli that constantly threaten his capacity to tolerate painful experiences.

The study of the external meanings of behavior requires a historical examination of institutions and their environments. The internal meanings of behavior also require a historical study, but of the individual and the legacies of his development. Leadership style is essentially the outcome of the developmental process and can be defined, following the psychoanalytic concept of "character," as *the patterned modes of behavior with which an individual relates himself to external reality and to his internal dispositions*.

One of the major contributions of psychoanalytic psychology has been to demonstrate the place of conflict in the individual's development. Each stage in the life cycle involves personal conflict, in which the individual has the task of giving up one set of gratifications and searching for alternatives that take account simultaneously of biological, psychological, and social challenges. Failure to relinquish gratifications impedes development, while overly rapid learning establishes a gap between instinctual emotional processes and cognitive-rational capacities. This gap leads often to low tolerance for drives and emotions and to a highly rigid set of conditions for the exercise of competence.

Forrestal Tragedy

The life and tragic death of James Forrestal is a case in point. Forrestal built a successful career on Wall Street and in government service. Toward the latter part of his service as the first Secretary of Defense, he developed a series of symptoms which later, when he left his post, took the form of manic-depressive psychosis with paranoid delusions. He took his life while under treatment, an end not uncommon in this type of illness.

Throughout his life, Forrestal, according to one biographer (Rogow, 1963), developed his capacity for work, but at the expense of achieving intimacy in his family. Forrestal broke with his parental family after completing college, in effect renouncing his past. Such breaks with the past usually occur only as a result of basic disappointments in the individual's experience with his development and his position in the family.

In Forrestal's case, while the data permit only reasoned speculations, they suggest the kinds of disappointments one finds in a harsh mother-child relationship. As the result of a complex psychological process, the individual renounces nurturance and other tender emotional exchanges, and substitutes instead a burning drive to achieve. If the individual has ability, as Forrestal clearly had in abundance, he may achieve leadership and success by any of the standards we use to evaluate performance, but the individual is vulnerable to continuing disappointment that may lead to breakdown. For Forrestal, the major disappointment in his career in government was probably his failure to achieve a power base independent of the President of the United States. He may even have harbored strong ambitions for the Presidency—a position beyond his reach, given the political realities in our society.

Consequently, Forrestal's relationship with Truman became competitive and led to his replacement following the 1948 election. Forrestal fell ill immediately on the acceptance of his resignation and Louis Johnson's appointment as Secretary of Defense. As an active, ambitious man stripped of his power, he suffered a major deprivation on severing the channels he had formerly used to guide his energies. Unfortunately, he had no alternative channels, and no human relationship with which he could heal his wounds and rebuild his life.

Mastery Process

The end need not have been tragic. Many great men work through their disappointments to emerge with greater strength and a heightened capacity for leadership. Winston Churchill suffered a similar disappointment during World War I. The disastrous campaign at Gallipoli became Churchill's responsibility and abruptly interrupted the career of this ambitious and powerful man. But he mastered this disappointment to become a leader during the supreme crisis of World War II. This process of mastery must have demanded from him the kind of psychological work which usually occurs in psychoanalysis. Here, the individual withdraws and refocuses energy and attention from the outer world to himself. The outcome, if successful, is reorganization of personality based on insight, and then the renewal of one's energy in work.

We know all too little about the self-curative processes which occur for "great men" in their struggle with disappointment (Erikson, 1958). But Churchill must have been aided immeasurably by his range of talents, not the least of which was writing. In other words, he did not have all his eggs in one basket. He also found strength in his relationship with his wife.

Similar processes must have occurred in the emergence of Franklin D. Roosevelt as a great leader. The injury he suffered—and I refer now to psychological injury as a result of the polio attack—was the critical episode in his career. But, again unlike Forrestal, he had the psychological resources and the relationships he needed for performing the curative work necessary in a personal crisis.

Two final examples will clarify the complex way disappointment acts in the adult years as the developmental crisis of a career. Disappointment is not simply a condition where the outer evidences of success are absent, or where failure to realize ambitions is the critical event.

In his autobiographical writing John Stuart Mill described the onset of his late adolescent depression. He was reflecting on life and his ambitions, and asked himself this question: "Suppose that all your objects in life were realized; that all the changes in institutions and opinions which you were looking forward to could be completely effected at this very instant: would this be a great joy and happiness to you?" (Mill, 1964). His answer was negative, and the outcome of his personal honesty was an intense depression which lifted only after he was able to mourn and express the grief underlying the psychological loss connected with his disappointments in fantasy.

Henry Ford seems to have experienced a similar disappointment in fantasy on the success of the Model T. That great achievement marked a turning point in his career. Where formerly he could channel energies and direct others, he became increasingly rigid and unrealistic in his thinking. He entertained omnipotent and somewhat paranoid ideas, as evidenced by the ill-fated venture of the Peace Ship and his acceptance and support of the anti-Semitic campaigns of the newspaper *The Dearborn Independent* (Jardim, 1970).

There are men who are spoiled by success and, as Sigmund Freud pointed out, develop symptoms only after major accomplishment (Freud, 1916). This phenomenon seems perverse or inexplicable to the naive observer but it becomes comprehensible when analyzed in relation to the individual's investment in his fantasies. To produce a car, become president of a company, or make a great scientific discovery is not a simple dream (Tartakoff, 1966), for such dreams may also contain the hope of restoring the individual to some state of happiness which he may have felt he once had, and then lost. Or he may be enveloped by a sense of entitlement from which he views other persons as barriers to getting what he feels he justly deserves. Such infantile wishes contained in a leader's actions are most dangerous: Hell hath no fury like a woman scorned, or a man whose ambitions are frustrated because his dreams cannot be realized no matter how hard he works, or how tangible his achievements. Ambitions which contain hopes for changing the past and reversing the psychological disappointments of youth are self-defeating. The best that any of us can do is to understand the past. It cannot be changed.

Attachment to Self

All human beings experience disappointment. If this hard fact of development were not so, it would be very difficult to explain the attractions of myth and legend. In myth we temporarily heal the wounds of disappointment and are restored to wishes once held and reluctantly abandoned in the interests of preserving attachment to reality and the objects we love. The psychology of the leader is therefore no different from that of other human beings in sharing an initial fate of injury and disappointment. But the psychology becomes different in the consequences of injury.

Most human beings accept disappointment and more or less content themselves with a collective engagement in which ritual and myth, along with work and human relationships, permit them to bear pain and loss. For creative people and those leaders endowed with special abilities, a sense of estrangement follows early experiences with developmental conflicts. Like Narcissus, who caught his image in a reflecting pool and fell in love with this ideal self—during their childhood leaders often direct their emotional investments inward. Their dreams and fantasies, translated in adulthood into ambitions, maintain them in their sense of being special. Very often these fantasies are part of an experience of destiny; their fate is to perform a great deed like Oedipus, who solved the riddle of the Sphinx, or the biblical Joseph, who interpreted the Pharaoh's dreams and predicted the famine.

The attachment to self leads to achievement, but only in conjunction with sharply developed talents, for without other qualities, such as the power to reason, to perceive the interplay of events in the environment, or to invent new solutions to old problems, the heightened sense of self would lead only to heightened frustration and, in the extreme, even madness. But the sense of self enters strongly into the personality of the leader and the ties others establish to him. What the leader does with his abilities and his investment in self is in fact the manifestation of what we call his style, with its special consequences for institutional management.

Resource or Hazard?

The nature of policy and strategy in business organizations is a direct outcome of the actions of leaders; it is not realistic to imagine that decisions are made in an impersonal way. Decisions are made by men who think and act in relation to the influence of authority figures who themselves are, as I have tried to indicate, bound to a general process of human development.

In reaching decisions and charting a course for a corporation, considerable clarity of vision and accuracy in perception are necessary. The heightened sense of self that I have identified as a major factor in the psychology of leaders is both a resource and a hazard in corporate management as well as in the fate of the individual. It is a resource in that the investment in self preserves the independence necessary to weigh opinions and the advice of others. However, while it is good common sense to encourage subordinates to offer recommendations, in the final analysis a major policy must be based on the convictions of the chief executive. How does he achieve the conviction necessary to seal a decision? If he is dependent on others because of an impoverishment of self-confidence, it will be very difficult indeed for him to guide the destiny of the organization.

The problem of investment in self as a psychological quality of leadership is one of degree. Too little self-investment amounts to overdependence and often to diffusion of purpose. The other extreme, overinvestment in self, poses problems as well, but in a more complex way than overdependence.

Freud in his study "Group Psychology and the Analysis of the Ego" (1921) described the primal leader as an individual who loves no one but himself. This imagery suggests the autocrat who keeps subordinates at a distance and allows them little independent action. This primal leader is not an archaic figure in business management. Although he is not idealized now as he was in the late nineteenth and earth twentieth centuries, nevertheless, he still persists with all his strengths and weaknesses in small enterprises as well as in large corporations. The autocrat provides direction, and if he selects a correct path, he usually manages a successful enterprise. As a leader, he tends to select subordinates in his own image, and they reflect all his virtues and vices.

The hazard facing the autocrat stems from the tendency for new ideas, information, and vision to find limited acceptance. Subordinates tell the primal leader only what he wants to hear, and he restricts opportunities for communication by his distance. If he continues to direct the organization by an incorrect or outdated strategy, then the future is in doubt. Precisely this set of conditions occurred in the Ford Motor Company, leading to its decline in the industry and to serious financial losses from the 1920's until World War II.

Balance and Perspective

At a more personal level the problem the primal leader faces is maintaining balance and perspective through inevitable disappointments—especially those which may occur at the height of his career. These disappointments may range from business setbacks to family problems—including the discovery that his sons and heirs are not made in his image and have distinct personalities and problems. These latter-day disappointments may produce a kind of psychic injury that reopens old wounds. The leader's response may be rage and restitutive thought patterns that we recognize as a false sense of omnipotence, and even delusions.

Evidently Harry Truman had some insight into the hazards of disappointment, particularly those a leader experiences when he becomes aware of the limitations of his power to control events and the actions of others. Neustadt (1960) describes Truman's sympathetic anticipation of Eisenhower's problems with the Presidency. Truman said, "He'll sit here and he'll say, 'Do this! Do that!' And nothing will happen. Poor Ike—it won't be a bit like the Army. He'll find it very frustrating" (p. 22). What Truman evidently recognized is that no matter how powerful the leader's position, the issue of influence is still problematic: whether things get done or not is beyond the magical thinking that equates authority with influence.

The Narcissus-like leader who invests only in himself does not necessarily behave overtly like an autocrat, nor does he necessarily detach himself from others. Frequently one observes leaders who have close relationships with subordinates, but we cannot conclude from superficial observation whether these relationships indicate a balance between investment in self and in others. Closer observation often shows that the ties are not in reality those between two separate individuals who cooperate in a rational and purposive endeavor, but instead, that the individuals who position themselves around the leader are to him only as reflected images of himself taken from his infantile past. These executive structures then become dramatic reenactments of fantasies that existed to restore the self-esteem of the individual during his early experiences with disappointment.

The structure and dynamics of these relationships have a variety of unconscious meanings that are carried forward into major episodes of corporate life. While the relationships may have adaptive value, they may also become central to the outbreak of pathological processes within the leader and the other key executives in the organization. And again I suggest that the pathologies involve the reexperience of disappointment and loss when the relationships shift or, under the influence of reality, fail as restitutive episodes.

While subordinates may be related to a leader in ways which become significant in the reenactment of fantasies, there is still room for modification. I am reminded of the tragedy of King Lear, who had to drive away those individuals who loved him most because he could not tolerate the intensity of his love for his youngest daughter, Cordelia. The only figure who remained close to Lear and who would tell him the truth was his fool. But the only way the fool could exist and speak the truth was as the castrated object who posed no threat to the power of the leader.

With this observation our problem shifts. Why would anyone give up his own self-esteem to serve another, even though in a paradoxical way he performs noble work in helping the narcissistic leader maintain his fragile hold on reality? To be the king's fool strikes me as an excessive price to pay for another man's contributions to society. There is still another way, and that is to maintain one's integrity, to speak the truth, and to let the chips fall where they may. Subordinates to narcissistic leaders sometimes succumb to their own restitutive fantasies as a way of rationalizing their position. We can be sure that where a close relationship persists, there are more reasons than we know about to account for the willingness of those involved to maintain object ties.

SELF-EXAMINATION NEED

Business managers, whether they know it or not, commit themselves to a career in which they have to work on themselves as a condition for effectively working on and with other people. This fact of the business career is so often neglected that we would do well to reexamine the implications of the need to work on oneself as a condition for the exercise of power.

The analysis presented in this study suggests that a significant area for personal and inner work on oneself is the experience with disappointment. The question we now have to explore is: How does an executive make the management of disappointment a catalytic experience for personal growth? Here are some leads and suggestions.

Preventive Aspects

First, as a preventive measure, one should examine carefully the personal goals behind the decision to assume responsibility in a position. If the goals are themselves unrealistic, then major disappointment is inevitable.

A number of years ago, a man who decided to change his career and take over a small enterprise told me that his reason for entering business was to put into practice the conceptions of good human relations in leadership to which he was personally dedicated. My question to him was this: How about going into business to manage a successful company and to make money? My intent was not to insult his noble purposes but, rather, to suggest that the way one formulates his personal goals has to do with the way he will practice his profession. In other words, a noble intention may enlighten work, but it is no substitute for competence. The investment in noble purposes may even prevent success, and finally set the stage for the traumatic experience with disappointment.

McGregor's Theories

A collection of essays by Douglas McGregor, published in 1966 following his death, offers by indirection some clues on how the clash between personal ideology and reality may obscure insight.

McGregor pointed out the difference between what he called Theory X and Theory Y. According to his persuasive arguments, many managers of complex organizations are acting on the basis of an outmoded conception of human nature and institutions. This conception, Theory X, sees man as a stubborn, recalcitrant being who has to be motivated to work toward organizational goals. Believing in this conception of man produces a self-fulfilling prophecy. That is, the type of leadership fostered by this "mechanical" man is apt to produce stubborn, recalcitrant individuals who sabotage the organization instead of contributing to its well-being.

In advocating the opposite view, Theory Y, throughout his essays, McGregor proposed that leaders should change their ideas about human nature. Basing his ideas on the findings of behavioral science, particularly psychology, McGregor appealed to managers to adopt a philosophy of leadership predicated on the assumption that individuals want to be self-actualizing and want to live in harmony with their environment. In this view the leader is an agronomist who cultivates the organizational environment so as to fulfill this more optimistic picture of man.

This powerful message lies at the root of McGregor's considerable stature as a management theorist. Its appeal lies in its humanness and in the subtle way it addresses itself to the underlying guilt which plagues men who exercise power in modern organizations. All too often, leaders are uneasy about the power they have over men and decisions, an uneasiness that is accompanied by a sense of guilt and a desire for reassurance, love, and approval from associates. It is as though leaders listen for voices outside themselves that will testify to their humanity in counterpoise to the disquieting inner voices that disapprove and accuse. In short, McGregor's message was designed to deal as much with a bad conscience as with the realities of work, authority, and decisions in organizations.

But how lasting and relevant are these external cures for a bad conscience? Whether in the name of religion or science, the cure is temporary as compared with the more arduous route of self-knowledge and mastery. Socrates' advice to "know thyself" is exceedingly relevant today for men of responsibility. Unfortunately, McGregor's theories avoid the inner conflicts and resolutions of leadership problems in their almost singular dedication to creating an ideal organization climate.

McGregor missed the point in the study of leadership because, while he was keen on talking to managers, he failed in a basic sense to identify with them. His identification was largely with subordinates; and in talking to managers, McGregor communicated the wish in all of us for benign and benevolent power figures. But to love and to be loved is not enough in the painful process of choice while exercising leadership.

McGregor did capture this idea during what must have been for him a period of intense stress. In his essay "On Leadership," written as he was about to leave the presidency of Antioch College after six years, he said:

> Before coming to Antioch, I had observed and worked with top executives as an advisor in a number of organizations. I thought I knew how they felt about their responsibilities and what led them to behave as they did. I even thought I could create a role for myself that would enable me to avoid some of the difficulties they encountered. I was wrong! . . . I believed, for example, that a leader could operate successfully as a kind of advisor to his organization. I thought I could avoid being a "boss." Unconsciously, I suspect, I hoped to duck the unpleasant necessity of making difficult decisions, of taking responsibility for one course of action among many uncertain alternatives, of making mistakes and taking the consequences. I thought that maybe I could operate so that everyone would like me—that "good human relations" would eliminate all discord and disappointment. I could not have been more wrong . . . [1966, p. 67].

The essay from which this quotation was taken appeared in May, 1954. The subsequent essays, written while McGregor continued a distinguished career as professor at M.I.T., suggest he had not assimilated the insight underlying his sense of disappointment. I suspect the insight got lost because McGregor was too hard on himself, as the brief quotation above suggests. In the later essays in this book, McGregor returns to the message through which he appealed to authority figures on behalf of subordinates.

Had he pursued the insight imbedded in the Antioch essay, he might have recognized that the essence of leadership is choice, a singularly individualistic act in which a man assumes responsibility for directing an organization along a particular path. He might also have recognized that as much as a leader wishes to trust others, he has to judge the soundness and validity of the positions his subordinates advocate. Otherwise, the leader is in danger of becoming a prisoner of the emotional demands of his subordinates, frequently at the expense of judging the correctness of policies and strategies.

McGregor's problem, I would suspect, developed out of his noble purposes. But nobility of purpose is not the first order of business in establishing one's position as chief executive of an organization. In the personal assessment of one's intention to lead, it is far better to assign the highest priority to discovering those things that need to be done, and then to devote oneself to engaging the commitments of others toward these goals. Of course, this does not rule out the possibility that historians can later look at this executive's work and discover the nobility which surrounded his leadership.

But no matter how hard one works on the preventive aspects, sooner or later disappointments occur, and the personal working through of these events then becomes the first order of business.

Facing Issues

The second suggestion I shall make is to face the disappointment squarely. The temptation and the psychology of individual response to disappointment is to avoid the pain of self-examination. If an avoidance pattern sets in, the individual will pay dearly for it later. Usually, avoidance occurs because this mode of response has been the individual's habitual way of dealing with disappointment from childhood days on. It also seems clear that those who have learned in childhood how to face loss are best equipped to deal with the personal issues that arise during experiences with disappointment in the executive career. Consider:

One line manager in a large corporation worked closely with a vice president, who in the course of events in business life came out second best in a rivalry. The vice president resigned, and his department was left in a vulnerable position, without a leader, and with a loss of status. The line manager, who was in his early forties, had spent his entire working career with this large corporation. He had an excellent reputation, and the senior executives were genuinely hopeful that he would remain with the company.

After thinking the issue through he decided to resign, recognizing that his commitments to the deposed vice president were so strong that they would not permit him to reestablish ties with others and to work effectively without paying too high a personal price. He discovered that his experience and talents were indeed in high demand, and he made a successful transition to another corporation where he soon became a vice president and senior executive in his own right.

The decision to remain or to leave was not the significant test of whether the line manager was actually facing his disappointment. Rather, the significant test came in his silent work of self-examination which he shared only with his wife, who matched his personal courage and willingness to take risks. In effect, this line manager learned to face events and to follow the sound financial principle of writing off a loss, and then setting forth on a new program.

Emotional Awareness

The key factor in mastering disappointment is the capacity to experience the emotions connected with the personal career losses (Zetzel, 1965). The flight from the work leading to mastery is usually connected with the individual's limited capacity to tolerate painful emotions. The third suggestion, therefore, is to become intimately acquainted with one's own emotional reactions.

An example of the issues implicit in attempting to face the emotional reactions following disappointment is poignantly described in *The Diaries of Harold Nicolson* (1967). Nicolson, a member of Parliament, held the post of Parliamentary Secretary in the Ministry of Information during the early years of World War II. Churchill asked for his resignation in connection with a series of top-level changes in the ministry resulting from public criticism and charges of mismanagement. Nicolson resigned, and the following day (July 19, 1941) he noted this entry in his diary:

> I wake up feeling that something horrible has happened, and then remember that I have been sacked from the Government. Go to the Ministry and start clearing out some of

my private possessions. Then attend the Duty Room, probably for the last time. I meet Gerald Campbell in the passage. 'I hear,' he says, 'that you have been thurtled?'[1] Everybody expresses dismay at my going.[2] I have a final drink in the Press Bar with Osbert Lancaster, and then lunch at the Travellers with Robin Maugham. He is as charming as he could be.

But I mind more than I thought I should mind. It is mainly, I suppose, a sense of failure. I quite see that if the Labour leaders have been pressing to have my post, there is good cause why they should have it. But if I had more power and drive, I should have been offered Rab Butler's job at the Foreign Office,[3] which I should dearly have loved. As it is, I come back to the bench below the gangway having had my chance and failed to profit by it. Ever since I have been in the House I have been looked on as a might-be. Now I shall be a might-have-been. Always up till now I have been buoyed up by the hope of writing some good book or achieving a position of influence in politics. I now know that I shall never write a book better than I have written already, and that my political career is at an end. I shall merely get balder and fatter and more deaf as the years go by. This is an irritating thing. Success should come late in life in order to compensate for the loss of youth; I had youth and success together, and now I have old age and failure.[4] Apart from all this, I mind leaving the Ministry where I did good work and had friends.

This space indicates the end of my ambitions in life. 'Omnium consensu capax imperii nisi imperasset.'[5]

According to the editor of the diaries, it took Nicolson some time before he could assimilate the disappointment and plunge anew into lesser responsibilities. But Nicolson's honesty and his

---

[1]Nicolson was replaced as Parliamentary Secretary by Ernst Thurtle, Labor M.P. for Shoreditch, who retained the office till the end of the war. Duff Cooper was succeeded as Minister by Brendan Bracken.

[2]Duff Cooper wrote to him, "I think you have received very shabby treatment, and I find that everybody shares that view."

[3]R. A. Butler, Under-Secretary of State for Foreign Affairs since 1938, was now appointed Minister of Education, and was succeeded at the Foreign Office by Richard Law.

[4]Nicolson was then fifty-four.

[5]Tacitus on the Emporor Galba: "Had he never been placed in authority, nobody would ever have doubted his capacity for it."

gifts as an observer of events evidently helped him during a difficult personal crisis.

Studies of individuals who get into trouble and present themselves for treatment to a psychoanalyst frequently show that the roots of their difficulties lie in a limited capacity to tolerate emotions, especially those connected with loss and disappointment. The business executive is especially vulnerable because he may have developed an unconscious strategy of forced activity or, more accurately, hyperactivity as a defense against emotional awareness. The hyperactive executive finds his rewards, of course, since in the conventional understanding of how an executive should behave, busy-ness is generally considered a good thing.

However good it is in some respects, it is bad if busy-ness also serves to build a wall between the inner worlds of thought and feeling. In the treatment of such individuals who are in trouble, the most positive indicator of progress is the appearance of sadness and depression. As the individual consciously assimilates the depression and relates it to his experiences with disappointment throughout his development, he becomes capable of undoing the ineffective patterns and of substituting more effective ways of dealing with the demands and stresses of responsibility.

CONCLUSION

No one is immune to encounters with disappointment. More significantly, individuals who want power and responsibility or who seek creative expression are especially vulnerable to episodes in which reality does not conform to one's wishes or intentions. As I have indicated in this article, far from being a prelude to continued failure in career, these critical episodes of disappointment may actually be occasions for accelerated growth, and even the beginning of truly outstanding performance.

But much depends on the quality of the psychological work the individual accomplishes under the stress of loss and bewilderment which frequently accompanies disappointment. As in all matters of personal development, the outcome turns on the quality of the man, the measure of courage he can mobilize, the richness of his talents, and his ability for constructive introspection.

It is no easy task to examine one's own motivations. In fact, the necessity seldom arises until one meets an impasse in life. At this juncture, one is confronted with two sets of personal concerns: those connected directly with the present disappointment, and those related to past experiences with disappointment. Usually a crisis in the present reopens problems from the past, and, in this sense the individual experiences a telescoping of time in which the psychological past and present tend to merge.

But the degree of telescoping is critical in judging the intensity of stress involved in handling disappointment. It is usually difficult enough to solve a current problem, with all its demands for accurate observation and realistic thought, but the difficulty increases when the route to solving current problems involves examination of one's history with loss or deprivation. Here the most effective step the individual can take is to seek competent help.

In the course of examining reactions to disappointment, a subtle change may take place in the individual's perspectives and attitudes. While he may come to recognize the impossibility of certain goals and be willing to relinquish their demands on his behavior, he may at the same time discover new, uncharted possibilities for productive work and pleasure. These immanent possibilities usually remain obscure so long as the individual is intent in his quest for restitutive rewards to make up for losses of the past.

There is irony in all of human experience, and no less in the solutions to the problem of disappointment. The deepest irony of all is to discover that one has been mourning losses that were never sustained and yearning for a past that never existed, while ignoring one's own real capabilities for shaping the present.

REFERENCES

Chandler, A. (1962), *Strategy and Structure: Chapters in the History of Industrial Enterprises*. Cambridge, Mass.: M.I.T. Press.

Erikson, E. H. (1958), *Young Man Luther*. New York: Norton.
Freud, S. (1916), Some Character-Types Met with in Psycho-Analytic Work. *Standard Edition*, 14:309-333. London: Hogarth Press, 1957.
────── (1921), Group Psychology and the Analysis of the Ego. *Standard Edition*, 18:65-143. London: Hogarth Press, 1955.
Jardim, A. (1970), *The First Henry Ford: A Study of Personality and Business Leadership*. Cambridge, Mass.: M.I.T. Press.
McGregor, D. (1966), *Leadership and Motivation*. Cambridge, Mass.: M.I.T. Press.
Mill, J. S. (1964), *Autobiography*. New York: New American Library.
Neustadt, R. E. (1960), *Presidential Power: The Politics of Leadership*. New York: Wiley.
Nicolson, H. (1967), *The Diaries of Harold Nicolson: The War Years, 1939-1945*. New York: Atheneum.
Rochlin, G. (1965), *Griefs and Discontents*. Boston: Little, Brown.
Rogow, A. A. (1963), *James Forrestal: A Study of Personality, Politics, and Policy*. New York: Macmillan.
Tartakoff, H. H. (1966), The Normal Personality in Our Culture and the Noble Prize Complex. In: *Psychoanalysis—A General Psychology: Essays in Honor of Heinz Hartman*, ed. R. M. Loewenstein, L. M. Newman, M. Schur, and A. J. Solnit. New York: International Universities Press.
Zetzel, E. R. (1965), Depression and the Incapacity to Bear It. In: *Drives, Affects, Behavior*, Vol. 2, ed. R. M. Loewenstein. New York: International Universities Press.

Section II
Theoretical Considerations

Adaptation as a criterion of mental health and, indeed, as a bridge to survival, is the underlying theme of this chapter by Levinson and Weinbaum, which starts off Section II. The authors examine how the individual adapts to the organization, as reflected in his reactions to the three basic forms of anxiety: ego, id, and superego anxiety. The role of the ego ideal—that image within the individual which contains the emotional map for the unfolding of his life pattern—is explored with reference to organizational identification.

12

The Impact of Organization on Mental Health

HARRY LEVINSON AND LOUIS WEINBAUM

Adaptation is basic to all of the formulations on mental health. It is a conception that might well serve as a "bridge criterion" because it has anchor points in biology, genetics, and physical health as well as in both the behavioristic and psychoanalytic schools of psychology.

Adaptation is the mastery of self and of external reality sufficient to ensure survival of the individual. It is not the same as adjustment, which often refers to removal of tensions (Mowrer and Kluckhohn, 1944; Rotondo, 1965; Hartmann, 1964). Nor is adaptation the same as job satisfaction, morale, motivation, and similar rubrics for describing externally observed behavior, for it refers in this context specifically to the management of anxiety. A man who has achieved a level of effective adaptation is likely

This chapter originally appeared in longer form in *Mental Health and Work Organizations*. Chicago: Rand McNally, 1970. By permission of Dr. Levinson.

to experience job satisfaction, and high morale, and be intensely motivated in his work. Conversely, he who has not adapted effectively may well have limited job satisfaction, low morale, and feeble work motivation. Yet, these two alternatives are not necessarily consequences of poor adaptation. Many a poorly adapted man has sacrificed his life to his work with great zeal. One could be dissatisfied with his job in the sense of not being particularly pleased with it, but be able to obtain other kinds of satisfactions and be touched in only a limited way by his job discontent.

Adaptation must be viewed in the environmental context in which it occurs. For example, a suspicious man may effect an excellent adaptation by becoming a detective. Removed from that situation, his suspiciousness, unintegrated with an occupation, might become a maladaptive life style. We must therefore speak of a man-in-environmental matrix.

One can conceive of maladaptation arising from many different kinds of conflicts and forces. The most comprehensive theory which embraces these conflicts and forces is psychoanalytic theory. According to psychoanalytic psychology, mental illness or psychological disequilibrium and impairment of maturation—all forms of maladaptation—arise from three kinds of anxiety: (1) ego anxiety; (2) id anxiety; (3) superego anxiety.

Ego anxiety refers to fear, threat of overwhelming loss from outside the person. Generally speaking, overwhelming loss from the ouside can be limited to two events. The first consists of those unexpected environmental phenomena like the explosion of a power plant, the fall of a scaffold or other traumatic accident. Such events are conducive to so-called traumatic neuroses (Modlin, 1959) because the ego is suddenly deprived of, or threatened with deprivation of, its environmental supports. If the supports are suddenly removed, as in an explosion, and the person is simultaneously experiencing an overwhelming onslaught of environmental stimuli, this so impedes the ego functions that the person no longer feels master of himself or of his immediate environment. He is unable to adapt; his survival is threatened. Psychologically, the behavior which follows is similar to an animal's retreat into a cave to lick its wounds.

The second event which precipitates ego anxiety or fear is a kind of overwhelming ego deprivation such as the loss of a job and subsequent unemployment. People who are unemployed increasingly withdraw from external stimuli. They become bored and apathetic. Important sources of support and gratification suddenly are no more. This experience is like having the maternal rug pulled out from under them. Physical relocation, severing established ties, has some of the same stresses for the same reasons.

In both instances, however, the effects of external events, providing they are not too overwhelming, can be counteracted by specific manipulations of the environment. It is a commonplace, for example, that if one is in an automobile accident he is urged to start driving again immediately. A fear-producing object may be removed, or a man be helped to find a job. A company may help a newly moved family in its introduction to a new community. By and large, then, ego anxiety or the threat of overwhelming loss on the outside, is not the difficult problem for occupational mental health.

The second major source of disequilibrium, id anxiety, refers to the threat of being overwhelmed by one's own aggressive or sexual impulses. More often the threat arises from the former. People go to great lengths to avoid the overt expression of aggression, the possibility that their hostile impulses may get out of hand. Although chronic provocation can produce intense feelings of hostility which may then explode, as reflected in the fact that most murders occur in families, rarely is there such intensity of relationship between a man and organization, or such chronic severe hostility that this becomes a threat to ego integrity. From time to time such feelings may be seen in violent strikes or the sabotage of products. There are, however, few other such circumstances.

This brings us, then, to the third major source of disequilibrium, superego anxiety. Superego anxiety refers to the threat from the conscience, the exacerbation of guilt feelings, or anger with self. These feelings may stem from the violations of one's own rules or society's rules, or from the failure to act according to one's values. It is with respect to these two themes—rules and values—that we ordinarily speak of conscience. In most such instances, however, conflicts about rules and values are conscious. Being aware of them, people can resolve them one way or another: by atonement, leaving the situation, or changing behavior.

In addition to rules and values, there is a third component of the superego: the ego ideal, that internal image of oneself as one would ideally like to be. One seeks, more than anything else, approval from the superego for meeting the ego ideal. He is unsatisfied with himself unless he is meeting the expectations and demands defined by the ego ideal. These are largely unconscious and are reflected in the aspirations of the person as well as those values to which he commits himself over a lifetime. The demands of the ego ideal have both short-term and long-term dimensions. A student who aspires to be a priest, for example, would become angry with himself (disappointed, disillusioned, frustrated) if he could not act even a small part of a priestly role while in training. Failure to meet the demands of the ego ideal results in the loss of self-esteem. Self-esteem may be understood as the span between the self-image and the ego ideal, or the gap between how a person perceives himself to be and how he thinks he ought to be.

One not only establishes an ideal for himself, but also seeks ideal others. Here Schafer's (1967) conceptions are apropos:

> Inherent in human thought is a tendency to create ideal images, to stabilize and elaborate them, however vaguely and unstably, to search the environment for their counterparts, and perceive and assess the environment (and the self) in terms of its correspondence to these ideal images. In this conception, *every wish creates an ideal*. Perhaps it is more precise to say that the ideal inheres in the wish, or in the fantasy or expectation that expresses the wish. This ideal includes an ideal self and an ideal object, or, alternatively, a self and object in an ideal wish-fulfilling relationship. Understanding of an object relationship should include a recognition of the ideal that exists alongside the experience, especially because the ideal inten-

sifies the relation to reality and partly determines what is experienced [pp. 160-161].

For example, in studies of the family, it is evident (Hess and Handel, 1967) that not only does an individual have an ideal for his own behavior, but he also forms conceptions of what he wants others to be. "Falling in love" is one such behavior. Thus, in addition to the discrepancy between how a person perceives himself and what he strives to be, there is also a discrepancy between his desired image of another person and what he finds the other to be. Our feelings about others are heavily influenced by the gap between what they are and what we, sometimes unconsciously, want them to be. The ideal images of others result in demands on the person, too. In a different vein, Byrnes (1966) relates the ego ideal to *role shock*, which he defines as "the frustrations and stresses associated with such discrepancies as between what a technical assistant views as the ideal role for himself and what he learns or finds the actual role to be abroad or between the role he expects to play abroad and the role he actually plays" (p. 96).

Since the development of one's ideal conception of himself becomes an integral and stable part of his personality, his effectiveness in adapting to any internal or external pressure for change is strongly influenced by that structure. The extensive research on psychotherapy by Rogers and his associates (1961) supports this notion. They found that it was primarily the self-concept, one's view of himself at present, which changes in their form of psychotherapy, not the ideal self. Brophy (1959) suggests that ". . . congruence in the intrapersonal relationship between the self-concept and the ideal self is one of the most fundamental conditions for both general happiness and for satisfaction in specific life areas" (p. 300).

If we posulate the ego ideal as a mediator between how the individual perceives the organization and his self-perceptions, this concept can provide us with a major mechanism by which the organization takes on meaning to those who are part of it. For example, Stagner (1966) ponders several questions: ". . . in what sense is the organization real? Can we identify the boundaries of the organization? What are the essential components, absence of which means a loss of identity?" (p. 146). Stagner finds that a useful conceptualization in dealing with such questions is one which identifies ". . . the organization with the percept, not of an observer, but of the participants, the members. Within such a framework, a group purpose and goals can be said to exist only to the extent that they are incorporated into the phenomenal fields of the members" (pp. 146-147). Yet, the "percept" is empty without an explanation of how it takes on meaning for the person, such as through his ego ideal.

We now turn from the self-esteem variable and the dimensions within the individual to which it may be related to find, with this concept, a point of conjunction among the various studies in the literature.

CONJUNCTION

What we are dealing with in the concept of the ego ideal is that image within the individual which sets forth the emotional map for the unfolding of his life pattern. If a person feels himself part of an organization in which he wishes to be, his work in it provides him with an opportunity to meet the requirements of his ego ideal by helping to attain the goals of the organization as a responsible, mature participant. It helps him further to meet the demands of the ego ideal by enabling him to discharge aggression into constructive tasks and relieve the pressures of the conscience by work per se. He views the organization's facilitation of his equilibrium-maintaining efforts as caring for him. This supports his tendency to idealize the organization. He gives the organization meaning. Therefore, the individual unconsciously views the organization as a loving parental surrogate (transference) from whom he can expect greater rewards, on whom he can make greater demands because of his loyal service. By identifying with the parental (organization) superego (goals and obligations), he has enlarged his own superego (the demands he makes upon himself on behalf of the organization). In return, the individual seeks to assuage the pressures of increased conscience by seeking more support, esteem, affection, and responsibility from the organization.

The individual can have dual relationships and loyalties to both management and unions. Conflict between the two would increase the intensity of conflict and guilt for the individual just as conflict between parents do so in the family (Levinson, 1965). Proxy fights, takeovers, mergers and similar events result in disillusionment, helplessness, and the experience of loss as the idealized organization demonstrates its weakness (Brooks and Smith, 1966). The organization can reinforce or depreciate the positive aspects of the individual's self-image. Depending on the correlation between his ego ideal and his organizationally influenced self-image, an individual may arrive at a confirmed self-identity which is reasonably satisfactory and healthy. On the other hand, the discrepancy between the two can precipitate acute stress or mental illness. The origins of convergence or contrast are found in the development of the psychological contract, because it defines the relationship between the individual and the organization.

A major problem is that much of psychological contract is unconscious. That part of it which may be conscious for the individual is often incomplete, somewhat vague, and lacking in explicit commitment from the other party, the organization.

In older, larger organizations, administrative policies and procedures are modes of fulfilling the psychological contract. In smaller organizations, face-to-face contact of the individual with the leader of the organization permits an informal personalized, day-by-day interpretation of mutual expectations, and an up-to-the-minute reporting of the status of the relationship between the individual and the organization. However, in contemporary organizations policies and procedures increasingly are refining the individual's obligation to the organization. There is little concomitant definition of the reciprocal: the organization's responsibility to the individual, other than the pay check and a nebulous aspiration to be a "good company to work for."

The relationship of the individual to the organization can be characterized as the relationship of the individual to a more knowl-edgeable powerful party. To the extent that this is true there is an inherent disparity in the resources of the individual vis-à-vis the organization. Thus the individual must have certain depen-dency needs which he expects the organization to fulfill. If the organization has a contrary view, the stage is set for a relationship which will ultimately prove to be less than fulfilling to the indi-vidual and therefore have a negative influence on his self-image, widening the gap between self-image and ego ideal.

Since most organizations are oriented primarily toward the fulfillment of some task other than the satisfaction of their indi-vidual member's needs, to the extent that an individual has press-ing psychological needs, he easily projects unrealistic assumptions about his relationship with the organization. For example, a de-pendent person may not understand and fully appreciate the effect on him of an atmosphere in which he and his fellow members are put into competition with each other for rewards or security. Not particularly competitive, he may be strongly attracted to such phrases as "We're one big happy family," when the reality is that there is much rivalry, manipulation, unpredictability, and inse-curity in his present and prospective organizational life. Because of his dependency bias, he may not be realistic in his assumptions about the durability of such organizational behavior. To that ex-tent, he is prone to perceive selectively those comments which tend to give him false assurance about his security in this rela-tionship.

Such distortion is further complicated by social distance be-tween superiors and subordinates, and by conflicting values and goals in large, complex organizations. Furthermore, because of rapid change, long-established traditions no longer adequately serve people in their organizational roles as well as formerly. Conversely, organizations find it difficult to maintain a current interpretation of what they expect of their members, what they expect of themselves, what the members should expect of the organization, and, presumably, what the individual members might expect of themselves. The psychological contract in such organizations is therefore more likely to be confused, inaccurate, and misinterpreted.

If individual and organizations can come to more explicit understanding of the need for continuous contract negotiation, and if the parties develop their understanding and skills appropriate to the task, the distance between self-image and ego ideal can be reduced, with consequent rise in self-esteem. It is in these terms that one can understand the meaning of participative management as well as the meaning of alienation. In participating, people can feel they are meeting the demands of their ego ideal, being fully responsible adults. When they feel alienated, they have no responsible participation in anything and cannot like themselves. Under such circumstances there is greater readiness to leave organizations.

It would appear that the organization has its positive image on the individual when it enhances the self-image, narrowing the gap between the self-image and ego ideal, that is, when it opens avenues for the person to act in keeping with the ego ideal and when it meets transference needs, and when it offers constructive avenues for aggression. On the other hand, it is conducive to mental illness when: (1) its actions create greater distance between the ego ideal and the self-image; or (2) it says to the individual that he will never meet the ego ideal, in which case the individual experiences psychological defeat of such proportion that he may psychologically die, and sometimes does so physically. It is the self-image, the ego ideal and the conscience, therefore, which are critical intervening variables for people at all levels and all occupations.

When the demands of the ego ideal are met, as is possible, for example, through the process of reciprocation, this results in what Erikson (1959) calls generativity. That is, it encourages spontaneous creativity, a wish for productivity and realization of potential in productivity. In addition, when one is able to like himself for what he is doing, to have hope and to flower as an individual, to be ensconced in a mutually complementary and facilitating relationship with an organization, he is then in a psychological state of readiness to create products of that relationship. That is, he is prepared psychologically to train his successor in an organization, to transmit his experiences, knowledge, and support to those whom he rears on behalf of the organization. Thus, there is a facilitation of the organization's capacity to regenerate itself, or the perpetuation of the species in social terms.

If biologically man's purpose in procreating is to ensure the survival of the species, in social terms his purpose is to build social instrumentalities and to provide for their regeneration so that those that are socially useful may endure. Thus, the individual attaches himself to an object—the organization—and the organization attaches itself to the individual. Though the individual may ultimately die or leave the organization, the organization endures for his contributions. Meanwhile, he has himself achieved purpose and hope in the process of mastery and meeting the demands of the ego ideal. He experiences identification and caring. He experiences a sense of competence (White, 1963). The skills and competences an individual acquires in maintaining and continuing this involvement with reality are then transferable to other aspects of his life, thus expanding the ego and furthering adaptation as we have defined it previously.

It is for this reason that participative management has such power, that democratic management is, for long-run purposes, more effective than autocratic management. Democratic management not only is conducive to the greater demand of people on the organization, but also vice versa. To be involved in making decisions about a task, one has to confront the external realities of the organization. In this way, one is himself continuously acting to meet the demands of his own superego, and particularly his ego ideal, and in the process pushes the organization to heights which under other circumstances the organization would not achieve.

APPLICATIONS

The concept of the ego ideal has served effectively to subsume the various studies of the impact of organization on mental health, to relate them to a systematic theory of personality, and to mental illness as well as mental health. However, this does not mean that all of the relationship between the organization and mental health may be viewed as related to the ego ideal alone. Such issues as sublimation, defenses, transference and many others (Levinson, 1965) are also part of the complex organization-individual interaction. These deserve to be carefully investigated. Inasmuch as data on these are sparse, and most of the work to date relates to the ego ideal, suggestions for further work will be limited here to that direction.

If the ego ideal is a pivotal concept, then it is obvious that we need a range of theoretical, highly sophisticated studies to define and delimit the ego ideal across social class, geographical, cultural, and similar lines. This will require the development of instruments similar to the Allport-Vernon Scale of Values, but of greater subtlety and refinement, coupled with clinical interviews and projective tasks. Such investigations should seek to specify the personal identification models of individuals, together with tacit as well as overt expectations such models hold for that person, and should examine inner signals to determine the direction toward which the person is being guided. This direction is in sharp contrast with conventional concern with aptitudes, interests and attitudes, which, however important, are less so than psychological direction. With respect to the impact of the organization on mental health, and indeed with career success, we should become more interested in internal images than in skills, in unconscious goals more than in conscious interests.

Studies of individuals should be complemented by psychologically sophisticated studies of organizations. With contemporary social science measures it is relatively easy to specify what behaviors various organizations support, reinforce or reject in keeping with an organizational image. This can result in the development of organizational profiles and the definition of organizational ideals, as well as more complex psychological configurations. Thus a new type of fit can be assessed between organization and individual, and further studies can be undertaken to weigh the significance of the emotional fit thus evolved.

In addition to problems of emotional fit, there are those of intraorganizational conflict. Specifically, organizations may urge all members to compete but limit competitive activity to only a certain class of people, e.g., those with college degrees. They may make sharp social class distinctions within their structure, thus lowering self-esteem. They may reward achievement, but punish initiative. These kinds of conflicts, some of which have already been discussed in the literature, must be carefully delineated by both survey studies and anthropological field work, with particular reference to their personal, organizational, and social costs. Many of the present studies, dependent upon questionnaires and often with limited populations, are too far from the complex realities and the plant floor experience to convey human import to executives and others who must do something about them. If the studies are to lead to action, they must be alive for the readers, and point to why and how the results will have specific effects on specific persons. In short, they must be related to the ego ideal as an intervening variable.

One of the key issues to be examined is the way in which dependency needs are satisfied in different organizations and in different roles within an organization. This factor is widely unrecognized in organizations, and almost no systematic efforts are made to take dependency needs into account, although every clinician knows how important they are and how carefully they must be managed. A topography of organizations could be constructed with just such differentiations. This, in turn, could contribute to more sensitive, more effective placement and more realistic—and thereby non-destructive—promotional policies. One facet of dependency is the person's relationships with authority figures and the practice of authority within a given company. That, too, must be more carefully specified to establish better fit and avoid stress.

We have many studies of group interaction. We have fewer of shared ideals. Peer groups do indeed share ideals as well as interests and tasks. Those who share a common ideal support each other toward transcendent goals. Another kind of fit, then, is that of individual and group in these terms.

A possible comprehensive study would look at several companies in one specific industry. It might then define in operational terms the business structure and business environment of the industry as well as the composition of the work force. Then one could assess the relationship between operationally determined attributes, the intervening ego ideal concept, and the occurrence of symptoms through various morale indices and destructive behaviors. The effects of social mobility and physical relocation might be better understood if they, too, were studied in this kind of a context.

Once such studies begin to yield information, we can begin to answer such questions as, "Is the organization responsible for a man's intensive work, or would he work as hard no matter what the organization did?" and, "Even if he were internally driven, could the organization not exert some form of control so that he would not be so destructive to himself, the organization, and his family?" Of course, this brings up the problem of how much an organization should be concerned about a man's family. Yet, inevitably the influence an organization exerts on an employee has its repercussions in the family just as it has on his individual health. The question is not whether the organization should or should not intrude; however tacitly, it does so already. Rather, the issue is how clearly an organization can recognize its impact and what responsibility it has for making that impact non-destructive. Psychological pollution is becoming as unacceptable as chemical pollution. Organizations will therefore have to be concerned about advising executives how to handle the stresses the work poses for their wives, about providing reward systems which diminish stresses for families, about weighing organizational change for its impact on families.

All this, in turn, means that the executive will need specific guidelines for enhancing mental health. The research studies will need translation into concepts and practices for application in the management of organizations. Such concepts and practices must then be incorporated into managerial training both in business schools and in in-service organization programs.

In addition, specific preparation of professionals for organizational consultation must be undertaken so that applications can be made through organizational intervention. The triggering effect of managerial actions on symptoms is well known. The managerial process itself, therefore, is one of the best arenas for intervention to reduce symptoms of mental illness.

Conclusion

In summary, the concept of the ego ideal enables us to make a conceptual bridge from the society, to the culture, to the family, or work organization and to the individual. The *values* of the society and culture are the key elements transmitted through the family and work organization to the individual. It is through these values, and behaviors based on these values, that the individual becomes civilized and defines who he is, where he is, and where he expects to go in his career, and what he expects to become. A person's feelings about himself affect his psychological equilibrium and the efforts he makes to maintain this equilibrium. The stability of this equilibrium, in turn, affects his psychological and physical health. Thus the concept is a critical intervening variable between the organization and the mental health of the individual, and opens avenues for both research and applications.

Given the limits of our knowledge about constitutional and developmental factors in mental illness, applications through education and intervention will not create a millennium with respect to mental illness any more than the abolition of smoking would itself mean the end of lung cancer. It is a truism within everyone's experience, however, that "things can be better" in all kinds of organizations, and that the "better" reduces symptomatology. Our task in this chapter has been to try to specify a major dimension of the "better" as an avenue for action.

References

Brooks, D., & Smith, R. (1966), *The Human Effects of Mergers*. London: Acton Society Trust.

Brophy, A. L. (1959), Self, Role, and Satisfaction. *J. Gen. Psychol.*, 59:263-308.

Byrnes, F. C. (1966), Role Shock: An Occupational Hazard of American Technical Assistants Abroad. *The Annals of the American Academy of Political and Social Science*, 368:95-108.

Erikson, E. H. (1959), *Identity and the Life Cycle*. [*Psychological Issues*, Monogr. 1.] New York: International Universities Press.

Hartmann, H. (1964), Psychoanalysis and the Concept of Health. In: *Essays on Ego Psychology*. New York: International Universities Press.

Hess, R. D., & Handel, G. (1967), The Family as a Psychosocial Organization. In: *The Psychosocial Interior of the Family*. Chicago: Aldine.

Levinson, H. (1965), Reciprocation: The Relationship between Man and Organization. *Administrative Science Quarterly*, 9:370-390.

Modlin, H. C. (1959), Trauma and Neurosis. *Postgraduate Medicine*, 25:A50-A62.

Mowrer, O. H., & Kluckhohn, C. (1944), Dynamic Theory of Personality. In: *Personality and the Behavior Disorders*, ed. J. M. Hunt. New York: Ronald Press.

Rogers, C. R. (1961), *On Becoming a Person*. Boston: Houghton Mifflin.

Rotondo, H. (1965), Adaptability of Human Behavior. In: *Environmental Determinants of Community Well-Being*. Pan-American Health Organization, Scientific Publication No. 123, December.

Schafer, R. (1967), Ideals, the Ego Ideal, and the Ideal Self. In: *Motives and Thought*, ed. R. R. Holt. [*Psychological Issues*, Monogr. 18/19.] New York: International Universities Press.

Stagner, R. (1966), New Design for Industrial Psychology. *Contemp. Psychol.*, 21:145-150.

White, R. W. (1963), *Ego and Reality in Psychoanalytic Theory*. [*Psychological Issues*, Monogr. 3.] New York: International Universities Press.

The organization has become a major point of identity in many lives, and since the work organization performs many basic functions, it has become an important psychological device as well. Individuals also use the organization to replace certain psychological losses and to serve as an object of transference. In presenting a further elaboration of the man-organization interface, Levinson discusses the role of unions and the functions of reciprocation, which establishes a psychological contract between persons and organizations. He devotes attention to the defensive, growth and mastery functions of reciprocation.

13

Reciprocation: The Relationship Between Man and Organization

HARRY LEVINSON

In keeping with the style of much of American and British psychology, industrial psychology places heavy emphasis on variables that lend themselves readily to measurement. This focus arises in part from the fact that traditionally, industrial psychology has had to deal with large numbers of people, and therefore to deal with them statistically rather than individually. The pragmatic tradition of industrial psychology gives more weight to empirical findings than to systematic theory. As a result, much has been learned about many aspects of the man at work, but for the most part, the study of his personality has been neglected (Dunnette and Bass, 1963).

Unconscious motivation, the twin drives of love and hate, the struggles with dependency and identity, and other important con-

This chapter originally appeared in *Administrative Science Quarterly*, 9:370-390, 1965.

cepts of personality, get scant attention in texts on industrial psychology. Although some of these topics have been touched upon by Argyris (1957), Jennings (1962), McMurry (1952), and Pederson-Krag (1955), among others, as interrelated topics they are left to be discussed in texts on clinical psychology and personality.

There are as yet few ways to make a bridge between these intrapersonal variables and the traditional interests of industrial psychology. Psychoanalytic theory is one way, and although it has limits as a bridge, it has promising possibilities. Many people believe it to be limited to the psychology of the inner man, but it is in fact a theory of man-environment relations. As Gill (1959) has noted, "The explicit theoretical accounting for the role of the organized social environment is relatively recent and it is true that only relatively recently has the effort begun to encompass object relationships systematically within psychoanalytic theory" (p. 3).

This paper attempts to realize some of the possibilities of this bridge, suggesting that what a work organization means to a person has an important bearing on the variables that have been of major interest to industrial psychologists.

IMPORTANCE OF ORGANIZATIONAL AFFILIATION

Social Change and Personal Loss

Increasing mobility, both social and geographical, has made it more difficult for people to establish relatively enduring friendships. Many who anticipate further moves from one area to another are reluctant to involve themselves deeply in friendships, to avoid the later pain of separation. Thus they lose some of the impetus for consistent ties with others, and therefore opportunities to give and receive affection.

The extended family unit is less likely to be found living in the same geographical area where family members can turn readily to each other for social activities and mutual aid. Family elders in many cases are too far away from their grandchildren to become models for identification and sources of psychological support. This means both fewer sources of support and less sense of family continuity. People who seek professional help when under stress frequently indicate this lack of support with "I have nobody to turn to."

Social services, voluntary health agencies, hospitals, and nursing homes have become progressively more institutionalized. These and similar organized efforts have taken the place of the more personal services and charitable acts characteristic of a previous era, "more personal" meaning that people believed there was more affection and concern in the noninstitutional services. The change therefore represents a perceived loss of certain sources of love—"Nobody really cares."

Even in work some sources of gratification are being lost. Rapid technical changes have altered the composition of work groups and work tasks. Occupational and status achievements are somewhat tenuous when skills can readily be made obsolete, or when their social value can depreciate rapidly as a result of technical changes and new industrial developments (Michael, 1962). Many of the services formerly performed by small entrepreneurs are now carried out by larger units of production and marketing. Movement from a small business to a larger enterprise usually means some loss of personal freedom. For those who were part of a work group, these changes contribute to the loss of a sense of group purpose about work and of group solidarity.

Replacement of Losses

Affiliation with an organization in which a person works seems to have become a major device for coping with the problems resulting from these economic, social, and psychological changes. Organizations have recognized and fostered the desire of employees to seek financial security in the organization by means of long service. Seniority advantages in union contracts, vested rights in pension funds, and promotion within a given organization rather than upward movement from one business to another have encouraged long-term affiliation with one organization. Indeed, often a man enters a work organization before he marries and remains in it long after his grandchildren are grown.

Instead of a geographical orienting point, many now have an organizational orienting point. They identify themselves with an organization—whether a company, church, university, or government department. In a man's movement from one neighborhood or community to another, the work organization is his thread of continuity and may well become a psychological anchor point for him.

Frequently his social friendships arise from his work associations. Old Navy men have long had a ready bond for friendship, and two strangers who work for IBM are already likely to have much in common. In the course of some research on mental health in utilities companies, it was found that a number of men who had moved from one electric generating station to another in the same company would frequently drive long distances on their days off to visit their old work buddies. They did not mention visiting others in their old communities.

It is not unusual for the company, both by means of its staff services and the personal interest of an employee's associates and superiors, to come to the assistance of a person in emergency circumstances. The "kitty" for emergencies is a ubiquitous phenomenon in organizations, whether raised by contributions or profits from coin machines. Fellow workers mobilize for blood transfusions as well as money, and in some instances the organization continues a man's salary beyond sick-leave provisions until he can return to work. When a man's fellow workers mobilize to help him, this support is seen by the recipient as the personal giving by good friends because of their common interest as organizational members.

If technical change eliminates a man's job, the company will often retrain him, thereby helping him to cope with the change and assuring him of long-term job security. Recent contractual innovations in the steel industry provide for cushions against job displacement as a result of technological obsolescence. Organizations recognize some obligation to help their employees, particularly those of long service, to cope with change.

In the past a man was introduced to others by his name or by identifying him with his trade. Today he is identified not merely as John Smith, but John Smith, foreman in the Midland Utilities Company, or more simply as being "with Midland Utilities." And mostly he will identify himself the same way. Together with the movement from small businesses to large organizations, this means relatively less recognition of the individual as an individual and relatively more recognition of the individual as part of an organization. It gives added weight to the importance of the relationship between a man and his work organization for gaining social power. Within that relationship, however, the individual seeks increasing individual recognition, consideration, and responsibility (McGregor, 1960; Likert, 1961), and looks to support from his supervisor to obtain them (Mann and Hoffman, 1960).

Affiliation seems to be as important to executives as it is to people on hourly wages. A far larger number of graduates of business schools go into companies than start their own businesses. A 1963 Bureau of the Census report indicates that salaried men now outnumber self-employed professional and businessmen in the income bracket that includes the top 5 percent of the earning population. Managers and salaried professionals, according to the report, account for half of these, whereas the self-employed number only one-fourth. These figures are a reversal of those of 1950 and reflect the growth of corporations and the increasing number of executives in them. Moreover, executives have social and economic influence only as long as they hold positions in organizations. This is one reason many give for not wanting to retire, for to retire means, as they put it, to become a "nobody."

Reinforcement of Defenses

Organizations have important social functions to perform: they produce goods or render services; they also provide the means for people to earn a livelihood. These are fundamental functions of organizations, and it is because these functions are basic that organizations become important psychological devices as well.

Jaques (1955) has observed that, in addition to serving the many economic, social, and psychological purposes already referred to, organizations reinforce individual defenses against unconscious anxiety. In this he follows Melanie Klein's (1935) conception that infants respond to early frustration by experiencing the outside world as hostile and potentially harmful. She calls the two kinds of resulting anxiety paranoid and depressive.

Jaques (1955) suggests that as people grow up, they are on guard against the recurrence of these anxieties and use social institutions as modes of warding them off. For example, dividing people into good and bad, commonly observed in clinical practice, is one way of handling paranoid anxiety. The "bad" impulses of people in an organization may thereupon be projected onto a "bad" figure or figures. Jaques calls attention to the way in which the first officer of a ship is commonly regarded by the crew as the source of all trouble, permitting the men to idealize the captain and identify themselves with him. There is often a similar polarity in the army between the executive officer and the commanding officer or "old man." Industrial psychologists will recognize key figures in other divisions of a company who are seen as the bad ones who cause all the problems.

Depressive anxieties can be dealt with by identifying with an organization which "does good" and by working hard at its activities, thus relieving guilt feelings. After the 1938 hurricane that devastated New England, employees of a major public utility came from many parts of the country to work long hours under dangerous conditions in unfamiliar territory to restore service. In their six weeks of intensive work there was not one accident. The work in itself was sufficiently guilt-relieving that accidents did not occur.

Whether one agrees with the specifics of Jaques' hypothesis about paranoid and depressive anxiety is of little consequence for this discussion. The point is that relating personality variables to organizational problems makes it possible systematically to inter-relate morale, motivation, leadership, and most of the other concerns of industrial psychology.

Transference

The question might arise, "How can you speak of man-organization relationships?" An organization is created as a legal fiction which meets certain requirements and has certain capacities, but, as Peter Drucker (1954) argues, it has no life of its own apart from people.

One can speak of man-organization relationships, first, because phenomena with typical features of transference can be observed; second, because many employees in their relationships with other people, act as agents of the organization. Transference means unconsciously bringing past attitudes, impulses, wishes, and expectations (particularly those usually experienced toward powerful parental figures), in exaggerated form into present situations, whether in or out of the consulting room, as shown by Freud (1912), Fenichel (1945), Hendrick (1958) and Anna Freud (1946). Transference phenomena occur constantly in everyday life. It occurs with respect to organizations and institutions just as it occurs with individuals; that is, people project upon organizations human qualities and then relate to them as if the organizations did in fact have human qualities. They generalize from their feelings about people in the organization who are important to them to the organization as a whole, as well as extrapolating from those attitudes they bring to the organization. Transference makes it possible to use a hospital as a therapeutic device simply because patients believe it to have therapeutic powers.

Selznick (1957) argues that organizations quickly become invested with psychological meaning for their members. Organizations could not endure for very long if this did not happen. Simmel (1929) discussing the management of a psychiatric hospital, spoke of creating "a positive attachment to the institution as such . . . so that the patient may be thus secure of a firm foundation. . ." [p. 78]. Reider (1953) reported that patients maintained ties to the psychiatric outpatient clinic rather than to the therapists who treated them. He said that "as soon as a medical institution achieves a reputation, it is a sign that an idealization and condensation of the magical power and the benevolent greatness of parental figures have been posited in the institution. . . . The phenomenon is widespread and *touches upon every type of institution which has any characteristics of benevolence* (italics mine)" [p. 60]. Reider sees such transference as a way of dealing with reality by participating in a great organization.

Wilmer (1962) speaking of transference to a medical center as a cultural dimension in healing, points out that, "One cannot understand staff-patient relationships in any institution without an appreciation of this important psychologic, social and, particularly cultural dimension of its healing powers. Physicians, just as patients, are enmeshed in transference feelings toward the institution. . ." [p. 173]. He adds that the institution can stand as the symbolic parental surrogate, and the positive or negative attitudes of the person toward the institution may well be, in part at least, transference reactions.

Transference is not new in relationships with other institutions. In this country some men seek to enroll their sons in their *alma maters* as soon as they are born. In England there is a similar attitude toward some clubs. In both countries some men look upon the Army as others would upon their college or club.

Describing the elements of an institution that contribute to transference feelings, Wilmer observes that a medical center is a great institution which occupies many large and impressive buildings and has certain institutional rites of introduction, examination, and treatment, which gratify the dependent and narcissistic needs of patients. The personality of the physician is endowed with the power of the center. The institution endures beyond and transcends the individuals who work there. The more famous the institution the greater the anonymity of the individuals representing it. "The very name of the institution is a cherished and sacred title, a powerful symbol to which much transference

feeling is attached." Then Wilmer adds a critical element: "It is
in *affiliation*—to take a son—that the whole phenomenon of transference to a center takes on new meaning and new members"
[p. 179].

The modern organization has some of the benevolent characteristics Reider discusses. It is a medium for recouping psychological losses in a rapidly changing society. Moreover, the
actions of individual people in an organization are viewed by
them, by the objects of the action, and by observers, as actions
of the organization. For example, if a local manager of Midland
Utilities cuts off someone's service for nonpayment, that action
is seen as the company cutting off the service. There are many
reasons why this should be so.

1. The organization is legally, morally, and financially responsible for the actions of its members as organizational agents.

2. The organization has policies which make for great similarity
in behavior by agents of the organization at different times and
in different geographical locations.

3. These policies are supplemented by precedents, traditions,
and informal norms as guides to behavior.

4. In many instances the action by the agent is a role performance with many common characteristics throughout that organization regardless of who carries it out; for example, the
personnel officer.

5. Selection processes in an organization tend to result in the
clustering of people whose personality structures have much in
common and who would therefore tend to act along some personality dimensions in the same general way. These factors result
in what is sometimes referred to as a "corporate personality," a
generalized mode of behavior on the part of employees in a given
company, recognized by others both in and out of the organization, which supports continuity of characteristic relations with the
organization.

6. There tends to be a consensus of perception of a given
employee by others in an organization as a result of discussions
among one another about their experiences with the man and

their review of his actions. This is particularly true if there are systematic appraisals in the organization.

7. As a legal and group entity, the organization has power independent of that of its agents. Often it also has financial and other resources which can be used on behalf of employees. The organization's capacity for aggressive and benevolent power can be perceived by its members, particularly when it is used either against employees or to support them in emergency situations.

8. It is often difficult for an employee to know who in the organization has done what to him. People speak of an undifferentiated "they" who make decisions and take action. Vague organization policy allows fantasies to come out.

9. Those who act within the power structure can often rationalize transference feelings that they act out. The boss who complains that his subordinates are too dependent may be treating them as children, using the product of his behavior as a rationale for continuing it. Another might justify his sadistic behavior with the familiar, "It hurts me more than it hurts you."

In *The Devils of Loudun*, Aldous Huxley (1952) states:

> But partisanship is a complex passion which permits those who indulge in it to make the best of both worlds. Because they do these things for the sake of a group which is, by definition, good and even sacred, they can admire themselves and loathe their neighbours, they can seek power and money, can enjoy the pleasures of aggression and cruelty, not merely without feeling guilty, but with the positive glow of conscious virtue. Loyalty to their group transforms these pleasant vices into acts of heroism [p. 23].

It was this thesis that permitted men of the church to torture a victim to death, all the while crying, 'Dicas' (Confess). Huxley adds:

> When Grandier criticized the monks of Loudun, it was, we may be sure, with a sense of righteous zeal, a consciousness of doing God's work. For God, it went without saying, was on the side of the secular clergy and of Grandier's good friends, the Jesuits [p. 24].

The generalized mode of behavior characteristic of organizational agents as they act on behalf of the organization, together
with the demonstration of the organization's power, make it possible for transference phenomena to occur which give the organization a psychological reality in the experience of the individual
members.

Transference from Organization to Employee

The very phenomena which are the necessary conditions for
the existence of transference phenomena in one direction also
make for transference in the other. Those who act on behalf of
the institution or organization have power and use their power
in the manner of parental surrogates, according to the folkways
of the organization. The purpose of a mental hospital, for example,
is to help patients get well. If a patient does not improve, the
staff may reject him. In a typical state hospital, he is consigned
to the back wards. In a more enlightened institution, the rejection
takes place informally, as happened in one short-term treatment
center on the West Coast, which admitted only acutely ill patients
and placed heavy emphasis on psychotherapy. The physicians,
who were serving their residency in psychiatry, clipped informal
notes to the log book for the officer of the day. Each resident was
officer of the day in turn, and the officer of the day was also the
admitting officer, so each had before him the notes of all the
others. These unofficial notes emphatically instructed the officer
of the day not to readmit certain patients who, in their judgement,
would not profit from treatment. As apprentice psychiatrists, they
naturally preferred to work with those patients who would be
most responsive to their efforts. Economics alone would make
this a reasonable point of view. This, however, does not explain
their strong feeling about those whom they were not able to help
and the indirect way they chose to keep them away, even when
the hospital had no formal policy of rejections.

In industry, there is a similar phenomenon. The management
of a major heavy manufacturing industry, for example, believes

that employees should want nothing from their jobs except their salaries. It complains that though it pays its people relatively well, they do not understand that the stockholders need a return on their money, and they keep demanding higher wages. "Look at all that we give them in fringe benefits," the management says, "Look how good we are to them. Why don't they understand our point of view and not keep demanding more money?" The parallel between this attitude and that of many parents is obvious. The industrial culture is replete with such examples.

In these illustrations of transference, those who have power in the organization perceive the individual as a member of the organizational family and react to him as such. Although an employee may be a complete stranger in the personal sense to other persons in the organization, at the very least, what the person does reflects on the organization and its members. The underlying reason for the appearance of transference phenomena from the organization to the person is the importance of the person to others in the organization, who, taken together comprise the organization as it relates to the person.

The relationship is important to the organization because the major concern of the top management of most business organizations is not today's profitability, though that is important, but the long-term survival of the organization. With larger capital investments that must be amortized over longer periods of time and with an emphasis on organizational growth and creative innovation as a means of surviving in a competitive economy, corporate managements encourage personnel to remain in the company. Their permanence will presumably make for greater loyalty, productivity, and willingness to assume increasing responsibility, and their psychological investment will make for greater creativity. Legal decisions relating to workmen's compensation and labor relations, pressures from labor unions, and concern about the company's public image, all tend to foster company interest in the individual, transcending the interest of any given management group. There is, in addition, a growing sense of social responsibility on the part of business executives,

partly because today's business leaders have higher levels of education than their predecessors, and partly because the corporation recognizes that it cannot afford to be irresponsible. Taken
together, these forces make the man-organization relationship
highly important to the organization.

In brief, the man-organization relationship is important to the
person because it meets certain needs; in addition, he uses the
organization to replace certain psychological losses, to reinforce
his psychological defenses, and to serve as a major object of transference. The relationship is important to people who comprise
the organization because of reverse transference phenomena toward organizational members, and because of the need for the
organization to survive.

Relation of Unions to the Man-Organization Relationship

Just as in the family, however, the relationship is not a simple
two-party one. It is not without good psychological reason that
one speaks of paternalism in industry, and that some companies
are referred to by their employees as "Mother (name of company)," and that companies called "Mother" by their employees
are benign and kindly and have either no union or a relatively
non-militant union. In fact, some of the kindliness of the organization is an effort to head off unionization. This tells something
about one psychological meaning of the union, namely its mothering function, which Purcell's (1953) dual-loyalty studies have
pointed up. Purcell notes that employees expect the union to
protect them and obtain security provisions for them; whereas
they look to management to run the business, and feel loyalty to
management for doing so.

When the union plays its mothering function well, it enhances
the employees' relationship to the organization. A good example
is the way in which the Scanlon Plan (Lesieur, 1958) conceived
by a union leader, involved employees in the survival efforts of
a company and saved the company from failure. This plan, incidentally, is the basis for the present Kaiser Steel pact. When the

union does not serve this function well, however, it either in-
adequately replaces the organization or deprives the worker of
significant psychological ties to his work.

Some of the major industrial unions are examples of the first
problem. They are highly militant, define the company as an
exploitative enemy, and, with unwitting cooperation from a too-
aggressive management, encourage the worker to identify with
them. Unions whose members are hired from their hiring halls
deprive their members of psychological ties to their work. Without a consistent relationship to any single producing organization,
most of these men work primarily for immediate monetary return
and do not have much interest in their work. They are among
those much criticized for featherbedding, for failing to use their
skills to produce high-quality work, and for their seemingly ex-
orbitant wage demands.

But even under the best of circumstances, the union cannot
provide the worker with the gratification that ideally he could and
should be getting from his work (Herzberg et al., 1959) because
the union does not manage productive processes. This discussion
is not to be construed as an argument against unions. Rather, it
illuminates some of the psychological meaning of the union and
the ways in which union-management relations can affect man-
organization relationships.

THE CONCEPT OF RECIPROCATION

Examination of some of the psychological meanings of the
man-organization relationship should make it possible to refine
the concept so as to contribute to the development of research
and to begin to integrate intrapersonal concepts with those of
industrial psychology.

The concepts of identification, transference, and psychological
defense, drawn from the literature of clinical psychology and psychiatry, were evolved to organize experiences going on psychologically within the person. They therefore have limitations when
extended beyond their original limits. Identification and trans-

ference account for only one side of a dual relationship, for only part of a process, referring to one person or group at a time, not to interaction. Identification already has a variety of meanings. No only did Freud (1921) use the concept in many different ways but others, such as Becker and Carper (1956), Bronfenbrenner (1960), and Sanford (1955), have added connotations. What is needed then, is a concept which encompasses a continuous two-way process, which can incorporate and accommodate other concepts, and which is not colored by previous connotations.

In a study of mental health in industry (Levinson et al., 1962), it was apparent that transference phenomena and people's efforts to fulfill various psychological needs in their relationship with a company arose out of efforts, by both parties, to fulfill expectations (only part of which were conscious). This process of fulfilling mutual expectations and satisfying mutual needs in the relationship between a man and his work organization was conceptualized as a process of *reciprocation*. Viewed another way, it is the process of carrying out a psychological contract (Menninger, 1958) between person and organization. It is a complementary process in which the person and the organization seem to become a part of each other. The person feels that he is part of the corporation or institution, and, at the same time, that he is a symbol standing for the whole organization. That is, he sees himself and is seen by others who are not fellow employees as the company personified. The public image of the organization is displaced onto the person and vice versa.

For example, a middle-management man in a medium-sized company, perhaps unknowingly speaking for all middle-management men, said, "After all, in this locale I *am* the company. Anything I say reflects back on the company." Another man at the same level in the same company observed, "You can't divorce your position from yourself. Various social groups catalogue you." He then enumerated the community activities and specific jobs within these activities which he had been asked to assume because he was a manager in his particular company. A foreman in the same organization had a similar experience, as do many line employees. "In your neighborhood, you are the company. The neighbors think if you weren't the right sort of a fellow, you wouldn't be with them. Most people think our salaries are above average, so you have to keep your place looking halfway decent, and your kids in shoes."

If reciprocation is a continuous process of fulfilling mutual expectations, of carrying out a psychological contract, and thereby, of enhancing the man-organization relationship, how can it contribute to integrating many of the heretofore disparate areas of industrial psychology?

FUNCTIONS OF RECIPROCATION

Reciprocation facilitates the maintenance of psychological equilibrium (defense), psychological growth, and the mastery of a part of one's world.

Defense

It is relatively easy to see defensive phenomena and how the organization may support the individual under stress. It is not so easy to see how the individual supports the organization under similar circumstances. An example would be the spontaneous mobilization of employees to help a public utility company keep its franchise in a community, though the employees would have no difficulty obtaining other jobs if the company lost its franchise.

Better understanding of defensive needs and the ways in which they shape the meaning of work and the work organization for the individual could be the basis for further development of aptitude, interest, and value inventories. In turn, also, a comprehensive theoretical basis for aptitude and interest studies would make it possible to relate them to studies of motivation and morale, making possible a better understanding of morale and defining it with greater precision. This conceivably could help us avoid such inadequate studies of morale as those reported by Brayfield and Crockett (1955).

Growth

Reciprocation fosters psychological growth in several ways. When the organization is functioning well, and the person feels an integral part of it, he is identifying with his superiors. This means that he is making some of their skills, experiences, points of view, and knowledge a part of himself. By making multiple identifications and reorganizing them in keeping with his own personality structure, a person grows more skilled and occupationally mature (Adelson, 1961).

When there is reciprocation, a man receives guidance from his superiors. If one interviews executives about their work, most will spontaneously mention some older person in an organization who took a special interest in him and "was like a father to me." Rarely do first-level workers spontaneously make the same comment, suggesting that the guidance of an experienced superior can make a difference in career progress.

Reciprocation opens up opportunities; for where the relationship between a man and organization is a good one, he is far more likely to move to greater responsibility than if reciprocation is not being fulfilled. Drucker (1954) cites the different degrees of progress made by comparable young management trainees in two different parts of the Sears organization where the psychological contract was fulfilled differently.

The organization also contributes to the growth of the person by the demands it makes upon him which stimulate him to new learning. Technical changes, new problems to surmount, and the changing functions of the organization all stimulate the person to grow.

The growth of the person contributes to the character of the organization. A man may identify himself with his superiors, but he also brings something of his own personality to the organization. As he grows more experienced, others will identify themselves with him. He leaves something of himself in the organization and thereby contributes to its growth.

The organization is stimulated to growth by the collective demands of its employees, which may force it to greater efficiency, as in the coal industry; by the determination of its employees to take on new challenges as in the Scanlon Plan (Lesieur, 1958) and by the behavior of its employees as they seek to use the organization for their own psychological needs. The contemporary trend toward more flexible and innovative management stems in part from the increasing rejection by employees of autocratic leadership.

These facets of the occupational growth of the individual are important considerations for management development, for supervisory training, for leadership selection, and for evaluation and appraisal. Too little attention has been given to the psychological values of the teaching functions in industrial leadership. Reciprocation makes it an imperative function of the executive. Management development activities cannot therefore be simply relegated to the training department (Levinson, 1962). With a *psychological* conception of the man-organization relationship, a psychologist's contributions are significant; with only an economic conception, they can have only a marginal purpose.

Mastery

Besides the psychological task of maintaining the equilibrium of ego-id-superego forces in their interaction with the environment, a person has the task of mastering enough of his world so that he can survive in it. His job is a major way of attaining and maintaining that mastery. Work that serves all of these purposes might be looked upon as creative adaptation.

When channels for constructive mastery of the organization are inadequate, efforts may be directed toward indirect controls. For example, one company supplied its men with new shovels of a type they did not like. These inadvertently were left in the field, run over by trucks, or disposed of in other ways. After that the men were consulted on the tools they wanted. Another group of men, dissatisfied with their manager's failure to obtain better physical facilities for their equipment repair shop, managed to collect enough surplus paint and other items to refurbish their shop, to the chagrin and embarrassment of higher management. Every company knows the problem of subtle empire building, and the *fait accompli* which commits the organization to actions never intended by official policy formulations. That people in organizations resist change and avoid responsibility by means of passive resistance is widely recognized.

Considerable attention has been given to mastery of the job with various forms of psychological engineering studies, achievement and performance measures, and appraisal practices. Herzberg and his colleagues (1959) in particular have shown how important it is to the employee to master his work. But with reciprocation, an important part of mastering the job is to master a part of the organization.

That the organization tries to make itself the master of the man is a problem that has been the focus of much recent research. The company requires that task demands be fulfilled, that some people accept the direction of other people. It also controls the ways in which people may behave on the job by how it allocates financial and production resources. It may even require certain off-job behaviors. The men who spoke of how they were expected to behave at home because they were employees of the company were not told they had to behave that way, yet they felt obligated to do so. Employees are not usually told they must believe in the free enterprise system, or that they must give to the United Fund, but there are powerful informal forces in the organization which influence them to do both.

While some people deplore the fact that the organization to some extent shapes the man, in reciprocation it is inevitable and not always undesirable; for the shaping can contribute to his growth. Moreover, the man is not merely a Galatea in the hands of an industrial Pygmalion; reciprocally he makes demands, too. If the organization does not meet his needs he can leave it. No department wants to be known for having high turnover or absenteeism. Work groups establish informal production norms and frequently control work processes and thereby production schedules, profitability, and other factors that presumably are under the control of management, as Whyte (1955) and Mechanic (1963) have shown. The ultimate direct-control technique of the employee is the strike. In some instances, the employee clearly exploits the organization and in effect forces it to adopt certain formal courses in its own defense. In other instances, as in the Scanlon Plan companies, employees have a more direct influence on shaping organizational processes and products.

SUMMARY

In reciprocation, each partner shapes the other to some extent. When one speaks of the alienation of the employee from his work in industry, one usually means that the employee does not feel he is making an impact on the organization (Pearlin, 1962). Conversely, if the organization feels it has little possibility of shaping the employee, that it is pretty much at his mercy, then organization leadership takes a hostile view of him, as is so common in the construction industry.

This mutual shaping of each party by the other is examined in detail from a sociological point of view by Bakke (1953). Taking role theory as his point of departure, he comes to similar conclusions. He describes the interaction of man and organization as the "fusion process." Other role theory formulations account for specific job behaviors as the result of the person's place in the formal structure of the organization. Such formulations, when they also allow for psychodynamics and the effect of the person on the role, as in the work of W. E. Henry (1948) and Daniel Levinson (1959) can be integrated into the concept of reciprocation.

If reciprocation facilitates the operation of psychological defenses, growth, and mastery in the individual, and if it contributes to similar processes in the organization, then it should have a significant relationship to the mental health of the employee and to the effective functioning of the organization. When the process is operating well, the employee obtains psychological support and stimulation to psychological growth from the organization. He has a contributing responsible role in the company and a continuing

opportunity for personal development. The company has his cohesive support and his creative investment in the organization's
tasks, therefore it gains the potential for both growth and survival.
When reciprocation between the two is inadequate, both man
and organization suffer.

REFERENCES

Adelson, J. (1961), The Teacher as a Model. *American Scholar*, 30:383-406.
Argyris, C. (1957), *Personality and Organization*. New York: Harper.
Bakke, E. W. (1953), *The Fusion Process*. New Haven: Labor and Management Center,
     Yale University.
Becker, H. S., & Carper, J. W. (1956), The Development of Identification with an Oc-
     cupation. *Amer. J. Sociol.*, 61:280-298.
Brayfield, A. H., & Crockett, W. H. (1955), Employee Attitudes and Employee Perfor-
     mance. *Psychol. Bull.*, 52:396-424.
Bronfenbrenner, U. (1960), Freudian Theories of Identification and Their Derivatives.
     Child Devel., 31:15-40.
Drucker, P. (1954), *The Practice of Management*. New York: Harper.
Dunnette, M. D., & Bass, B. (1963), Behavioral Scientists and Personnel Management.
     Industrial Relations, 2:115-130.
Fenichel, O. (1945), *The Psychoanalytic Theory of the Neuroses*. New York: Norton.
Freud, A. (1946), *The Ego and the Mechanisms of Defense*. New York: International
     Universities Press.
Freud, S. (1912), The Dynamics of the Transference. *Standard Edition*, 12:97-108. Lon-
     don: Hogarth Press, 1958.
——— (1921), Group Psychology and the Analysis of the Ego. *Standard Edition*, 18:65-
     143. London: Hogarth Press, 1955.
Gill, M. M. (1959), The Present State of Psychoanalytic Theory. *J. Abnorm. Soc. Psychol.*,
     58:1-8.
Henry, W. E. (1948), Executive Personality and Job Success. *Personnel Series*, No. 120.
     New York: American Management Association.
Hendrick, I. (1958), *Facts and Theories of Psychoanalysis*, 3rd Ed. New York: Knopf.
Herzberg, F., Mausner, B., & Synderman, B. (1959), *The Motivation to Work*. New York:
     Wiley.
Huxley, A. (1952), *The Devils of Loudun*. New York: Harper.
Jaques, E. (1955), Social Systems as a Defense Against Persecutory and Depressive Anx-
     iety. In: *New Directions in Psychoanalysis*, ed. M. Klein et al. New York: Basic
     Books.
Jennings, E. F. (1962), *The Executive: Autocrat, Bureaucrat, Democrat*. New York: Har-
     per.
Klein, M. (1935), A Contribution to the Psychogenesis of Manic-Depressive States. In:
     Contributions to Psychoanalysis, 1921-1945. London: Hogarth Press, 1948.
Lesieur, F. G. (1958), *The Scanlon Plan*. New York: Wiley.
Levinson, D. (1959), Role, Personality and Social Structure in the Organizational Setting.
     J. Abnorm. Soc. Psychol., 58:170-180.
Levinson, H. (1962), A Psychologist Looks at Executive Development. *Harvard Business
     Review*, 40:69-75.

————, Price, C. R., Munden, K. J., Mandi, H. J., & Solley, C. M. (1962), *Men, Management, and Mental Health*. Cambridge, Mass.: Harvard University Press.

Likert, R. (1961), *New Patterns of Management*. New York: McGraw-Hill.

Mann, F., & Hoffman, R. (1960), *Automation and the Worker*. New York: Holt & Dryden.

McGregor, D. (1960), *The Human Side of Enterprise*. New York: McGraw-Hill.

McMurray, R. N. (1952), The Executive Neurosis. *Harvard Business Review*, 30:33-47.

Mechanic, D. (1963), The Power to Resist Change Among Low-Ranking Personnel. *Personnel Administration*, 26:5-11.

Menninger, K. (1958), *Theory of Psychoanalytic Technique*. New York: Basic Books.

Michael, D. N. (1962), *Cybernation: The Silent Conquest*. Santa Barbara: Center for the Study of Democratic Institutions.

Pearlin, L. I. (1962), Alienation from Work: A Study of Nursing Personnel. *Amer. Sociol. Rev.*, 27:314-326.

Pederson-Krag, G. (1955), *Personality Factors in Work and Employment*. New York: Funk & Wagnalls.

Purcell, T. (1953), *The Worker Speaks His Mind on Company and Union*. Cambridge, Mass.: Harvard University Press.

Reider, N. (1953), Transference to Institutions. *Bull. Menn. Clin.*, 17:58-63.

Sanford, N. (1955), The Dynamics of Identification. *Psychol. Rev.*, 62:106-118.

Selznick, P. (1957), *Leadership in Administration*. New York: Row, Peterson.

Simmel, E. (1929), Psychoanalytic Treatment in a Sanitarium. *Internat. J. Psycho-Anal.*, 10:70-89.

Whyte, W. F. (1955), *Money and Motivation*. New York: Harper.

Wilmer, H. A. (1962), Transference to a Medical Center. *Cal. Med.*, 96:173-180.

Zaleznik and Kets de Vries contend that executive action cannot be treated simply as an attribute of structure, but must be considered as an outcome of the individual's behavior within a structure. An individual's effect on the organization is determined by distribution of authority, management control, and by the use of power. They illustrate this view by examining the leadership styles of several political and business leaders, arguing that a psychopolitical approach to executive action is the problem of the person-position encounter, and that it relates to both structural and personality variables.

14

Leadership and Executive Action

ABRAHAM ZALEZNIK AND MANFRED F. R. KETS DE VRIES

A man who wishes to make a profession of goodness in everything must necessarily come to grief among so many who are not good. Therefore, it is necessary for a prince, who wishes to maintain himself, to learn how not to be good, and to use this knowledge and not use it, according to the necessity of the case. . . .

—*Niccolò Machiavelli*

The critical ingredient in Machiavelli's prescription for leadership is the discernment of the "necessity of the case." What complicates matters is the fact that the case cannot be isolated from the character of the leader. Inevitably, his vision or blind spots determine the limits of his actions. So the proper object of the study of leadership is the individual in a situation—the "case,"

This chapter originally appeared in *Power and the Corporate Mind* by Abraham Zaleznik and Manfred F. R. Kets de Vries, Copyright © 1975 by Abraham Zaleznik and Manfred F. R. Kets de Vries. Reprinted by permission of Houghton Mifflin Company.

so to speak. The case also includes the people close to the leader, people who offer or withhold advice based on their position and personality. In the words of Homans (1964), the need in the analysis of organizations is "to bring man back in." Man has been left out in the interests of clarifying structure and process, which has led some to attribute more to the powers of rationality than experience warrants.

An analysis of leadership must concern itself more with individual action in human situations than with structure in relation to impersonal forces. It is true that there are impersonal factors that seem to put pressure on people to act in selected ways. But if the key to initiative lies in the experience of forces outside persons, that judgment is sustained by insight. Insight blends the external and objective with self-knowledge, so the personal strengths and weaknesses of the leader enter the case realistically.

There are three problems, common to all organizations, that test definitions of what is impersonal and personal in executive action. The first is the decision to organize, which establishes the formal structure and distributes authority. The second is control—the regulation of behavior and the willingness of people to meet expectations. The third is action itself—the crucial meeting of man and situation where, for whatever reasons, leaders decide to commit themselves to certain alternatives and to exclude others. These problems appear and reappear in organizations, reflecting the tensions between individual interests, and the needs and demands of other people and the organization. Machiavelli's "necessity of the case" governs when executives face issues of organizing, controlling the actions of others, and becoming personally involved in weighing options and making decisions.

THE DISTRIBUTION OF AUTHORITY

Directing an organization means that one must arrive at some basis for allocating authority so that relative power is proportional to responsibility and competence. Any allocation must meet two criteria: first, the allocation must be rational, and second, the allocation must be just. Rationality means that the distribution of authority is consistent with the goals and objectives of the organization and that resources are used economically. A sense of justice and equity in the distribution of authority is a condition of cooperation; authority and its uses will then be seen as legitimate and worthy of commitment and work.

Although rationality and justice may appear, in principle, absolute, ambiguities arise in their implementation. People will often spend hours improving the criteria upon which rational decisions are supposedly made, while ignoring the conflict inherent in converting abstract principles into concrete action. There are practical limitations to pure rationality and justice; if there were not, decisions concerning the allocation of authority could be programmed for a computer as a simple problem: producing the greatest output from the least input of human effort.

The limitations to rationality in the establishment of an organizational structure are imposed by several factors. First, the distribution of authority is only in part a quantitative problem (that is, how much authority to allocate among the various levels in a hierarchy). The quality of authority figures is also an important part of the problem.

We can thank Weber (1947) for his theoretical formulations on authority and bureaucracy, which outlined the types of authority existing in organizations. He discusses three types: traditional, legal, and charismatic.

Traditional authority, Weber says, is based on historical precedents that sanction certain individuals by birth and succession to the rights and responsibilities in governing. Implicit in traditional authority is the extrarational basis on which custom and prerogative depend. By contrast, legal authority formally prescribes the rights of individuals occupying positions in the structure to issue commands. The formal rights and obligations can be found in such documents as the Constitution of the United States. Other forms of legal authority exist in the charters of corporations and in their bylaws. These documents specify offices, powers, rules of tenure, methods of selection, and, perhaps most important, the means by which modifications may be made in the structure of legal authority (in the form of amendments, additions, and deletions to the bylaws).

The third type of authority in Weber's scheme is charismatic. Some individuals have authority, that is, the ability to influence by the nature of their personality, which seems to project a kind of spiritual or inspired leadership. Great mystics, religious leaders, and political leaders exert influence by the force of their personality. For example, Rasputin had an enormous influence in the court of the last Russian tsar because of his emotional hold over the tsarina and the hope he proffered for the cure of her hemophiliac son. The emotional basis of charisma is a subject to which we shall often return, especially since the interaction of charisma and legal or traditional authority is of special interest in modern organizations. For the present, we can refer to Freud's study "Group Psychology and the Analysis of the Ego" (1921), in which he likened the charismatic effect to the primary emotional ties of the child to the parent.

Weber's work on authority and bureaucracy provided a framework for the analysis of modern organizations, which are products of such broad technological, economic, and political forces as the Industrial Revolution, the stabilization of the nation-state, and the separation of ownership and management in large-scale enterprise. As with other theories based on ideal types, Weber's analysis spawned a generation of studies that showed how far from reality were the ideal types of bureaucracy. In Weber's ideal bureaucracy, legitimacy and acceptance of authority rested on the clear relationship of organizational resources to explicit objectives (rationality), and on the enforcement of rules designed to overcome the tyranny of men's passions and ambitions. Rationality and justice are, indeed, ideals; but, as a generation of researchers showed, the real world falls short of the ideal. The best people are not necessarily selected to exercise authority, and, instead of assuring equity, rules dominate bureaucracies and weaken the capacity of men to perform.

Any discussion of the rules for the allocation and exercise of authority does not account for motivations that bind people in authority relationships. The need for dependency, a human need seldom acknowledged in employment contracts, is characteristic to some degree of persons at work in all levels of the hierarchy. Dependency needs may be expressed in the desire for approval and for close relations with an authority figure, or in the wish to have satisfying relations with equals.

Departures from ideal bureaucracy also result from the complexity and specialization of work roles in modern organizations, which has led to the recognition of professional authority or expertise as a basis for power and influence in organizations. Professional authority differs from hierarchical or positional authority because it is based on the applications of expert knowledge to the work of the organization. As Selznick (1949) has shown in his study of the Tennessee Valley Authority, those who use knowledge and skill rather than hierarchical position for influence tend to develop their own goals and to seek independence from the dominant authority structure. It is a small step from independence to competition; one can view an organization as an arena for internal competition as well as for cooperation.

The culture of professional authority favors equality over hierarchy, and builds on the notion of a "flat," "organic" organization structure. The number of authority levels between the top and the bottom of the organization are fewer in flat as compared with pyramidal, "mechanistic" structures, which are built on the principle of chain of command—a rational principle derived from an optimal number of subordinates who can report to one executive. Lateral communication is emphasized, as is the use of committees and ad hoc work groups or task forces with rotating membership. The ideals of an egalitarian culture are flexible leadership and functional influence, in which the type of leadership a group needs, depending upon its task and emotional problems, comes from appropriate members, regardless of their hierarchical position and of the formal lines of authority. Indeed, leadership, especially of the type vested in position, becomes ambiguous, if not blunted, and there is a reduction of the social distance that exists in pyramids, with their clearly delineated status differences from level to level in the organization.

This brings us to another motivational constraint in the operation of different systems of authority. Social distance and status differences tend to produce anxiety—the fear of isolation felt by the leader, and the uncertainties of self-esteem suffered by the subordinate. The formation of informal groupings and cliques as a socially contrived means for buffering the effects of anxiety, counteracts the effects of social distance. To put the problem in another way, "love flees authority"; for many individuals, it is easier to get help from an equal than from a boss. Given the potential hazards of anxiety, especially when the nature of work requires interaction, informal groups and affiliations spring up to counterbalance the effects of hierarchy and its implications of evaluation, control, and damaged self-esteem.

The discovery (and rediscovery) of informal organization highlights the weaknesses of the various rationalistic models (including ideal-type bureaucracy) of organization and authority. An unfortunate result of the new awareness of informal organizations is the sense that they arise as a nonrational, if not irrational, response to authority. Informal structures may be irrational because they often oppose in form and content the explicit goals of the organization. But they may also be adaptive, since they siphon off tensions that, if allowed to build up, would soon impair the capacity of members to cooperate even minimally. The celebrated case of the workers on the assembly line in the Vega plant in Lordstown, Ohio, is a good case in point. The workers slowed down or refused to work, contrary to agreements in the collective bargaining contract, because the social structure—evidently—had no adaptive mechanisms to bring grievances to light and to resolve them; hence the only means available to the workers were slowdowns and strikes. The failure suggests the limitations of formal authority and rational organizational design as the sole regulator of human relations.

What the Lordstown phenomenon further suggests, an idea that is buttressed by the exquisite analysis in Crozier's study *The*

Bureaucratic Phenomenon (1964), is a broader concept of rationality in authority relations, incorporating the universal need for power and control as motives in the formation of groups in organizations. Instead of the individual's passive compliance with an organizational structure that establishes the distribution of authority, means can be developed for the active pursuit, whether by the individual or groups, to accumulate power for security and control. Man's striving for power may be a tactic of conservation, that is, a protection against encroachments, or it may be a competitive one, an expedient means for increasing the capacity to control and initiate. So organizations operate as political structures. Instead of authority as a means of using resources for organizational purposes, authority becomes a scarce commodity that individuals seek to obtain for their uses.

Jockeying for power often takes place in business firms when the decision must be made to centralize or decentralize authority. When an organization reaches the stage of growth at which it comprises several independent divisions, then the problem of centralization has to be faced. In the typical multidivisional company, the problem of distributing authority begins with the split between corporate and divisional management. The corporate organization is a superstaff, with responsibility for monitoring performance at the division level (the profit centers), approving budgets (operating and capital expenditures), financial planning, and long-range planning, including new ventures and acquisitions. There is line responsibility between the division heads and the corporate chief operating officer, but the latter cannot easily acquire the knowledge and intuitions necessary to monitor division activity closely. Moreover, the requirements of planning generally lead to the formation of a corporate staff made up of functional specialists. Or, if the corporation is large enough, there will be a new hierarchical position between the chief operating officer and the divisions, filled by a group president—a group consisting of a collection of profit centers, each with an operating head.

Because of the need for communication, both formal and informal, the division heads tend to create their own staffs to gather information and to prepare positions either in response to, or in anticipation of initiatives coming from corporate headquarters. The proliferation of staffs, each with its own authority base, tends to act on behalf of constituents within its own organization. The constituency relationship, in turn, fosters dependencies because of the sheer weight of communication that characterizes the carrying out of business in complex organizations. A structure arises, therefore, of countervailing power, which cannot be explained by conventional rationality. In fact, it may be useful to recognize the several levels where judgments about rationality may be made. First, there is rationality at the level of the total organization, where appraisals of the effective utilization of resources may be made. Second, rationality operates at the level of the group of individuals with a common responsibility or set of interests. Third, rationality exists at the level of the individual.

These three levels of rationality, often in conflict, exist simultaneously, which accounts for many serious problems in leadership. For example, in the problem of centralization and decentralization of authority, the existence of powerful corporate staffs is often a nonrational (and even irrational) response by chief executives to their anxiety, which is created by the need to control decisions at the group and even divisional level. The corporate staffs become the "training ground" for future group and divisional officers who, while responsible for profit centers, are also loyal to their benefactors in corporate management. Treading the mobility route of corporate staff from specialist to line positions may also erode the integrity of professional authority. There is a kind of corporate version of Gresham's law. That is to say, in organizations, hierarchical authority tends to drive out professional authority in direct relationship to the mobility of specialists from corporate staff to line jobs. The task, in theory at least, of rational decision making lies with the ideals of staff specialists. But as the specialists make their assessments of rationality at the group and individual level, the ideal often suffers and further obscures definitions of rationality of the total organization.

Conflicts in assessing rationality in the distribution of authority at the organization, group, and individual levels arise with seeming regularity when decisions are made about the establishment of a formal organization structure. Here, decisions concerning the centralization of functions affect the definition of initiatives and power at all levels of the organization. Besides these structural considerations, the formal organization also reflects the ideals of the chief executive and his staff. There will be new conflicts, for example, over the issues of democracy and participation on the one hand, and efficiency and control on the other. But the problems are seldom clear-cut; they are not free of internal power conflicts nor are they unaffected by the anxieties of the main actors in such corporate dramas.

There is now available an impressive array of studies involving the redistribution of authority by structural and ideological decisions. All of these studies involve the shift from pyramidal to flat organization structures, which are designed to shift the levels of decision making downward in the organization, and to secure wider participation and commitment from those who have increased authority. The ends sought are greater output and the improved quality of decisions. These ends speak to rationality at the level of the total organization. In conflict with this aim, however, is the underlying effect of such decisions in squeezing senior and middle management and reducing their power. Observations of such changes, both structural and ideological, call into question the motives of executives who initiate the moves. In a significant number of cases, there appears to be confusion between what is good for the organization and what is necessary for the chief executive and his staff (given the problems of developing confident relationships with people who, at the outset, are not dependent upon the chief executive exclusively for their power base and autonomy). The squeeze, although justified by bureaucratic rationalization (an intellectual defense of one's thoughts and actions), can be understood more fully through the language of rivalry, anxiety, and the other metaphors of power conflicts.

A decision to structure and distribute authority in formal or-

ganizations can be seen as an abstract event, an outcome of impersonal forces in which the logic of costs and benefits determines
the outcome. Nothing can be further from reality. How to organize
is seldom a one-time decision but rather a continuous evolution
that reflects, besides the "macro" forces of economics, technology,
and the marketplace, the "micro" forces of human personalities
that filter and define realities through conscious intentions and
unconscious conflict. The myth of formal organization and the
distribution of authority as a rational event dies hard. One reason
the myth persists is that executives in the midst of power moves
seldom evince interest in what is true; they are generally too busy
justifying and persuading instead of trying to understand or explain. There is, in fact, less interest in the "truth" and more in
rationalization than one would expect in this age of science.

People who manage organizations are less concerned with why
things happen than how they are to make things happen. They
tend to be concrete in their patterns of thinking, not abstract.
They prefer the "here and now" to the "there and then." Consequently, they seek to justify actions that they perceive, intuitively, as a means for persuading others to accept initiatives.
Persuasion all too often depends on the ability of the management
to obscure conflicting group and individual interests, especially
when individuals cannot negotiate conflicts of interest. The reason
so much time is devoted to persuasion, even though it might
obscure rather than clarify issues, is the desire to avoid the direct
and naked evidences of power. Power used directly is divisive,
subjecting the initiator to retaliatory measures. Therefore, the
tendency is to rationalize actions, to appeal to overriding common
interests, particularly in those decisions that affect the distribution
of authority and the balance of power in organizations.

MANAGEMENT CONTROL

One of the most important developments in managerial practice, still not fully articulated, is the concept that organizational
structure is only one of a number of ways to influence and control

behavior. This more balanced view suggests that authority should be distributed in harmony with specific purposes, technologies, individual motivations, work climates, and leadership styles. Flexibility, along with the capacity to adapt structure to new realities, overrides notions of optimal form, often at the expense of what Simon (1965) has called the traditional "proverbs" of organization structure. Instead of such relatively inflexible principles as "span of control" to guide organizational planning, notions of designing the organization to enhance the capacity for appraising performance and results have come to dominate present-day thinking.

Control systems and procedures, such as budgets and monthly profit-and-loss statements, would be ineffective without the structural means to pinpoint responsibility. Therefore, organizational structure is built upon performance, or "profit" and "cost" centers, each with a clearly designated head and his appropriate staff.

The idea of performance centers permits a wider choice of formal structures and, perhaps most important, greater latitude for an executive to develop a leadership style consistent with his personality, rather than with external imperatives which may constrain his behavior. For certain purposes, organizations may be "flattened", with many heads of performance centers reporting to one executive, as contrasted with pyramid structures, which create multiple status levels and increase the social distance between the planners and policy-makers and the performers.

But flat organizations imply a high degree of autonomy at the operational level that is, perhaps, more apparent than real. There may be wide latitude with respect to day-to-day administration of the unit, but very little latitude in the techniques of work, in capital expenditures, and even in methods of communicating and evaluating results. The techniques of work can be governed by staff personnel, who themselves develop new methods and procedures, and program their use in routine operations. The policy manual may indicate that the local manager has a final say on the adoption of new initiatives on the part of staff people, but it would be an especially strong (or foolhardy) manager who would defy staff directives, no matter how tactfully they may be couched as "suggestions." The reason staff directives have clout is that line managers tend to protect their flank, particularly when there are uncertainties about achieving expected performance.

The use of capital budgeting and allocation procedures also exerts considerable control over the direction local managers take. Generally speaking, the money limit above which the local manager cannot act without top-level approval is strict. Approval of capital expenditure requests requires justification, either in budget allocations or in special appropriation requests. Whether initially or specially allocated, capital expenditures must pass certain tests, for example, return on investment, before approval is granted. Even when they meet such tests, capital requests may be deferred in order to give priority to some other groups in the corporation, especially when capital funds are short.

The process of reviewing capital budgets and requests usually falls to corporate staffs. Here again, the monitoring function is delegated to staff specialists, even though final action in the form of approvals, disapprovals, or deferrals is given by line executives and the board of directors. When competition for funds becomes intense, the displacement of aggression onto staffs and away from the line authority acts to guard the authority structure while maintaining the myth of local autonomy. If local initiatives are blocked, pleas for cooperation may be the signal to all concerned to end contentions and to accept proposed solutions, which are usually compromises among competing line groups and staff officers.

The use of formal operating budgets as a management control technique deserves careful attention. Budgets work by committing the heads of profit centers to a stated level of sales and profits. In a literal sense, then, the budget procedure brings executives to the point of decision, committing men to action throughout the organization.

Budgets also function symbolically, a perspective that merits emphasis in managerial psychology. The symbolism underlying the budgetary approach starts with conflicts between realistic thinking and sentiment. A chief executive who, for example, is intent upon rapid growth may inform all heads of performance centers that a growth rate under 15 percent per annum in sales and profits is an unacceptable projection. Because rates of growth are under the influence of general conditions in the economy and other forces outside the manager's control, the tendency to project unrealistic forecasts curries the chief executive's favor at the expense of reality. Under such circumstances, staffs usually protect the exposed manager when the chances of meeting forecasts are slim. If the manager were held strictly accountable, he would be the victim of a "double bind"; he makes unrealistic commitments to conform to a philosophy while, at the same time, he allows himself to be vulnerable to punishments for the failure to meet projections. To protect the exposed manager, staff people encourage him to make the forecasts, and they prepare everyone for the more probable outcome. This avoids damaging the reputation or the future of heads of performance centers.

Of course, if unreality persists in the preparation of operating budgets and forecasts, the bubble is bound to burst, as the fates of the so-called growth companies and conglomerates have shown. These have often based their strategy on expanded profits and rising stock prices. The high-multiple stock prices have been used to acquire companies with stocks valued at a lesser multiple. But once the profit realized falls short of projections and the stock prices fall, the strategy no longer works. If the acquisitions and patterns of growth make little inherent sense, and if the management is spread over unfamiliar areas of operation, the result may be disastrous.

Budgets reduce basic decisions about corporate strategy to numbers. Accordingly, the budget only symbolizes a deeper thought process concerning goals, purposes, and instruments. The comfort in concrete numbers, with their appearance of objectivity, will be illusory if one is unaware that there may be hidden problems in commitments made and opportunities foregone in arriving at forecasts and operating plans. Some chief executives, conscious of the symbolic aspects of budgets, purposely hold planning meetings, "think tanks," and "blue sky" sessions to break out of the molds that budgeting forms around thinking.

Another symbolic and often obscured issue in the use of budgets involves cooperation and competition. In large organizations, it is not uncommon for one division to be the customer of another division; there can be contentions about the internal market and pricing structure that should be adhered to and reflected in operating budgets and profit forecasts. Because of certain internal political considerations, the "seller" may be given an advantage in the marketplace by directives that force the "buyer" to seek his supply exclusively within the corporation. Strict control through the measurement of performance demands that a manager be free concerning decisions in buying. The rule of the marketplace and competition should govern the decision to buy inside or outside. But such hard-and-fast rules are naive. Where, for example, the decision to buy outside could literally destroy allied performance centers, a free market has to give way to protectionist policies. Over the long run, however, the discipline of comparing transfer and market prices permits healthy competition to rule within as well as outside the corporation.

Conflicts of interest and internal competition can be put to good use, provided there is an effective information system to expose to realistic appraisal the bases on which forecasts are made and costs are distributed within an organization. If management information is inadequate, the internal conflicts of interest can destroy organizations by making them unable to channel aggression and competition. In the final analysis, the operating results determine how executives are rewarded. The use of money incentives is a powerful device to control actual performance. When the information system is poor, the reward structure collapses, as does the confidence necessary to maintain authority in organization.

The problem of rewards and compensation deserves a more intensive treatment than we are prepared to offer here. We raise it briefly because underlying any program of compensation is the ultimate objective of maintaining motivation and influencing executive behavior.

Executive compensation plans are not unmixed blessings. On

the one hand, they are designed to provide rewards commensurate with performance by using profit-sharing and bonus plans. (Base salaries reflect the market, both internal and external, available to the corporation, and they indicate how much money it takes to get and to keep an executive in the race for higher rewards). On the other hand, when executives elevate their standards of living to meet—and often exceed—their earnings, they can mortgage their egos beyond their capacity to live with the stress they themselves engender. Instead of independence, the mortgage may foster conformity, getting along, and avoiding the dangers inherent in the errors of commission. A concrete example of such mortgaging can be seen in the sad situation of executives who exercised stock options, sometimes borrowing money to buy the stock, only to discover that stock prices go down as well as up. The result is the anxiety of debt and current interest payments, not the sought-after security of assets that can be converted to cash and retained after the smaller capital gains tax. With the realization that stock options hold perils as well as potential security, and with the maximum income tax rate at 50 percent of taxable income, the virtue of money in the hand in the form of high salaries has once again become attractive. If the executive can discipline himself to a more modest standard of living and save the residue of his income above expenses and taxes, he will not get rich, but he will avoid trapping himself in a corporate structure that, while demanding autonomy on his part, is often just as glad to see him somewhat dependent and, therefore, more controllable when he makes judgments and undertakes actions.

As formal control systems become even more sophisticated and are subtly intertwined in the basic functions of strategy and decision making, the process of using information to control behavior will deserve even more careful study. The burden of analysis, we suggest, is to look beneath the surface in order to understand the psychological forces that act on individuals in their uses of authority and power.

EXECUTIVE ACTION

The problem of executive action is directly concerned with how individuals mobilize and use power derived from position, competence, and personality. Ideally, only the man best qualified to hold an office should have it, and the authority of position therefore assumes paramount importance. The assumed harmony between position and competence is naive, because position controls the flow of reward. (Subordinates follow directives because the superior, acting from a position of authority, can reward and punish). The effects of disharmonies between designated authority and competence, and the psychological conflicts engendered in subordinates, are tellingly portrayed in novels like *The Caine Mutiny*.

The discrepancy between what is ideal and what is real leads inevitably to revisions in theory. One such revised theory holds that "authority is another name for the willingness and capacity of individuals to submit to the necessities of cooperative systems." Accordingly, Barnard (1938) distinguishes two dimensions of authority: "authority of position" and "authority of leadership." The first depends on a central location in the organization's communications system; the second depends upon the superior ability of the leader. Taken together, authority of position and of leadership determine the extent to which a superior's directives will be followed.

But the problem of executive action cannot be resolved by concentrating on, eliminating, or varying any single factor, whether it be authority of position or voluntary acceptance of authority by subordinates (itself a consequence of the use of authority inherent in competence and personal attractiveness). The problem of action boils down to the problem of how and for what purpose an executive generates and mobilizes the power and authority vested in his position, his level of competence, and the personal appeal with which he may be endowed.

As has been indicated previously, the fundamental view here is that executive action cannot be treated as simply an attribute of structure, but must be considered as an outcome of the individual's behavior within a structure. Illustrations of this view can be found in the work of political analysts, whose accounts of chief executives in office provide the clearest indication of the extent to which individual predispositions and personality have shaped and reshaped an office. Political analysts point out that the positional power of the President of the United States is always present, but that there are marked variations in the ways incumbents have used their powers; the differences lie not simply in the ways in which power is exercised, but also in the individual's awareness of power processes.

As a guide in comparisons of leaders in their exercise of power, political analysts have used the concept of "style." One can define style, following the psychoanalytic concept of "character," as *the patterns of behavior with which an individual relates himself to external reality and to his own internal dispositions*. First, we shall examine descriptions of Presidents in office and the styles of leadership with which they respond to the functional demands of their positions. The discussion will then move from what actually happens in the encounter between the individual and the situation to why it appears to happen in the way that it does.

In his book *Presidential Power* (1946), Neustadt gives a clear account of the functions a President must serve, of the means available to him for the purpose, and of the leadership styles of three different Presidents as they used their power in the execution of policy.

The President is, of course, acting within a structure, and Neustadt, identifying the constitutional functions that he must serve, also brings into perspective one of the crucial dilemmas of power and position:

> In form, all Presidents are leaders nowadays. In fact, this guarantees no more than that they will be clerks. Everybody now expects the man in the White House to do something about everything. Laws and customs now reflect acceptance of him as the Great Initiator, an acceptance quite as widespread at the Capitol as at his end of Pennsylvania Avenue. But such acceptance does not signify that all the rest of the government is at his feet. *It merely signifies that other men have found it practically impossible to do their jobs without assurance of initiatives from him*. Service for themselves, not power for the President, has brought them to accept his leadership in form [p. 6; italics added].

The "constituents" of the President, those who look to him for initiatives, come from six groups: executive officialdom, Congress, political partisans, citizens at large, the press, and officials in foreign countries. Representatives of each of these constituent groups seek to develop claims on the Chief Executive in ways that enable them to act, and the President himself seeks to establish claims on their actions.

Presidential power, or the power to initiate successfully, is, according to Neustadt,

> influence of an effective sort on the behavior of men actually involved in making public policy and carrying it out. Effective influence for the man in the White House stems from three related sources: first are the bargaining advantages inherent in the job with which he persuades other men that what he wants of them is what their own responsibilities require them to do. Second are the expectations of those other men regarding his ability and will to use the various advantages they think he has. Third are those men's estimates of how his public views him and of how their public may view them if they do what he wants [p. 179].

The use of these powers, however, depends on an individual's conception of his role. Neustadt provides a striking example of this in his discussion of the leadership styles of Roosevelt and Eisenhower:

> Eisenhower wanted to be president [although] what he wanted from it was a far cry from what F.D.R. had wanted. Roosevelt was a politician seeking personal power; Eisenhower was a hero seeking national unity. . . . He genuinely thought the President was or ought to be the source of unifying, moderating, influence above the struggle [pp. 165-166].

Eisenhower's presidential style was that of a leader above the struggle. He established a staff system in the White House that

> imparted more superficial symmetry and order to his flow of information than was ever done before. Therefore, he became typically the last man in his office to know tangible details and

the last to come to grips with acts of choice. His one-time chief assistant in the White House, Sherman Adams, is reported to have told a close associate: "I count the day lost when I have not found some new way of lightening the President's load" [pp. 158-159].

Unlike Roosevelt, Eisenhower did not want the details of every factor that could affect a decision. He wanted the details already weighed and only the final alternatives presented to him. These alternatives often reflected other men's interests more closely than his own, as Neustadt's description of the circumstances surrounding Eisenhower's 1957 budget shows. The system limited Eisenhower's ability to exploit the power available to him, since he lacked information on how and where it should be applied.

In his article "The Concept of Power" (1957), Dahl stresses that a power base is inert or passive; it must be exploited in some way if the behavior of others is to be affected. He defines the means of power as "a mediating activity by A between A's base and B's response," and he illustrates this by suggesting that

> in the case of the President, the means would include the promise of patronage, the threat of veto, the holding of a conference, the threat of appeal to the electorate, the exercise of charm and charisma, etc. . . [p. 203].

The bases of power in position, competence, and charisma are apparent, but in Eisenhower's case they went largely unused. Roosevelt, on the other hand, was a man bent on taking the initiative. The Roosevelt of the nineteen thirties wanted to make new departures, and he exploited every base of power available to him to rally support for his decisions.

> The first task of an executive, as he evidently saw it, was to guarantee himself an effective flow of information and ideas. . . . Roosevelt's persistent effort, therefore, was to check and balance information acquired through official channels by information acquired through a myriad of private, informal, and unorthodox channels and espionage networks.

At times he seemed almost to pit his personal sources against his public sources [Schlesinger, 1959, pp. 522-523].

In doing this, however, he not only checked and balanced the flow and validity of his information, but also insured for himself a position of the utmost centrality at every stage in the decision-making process. He could assess who wanted what and why they wanted it. He could establish his priorities and make his choices, guided by clear indications as to where his power should be directed in order to secure support. At the same time, Roosevelt's style of leadership was not just that of an initiator; it involved the use of ambiguity in interpersonal relations. The use of ambiguity provided a means for maintaining a central position in the communications network and flexibility in negotiation and decision making.

A President can also attempt to assume the initiative with an interpersonal style that is aloof and distant. In *Woodrow Wilson and Colonel House* (1964), Alexander and Juliette George make it clear that Wilson was dramatically aware of the Chief Executive's function as initiator. In fact, whatever leadership position he attained, whether as president of Princeton University, governor of New Jersey, or President of the United States, Wilson initiated reforms of a sweeping nature. His style of initiation, however, reflected an emotional attachment to abstract ideals, such as justice and democracy, and his expression of these ideals involved an emotional bond between himself and the public. This narcissistic transaction proceeded through the spoken word, the "giving" in verbal imagery of strong emotional currents that mobilized and sustained idealism. The "getting" in this exchange involved the adoration of the electorate, to reinforce a self-image built on the theme of the warrior overcoming malevolent forces that impede man's struggle for justice and equality. Wilson could not function freely when action depended on negotiation and persuasion in close, face-to-face relationships. In the earlier stages of his presidency, he depended on Colonel House to deal with the hard realities of negotiation, and in this sense established a relationship involving complementary role performances.

In all organizations, executives face the problem of fusing a personal style with structural realities when they assert power. Executives may or may not be conscious of the functions that they are really called upon to serve. The structure does not necessarily make clear and unequivocal what are the preferred actions. Consequently, an individual may or may not be aware of the bases of power available to him, or, as in Wilson's case, he may rely on a particular base, ignoring others that are equally available and, indeed, are more appropriate means of achieving objectives.

A PSYCHOPOLITICAL APPROACH TO EXECUTIVE ACTION

A psychopolitical approach to executive action is the problem of the person-position encounter, which must take into account both structural and personality variables. The structure provides the elements for a power base as well as the definition of issues for attention. Personality is synonymous with style; it helps determine how an organization gets built, the priorities attached to objective issues, and the underlying attachments to images of the organization.

There are three basic leadership strategies: homeostatic, mediative, and proactive. The homeostatic strategy addresses the need for preserving the organization—to insure its internal stability and continuity in the face of internal disruption. The mediative strategy aims at change in the organization, made under the impact of external pressures. The proactive strategy, rather than reacting to environmental pressure, induces change in the environment to use creatively the resources of the organization. Proaction is the strategy of major innovation, which tends to induce resistance, aggression, and, in some cases, outright hostility within the organization: it forces disruption of internal relations in the interests of changing the environment.

Historically, organizations move through phases of all three images. For example, a brief study of management succession in Sears, Roebuck by Stryker (1961), provides an account of the correlation between management succession and changes in corporate strategy.

Richard W. Sears, the chief executive from 1893 to 1908, founded the company in partnership with Roebuck, selling watches by direct mail. As the business grew, Sears introduced basic innovations in mail-order selling, not least of which was insisting that the quality of his goods met the hyperbolic advertising copy, and this at a time when, as Stryker writes, "fleecing yokels was standard business practice." Sears kept his prices low and his markup small, and depended on high-pressure advertising to increase turnover. His advertising changed tastes and formed new ones. To compete with Sears's merchandising tactics, businessmen in the cities and small towns improved their sales and service policies, often copying his techniques outright. Sears was a proactive leader who changed the environment that merchandisers until then had taken for granted.

The man who succeeded Sears, however, adopted a different strategy. Julius Rosenwald bought a half-interest in the company in 1895 and found Sears's methods increasingly disruptive of what was, in Rosenwald's view, efficient management. Sears's advertising and promotion had sparked such a volume of orders that in ten years the company's sales jumped from three-quarters of a million dollars to nearly $40 million. The buying and shipping departments were overburdened and confused. When sales fell in the Depression, Sears argued strongly for even larger expenditures on advertising, but Rosenwald prevailed over him and began a drastic cost-cutting program. After Sears resigned, Rosenwald assumed control and stressed the importance of developing internal stability, a homeostatic position. His most far-reaching innovation improved methods of quality control, but even these were later eliminated as part of an economy drive.

Rosenwald's eventual successor was Robert E. Wood, who, as vice president of Montgomery Ward, had begun to apply statistical analysis to the mail-order market and had foreseen that the declining rural population was reducing the need for mail-order services, while, at the same time, the shift in population was increasing the need for retail stores in suburban towns. Realizing that competition from chain stores was intensifying, Wood became convinced that the future of mail-order services lay in changing the emphasis to retailing; after joining Sears, Roebuck, he immediately began to move the company into the retail trade. In 1928, the number of company-owned stores rose from 27 to 192, and the chain grew to more than 630 over the next twenty years, accounting for approximately three-quarters of Sears's total sales. Wood's contribution to the company lay in implementing a mediative strategy, adapting the business to an environment that had changed substantially. He foresaw trends and moved the organization to meet them.

In 1954, Theodore Houser succeeded Wood. As chief merchandiser of Sears under Wood, Houser had devised an unusual strategy of "basic buying," which called for close cooperation with the company's suppliers in the design of products and in the costing of materials, labor, overhead, and profit. Houser aimed to develop low-cost suppliers capable of making a steady profit for themselves. These suppliers were so located that they could save distribution costs and, assisted by Sears, Roebuck's research and volume orders, reduce their operating costs. Thus, Houser viewed Sears's suppliers as part of the company's structure, with Sears assisting each to become a more efficient producer, rather than just a source of goods at the lowest possible price.

The evolution of Sears illustrates some of the differences between mediation and proaction as business strategies. A further innovation by Houser makes the distinction even clearer. Sears had long been criticized for the cash drain its mail-order sales imposed in many rural areas. Houser found, for example, that Sears was spending less than $500,000 a year in Mississippi, while selling $8 million to $9 million worth of goods there. He felt that Sears could change the situation. Instead of continuing to rely on one very large supplier, he instituted buying policies that would encourage the establishment of several small plants spread over a wide area. On this basis, Sears acquired suppliers across the country, bringing sales and purchases into a more even balance. In the Southeast alone, Sears helped to establish nearly a hundred small factories, increasing its purchases to the point where they were nearly in line with the company's sales in the area.

The discussion shows that, under its founder, Sears, Roebuck changed the mail-order environment; the organizational strategy unconsciously influencing its leadership was proactive. The internal disruption that ensued led to a homeostatic counterrevolution under Rosenwald, which was followed by Wood's successful attempts to adapt the company to an environment that had changed appreciably. Houser, in turn, reverted to proaction and innovation.

If one considers that these strategies, converted into action and decision, represent organizational reality for an executive, then we need to consider the means by which they meet or avoid functional demands. The situation in which these demands appear is interpersonal, but the first stimulus is necessarily intrapersonal, arising from the images of power formed with the personality of the chief executive.

The functional demands of organizations, described in the language of economic, political, and social realities, interact with the executive's tendencies to assume certain roles. Taking a role should not be confused with play-acting on the stage. The conscious and deliberate enactment of a role as a theatrical performance is bound in time and, although it involves the individual, it is a highly limited performance. Role-taking in organizations is part and parcel of character structure, the habitual modes of responding to internal and external stimuli. Therefore, the individual's performance serves defensive as well as adaptive purposes. Unconscious motives determine the role, and they are products of developmental conflicts as well as maturation.

The process of dovetailing individual predispositions for roles within the strategies of organizations leads to three types of objects that engage the emotions and intellect: people, tactics, and ideas. The mutual compliance of men and situations (a "best fit") can be represented in a matrix like the one shown in Figure 1.

Some individuals direct their emotional energy toward tasks; they invest their attention and energies in ideas, solving problems, and devising systems of doing work. They are uninterested in people and need to avoid human relationships in order to

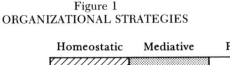

Figure 1
ORGANIZATIONAL STRATEGIES

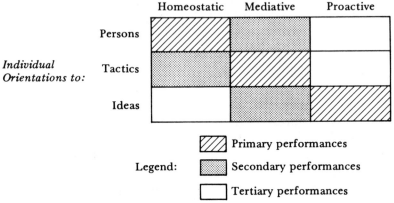

regulate their anxieties. The opposite orientation directs emotional investment toward human relationships. Tasks are unimportant to the individual's inner needs and values, and, in fact, the cognitive-technical aspects of work provoke anxiety because work seems detached from people. The third orientation is the concern for tactics, how to get things done through people. Here, the individual in his inner world weighs both persons and ideas as important to him and blends them in a concern for solving problems in a real world (Moment and Zaleznik, 1963).

Although individuals can shift responses to changing situations, they still select, unconsciously, a mode of acting in situations. The person-oriented individual performs most comfortably when regulating the internal relations of people to maintain a steady state. Such an individual avoids initiatives except under severe stress because he unconsciously needs to avoid aggressive behavior in his relations with others. The idea-oriented individual, on the other hand, performs most easily in initiating change, that is, in acting under circumstances in which aggression and dominance govern human relationships. Anxiety mounts when he forms attachments to people, so he avoids homeostatic functions. Organizational effectiveness would seem to require some mix in executive performance to insure that things get done and that the internal capacities of the organization are maintained.

Leadership style is the selective orientation of an individual toward a particular strategy. The means by which style becomes apparent are the ways in which the individual makes use of the bases of his power. Implicit in Neustadt's analysis of the Presidency, for example, is the degree to which its effectiveness, its "success," is dependent on proactivity; the system turns on presidential initiative. But for the President to win support for his initiatives, he must be able to use the power available to him, and this, in turn, depends on his awareness of the demands placed on him and on the way in which these demands coincide with the personal predispositions that he brings to the office.

Thus to speak of Roosevelt as "a politician seeking personal power" is to do him an injustice (Neustadt, 1964, p. 165). In Roosevelt, a predisposition for change and the functional demands of his office were effectively fused. He was psychologically free to achieve his objectives through the use of all the bases of power available to him. He could use people.

> His favorite technique was to keep grants of authority incomplete, jurisdictions uncertain, charters overlapping. The results of this competitive theory of administration were often confusion and exasperation on the operating level; but no other method could so reliably insure that in a large bureaucracy filled with ambitious men eager for power the decisions, and the power to make them, would remain with the President [Schlesinger, 1959, p. 528].

In this respect, Franklin D. Roosevelt differed fundamentally from Woodrow Wilson. Wilson's emotional investment in ideas was fraught with inner conflict over the challenge to his authority that he felt in relationships with other men; in the Presidency he dealt with this problem by referring it to his close associate, House, or by avoiding it entirely and relying instead on charismatic power to forge an alliance with the electorate as a means of achieving political objectives.

Neustadt's (1964) description of Eisenhower's style also suggests the contrasts with Roosevelt's:

Eisenhower's use of men tended to smother, not enhance, the competition roused by overlapping jurisdictions. Apparently this was intention. . . . Eisenhower seemingly preferred to let subordinates proceed upon the lowest common denominators of agreement than to have their quarrels—and issues and details—pushed up to him [p. 161].

Eisenhower evidently tried to avoid conflict and aggression, and his conscious attitude was one of altruism rather than the egoism of Franklin Roosevelt. Personal power—the means by which an idea orientation is transformed into a proactive style—held no attraction for Eisenhower. Doubting his own judgment, he relied on that of the people around him.

Another illustration of the meshing of functional demands with individual predispositions can be found in the alliances chief executives establish with their close associates. For example, in an important teaching and research hospital, three executives, all doctors who had gained recognition in their fields, were in the key positions of superintendent, clinical director, and director of research (Hodgson, et al., 1965). The superintendent was an active, assertive, and dominating figure, who specialized in external relations. He viewed himself very much as a builder, one who could put things together and make them run. He talked of his many activities and commitments as means to building the future of psychiatry. His memberships in professional societies, which were of immediate interest and value to him, were also part of his larger design to influence his profession. Thus, the superintendent contributed a sense of action and movement, but more than a few of his subordinates feared him for his very qualities of assertiveness. They avoided him and weakened his lines of communication throughout the organization.

To a large extent, the cost of the superintendent's style were offset in the person of the clinical director, a warm, quiet figure with close emotional ties to people in the organization and an intimate knowledge of what went on in their daily lives. The third person in this alliance, the director of research, assumed the position of a friendly uncle who gave practical advice on careers while he encouraged research work.

In general, a chief executive structure usually consists of a small number of key individuals who make up an inner circle. The word "constellation," rather than "group," emphasizes the significance of the personal relations among key executives; that is, the emotional climate of the group and the psychological properties of the interactions that define the group. Constellations involve role specialization of executive members, differentiation among individual roles, and complementary roles. An executive constellation or alliance is seldom formed by individuals who are unable to define themselves in recognizable and complementary identities.

The way in which executives mobilize and redistribute power in interpersonal structures must meet the strategic problems of the organization. Taking a part in a strategy—homeostatic, mediative, or proactive—is closely related to personality structure and dynamics and, in its manifestation as a style of executive action, involves the uses of organizational power itself.

Executive constellations as structures for using power can take a variety of forms, each with its symbolic meaning to the actors in the situation. The types of constellations include the patriarchy, built around the dominant leader as the central figure; the group, an executive system of equals; and the pair, a structure, often encountered, in which two executives relate to each other and their subordinates symbolically as parents in a family.

The acceptance of roles in constellations (this is not a reference to formalistic job descriptions, but to the functional roles that keep organizations moving) is a consequence of unconscious attachments to power. The executive acting in organizations is the center of a psychopolitical drama in which power is the focus of his attention and that of his subordinates. How he perceives power in conscious and unconscious imagery defines his mode of relating to others and his way of making decisions. The need for power does not originate in the attempts to build a career. If it did, there would be a greater degree of self-control in the executive than one usually finds. Executives appear driven in their search for power and only too painfully aware that their motives warrant some explanation beyond their reach.

REFERENCES

Barnard, C. (1938), *The Functions of the Executive*. Cambridge, Mass.: Harvard University Press.
Crozier, M. (1964), *The Bureaucratic Phenomenon*. Chicago: University of Chicago Press.
Dahl, R. A. (1957), The Concept of Power. *Behav. Sci.*, 2:201-215.
Freud, S. (1921), Group Psychology and the Analysis of the Ego. *Standard Edition*, 18:65-143. London: Hogarth Press, 1955.
George, A. L., & George, J. L. (1964), *Woodrow Wilson and Colonel House: A Personality Study*. New York: Dover.
Hodgson, R. C., Levinson, D. J., & Zaleznik, A. (1965), *The Executive Role Constellation: An Analysis of Personality and Role Relations in Management*. Boston: Harvard University Graduate School of Business Administration, Division of Research.
Homans, G. (1964), Bringing Man Back In. *Amer. Sociol. Rev.*, 29:809-818.
Moment, D., & Zaleznik, A. (1963), *Role Development and Interpersonal Competence*. Boston: Harvard University Graduate School of Business Administration, Division of Research.
Neustadt, R. E. (1964), *Presidential Power: The Politics of Leadership*. New York: Wiley.
Schlesinger, A. M. (1959), *The Age of Roosevelt. Volume 2: The Coming of the New Deal*. Boston: Houghton Mifflin.
Selznick, P. (1949), *T.V.A. and the Grass Roots*. Berkeley: University of California Press.
Simon, H. A. (1965), *Administrative Behavior*. New York: Free Press.
Stryker, P. (1961), *The Character of the Executive*. New York: Harper and Row.
Weber, M. (1947), *The Theory of Social and Economic Organization*, ed. T. Parsons. New York: Oxford University Press.

In this chapter Zaleznik elaborates the view that organizations are political structures which operate by distributing authority and by providing a platform for the exercise of power. If the quality of organizational life is to be improved, the importance of personality factors must be recognized as well as the balanced use of the strengths and limitations of people in making decisions on power distribution. Various expressions of power conflicts are described, and a problem-solving approach to organizational structure is suggested.

15

Power and Politics in Organizational Life

ABRAHAM ZALEZNIK

While managers purport to make decisions in rational terms, most observers and participants know that personalities and politics play a significant, if not an overriding role in decision making. Whatever else organizations may be (problem-solving instruments, sociotechnical systems, reward systems, and so on), they are political structures. This means that organizations operate by distributing authority and setting a stage for the exercise of power. It is no wonder, therefore, that individuals who are highly motivated to secure and use power find a familiar and hospitable environment in business.

At the same time, executives are reluctant to acknowledge the place of power both in individual motivation and in organizational relationships. Somehow, power and politics are dirty words. And in linking these words to the play of personalities in organizations, some managers withdraw into the safety of organizational logics.

As I shall suggest in this chapter, frank recognition of the importance of personality factors and a sensitive use of the strengths and limitations of people in making decisions on power distributions can improve the quality of organizational life.

POLITICAL PYRAMID

Organizations provide a power base for individuals. From a purely economic standpoint, organizations exist to create a surplus of income over costs by meeting needs in the marketplace. But organizations also are political structures which provide opportunities for people to develop careers and thereby provide platforms for the expression of individual interests and motives. The development of careers, particularly at high managerial and professional levels, depends on accumulation of power as the vehicle for transforming individual interests into activities which influence other people.

Scarcity and Competition

A political pyramid exists when people compete for power in an economy of scarcity. In other words, people cannot get the power they want just for the asking. Instead, they have to enter into the decisions on how to distribute authority in a particular formal organization structure. Scarcity of power arises under two sets of conditions: (1) where individuals gain power in absolute terms at someone else's expense; (2) where there is a gain comparatively—not literally at someone else's expense—resulting in a relative shift in the distribution of power.

In either case, the psychology of scarcity and comparison takes over. The human being tends to make comparisons as a basis for his sense of self-esteem. He may compare himself with other people and decide that his absolute loss or the shift in proportional shares of authority reflects an attrition in his power base. He may also compare his position relative to others against a personal standard and feel a sense of loss. This tendency to compare is deeply ingrained in people, especially since they experience early in life the effects of comparisons in the family where—in an absolute sense—time and attention, if not love and affection, go to the most dependent member.

Corporate acquisitions and mergers illustrate the effects of both types of comparisons. In the case of one merger, the president of the acquired company resigned rather than accept the relative displacement in rank which occurred when he no longer could act as a chief executive officer. Two vice presidents vied for the position of executive vice president. Because of their conflicting ambitions, the expedient of making them equals drove the competition underground, but not for long. The vice president with the weaker power base soon resigned in the face of his inability to consolidate a workable definition of his responsibilities. His departure resulted in increased power for the remaining vice president and the gradual elimination of "rival camps" which had been covertly identified with the main contenders for power.

The fact that organizations are pyramids produces a scarcity of positions the higher one moves in the hierarchy. This scarcity, coupled with inequalities, certainly needs to be recognized. While it may be humane and socially desirable to say that people are different rather than unequal in their potential, nevertheless executive talent is in short supply. The end result should be to move the more able people into the top positions and to accord them the pay, responsibility, and authority to match their potential.

On the other side, the strong desires of equally able people for the few top positions available means that someone will either have to face the realization of unfulfilled ambition or have to shift his interest to another organization.

Constituents and Clients

Besides the conditions of scarcity and competition, politics in organizations grows out of the existence of constituencies. A superior may be content himself with shifts in the allocation of resources and consequently power, but he represents subordinates who, for their own reasons, may be unhappy with the changes. These subordinates affirm and support their boss. They can also withdraw affirmation and support, and consequently isolate the superior with all the painful consequences this entails.

While appointments to positions come from above, affirmation of position comes from below. The only difference between party and organizational politics is in the subtlety of the voting procedure. In a large consumer products corporation, for example, one division received almost no capital funds for expansion while another division, which had developed a new marketing approach for products common to both, expanded dramatically. The head of the static division found his power diminished considerably, as reflected in how seriously his subordinates took his efforts at influence (e.g., in programs to increase the profit return from existing volume). He initiated one program after another with little support from subordinates because he could not make a claim for capital funds. The flow of capital funds in this corporation provided a measure of power gains and losses in both an absolute and a relative sense.

Power and Action

Still another factor which heightens the competition for power that is characteristic of all political structures is the incessant need to use whatever power one possesses. Corporations have an implicit "banking" system in power transactions. The initial "capitalization" which makes up an individual's power base consists of three elements:

1. The quantity of formal authority vested in his position relative to other positions.

2. The authority vested in his expertise and reputation for competence (a factor weighted by how important his expertise is for the growth areas of the corporation as against its historically stable areas).

3. The attractiveness of his personality to others (a combination of respect for him as well as liking, although these two sources of attraction are often in conflict).

This capitalization of power reflects the total esteem with which others regard the individual. By a process which is still not too clear, the individual internalizes all of the sources of power capital in a manner parallel to the way he develops a sense of self-esteem. The individual knows he has power, assesses it realistically, and is willing to risk his personal esteem to influence others.

A critical element here is the risk in the uses of power. The individual must perform and get results. If he fails to do either, an attrition occurs in his power base in direct proportion to the doubts other people entertained in their earlier appraisals of him.

What occurs here is an erosion of confidence which ultimately leads the individual to doubt himself and undermines the psychological work which led him in the first place to internalize authority as a prelude to action.

What distinguishes alterations in the authority structure from other types of organizational change is their direct confrontation with the political character of corporate life. Such confrontations are real manipulations of power as compared with the indirect approaches which play on ideologies and attitudes. In the first case, the potency and reality of shifts in authority have an instantaneous effect on what people do, how they interact, and how they think about themselves. In the second case, the shifts in attitude are often based on the willingness of people to respond the way authority figures want them to; ordinarily, however, these shifts in attitude are but temporary expressions of compliance.

One of the most common errors executives make is to confuse compliance with commitment. Compliance is an attitude of acceptance when a directive from an authority figure asks for a change in an individual's position, activities, or ideas. The individual complies or "goes along" usually because he is indifferent to the scope of the directive and the changes it proposes. If compliance occurs out of indifference, then one can predict little difficulty in translating the intent of directives into actual implementation (Barnard, 1938).

Commitment, on the other hand, represents a strong motivation on the part of an individual to adopt or resist the intent of a directive. If the individual commits himself to a change, then he will use his ingenuity to interpret and implement the change in such a way as to assure its success. If he decides to fight or block the change, the individual may act as if he complies, but reserve other times and places to negate the effects of directives. For example:

In one large company, the top management met regularly for purposes of organizational planning. The executives responsible for implementing planning decisions could usually be counted on to carry them out when they had fought hard and openly in the course of reaching such decisions. When they seemed to accept a decision, giving all signs of compliance, the decision usually ended up as a notation in the minutes. Surface compliance occurred most frequently when problems involved loyalties to subordinates.

In one instance, a division head agreed to accept a highly regarded executive from another division to meet a serious manpower shortage in his organization. When the time came to effect the transfer, however, this division general manager refused, with some justification, on the grounds that bringing someone in from outside would demoralize his staff. He used compliance initially to respond to the problem of "family" loyalties to which he felt committed. Needless to say the existence of these loyalties was the major problem to be faced in carrying out organizational planning.

Compliance as a tactic to avoid changes, and commitment as an expression of strong motivation in dealing with organizational problems are in turn related to how individuals define their interests. In the power relations among executives, the so-called areas of common interest are usually reserved for the banalities of human relationships. The more significant areas of attention usually force conflicts of interest, especially competition for power, to the surface.

INTEREST CONFLICTS

Organizations demand, on the one hand, cooperative endeavor and commitment to common purposes. The realities of experience in organizations, on the other hand, show that conflicts of interest exist among people who ultimately share a common fate and are supposed to work together. What makes business more political and less ideological and rationalistic is the overriding importance of conflicts of interest.

If an individual (or group) is told that his job scope is reduced in either absolute or proportional terms for *the good of the corporation*, he faces a conflict. Should he acquiesce for the idea of common good or fight in the service of his self-interest? Any rational man will fight (how constructively depends on the absence of neurotic conflicts and on ego strength). His willingness to fight increases as he comes to realize the intangible nature of what people think is good for the organization. And, in point of fact, his willingness may serve the interests of corporate purpose by highlighting issues and stimulating careful thinking before final decisions are reached.

Secondary Effects

Conflicts of interest in the competition for resources are easily recognized, as for example, in capital budgeting, or in allocating money for research and development. But these conflicts can be subjected to bargaining procedures which all parties to the competition validate by their participation.

The secondary effects of bargaining do involve organizational and power issues. However, the fact that these power issues follow debate on economic problems rather than lead it creates a manifest content which can be objectified much more readily than in areas where the primary considerations are the distribution of authority.

In such cases, which include developing a new formal organization structure, management succession, promotions, corporate mergers, and entry of new executives, the conflicts of interest are severe and direct simply because there are no objective measures of right or wrong courses of action. The critical question which has to be answered in specific actions is: Who gets power and position? This involves particular people with their strengths and weaknesses and a specific historical context in which actions are understood in symbolic as well as rational terms.

A large corporation, General Motors in fact, inadvertently confirmed what every seasoned executive knows: that coalitions of power to overcome feelings of rivalry and the play of personal ambitions are fragile solutions. The appointment of Edward Cole to the presidency followed by Semon Knudsen's resignation shattered the illusion that the rational processes in business stand apart or even dominate the human emotions and ties that bind men to one another. If any corporation prides itself on rationality, General Motors is it. To have to experience so publicly the inference that major corporate life, particularly at the executive levels, is not so rational after all, can be damaging to the sense of security people get from belief in an idea as it is embodied in a corporate image.

The fact that Knudsen subsequently was discharged from the presidency of Ford (an event I shall discuss later in this paper) suggests that personalities and the politics of corporations are not so much aberrations as they are conditions of life in large organizations.

But just as General Motors wants to maintain an image, many executives prefer to ignore what this illustration suggests: that organizations are political structures which feed on the psychology of comparison. To know something about the psychology of comparison takes us into the theory of self-esteem in both its conscious manifestations and its unconscious origins. Besides possibly enlightening us in general and giving a more realistic picture of people and organizations, there are some practical benefits in such knowledge. These benefits include increased freedom to act more directly—that is to say, instead of trying to "get around" a problem, one can meet it—and greater objectivity about people's strengths and limitations, and, therefore, the ability to use them more honestly as well as effectively.

More effective planning in organizational design and in distribution of authority; instead of searching for the "one best solution" in organization structure, one accepts a range of alternatives and then gives priority to the personal or emotional concerns that inhibit action.

POWER RELATIONS

Organizational life within a political frame is a series of contradictions. It is an exercise in rationality, but its energy comes from the ideas in the minds of power figures the content of which, as well as their origins, are only dimly perceived. It deals with sources of authority and their distribution; yet it depends in the first place on the existence of a balance of power in the hands of an individual who initiates actions and gets results. It has many rituals associated with it, such as participation, democratization, and the sharing of power; yet the real outcome is the consolidation of power around a central figure to whom other individuals make emotional attachments.

Faulty Coalitions

The formal organization structure implements a coalition among key executives. The forms differ, and the psychological significance of various coalitions also differs. But no organization can function without a consolidation of power in the relationship of a central figure with his select group. The coalition need not exist between the chief executive and his immediate subordinates or staff. It may indeed bypass the second level, as in the case of Presidents of the United States who do not build confident relationships within their Cabinets, but instead rely on members of the Executive staff or on selected individuals outside the formal apparatus.

The failure to establish a coalition within the executive structure of an organization can result in severe problems, such as paralysis in the form of inability to make decisions and to evaluate performance, and in-fighting and overt rivalry within the executive group.

When a coalition fails to develop, the first place to look for causes is the chief executive and his problems in creating confident relationships. The causes are many and complex, but they usually hinge around the nature of the chief executive's defenses and what he needs to avoid as a means of alleviating stress.

The "palace revolt" which led to Semon Knudsen's departure from Ford Motor Company is an illustration of failure in the formation of a coalition. While it is true that Henry Ford II named Knudsen president of the company, Knudsen's ultimate power as a newcomer to an established power structure depended on forming an alliance. The particular individual with whom an alliance seemed crucial was Lee Iacocca. For some reason, Knudsen and Iacocca competed for a power base to which both contributed, as is the case with most workable coalitions. In the absence of a coalition, the alternate postures of rivalry and battle for control erupted. Ford ultimately responded by taking sides.

As I have indicated, it is not at all clear why in Knudsen's case the coalition failed to develop. But in any failure the place to look is in the personalities of the main actors and in the nature of their defenses which make certain coalitions improbable no matter how obvious their necessity.

But defensiveness on the part of a chief executive can also result in building an unrealistic and unworkable coalition, with the self-enforced isolation which is its consequence. One of the most frequently encountered defensive maneuvers which leads to the formation of unrealistic coalitions or to the isolation of the chief executive is the fear of rivalry.

A realistic coalition matches formal authority and competence with the emotional commitments necessary to maintain the coalition. The fear of rivals by chief executives, or subordinates, jealousy of the chief executive's power, can at the extreme result in paranoid distortions. People become suspicious of one another, and through selective perceptions and projections of their own fantasies create a world of plots and counterplots.

The intrusion of personal concerns onto substantive material in decision making is potentially the most dangerous form of defensiveness. The need for defense arises because people become anxious about how they are rated in existing power coalitions. But perhaps even more basic is the fear and the rivalry to which all coalitions are susceptible given the nature of investments people make in power relations. While it is easy to dismiss emotional reactions like these as neurotic distortions, their prevalence and impact deserve careful attention in all phases of organizational life.

Unconscious Collusions

All individuals and consequently groups experience areas of stress which mobilize defenses. The fact that coalitions embody defensive maneuvers when stress goes beyond the level of tolerance is not surprising. An even more serious problem, however, occurs when men rally together to defend against or to act out the conflicts which individuals cannot tolerate alone.

Where coalitions represent the aggregation of power with the conscious intention of using the abilities of members for constructive purposes, collusions, on the other hand, represent predominance of unconscious conflict and defensive behavior. In organizational life, collusion and its causes often becomes the knot which has to be unraveled before any changes can be implemented.

The collusion of latent interests among executives can become the central theme and sustaining force of an organization structure of top management. For a collusion to take hold, the conflicts of the "power figure" have to be communicated and sensed by others as an overriding need which seeks active expression in the form of a theme. The themes vary, just as do the structures which make a collusion. Thus one common theme is the need to control; another is the need to be admired and idealized; and still another is the need to find a scapegoat to attack in response to frustrations in solving problems.

If people could hold onto and keep within themselves areas of personal conflict, there would be far fewer collusions in organizational life. But it is part of the human condition for conflicts and needs to take over life situations. As a result, we find numerous instances of collusions controlling the behavior of executives. To illustrate:

A multidivisional corporation found itself with a revolution on its hands. The president was sensitive to the opinions of a few outside board members representing important stockholder interests. He was so concerned that he would be criticized by these board members that he demanded from vice presidents full information on their activities and complete loyalty to him. Over a period of years, he moved divisional chief executives to corporate headquarters so he could assure himself of their loyalty. Other executives joined in to gratify the president's need for control and loyalty.

The result of this collusion, however, was to create a schism between headquarters and field operations. Some of the staff members in the field managed to inform the board members of the lack of attention to and understanding of field problems. Discontent grew to such an extent that the board placed the president on early retirement.

Subsequently, the new president, with the support of the board, decentralized authority and appointed new division heads who were to make their offices in divisional headquarters with full authority to manage their respective organizations. One of the lingering problems of the new president was to dissolve the collusion at headquarters without wholesale firing of vice presidents.

Just as power distributions are central to the tasks of organizational planning, so the conservation of power is often the underlying function of collusions. Thus:

A manufacturing vice president of a medium-sized company witnessed over a period of fifteen years a procession of changes in top management and ownership. He had managed to retain his job because he made himself indispensable in the management of the factory.

To each new top management, he stressed the importance of "home rule" as a means of assuring loyalty and performance in the plant. He also tacitly encouraged each supervisor to go along with whatever cliques happened to form and dominate the shop floor.

However, over time a gradual loss of competitive position, coupled with open conflict among cliques in the form of union disputes, led to the dismissal of the vice president. None of his successors could reassert control over the shop, and the company eventually moved or liquidated many of the operations in this plant.

"LIFE DRAMAS"

Faulty coalitions and unconscious collusions, as I have illustrated, can result from the defensive needs of a chief executive. These needs, which often appear as a demand on others to bolster the self-esteem of the chief executive, are tolerated to a remarkable degree and persist for a long time before harmful effects become apparent to outside stockholders, bankers, or boards of directors which ultimately control the distributions of power in organizations. Occasionally, however, corporations undergo critical conflicts in organizational politics which cannot be ignored in the conscious deliberations which affect how power gets distributed or used.

Intertwined with the various expressions of power conflicts in organizations are three underlying "life dramas" deserving careful attention:

The *first* portrays stripping the powers of a *parental figure*.

The *second* portrays the predominance of *paranoid thinking*, where distortions of reality result from the surfacing of conflicts which formerly had been contained in collusions.

The *third* portrays a *ritualistic ceremonial* in which real power issues are submerged or isolated in compulsive behavior but at the cost of real problem solving and work.

Parental Figure

The chief executive in a business, along with the heads of states, religious bodies, and social movements, becomes an object for other people. The term "object" should be understood, in a psychological sense, as a person who is the recipient of strong emotional attachments from others. It is obvious that a chief executive is the *object* because he controls so many of the levers which ultimately direct the flow of rewards and punishments. But there is something to say beyond this obvious calculation of rewards and punishments as the basis for the emotional attachments between leader and led as object and subject.

Where a leader displays unusual attributes in his intuitive gifts, cultivated abilities, or deeper personal qualities, his fate as the object is governed by powerful emotions. I hesitate to use the word "charismatic" to describe such a leader, partially because it suggests a mystique but also because, in its reference to the "great" man as charismatic leader, it expands to superhuman proportions what really belongs to the psychology of everyday life.

What makes for strong emotional attachments is as much in the need of the subject as in the qualities of the object. In other words, the personalities of leaders take on proportions which meet what subordinates need and even demand. If leaders in fact respond with the special charisma that is often invested in them at the outset, then they are parties to a self-fulfilling prophecy. Of course, the qualities demanded have to be present in some nascent form, ready to emerge as soon as the emotional currents become real in authority relationships.

The emotional attachments I am referring to usually contain mixtures of positive and negative feelings. If the current were only of one kind, such as either admiration or hostility, the authority relationship would be simpler to describe as well as to manage. All too often, however, the way positive feelings blend into the negative sets off secondary currents of emotion which intensify the relationships.

On the one side, subordinates cannot help but have fantasies of what they would do if they held the No. 1 position. Such fantasies, besides providing fleeting pleasures and helping one to regulate his ambitions, also provide channels for imaginative and constructive approaches to solving problems. It is only a short step from imagining what one would do as chief executive to explaining to the real chief executive the ideas which have been distilled from this flight into fantasy. If the chief executive senses envy in back of the thoughts, he may become frightened and choke off ideas which can be used quite constructively.

But suppose a situation arises where not one but several subordinates enjoy the same fantasy of being No. 1? Suppose also that subordinates feel deprived in their relationship with the chief executive? Suppose finally that the organization faces substantive problems which are more or less out of control. With these three conditions, and depending on the severity of the real problems besetting the enterprise, the stage is set for a collusion which, when acted out, becomes a critical episode of displacing the parental figure. To demonstrate:

In November, 1967, the directors of the Interpublic Group, a $700-million complex in advertising and public relations, moved for the resignation of the leader and chief executive officer, Marion Harper, Jr. Briefly, Harper had managed over a period of eighteen years to build the world's largest conglomerate in market services, advertising, and information on the base of a personally successful agency career. In expanding from this base, Harper made acquisitions, started new companies, and widened his orbit into international branches and companies.

As often happens, the innovator and creative person is careless in controlling what he has built so that financial problems become evident. In Harper's case, he appeared either unwilling or unable to recognize the seriousness of his financial problems and, in particular, the significance of allowing cash balances to go below the minimum required in agreements with lending institutions.

Harper seemed careless in another, even more telling, way. Instead of developing a strong coalition among his executive group, he relied on individual ties to him in which he clearly dominated the relationship. If any of the executives "crossed" him, Harper would exile the offender to one of the "remote" branches or place him on partial retirement.

When the financial problems became critical, the aggrieved executives who had once been dependent on Harper and then cast out, formed their own coalition, and managed to garner the votes necessary to, in effect, fire the head man. Although little information is available on the aftermath of this palace revolution, the new coalition had its own problems—which, one would reasonably judge, included contentions for power.

A cynic viewing this illustration of the demise of a parental figure could conclude that if one seeks to maintain power by dominance, then one had best go all the way. This means that to take some but not all of the power away from rebellious sons sets the stage for a cabal among the deprived. With a score to settle, they await only the right circumstances to move in and depose the aggressor.

While this cynical view has its own appeal, it ignores the deeper issues of why otherwise brilliant men fail to recognize the realistic needs for coalitions in the relationships of superior and subordinates. To answer this question we would need to understand how powerful people operate with massive blind spots which limit vision and the ability to maneuver in the face of realistic problems.

The one purpose that coalitions serve is to guard against the effects of blind spots, since it is seldom the case that two people have identical limitations in their vision and their ability to respond. The need to control and dominate in a personalistic sense is perhaps the most serious of all possible blind spots which can affect a chief executive, because he makes it difficult for people to help him, while creating grievances which sooner or later lead to attacks on him.

The unseating of a chief executive by a coalition of subordinates seldom reduces the emotional charge built up in the uncertain attachments to the ousted leader. A new head man has to emerge and establish a confident coalition. Until the contentions for power subside and the guilt reactions attached to deposing the leader dissolve, individuals remain vulnerable to their own blind spots and unconscious reactions to striving for power.

The references to a parental figure in the preceding discussion may appear to exaggerate the meaning of power conflicts. In whatever ways it exaggerates, it also condenses a variety of truths about coalitions among executives. The chief executive is the central *object* in a coalition because he occupies a position analogous to parents in the family. He is at the nucleus of a political structure whose prototype is the family in which jealousy, envy, love, and hate find original impetus and expression.

It would be a gross error to assume that in making an analogy between the family and formal organizations the parental role is strictly paternal. There are also characteristics of the mother figure in certain types of chief executives and combinations of mother-father in the formation of executive coalitions.

Chief executives can also suffer from depersonalization in their roles and as a result become emotionally cold and detached. The causes of depersonalization are complex but, in brief, have some connections to the narrow definitions of rationality which exclude the importance of emotions in guiding communication as well as thought.

For the purpose of interpreting how defensive styles affect the behavior of leaders, there is some truth to the suggestion that the neutrality and lack of warmth characteristic of some leaders is a result of an ingrained fear of becoming the *object* for other people—for to become the *object* arouses fears that subordinates will become envious and compete for power.

Paranoid Thinking

This is a form of distortion in ideas and perception to which all human beings are susceptible from time to time. For those individuals who are concerned in their work with the consolidation and uses of power, the experience with suspiciousness, the attribution of bad motives to others, jealousy, and anxiety (characteristics of paranoid thinking), may be more than a passing state of mind.

In fact, such ideas and fantasies may indeed be communicated to others and may even be the main force which binds men into collusions. Organizational life is particularly vulnerable to the effects of paranoid thinking because it stimulates comparisons while it evokes anticipations of added power or fears of diminished power.

To complicate matters even more and to suggest just how ambiguous organizational decisions become, there may be some truth and substance in back of the suspicions, distrust, and jealousies which enflame thinking. Personality conflicts do affect decisions in allocating authority and responsibility, and an individual may not be distorting at all to sense that he had been excluded or denied an ambition based on some undercurrents in his relationships with others. To call these sensitivities paranoid thinking may itself be a gross distortion. But no matter how real the events, the paranoid potential is still high as a fallout of organizational life.

Paranoid thinking goes beyond suspiciousness, distrust, and jealousy. It may take the form of grandiose ideas and overestimation of one's power and control. This form of distortion leads to swings in mood from elation to despair, from a sense of omnipotence to helplessness. Again, when acted out, the search for complete control produces the tragedies which the initial distortions attempt to overcome. The tragedy of Jimmy Hoffa is a good case in point.

From all indications, Hoffa performed brilliantly as president of the teamsters' union. He was a superb organizer and bargainer, and in many ways a highly moral and even prudish man. There is little evidence to support allegations that he used his office to enrich himself.

Hoffa's troubles stemmed from his angry reactions when he could not get his way in managing the union's pension fund, and from his relations with the government. In overestimating his power, Hoffa fell victim to the illusion that no controls outside himself could channel his actions. Consequently, Hoffa had to serve a sentence in Lewisburg Penitentiary, having been found guilty of tampering with a jury.

It is interesting to note that Hoffa's successor delegated considerable authority to regional officers, a step that removed him from direct comparisons with Hoffa and served to cement a coalition of top officers in the teamsters.

Executives, too, can be victims of their successes just as much as of their failures. If past successes lead to the false sense of omnipotence which goes unchecked in, say, the executive's control of the board of directors, then he and his organization become the victims of changing times and competitive pressures along with the weakening in perception and reasoning which often accompanies aging.

One could speculate with some reason that paranoid distortions are the direct result of senility and the inability to accept the fact of death. While intellectually aware of the inevitability of death, gifted executives can sometimes not accept emotionally the ultimate in the limitations of power. The disintegration of personality in the conflict between the head and the heart is what we come to recognize as the paranoid potential in all forms of our collective relations.

Ritualistic Ceremonial

Any collective experience, such as organizational life with its capacity for charging the atmosphere in the imagery of power conflicts, can fall victim to rigidities. The rigidities I have in mind consist mainly of the formation and elaboration of structures, procedures, and other ceremonials which create the illusion of solving problems but in reality only give people something to act on to discharge valuable energies.

The best example of a ritualistic approach to real problems is the ever-ready solution of bringing people together in a committee on the naive grounds that the exchange of ideas is bound to produce a solution. There are even fads and fashions to ritualism, as in the sudden appearance of favorite words like "brainstorming" or "synergism."

It is not that bringing people together to discuss problems is

bad. Instead, it is the naive faith which accompanies such proposals, ultimately deflecting attention from where it properly belongs.

In one research organization, professionals faced severe problems arising from personal jealousies as well as differences of
opinion on the correct goals and content for the research program.
Someone would periodically suggest that the problems could not
be solved unless people came together, preferably for a weekend
away from the job, to share ideas and really get down to the basics
of the problem. The group would indeed follow such suggestions
and typically end the weekend with a feeling of euphoria brought
on by considerable drinking and a sumptuous meal.

The most concrete proposal for actions was in the idea that
the basic problem stemmed from the organization's increased size
so that people no longer knew one another and their work. The
solution which appeared, only shortly to disappear, was to publish
a laboratory newsletter that would keep people abreast of their
colleagues' newest ideas.

In a more general vein, ritualism can be invoked to deal with
any real or fancied danger, with uncertainty, ambivalent attitudes,
or a sense of personal helplessness. Rituals are used even in the
attempt to manipulate people. That power relations in organizations should become a fertile field for ritualism should not surprise anyone.

As I have tried to indicate, the problems of organizational life
involve the dangers associated with losses of power; uncertainties
are legion, especially in the recognition that there is no one best
way to organize and distribute power, and yet any individual must
make a commitment to some form of organization.

Ambivalent attitudes, such as the simultaneous experience of
love and hate, are also associated with authority relationships,
particularly in how superior-subordinate become the subject and
object for the expression of dependency reactions. In addition,
the sense of helplessness is particularly sensitized in the events
which project gains and losses in power and status.

Finally, superior and subordinate in any power structure are constantly tempted to manipulate each other as a way of gaining control over one's environment, the more so when there is a lack of confidence and credibility in the organization's efforts to solve problems in realistic ways.

The negative effects of ritualism are precisely in the expenditure of energy to carry out the rituals and also in the childlike expectation that the magic formulas of organizational life substitute for diagnosing and solving real problems. When the heads of organizations are unsure of the bases for the exercise of power and become defensive, the easy solution is to play for time by invoking rituals which may temporarily relieve anxiety.

Similarly, when executives fail to understand the structure and potential of the power coalitions they establish (either consciously or unconsciously), they increasingly rely on rituals to deflect attention away from their responsibilities. And, when leaders are timid men incapable of initiating or responding, the spontaneous reaction is to use people to act out rituals. Usually, the content and symbolism in the rituals provide important clues about the underlying defensiveness of the executive.

Obsessional Leaders

The gravitational pull to ceremonials and magic is irresistible. In positions of power, obsessional leaders use in their public performance the mechanisms of defense which originate in their private conflicts. These defenses include hyper-rationality, the isolation of thought and feeling, reactive behavior in turning anger into moral righteousness, and passive control of other people as well as of their own thought processes.

Very frequently, particularly in this day and age of psychologizing conflict, obsessive leaders "get religion," and try to convert others into some new state of mind. The use of sensitivity training with its attachment to "openness" and "leveling" in power relations seems to be a recent favorite.

What these leaders do not readily understand is the fallacy of imposing a total solution for the problem of power relations where reality dictates at best the possibility of only partial and transient solutions. To force openness through the use of group pressure in therapy groups and to expect to sustain this pressure in everyday life is to be supremely ritualistic. People intelligently resist saying everything they think to other people because they somehow have a deep recognition that this route leads to becoming overextended emotionally and, ultimately, to sadistic relationships.

Intelligent Uses of Power

The choice fortunately is not between ritualistic civility and naive openness in human relationships, particularly where power is concerned. In between is the choice of defining those partial problems which can be solved and through which bright people can learn something about the intelligent uses of power.

We should not lose sight of the basic lesson that people in positions of power differ from "ordinary" human beings mainly in their capacity to impose their personal defenses onto the stage of corporate life. Fortunately, the relationships are susceptible to intelligent management, and it is to the nature of this intelligence that I wish to address the conclusion of this paper.

COMING FULL CIRCLE

The main job of organizational life, whether it concerns developing a new political pyramid, making new appointments to executive positions, or undergoing management succession at top levels, is to bring talented individuals into location for the legitimate uses of power. This is bound to be a highly charged event in corporate relationships because of the real changes in power distributions and the emotional reactions people experience along with the incremental gains and losses of power.

The demand, on the one hand, is for objectivity in assessing people and needs (as opposed to pseudorationality and rationalizing). This objectivity, on the other hand, has to be salvaged from the impact of psychological stresses which impel people to act out fantasies associated with power conflicts. The stresses of change in power relations tend to increase defensiveness to which counterreactions of rationalizing and of mythmaking serve no enduring purpose except perhaps to drive underground the concerns which make people react defensively in the first place.

Stylistic Biases

Thought and action in the politics of organizational life are subject to two kinds of errors commonly found in practical life: the errors of omission and commission. It is both what people do and what they neglect to do that result in the negative effects of action outweighing the positive. But besides the specific errors of omission and commission (the tactical aspects of action), there are also the more strategic aspects which have to be evaluated. The strategic aspects deal both with the corporate aims and objectives and with the style of the leaders who initiate change.

In general, leaders approach change with certain stylistic biases over which they may not have too much control. There is a preferred approach to power problems which derives from the personality of the leader and his defenses as well as from the realities of the situation. Of particular importance as stylistic biases are the preferences for partial, as contrasted with total, approaches and the preferences for substance over form.

Partial vs. Total

The partial approaches attempt to define and segregate problems which become amenable to solution by directive, negotiation, consensus, and compromise.

The total approaches usually escalate the issues in power relations so that implicitly people act as though it were necessary to undergo major conversions. The conversions can be directed toward personality structure, ideals, and beliefs, or toward values which are themselves connected to important aspects of personal experience.

When conversions become the end products of change, then one usually finds heightened concern over such matters as who dominates and who submits, who controls and who is being controlled, who is accepted and who is rejected. The aftermath of these concerns is the heightening of fantasy and defense at the expense of reality.

It may come as something of a disappointment to readers who are favorably disposed to psychology to consider the possibility that while organizations do have an impact on the attitudes of their constituent members, they cannot change personality structures or carry out therapeutic procedures. People may become more effective while working in certain kinds of organizations, but only when effectiveness is not dependent on the solution of neurotic conflict.

The advocates to total approaches seem to miss the point in their eagerness to convert people and organizations from one set of ideas to another. It becomes a good deal wiser, if these propositions are true, to scale down and make concrete the objectives that one is seeking to achieve.

A good illustration is in the attention given to decentralization of authority. Decentralization can be viewed in the image of conversion to certain ideals about who should have power and how this power should be used responsibly, or through an analytical approach to decide selectively where power is ill-placed and ill-used and to work on change at these locations. In other words, the theory of the partial approach to organizations asserts priorities and depends on good diagnostic observation and thought.

Substance vs. Form

Leaders can also present a stylistic bias in their preference for substance or form. Substance, in the language of organizations, is the detail of goals and performance—that is, who has to do what with whom to meet specific objectives. Form directs attention to the relationship of "who to whom" and attempts to achieve goals by specifying how the people should act in relation to each other.

There is no way in which matters of form can be divorced from substance. But students of organization should at least be clear that attention to form *ahead* of substance threatens a person's sense of what is reasonable in undertaking actions. Attention to form may also present an implicit attack on one's conception of his independence and freedom from constraint.

Making form secondary to substance has another virtue: it can secure agreement on priorities without the need of predetermining who will have to give way in the ultimate give-and-take of the negotiations that must precede decisions on organization structure.

The two dimensions of bias, shown in Figure 1, along with the four cells which result, clarify different executive approaches to power. The two dimensions define the executive's cognitive biases in: (1) selection of goals (partial vs. total), and (2) orientation toward action (form vs. substance).

Figure 1
COGNITIVE MANAGEMENT STYLES IN ORGANIZATIONAL LIFE

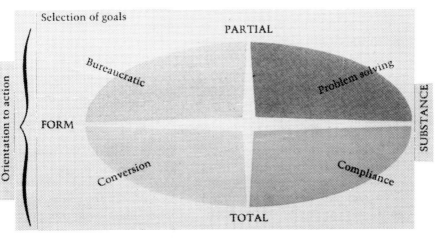

In the *bureaucratic* approach—that is, partial goals and attachment to form as a mode of acting—the emphasis is on procedure and the establishment of precedent and rule to control the uses of power.

The appeal of this approach is its promise of certainty in corporate relationships and in the depersonalization of power. The weaknesses of the bureaucratic approach are too familiar to need detailing here. Its major defect, however, is its inability to separate the vital from the trivial. It more easily commands energy over irrelevant issues because the latent function of the bureaucratic approach is to bypass conflict.

My contention here is that few important problems can be attended to without conflict of ideas and interests. Eventually organizations become stagnant because the bureaucratic approaches seldom bring together power and the vital issues which together make organizations dynamic.

The *conversion* approach (total-form) is notable through the human relations and sensitivity training movements as well as ideological programs, such as the Scanlon Plan and other forms of participative management. The popularity of "management by objectives" bears some scrutiny as a conversion movement directed toward power figures.

Another "total" approach which differs from conversion in its emphasis on substance is *compliance* with the directives of the powerful leader. This is the arena of the authoritarian personality (in both the leaders, who have the power, and in the led, who seek submission), for whom personal power gets expressed in some higher goal that makes it possible for ends to justify means. The ideals may, for example, be race, as with dictator Adolf Hitler, or religion, as with Father Charles Coughlin, a dictator-type orator of the Depression. In business, the illustrations are of a technological variety as with Frederick Winslow Taylor's "scientific management" and Henry Ford's automobile and assembly line.

Almost any technology can assume the proportions of the total approach if it is advanced by a charismatic leader and has deep emotional appeal. This explains the popularity of "management information systems," "value analysis," and "program planning and budgeting," which lead to a belief that the system itself is based on order, rationality, and control; therefore, the belief in turn helps to counteract the fears of chaos and lack of control which make people willing to demand total dependence and compliance in power relations. The effects of this fear on how people seek to arrange power relations in business, government, and the community cannot be overestimated.

Problem-Solving Approach

It should be obvious by now that my favored approach to organizational life combines the biases in Figure 1 of the partial substantive quadrant which I have designated "problem solving." From observation of competent business executives, we know it is precisely their ability to define problems worthy of thought and action and to use their organization to evolve solutions which characterize their style.

The contrary notion that executives are primarily caretakers, mediators, and seekers of consensus is more a myth than an accurate portrayal of how the competent ones attach themselves to power. To have power and not direct it to some substantive end that can be attained in the real world is to waste energy. The difficulties with the problem-solving approach are in risking power in favor of a substantive goal.

While there are no absolute right answers in problem solving, there are ways of evaluating the correctness of a program and a plan. With a favorable average, the executive finds his power base enhanced and his ability to take risks increased.

The problem-solving approach to organization structure operates according to certain premises:

1. That organization structure is an instrument rather than an end. This means that a structure should be established or modified quickly instead of stringing out deliberations as though there actually exists a best and single solution for the problem of allocating power.

2. That organization structure can be changed but should not be tinkered with. This means that members of an executive organization can rely on a structure and can implement it without the uncertainty which comes from the constant modification of the organization chart.

3. That organization structure expresses the working coalition attached to the chief executive. In other words, the coalition has to be established de facto for the structure to mean anything. If the structure is out of line with the coalition, there will be an erosion of power and effectiveness. If no coalition exists in the minds of participants, putting it on paper in the form of an organization chart is nothing more than an academic exercise and a confusing one at that.

4. That organization structure represents a blend of people and job definitions, but the priority is in describing the structure to accommodate competent people. The reason for this priority lies in the fact that competent executives are hard to find. Therefore, as an action principle, one should ensure the effective uses of the scarcest resources rather than conform to some ideal version of power relations.

5. That organization structure is a product of negotiation and compromise among executives who hold semiautonomous power bases. The more the power base of an executive is his demonstrated competence, the greater his autonomy of power and therefore capacity to determine the outcome in the allocations of power. The basic criticism of the problem-solving approach is in the danger of defining issues narrowly and ultimately undermining the moral-ethical basis of leadership. This criticism is valid, but as with so many problems in practical affairs, it can be overcome only by leaders who can see beyond the limits of immediate contingencies. In fact, I have tried to show throughout this paper how the limitations of leaders, in both their cognitive and their emotional capacities, become the causes of power problems.

We have therefore come full circle in this analysis: because power problems are the effects of personality on structure, the solutions demand thinking which is free from the disabilities of emotional conflicts. This insight is often the margin between enduring with what exists, or taking those modest steps which align competence with institutional authority in the service of human needs.

REFERENCE

Barnard, C. (1938), *The Functions of the Executive*. Cambridge, Mass.: Harvard University Press.

Larçon and Reitter view the man-organization relationship in the context of corporate imagery and corporate identity. The authors examine the foundations of this imagery and look into the questions of how it changes with time and how its identity can be created or altered. The relationship between an organization and its members is a continuously evolving process, and the collective corporate identity that emerges is manifested in myth, rituals, and taboos. The authors also discuss the relationship between organizational imagery and its functioning, in particular its capacity for increasing adaptation. Their study of a French furniture company shows how an organization's capacity to adapt is affected by its identity and the images its employees hold of it. (See also Chapter 12 on the role of the ego ideal in organizational identification.)

16

Corporate Imagery and Corporate Identity

JEAN-PAUL LARÇON AND
ROLAND REITTER

In any organization, the relationship between strategic, structural, and psychological factors centering around a common core of abilities leads us to postulate the existence of a "corporate identity" which, in the same way as an individual's personality, deeply influences its development. Corporate identity seems to be a series of interdependent characteristics of the organization from which it draws its specificity, stability, and unity.

No one would deny that in the history of Renault or of General Motors there is a specificity, a stability, and a unity which provide each of these firms with its own identity and permanence despite

---

This chapter was written expressly for this book.

fluctuations in the general industrial situation. Whether seen from the viewpoint of its managers (i.e., Louis Renault or Pierre Dreyfus), or of academics or trade unionists, the firm appears as an entity having specific sociological, psychological, and political characteristics which themselves determine choices of product policy, trade-union relations, and industrial strategies.

What, then, are the foundations of this organizational identity, and how does it change with time? How can such an identity be created or altered? These are all fundamental questions for the managers, consultant, or researcher.

The practitioner generally uses his intuition to understand the identity of the organization with which he is concerned, but we must take our study further than this intuitive approach in order to comprehend this fundamental aspect of the life of the organization.

Let us start with the individual executive. Once he has reached a certain level in the hierarchy, his life within the organization assumes crucial importance for his own self-image to the extent that he assumes responsibilities, has complex power relationships and exerts some influence on the activities of the company. His problems, successes, and failures have a profound effect upon his ambition and psychological equilibrium. The organization is part of his emotional life.

Now, the individual's life in the organization has three aspects: first, he is generally part of a restricted work group in which he spends most of his time and experiences most of his emotions (group identity); second, he encounters specific problems in his job which bring him specific satisfactions (role identity); finally, he is a member of the organization as a whole, and as such he shares his problems with others and obeys the rules of the game (corporate identity). These three elements determine the images the individual forms about his life within the organization. Of course, all these representations are both conscious and unconscious; they are important contributing factors to overall organizational identity.

As a member of a work group, the individual is emotionally

involved; tasks are distributed and in turn received; places are assigned and coalitions are formed. The work group receives a certain amount of power related to the task to be done, and within the group a new division takes place. A certain mental effort is made. The group gradually works out a common mental definition, a common image of the structure of the group in which every member can find a place to his satisfaction. Thus everyone will have a specific and stable image of his group, and of himself as a member of this group.

The individual also carries on a professional role in which he exhibits the personal skills he has developed. This professional role is necessary for the execution of the task which the organization has set itself. The individual soon acquires the qualities necessary to carry on this role; he shares the rules of his professional role with others; he knows the pitfalls to avoid; he acquires an impression of what "we" are—"we" being his professional group, such as IBM systems analysts, or researchers at Polaroid.

Finally, the individual has an image of the organization as a whole, of what it is and what he himself is as a member of the organization. This image of the organization is the fruit of the individual's experiences and of his working life within the firm. It is formed from numerous messages which he decodes. These messages can be grouped according to their origin, for they come from two important and connected spheres in the life of the organization: the political power and the organizational context.

The political power is often differentiated. Behind the senior management there is a controlling power representing the owners, whether public or private. The strength, clarity, and cohesion of this "power constellation" is of interest to every individual in the organization. The very personality of the chief executive, his values, beliefs, attitudes, and personal conflicts cannot be a matter of indifference to those who depend on him, in the sense that it is he who eventually makes the major decisions for the organization and defines its aims and future.

We cannot lay too much stress on the fact that the strategy of an organization partly constitutes the basis of its future identity.

It is therefore vital for each individual to know clearly the firm's aims and how it hopes to achieve them, to the extent that the individual's own identity depends partly on the identity of the organization.

This identity of the organization must be seen in what we can call the organizational structure, that is, the structuring of the life of the organization. Every practitioner knows that it is extremely important for the structure of an organization to be in harmony with its strategy and to be based on systems of management —administrative direction, selection, evaluation, remuneration of personnel, system of planning, etc.—which form a coherent whole and which can provide the individuals in the organization with a coherent and acceptable view of the rules of the game within their organization. If we add to this the working context and the manner in which time and space are treated, we arrive at a composite whole which is nevertheless felt by the individual to be one entity: the organizational structure, within which he acts.

Let us take some examples of the major themes on which the impressions of the organization's identity will be based:

—The institution may appear to be fragmented or, on the other hand, to form a coherent unit: if fragmented, it contains parts which are alien, different, difficult to understand, mysterious, even hostile; if a coherent unit, it forms a familiar world, smooth in operation and presenting few dangers.

—The organization may appear powerful or weak. If powerful, some of its power will reflect back on to its members, unless it scares them. If weak, its members will experience its lack of power, unless they find in this an additional motive to fight the organization's cause.

—It can also be just or unjust, "good" or "bad." It can confer many or few benefits on its members.

—It may select and exclude, or attract and include people, it may give the impression that the hierarchy is important and rigid or, on the contrary, it may smooth over differences and conceal them, treating all its members as equals.

—The organization may be dynamic or inert. It may give its members the impression that they are in control of their environment, or, on the other hand, that they are very dependent on it.

—The organization may be strict or relaxed in the supervision of its employees. Does it follow a manager's movements closely, or does it allow a certain freedom of action? Does it allow for self-expression? Conversely, if the manager loses control over his emotions, how is he allowed to behave? Does it allow for a certain amount of distress? How does it deal with unconventional behavior? Are weaknesses allowed? Is there provision for regression in moments of stress?

—Does the organization permit confrontation and open conflict or does it rather impose a maze of bureaucratic procedures which stifle the shouldering of responsibility and the expression of conflict?

—Is the organization really special and different? Does it permit its members to be so in contacts with outsiders? Or is the manager merely one of many?

These are a few major themes. We shall take one example to illustrate their formation. Let us take the first of the themes we have just mentioned: a fragmented or unified impression of the organization—and relate it to the different categories of messages studied: what is it that makes an organization appear fragmented?

—Disagreement between the owners over what the identity of the firm should be and internal political conflict: this is frequently the case in France where joint ventures are favored (the company Genvrain constitutes a good example).

—Lack of unity at managerial level. First of all, of course, if there is a dyad or triad at the top and if the divisions between senior management are visible, the direction of the firm may be unclear and become a source of distress to those whose position in the firm is in jeopardy.

—However, even without multiple leadership at the top, there may be extreme ambivalence as expressed by the president. He may have doubts about himself and his own ability to act; he may be unconsciously trying to punish himself for his failures and even for his successes.

—The way strategy is determined. Some plans are ambiguous or obscure, or too many directions are issued at the same time. When the members of an organization ask themselves what their firm is doing—or what it is—and they receive conflicting messages without priorities for action, the firm may be seen as lacking identity or unity.

—The administrative systems and procedures. We have approached this subject via the topic of conflicting plans. Even if there is no conflict in the plans themselves, procedures may appear to contradict themselves or the plans. For example, a firm cannot at the same time preach the individual responsibility of employees, and then control their every action.

—Naturally those policies which relate to the process of differentiating or integrating units or to the solving of internal conflicts, also directly influence the perception of the firm's unity or lack of unity.

—Contradiction between the information which the firm issues about itself and the everyday reality of the situation. For example, the firm which tries to persuade itself that it has no conflicts will evolve rituals and taboos to conceal them; it preaches and publicizes certain values, but those who speak openly of conflict are rejected.

This lack of cohesion within the organization, which is also a lack of cohesion within oneself, is experienced traumatically by its members, and may lead to serious disturbances in behavior, such as psychological withdrawal, whereby the individual avoids suffering by refusing to make an emotional commitment, and seeks satisfaction outside the organization.

This last point leads us to a discussion of the relations between the organization's imagery, and the very functioning of the organization, in particular its capacity for strategic adaption. When the researcher looks at an organization, he does not at first see the imagery of the organization's members. What he sees are the concrete collective results of their actions and he can trace the daily habits revealed by what Crozier and Friedberg (1980) call organizational games. He can inquire as to the visible external symbols of the organization's culture. We feel that these fundamental aspects of the organization's functioning are closely dependent on its internal images.

A firm's ability to implement its strategy depends on the ability of its members, both individuals and groups, not only to carry out the specific job assigned to them, but also to coordinate and integrate their efforts—and adapt to external developments. In other words, the practices of each member must be in harmony with the organization's strategy. The games practiced by the individuals and groups must be stable and regulated, while at the same time they must be capable of evolving, if necessary. In short, an organization must have the ability to learn, and it is only able to learn if the structure of its policy games is not too inflexible, for reasons either rational (e.g., conflicting interests) or emotional.

These practices are not the only interesting aspect of organizational functioning. Like all human groups, the organization has a collective life style—a culture—which it manifests in symbolic form: myths, rituals and taboos. These symbols are very important since they provide clues to the collective imagery, their usual function being to allow for the tensions which may arise in the group from the organization's basic choices, and to assert the unity of the group over and above these differences and tensions.

The business firm, like any other human group, engenders myths, that is, stories about its history. The origins of the firm naturally constitute an ideal subject for myths, for it is there that the firm's values generally have their origin. But other key periods may also be evoked: economic crises, wars, interventions by governments (or approaches to governments). In very broad terms the purpose of the myth is to create—or to support—an ideal image of the firm. This image will cover problematic or obscure aspects and show them in a favorable light. The myth itself creates values.

Rites are practices which reflect the myth and which have no significance in themselves other than providing an occasion for a consensus on the important problem which the rite masks. A very good example is dissected by Trepo (1973). Taking four case studies of firms, he shows how a management style which is participative with regard to objectives may turn into a ritual when superiors and subordinates share anxiety regarding their respective situations of power and dependence; a system of Management by Objectives may enable them to hide this anxiety and this situation behind a screen of participation and "modern management." It is also very revealing to note how much such practices become emphasized when they have become rituals, for when an M.B.O. system is really successful, little is said about it. The same goes for the whole phraseology of "modern management": a real manager does not constantly boast of what he is doing.

Taboos can pinpoint the organization's sensitive spots; only those things which strike at the heart of the organization—its basic values, its secret conflict, its contradictions, its traumas—are taboo. Since the taboo is what should be denied, hidden, exorcised, wiped out, it is a fundamental part of the equilibrium of a company.

More generally, organizations have their own distinctive life style. They draw up their own code of values, their code of speech, their code of dress, which is not necessarily that which senior management would like to see applied. For the student of organizations, these symbols constitute an important aspect of identity; they are messages from the organization's core. Thus the organization's identity appears as an aggregate of its interdependent characteristics, which give its specificity, stability, and unity. Of these characteristics, the policy and structural factors form the bases of the identity, whereas the imagery and the functioning of the organization are two facets of the reality of the identity (see Figure 1).

This chart is not easy to use. Policy and structural data must be collected with the patience of an entomologist in order to understand their unity and complexity. At the level of imagery, the researcher deals with human feelings and the unconscious, which is never easy to comprehend. A certain relationship inev-

Figure 1
ORGANIZATIONAL IDENTITY

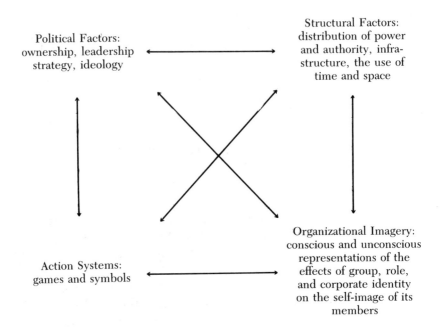

itably develops between the researcher and the persons interviewed, in which the researcher takes on the role of a psychoanalyst,
but in a very ambiguous context. These phenomena (transfer-
ences, countertransferences) are in themselves highly interesting
to analyze. Finally, when the researcher examines the organization's functioning, he is both entomologist and analyst: he observes and describes practices, but he also interprets them in the
realm of the actors' private mental world. He is doomed to move
uneasily back and forth between these two positions.

  We should like to illustrate this grid by briefly considering the
case of Knoll France. Knoll, a firm well known in France for the
sophistication of its contemporary furniture, belongs to an Amer-

ican company, Knoll International, which itself belonged from 1967 to 1975 to a conglomerate, the Walter E. Heller group. In 1973, Knoll France was a firm which had its own traditions and a very personal style within this group, a style created by one of its senior managers of the Sixties, Yves Vidal. At that time most individuals within Knoll France saw themselves as artists and Knoll as a design firm selling "craft works," mainly to the upper class. Organizational life seemed like a continuous party. Pedestrian concerns such as costs were unknown. Knoll meant beauty coming from Bauhaus; Knoll was not just a merchant. The 1972 exhibition of Knoll furniture held at the Louvre symbolized this tradition.

Knoll International, however, the parent company, was more concerned with mass marketing, and has mainly been involved in the office furniture market in the United States. This difference did not matter so long as the whole organization was profitable and shared the same long-term goals, but things became complicated when Walter Heller—who wanted to sell Knoll International—put on pressure to improve the group's short-term profits. Knoll International then informed Knoll France that they must "mass produce or die."

This mass production approach, more commercial than artistic, was achieved, not without difficulty, between 1973 and 1977 by a new management team which day after day came up against the old tradition and the image of "their" firm which is still held by its employees today, especially those on the marketing side. The launching of the "Pillorama" in 1976 can be seen as the symbol of these difficulties. Pillorama was a set of cushions which could be arranged in different ways to form a flexible and mobile system of interior furnishing. There is no doubt that this product corresponded to a developing section of the market and provided an original solution to the furnishing problem for people seeking a new lifestyle. This product, sold at a "moderate" price, was designed in the U.S. to appeal to a very large public. The new chairman of Knoll France, applying the new strategy of mechanization, was one of the first to mobilize his forces to sell this product. It was then that the effects on the individual internal image of Knoll France were suddenly experienced: the French salesmen felt that this product did not correspond to the image of quality or style which they had formed of "their products," and the production department saw the product as unfinished, slapdash, contrary to their tradition. Knoll agents thought the product "clashed" with other products in their shops. In short, it was generally felt that Pillorama was not "Knoll." This conflict in internal imagery might have been one of the contributing factors for the poor performance of Pillorama in France. However, by an irony of fate, an impressive order was won from the head of an important Arab state (where the cushion is a traditional product) for a personalized and luxurious version of the product. The desired "mass-produced" product once more became a "deluxe craft item." The organization had achieved a product in keeping with its identity and that still contributed to the company's success.

Thus it would seem that the firm's capacity to evolve and adapt to external conditions is profoundly affected by its identity, and in particular by those images which the employees form of the organization. A series of studies we made in medium-sized business concerns (Larçon and Reitter, 1979), of about 2,000 employees, has shown in particular that these images have a considerable bearing on the quality of commitment to the firm's general objectives, and on how choices are made between individual objectives and the interests of subgroups—subsidiaries, departments or sections—in relation to the aims of the organization as a whole. The imagery of the organization's members influences attitudes regarding the possible risks involved in investment decisions, diversification projects, the evaluation of new opportunities, the launching of new products. The imagery is decisive in matters of horizontal communication, interdepartmental relations, and cooperation between departments. This concept also appears to be very important when general management wishes to develop cooperation between different departments or to establish close internal cooperation on a specific project.

According to whether the organization appears to be united by a leader, purpose, or strategic plan, or fragmented into disparate activities or into competing feudal units, the attitude of its employees becomes more personal and political, or more cooperative and more oriented towards action and results.

While the small firm is relatively sheltered from these considerations to the extent that allegiance is directed towards the personality of the employer and the range of its products and markets is small, the firm which is both large and diversified may, on the other hand, create for its employees an image which is confused and in itself uninspiring.

One is astonished to discover to what extent objectives which appear clear at the level of general management are misunderstood or distorted at lower levels. The information and communications policy no doubt is partly to blame, but this rift between the firm's real or desired identity and the feeling of identity actually experienced by its members is far more than a simple matter of internal information. The image which employees form of the firm often reflects real inadequacies or contradictions in strategy, in styles of authority, and in the structure of the organization, or above all in the links between these three elements. Thus an analysis of this identity as experienced by others reveals to the chief executive the quality of the employees' participation in the firm's or subsidiary's overall policy and at the same time, the difficulties involved in achieving change. The identity of the firm constitutes a key factor in its survival, a force of inertia or a dynamic factor in its development.

REFERENCES

Crozier, M., & Friedberg, E. (1980), *L'Acteur et le Système*. Paris: Seuil.
Larçon, J.-P., & Reitter, R. (1979), *Structures de Pouvoir et Identité de l'Entreprise*. Paris: Nathan.
Trepo, G. (1973), Management Style à la Française. *European Business*, Autumn.

Section III
Effecting Change

In recent years there has been considerable concern with organizational change and organizational development. Levinson warns against organizational development programs based on insufficient understanding of both the organization and its members. He advocates the formulation of a comprehensive diagnostic technique, arguing that an effective consultant should be familiar with both individual motivation and organizational and small-group theory. He cites many case examples of the dangers of organizational consultation without adequate diagnosis, and offers a five-step diagnostic process based on the clinical case-study method.

17

Organizational Development versus Organizational Diagnosis

HARRY LEVINSON

If issues of individual and organizational adaptation are valid, then it becomes imperative to have sufficient understanding of both individuals and organizations to bring about the effective interaction of both for their mutual benefit. I want to suggest caution about the disproportionate emphasis on one or the other, particularly, given the contemporary emphasis on organizational development, on that preoccupation with organizational change which does not take into account conceptions of psychological man. I think it is important to alert managers and executives to the hazards and risks of disproportionate emphasis so that they may make their choices of consultants and processes more wisely.

This chapter originally appeared in slightly different form as "The Clinical Psychologist as Organizational Diagnostician" in *Professional Psychology*, Winter, 1972, pp. 34-40. Copyright © 1972, by the American Psychological Association. Reprinted by permission.

It is not my intention here to condemn, but to balance. Just as a physician may treat a physical pain with medication, without raising questions about psychological issues which may have precipitated it, similarly many people may become involved in treating an organizational pain on the basis of interventions that do not adequately take into account the psychology of the individuals involved or the comprehensive conception of what the organization is all about. The manager or the executive has the ultimate responsibility for what happens to him and his organization. He cannot leave that to specialists who, after all, by definition are just that—experts in one area.

In recent years there has been considerable concern with organizational change and organizational development. Much of this concern has stemmed from the group dynamics movement, and those who have practiced organizational development have been largely social psychologists, sociologists, and others in a variety of disciplines who have applied variations of group dynamics techniques. A limited number of clinical psychologists have also been involved in this new direction.

Like nondirective counseling, organizational development practices concentrate largely on having people talk to each other about their mutual working interests and problems; on working together on the resolution of common problems; and on having people weigh, out loud and with each other, their organizational aspirations and goals. These efforts are largely devoid of systematic theory. They are often problem-specific and frequently intuitive. It is presumed by their practitioners that the same general methods will apply to all organizations.

The field of organizational development is presently in a fluid state, marked primarily by ad hoc problem-solving efforts and by a heavy emphasis on expedient techniques ranging from games to confrontation. Frequently, the rationale behind these techniques is poorly thought through, and the fact that the techniques sometimes precipitate untoward consequences is either unrecognized or denied by many who claim to be experts in organizational development. However, as any skilled clinician knows, not all patients will prosper equally well with the same therapy, and there are severe limitations to that kind of intervention that merely enables people to clarify their conscious feelings and to work on problems consciously perceived. For dealing with more complex problems at deeper levels, the clinician—whether psychologist or psychiatrist—requires a comprehensive theory of personality and a range of interventions from which to choose techniques flexibly as the therapy progresses.

Little of what is presently called organizational development involves anything like formal diagnosis. For example, while it is traditional for a responsible clinical psychologist to evaluate his client or patient both from the point of view of that person's problems and the capacity he has for dealing with them—and most psychologists would find it irresponsible to work with clients or patients without formulating an understanding of what they are dealing with—such processes are not within the purview of most people involved in organizational development. It is my contention that a professional cannot act responsibly in consultation, whether individual or organizational, unless he maintains a scientific point of view about what he does. To me, this means that he must formulate a diagnosis, which is essentially a working hypothesis about what he is dealing with. Then he must formulate methods—whether they be treatment, intervention, training experiences, or other devices—that will be effective tests of the hypothesis he proposed or that will compel him to revise his hypothesis and change his methods accordingly.

A diagnosis, whether of an individual or an organization, requires a comprehensive examination of the client's system. That examination of the individual who is a client will frequently involve measures of intelligence and intellective or cognitive functions and modes of assessing psychological defenses and coping mechanisms, managing emotions, and pinpointing focal conflicts. A thorough examination will also require understanding personal history as the context for character formation and styles of adaptation. The examination will frequently involve psychological testing and often consultation with a neurologist, pediatrician, or psychiatrist. Indeed, some psychologists specialize in diagnosis alone, a process so helpful that in many of the best kinds of psychological and psychiatric clinics such diagnostic formulations guide the therapy regardless of who conducts it. Thus, a comprehensive examination, leading to a sensitive and sophisticated diagnostic statement, becomes the basis for predicting the best kind of therapeutic process, its likely course and outcome, and possible danger points. That process also permits the professional to review what goes on in his relationship with his client, to modify his behavior and activity in keeping with changes in his diagnostic hypotheses, and, ultimately, to compare his examinational finding at different points in time to measure progress.

It is quite unfortunate that this process seems not to be an intrinsic part of contemporary organizational development, but there are a number of reasons why. There is no systematic body of professional knowledge about organizational development. Most books on the subject are fragmentary, made up of unintegrated papers. Most techniques are ad hoc, with limited rationale. Many, if not most, people who work with organizational development have had limited training, some having no more than attended sensitivity training groups or, at best, having had only a brief internship in conducting sensitivity training. Most have had no training in depth to understand the dynamics of individual personality (even those who have degrees in social psychology or sociology), let alone any sophisticated understanding of group processes. Many lean heavily on psychological cliches like "self-actualization" or similar slogans derived from rubrics used in psychological research without refining these rubrics into syndromes or formulations that create the conditions for intervention. Finally, much organizational development seems to hinge on one device, namely, confrontation, which, when it is the single technique for all problems, necessarily becomes merely a gimmick. With respect to organizational development, we are at that point in time comparable to the use of leeches in medicine. Just as they served the purpose of drawing bad blood, so the single technique in organizational development seems to be justified in terms of serving the purpose of drawing out bad feelings or emotions.

FAILURE TO DIAGNOSE AND THE CONSEQUENCES

This state of affairs inevitably leads to certain kinds of failures, disillusionments, destructive consequences, and other negative outcomes that ultimately cause the public—in this case, the companies or other institutions—to withdraw, as many have, from sensitivity training and encounter techniques. Following are some case examples where the failure to diagnose led to untoward consequences.

A rigid, authoritarian company president, who built his organization into prominence, was disappointed by the fact that he could not seem to retain a corps of young managers who had top management executive potential. While he hired many, they left after two or three years with the organization, usually moving up into higher level roles in other companies. He himself attributed this loss to an inadequate management development program and sought the help of a social scientist well versed in the concept of confrontation. Certain that the problem was the president himself, and equally that he would profit by attack from his subordinates, the social scientist arranged an organizational development program whose first steps included just that kind of confrontation. In the course of the experience, the president became livid with frustrated rage, angry that his paternalism was unappreciated, and abandoned his efforts to develop the company further. In impulsive anger, he sold it, in a merger that ultimately cost him dearly and that enmeshed his management in the problems of adopting the company to its new role as merely an appendage of a larger organization.

A major division of a large corporation undertook, with the help of a prominent and responsible consultant, an organizational development program intended to "open things up" in order to foster group cooperation. Shortly after this development effort, the division head was removed from his position because it was discovered that he had manipulated and exploited his subordinates, that he had sponsored orgies at sales meetings in violation of company ethics, and that he had, in various other psychopathic ways, acted irresponsibly and manipulatively. The consultant, however well qualified in working with groups, knew nothing about individual psychology and, as a result, his efforts to "open people up" served only to make people potentially more vulnerable to exploitation. Under such circumstances that group of managers would have been much better off to have learned ways of becoming more highly guarded and protected.

A company president, in an effort to solve a problem of long-standing conflict between himself and two vice presidents reporting to him (whom he could not discharge), sought occasional professional advice on how to deal with this problem. The severely intense nature of the conflict reflected not only chronic irritation but certain obvious neurotic problems that required individual therapy for two of the three men involved. Both disdained such help. One of the vice presidents, impressed with the work of a trainer involved in team building in a division, persuaded the president to use the trainer to help the three of them resolve their conflict. The president agreed. The trainer's mode of working was to attack and pry loose the feelings of hostility, which he then required to be exhibited publicly. This mode of attack, like evangelistic fervor of old, served the purpose of making the president confess his "guilt" and his inadequacies, which the trainer required to be done not only in the presence of the two vice presidents but, subsequently, in the presence of the whole group of managers who reported to them. The president became increasingly depressed and was referred for psychiatric consultation. Meanwhile, the remaining managerial group, now subject to psychological attack from the president and vice presidents, as well as from the trainer (who made it known to all that he was making the decisions about managers' careers), awaited apprehensively their turn to be exposed. Furthermore, as the president became increasingly depressed, the story started circulating in managerial ranks that the vice president who brought the trainer in was using him to destroy the president. When the trainer was confronted by others about the destructive effect on the president of what he was doing he denied that he needed to have knowledge about such effects, saying that he was only "training" people and did not claim to be a psychologist (though he was a member of the American Psychological Association) or a psychiatrist.

A major consulting organization undertook to advise on the drastic reorganization of a client firm. The consequence of this drastic reorganization was that many people who had previously held power were successfully emasculated of their power although they retained their positions. The firm traditionally had insisted on and rewarded compliance so these men did not openly complain, but there was widespread depression and anger among them for which the consulting firm assumed the responsibility. In fact, it is doubtful whether their development efforts included any recognition of the psychological consequences of what they did.

As part of a developmental effort in a company, thought to be a wise course to "open people up," a trainer undertook encounter experiences that involved having the executives touch each other and engage in activities that brought them physically closer to each other. Two executives, whose latent homosexual impulses (unconscious and well controlled) could not tolerate such closeness, had psychotic breaks, and had to be hospitalized.

A trainer undertook a two-day intensive session with a group of managers in a company and required them to tell each other what problems they had with other managers and what they thought of each other's on-the-job behavior. This was, in many respects, a cathartic session, which discharged much hostility, presumably in preparation for cooperative work. However, when the management in the organization failed to follow up and, indeed, began to see the now "opened up" group as a threat to its power and tried to disband it as an effective group, the participants became disillusioned and angry and now pulled farther away from each other. Having expressed their hostility to each other for the purpose of common good, they now had to live with their hostile expressions when there was no longer a common good. They began to avoid each other and to feel guilty for their expressions as they awaited retaliation from those whom they had criticized.

The cases just cited are examples of the destructive conse-

quences of organizational consultation without diagnosis. I could
offer many more examples, but these will suffice.

FORMAL DIAGNOSTIC PROCESS

In order for a consultant to avoid these kinds of consequences,
he must have a systematic knowledge of individual motivation,
as well as organizational and small-group theory, and be able to
evolve modes of intervention based on diagnoses that include that
multiple level understanding. Now, by way of contrast, I will
illustrate, with several cases, what I think a formal diagnostic
process should provide.

The State Department has been subject to widespread criticism, study by several outside commissions, sensitivity training,
and a variety of other interventions, to little or no avail. The
problems of this bureaucracy remained and still had to be dealt
with. Diagnosis of that system indicated that an organizational
structure was unlikely to be changed by pressure from the outside
alone, pressure from the inside alone, or pressure from leadership
alone. It could not be altered significantly by sensitivity training
methods alone, as had already been demonstrated, or by leadership. If the problems were structural, that is, bureaucratic, then
change could occur only by altering the whole structure and by
evolving mechanisms for keeping it open. This conception led to
the establishment of thirteen task forces (including about twenty
people each) operating simultaneously. Thus, some 250 people
were turned loose in a self-appraisal of their own structure. They
produced from this a 600-page volume and have since had a series
of follow-up outcome statements on their recommendation. There
was minimal work by the consultant, which consisted largely in
his instructing the task force leaders, supporting organizational
leadership, and helping the task force leaders and the organizational leadership anticipate the kinds of hostility they were going
to encounter.

A president with a good managerial history was brought in to
head a scientific company whose key men neither understood nor

wanted to be subject to professional management. When they threatened to resign, and some did, urgent consultation was requested. Diagnosis of this situation took into account organizational history and scientific values, desertion by the company's founders, exploitation by a previous president, cohesion of the in-group, and the need to retain adaptive profitability. On the basis of a comprehensive assessment, it was decided to hear the men out in individual interviews, then summarize those interviews and present them simultaneously to the interviewees and the president. This procedure produced problems and issues to be dealt with, without subjecting the group to the possible exploitation of the president, whom they feared, and without running the risk of their destroying him under confrontation attack. The consultant became, in effect, an intermediary. On the one hand, his job was to help the president understand the nature of the complaints and the kinds of people he was dealing with as well as certain basic psychological principles. On the other hand, his task was to help the group recognize its need for a professional manager and to offer these men more constructive ways of giving the president support and guidance. After the initial contact of three, three-day sessions, the consultant maintained a distance from the group so that he would not be seen as "running the company." Many of the key managers individually took part in executive seminars to learn more about the psychology of management, and the consultant was available to all of them as individuals by phone or personal contact. This enabled the president and his key figures to develop a working relationship in which all could count on the distant but supportive influence of the consultant and the new and consistent pattern of leadership the president established.

Once general comfort was attained in these relationships and the men could come to trust the president (in part because the consultant drew off some of their hostility toward him), they decided that it would be wise to get together as a group at monthly intervals in order to open up avenues of communication, which they knew needed opening but which would have been destructively explosive had they been opened before. The group continues to function effectively together, now more closely than ever. However, this process of carefully differentiated steps extended over a three-year period.

Following the devastating effect of the reorganization of a company (mentioned in the fourth case in the previous discussion) and a subsequent year of turmoil, a consultant was asked to undo the situation. Initial interviews with the executives indicated the severity of the depression each was experiencing and provided information on the turmoil in the rest of the organization. Building upon a clinical understanding of depression following the experience of loss, an appreciation of the sense of responsibility the managers in the organization felt, the sensitivity of the new leadership, and important changes in external forces which the organization now confronted, the consultant recommended that the 100 top management people be brought together for a meeting to last several days. During this meeting, on the consultant's recommendation, the chief executive officer presented the history of the organization, its achievements, its present state, and its future potential, and indicated clearly what was happening in the outside environment and what drastic changes had to be made. This was followed by an opportunity for the 100 men, in small groups, to discuss and analyze what they had heard and to mourn the loss as well as to confront reality. While regretting the past, they could begin to see clearly what the future held and what kinds of adaptive efforts might have to be made.

They were then reconvened to hear presentations about future trends in their field, as well as in society at large, and to set in context what they were up against. They then had the opportunity to discuss and digest their impressions and to see how such forces related to them. On the basis of those small-group discussions, they established priorities for action, brought them together in large plenary sessions, and evolved a charter for their functional operations. Thus, they began to turn their aggressions outward on real problems, which they faced together, while working through their sense of loss and depression.

The president of a small corporation, wanted to develop an adaptive executive team on the one hand but, on the other, had the paranoid feeling that such a group would steal his business from him. I say paranoid because that was an important component of his personality. The consultant's diagnosis was that open confrontation would only reinforce his paranoid feelings and frighten him into withdrawing from his people further. Instead, the consultant chose to work directly with the president for a time, helping him spell out his fears and testing his suspicions of the consultant in a one-to-one relationship. Once that relationship could contain the suspicious hostility of the president, the consultant met with the vice presidents who reported to the president, got their view of the working relationship, and translated that for the president in ways that enabled him to understand the effects of his behavior without feeling attacked. Subsequently, the vice presidents and president were brought together to talk about these issues, with the consultant as a medium for trust and control. With that kind of process in motion, the consultant began to work with the twenty men who were the third echelon, taking them as a group through their working relationships and their managerial skills, now less afraid that they might be attacked by a suspicious, impulsive president for asserting their independence.

I cite these examples, not to illustrate in detail a diagnostic process, but to indicate that one was in motion which required different interventions for different organizations and with different people under varying circumstances. Whether the diagnoses made were the correct ones is not the point. Inasmuch as they were made consciously, they could exist as testable hypotheses, always subject to change. The consultant could then make interventions of choice. In effect, he exercised control over what was happening, testing his choices rather than assuming that one method worked equally well in all circumstances.

DEALING WITH PSYCHOLOGICAL POLLUTION

There is a devastating trend of psychological pollution in contemporary organizational circles. Destructive influences arise out

of merger, reorganization, individual and organizational obsolescence, and change. These forces will continue for the foresee-
able future. That kind of pollution can be dealt with through the
medium of organizational intervention, providing the consultant
has sufficient understanding of diagnostic and therapeutic conceptions to discern the phenomena he is dealing with and to be
able to act on them. We cannot afford the continued blundering
by untrained people, which is destructive to organizations and to
individuals, but we do have resources to deal with the problems.

First, executives can draw more heavily on clinically trained
personnel. The clinical psychologist and psychiatrist, trained as
they are in individual diagnosis and therapy, have a basic frame
of reference for looking at organizational problems in the same
way. Many are already working with families as systems. If encouraged to do so, many can extend their knowledge and, subsequently, their efforts to include organizations as systems. Such
work requires a formal diagnostic process built on clinical skills
but expanded to view the organization as the client system and
to include group and organization processes.

Clinicians can extend their diagnostic frame of reference, as
I have recently done (Levinson, 1972), by evolving a five-step
procedure. This procedure should include: (1) a detailed organizational history that will delineate both the forces impinging on
the organization over time and its characteristic adaptive pattern
and its modes for coping with crisis; (2) a description of the organization that would include its organizational structure, physical
facilities, people, finances, practices and procedures, policies,
values, technology, and context in which the organization operates; (3) an interpretation of observations, interviews, questionnaires, and other information about the organization's characteristic
ways of receiving, processing, and acting upon information, as
well as the personality characteristics of the dominant organizational figures and the style of organizational personality; (4) a
summary and interpretation of all these findings with a diagnostic
formulation; (5) a feedback report to the organization to establish
a basis for organizational action toward solving its problems.

Such a process is extended from and based on the clinical case study method. It views the organization as an open system with a range of semi-autonomous interacting subsystems. Both the subsystems and the organization as a total system can be evaluated in terms of how effectively they adapt to the environments in which they operate, where organizational and subsystem strengths and weaknesses lie, and what kinds of steps can be delineated to utilize the assets to cope with the weaknesses. In undertaking this kind of organizational diagnostic process, the clinician must give careful attention to the psychology of the individuals involved and to the collective psychology of groups, since many people working in the same organization share common elements of personality.

Second, the nonclinician familiar with group and organizational processes but unfamiliar with personality theory and clinical diagnostic practice can expand his learning to include both. There are clinical training resources in most large communities. There are also many individual clinicians who can serve as training consultants for people who need that kind of preparation.

The ultimate practice of organizational development might better be called "applied clinical sociology." The executive who is to make use of such techniques should therefore be certain his consultant is well trained in both dimensions—clinical and organizational. In practice, such a consultant usually gives careful attention to leadership and to continued work with the leadership. His feedback of his diagnosis to the client system or his guidance of an organizational team to formulate a diagnostic statement becomes the basis for formulating common action. He deals with both positive and negative unrealistic expectations of himself. In the last analysis, such a consultation is the management of a relationship between the consultant and the organizational system—thus a problem of clinical management for therapeutic purposes.

The need for such a diagnostic process is imperative because of disillusionment not only with organizational development but with many aspects of community change. Despite much talk, community psychology, community psychiatry, and other forms of community organizational development, have not had a significant impact on social systems, such as churches, schools, and similar community agencies. No amount of ad hoc expedience, no amount of talking about "growth," and no amount of depreciating the old as being "in the medical model" will substitute for solid knowledge systematically organized, interpretations based on a comprehensive conceptual system, and diagnostic hypotheses amenable to continuous testing and alterations. Only with a solid clinical base can one come at community and organizational development with a prospect of long-term gain. Inevitably, if he is to have a community impact, the clinician must become an organizational diagnostician, and the organizational development man, a clinician. The wise executive can facilitate that combination of skills by demanding the level of performance that requires it.

CONCLUSION

Many efforts to change organizations are based on economic-man or self-actualizing-man conceptions. These result in organizational restructuring, manipulation of rewards and punishments, or efforts to foster group interaction and group problem solving. However, based on limited understanding of the individual personality, they frequently produce unintended consequences. These efforts toward change cannot deal with problems where complex psychological issues are at play. Scientifically based interventions require formal diagnostic formulations and choice of methods of change based on such formulations. These require a conception of psychological man to take into account both individual and group processes. The executive who seeks organizational development consultation should require both individual and group levels of sophistication.

REFERENCE

Levinson, H. (1972), *Organizational Diagnosis*. Cambridge, Mass.: Harvard University Press.

Brocher elaborates on the theme of organizational diagnosis, emphasizing the effects of organizations on individuals. Organizations, created to serve human needs, acquire a life of their own, a functional autonomy which enables them to play a profoundly important role in shaping the personalities of those who work within them. He argues for a multidisciplinary approach to diagnosis, pointing out the pitfalls in applying to whole organizations methods of diagnosis which are appropriate to individuals, and he identifies the basic functions of organizations and describes the nature of their interrelationship.

18

Diagnosis of Organizations, Communities, and Political Units

TOBIAS BROCHER

The evolution of psychiatric diagnosis has been affected by more than twenty-five years of intensive research in the area of collective influence and group impact on individual behavior. Classic publications (Asch, 1940, 1951, 1952; Bion, 1948a, 1948b, 1949a, 1949b, 1950a, 1950b, 1952; Cartwright and Zander, 1960; Lewin, 1951; Lewin et al., 1939; Sherif and Sherif, 1953) have produced a tendency to question the idealized autonomy of the individual. Freud was accused by his contemporaries of having caused a serious narcissistic injury to individual self-esteem by diagnosing the dependency of the ego as a continuous struggle with two powerful adversaries: the "upward" drive impulses of the id, and their "downward" control by the superego as the heir of early aggression. In his first publication on groups, "Group

This chapter originally appeared in the *Bulletin of the Menninger Clinic*, 40:513-530, 1976.

373

Psychology and the Analysis of the Ego" (1921), Freud stated that group members follow the same ego ideal. Thus, group members reduce ingroup tension and aggression by unifying their individual aggressive drive needs which can then be directed toward an outside object—a particular outgroup or cause. The reduction of infighting and the increase in group cohesion enable the designated leader to use and direct the group's collective power to facilitate the group's success in reaching its goals.

Of course, the individual can become the victim of collective irrational assumptions by being unable to resist the group's pressure. As long as a group is not subject to appropriate control by external reality factors, its members are blinded in their cohesion by the same ego ideal, which is never questioned in terms of reality and group environment. One of the most terrifying collective experiences in recent history was the deliberately planned mass seduction of Germany. Nazi "group think" (Janis, 1958) misled millions of people who considered themselves intelligent human beings into a dehumanizing racism that ended in holocaust and cold-blooded slaughter. Sherif and Sherif's (1953) group experiments and Milgram's (1965) punishment research have demonstrated the impact and consequences of irrational premises and group assumptions on individual behavior. It is possible to destroy or divert individual insight and to prevent reality perceptions by creating social dependency needs, thereby forcing the individual into primary process operations through collective regression in the interest of collective unconscious drive needs and satisfaction.

Mental health professionals have been confronted with a whole new area of psychiatric diagnosis which can no longer be handled exclusively by isolating one individual from the group and treating him with traditional methods. The usual argument for limiting diagnosis to single individuals is: Since it is so difficult to determine the intrapsychic dynamics and to understand the motivation and functions of a single person, and since the functioning of organizations is determined by so many different persons, how can we dare to try to understand the functioning of organizations, communities, and political units? The dynamics of these interpersonal and intergroup relationships are predetermined by the perception and reaction formations of individuals who form any group, independent of its size. However, the whole is more than the sum of its parts because the various relationships between individuals within the system or organization determine the analytical approach to organizational diagnosis.

In the various approaches used to diagnose organizations, one serious pitfall has been to transfer methods appropriate to an individual patient to whole organizations—applying unchanged psychiatric statements which are based on the assumption that psychiatry and psychology have a valid, objective yardstick for what can be labeled "normal" or "sick." However, such statements do not include the premise that these sciences are part of the same society, with their own organizations which do not function any better than the society, and which share many basic assumptions with other groups and organizations within the same culture. The obstacle blurring our diagnostic vision is precisely "our acquired psychology—the programmed set of needs, values, attitudes, and prejudices . . . which have been shaped and deeply fixed by our existent social institutions" (Marmor, 1974, p. 429) and by the organizational mechanisms which we claim to diagnose and change. The question is: How much is the tendency to act to our own advantage or in our own defense connected with the specific needs of the societal group we serve? Psychiatry as an organization will have to redefine its primary task in relation to the environment in terms of reality control.

Organizations created to serve and facilitate human needs "acquire a life of their own, a functional autonomy . . . by virture of which they thenceforth play a profoundly important role in shaping the personalities of human beings who grow up in their sphere of influence" (Marmor, 1974, p. 421) and who begin to serve and maintain it without recognizing the destructive nature of an autonomous organization that neglects human needs. The myth of the machine prevails when the individual submits himself to the autonomy of the institution without questioning the validity of this abstraction. The preliminary diagnostic question, therefore, deals with the relationship between the individual and the organization. It is difficult to give a clear definition of the term *organization* because it is used in such varying contexts. For psychiatric diagnosis, organization must be more narrowly defined than in sociology or anthropology.

In defining the four pure types of complex formal organizations, the distinctions are between variations in costs, benefits, and transactions with recipients. Although most real organizations' actions fulfill the definition of more than one type, they are mixtures and not compounds.

> a. A *cooperative organization* is one whose sponsors are the recipients of its outputs and whose sponsors' goal is their own welfare as recipients . . . . the costs and benefits [are assigned] to them in their role as recipients, not as sponsors, since it is only to receive its outputs that they sponsor the organization. . . .
>
> b. A *profit organization* is one run in the interests of its sponsors, who except incidentally are not the same people as the recipients and whose outputs go to recipients on the basis of selfish transactions.
>
> c. A *service organization* is one whose outputs go to recipients on the basis of generous transactions. In the pure case . . . the outputs are pure gifts whose costs are born solely by the sponsors.
>
> d. A *pressure organization* is an organization . . . whose outputs go directly or indirectly to [a] recipient . . . for the purpose of improving the position of [the sponsor] . . . in a transactional relation with [the recipient]. . . . The sponsor . . . or his agent bears the cost . . . of the pressure activity . . . which is the output of the organization [Kuhn, 1974, p. 323].

Diagnosis is based on organizational analysis which includes two distinct types: ". . . the system concepts to deal with the organization viewed as a unit and the intersystem concepts of communication and transaction to deal with the interactions of its parts and its own interactions as a unit with other systems" (Kuhn, 1974, p. 327). The role of the psychiatrist and psychologist is limited to dealing with the intersystem concept. Nevertheless, the psychiatric or psychological consultant must compare his data with the prevailing sociological concept of the total organization as a unit.

However, in spite of the fact that the psychiatrist working as a consultant in business, industry, and government has to cope with the individual organization as a whole, his task is limited to specific aspects. For example, the psychiatrist examines the intra- and intergroup relationships relevant for the functioning of the organization. He looks at an individual's internal processes and at his maintenance system in contrast to the control system. "In all his communications and transactions the individual human acts as a unit—even if with vacillations, contradictions, and unconscious components" (Kuhn, 1974, pp. 297-298). By contrast, an organization's external interactions can be carried on simultaneously by different levels of the system. Organizational diagnosis follows these specific patterns by attending separately to the main or whole-system level and the subsystem level while dealing also with the intra- and intersystem aspects at each level. In addition, the distinction between formal and informal organizations and between controlled and uncontrolled systems must be made. Since it is possible to gather information about the goals, the internal and external constraints of formal organizations, a detailed theory could be built around formal organizations; however, applying any such theory to informal organizations such as political groups and subgroups would be difficult.

The sociologist has two main choices in the analysis of complex organizations when their complexity becomes too unwieldy to apply a tight analytic mode. He can either use statistical generalizations based on empirical observations of particular types of organizations and their behavior, or he can develop a special purpose or simulation model constructed from the same analytic building blocks. Sociological organization theory can still miss relevant aspects important for the diagnostic process because it is less related to organizational structure than to human needs. The diagnostic gap in sociological and economic or structural organization analysis has been the human factor. Gouldner (1965) describes the first steps to correct the sociological model, but his description does not clarify the importance of psychoanalysis as an applied psychology and behavioral science. Gouldner points out the characteristic differences between the social engineering model and the clinical model, including psychoanalysis. The traditional management consultant firm often takes the client's own formulation of the client's problems at face value, thereby paradoxically preserving the tensions and neglecting the breakdown in informal organization. In contrast, practitioners employing the clinical model do not accept "their clients' own formulation of their problem . . . at face value. Instead . . . [they take] their clients' complaints and self-formulations as only one among a number of 'symptoms' useful in helping them to arrive at their own diagnosis of the clients' problems" (Gouldner, 1965, p. 13). Thus the social engineer tends to study what the client tells him to, while the clinician necessarily arrives at an independent identification of the group's or organization's problems.

Before discussing more specific details, I should define the general framework within which the psychiatrist can operate to achieve an appropriate organizational diagnosis.

> Social scientists who use survey methods in their research on complex organizations do not think of themselves as having much in common with clinicians . . . [The distinction seems to be apparent in the] quantitative, statistical, content-specific approach . . . [of the social scientist and] the qualitative, non-statistical, more encompassing approach of the clinician . . . [Both social scientists and clinicians] are interested in understanding what factors are related to organizational functioning and individual member behavior . . . [and] in individual and organizational variables, how they relate to one another, and how these relationships change over time [Neff, 1965, p. 23].

By the term diagnosis the psychiatrist means

> . . . the process of examining various characteristics of an organization and its members to provide an accurate description of how things stand or are proceeding . . . [Diagnosis requires]

the collection of valid information . . . evaluation of that information, and assignment of priorities to courses of action which might be taken to improve the state of the organization. A diagnosis . . . is conditioned by the purpose, method, and sophistication of those making it [Neff, 1965, p. 25].

Most organizations are

> . . . hierarchically structured. This structure can be thought of as a pyramid of "organizational families." Each family is composed of a supervisor and the people who report to him, starting with the president and going down through the "linkpins" (member of one family, head of the next lower) to the first line supervisor and his subordinates (Neff, 1965, p. 28).

This structure serves as a communication link upward and a boundary function downward.

The typical member of an average company rarely has full qualitative and quantitative data about the state of the organization's structure. Nevertheless, each subgroup or subsystem within an organization follows certain assumptions that are related to specific reference groups. These reference groups serve as a yardstick of comparison for negative or positive aspirations. Hence, the willingness to identify with an organization's overall goals and objectives demonstrates a specific gradient which decreases from the top level down to the production line worker—a factor based on the amount of knowledge and information about the whole. The most striking result of this identification process is the development of an organizational ideology or myth which often shows characteristics of the leading group's values and beliefs. These values are unconsciously shaped by the leader's early object relationships and by historical figures—a sort of "tribal" value. Even the "tribal totem" appears as a trademark, logo, or traditional identifying symbol, just as the unwritten taboos determine inclusion or exclusion from the leading part of the organization.

In the last fifty years most industrial and business organizations have shifted from family enterprise to management systems. For instance, at the beginning of this century one of the largest companies had 1,000 employees, but today the average employee does not know the size of the corporation for which he works. In the family enterprise, identification with the founder contributed to the traditional, emotionally rooted feelings of belonging; the exchangeability, anonymity, and the functional concepts of management systems have taken away this emotional potential for personal relationships, creating instead feelings of alienation, isolation, and anxiety that cannot be shared openly with others. Nevertheless, complex organizations are still managed by people. Despite the increase in size and the diversification of production within large corporations, most organizations still consist of clearly distinguishable subsystems which are functionally connected. In addition to the imprinting quality of leadership styles within top management, this connecting function—the "link-pin"—between subsystems is most significant for organizational diagnosis.

In contrast, communities cannot be considered formal organizations. Although the community has a formal leadership and administration, both are only part of the whole, while the population forming the community remains an uncontrolled system. When a team from the Menninger Foundation intervened in the clashes between police and demonstrators in the community of Lawrence, Kansas (Satten et al., 1970-1971), it became evident that a diagnostic assessment of community conflict must take into account the unstructured and uncontrolled parts of community systems. The formal organization of the unrecognized opinion leaders within the community who had no official function proved to be more important for gathering diagnostic data than the formal administrative structure. Similar experiences in other larger communities (Green et al., 1972) confirm the importance of making the communication gaps present in intergroup conflicts the primary diagnostic focus. Although this information cannot be obtained by observation—it must be provided by individuals—the human factor is often neglected. No intervention is possible without clarifying the interpersonal motivation of intra- and intergroup conflicts.

When dealing with communities or political units like city councils or school boards as compared with industrial or business organizations, the diagnostic approach employed must take into account the relevance of highly complex informal and uncontrolled structures which are difficult to identify. A recent diagnostic study of a community by another Menninger Foundation team (Brocher et al., 1975) demonstrates the serious consequences of failing to identify and involve informal groups and opinion leaders. Not only is the relevance of informal subgroups often misjudged or unrecognized by traditional, formal community leaders, but their impact and influence on decision-making processes is frequently underestimated. The residuals of powerful authoritarian leadership assumptions are counterproductive to the intended goals.

When William C. Menninger (1947) studied the leadership styles of military commanders, he made discoveries similar to Bion's (1948a, 1948b, 1949a, 1949b, 1950a, 1950b)—that the derivatives of early object relations in the individual leader determine the preferred, irrational basic assumptions of the group. The more differentiated findings also confirmed the reciprocity between the individual valences of group or unit members and the specific valence of the group leader. Further development of group theories led to a more differentiated hypothesis of group functioning. Special identifiable functions can be recognized within groups and subsystems independent of the technical content or professional task. We call the role of the formal group leader within an organization the "alpha function." It is necessarily accompanied by a number of "alpha variations" taken by leaders of subsystems who are identifying themselves with the primary "alpha." The "alpha function" could not exist without the majority of followers whose activities comprise the "gamma function." The relationship of all "gamma functions" to the various "alpha functions" depends on two factors: (1) the relationship between "alpha functions" and "omega functions," i.e., the relation between the leading part and the weakest, most endangered, or temporarily dysfunctional parts of an organization; and (2) the relationship between "alpha functions" and "beta functions," i.e., the specific relation between the leading part and its critical opponent.

The "beta function" represents the independent reality control within a group and introduces the neglected or denied awareness of irrational group assumptions based on emotional group needs without appropriate realistic data. It is usually the most rejected function although the data base stems from realistic observations of how "omega functions" are treated by "alpha" and consequently by "gamma." The importance of the "beta function" becomes more understandable in light of the consequences of the "alpha-omega" relationship. The leader's perception of and actual behavior toward "omega" is a mirror image of his own relationship or the relationship of the leading group to the organizational environment, caused and shaped by the prevailing early object relationships and their derivatives.

The same organizational hierarchy is repeated in the organization's subgroups. The "link-pin" performs the "alpha function" in his own organizational family. His role change often leads to highly unconscious ingroup competitiveness because the qualities and valences the "link-pin" must adopt in assuming the "alpha function" on the lower level persist when he adopts his boundary function even though different qualities and valences must be mobilized if he is to function as the connecting link between the organization's various levels. Although the organization may have highly technical goals, and the primary task is clearly defined by reality demands from the environment, it is no surprise when organizational decisions are influenced by individual character structures, although this irrational influence is usually unrecognized.

An example may help demonstrate this point. A vice president in charge of the research department of a large company refused to move to the top executive suite in the main building. In his resistance against a newly appointed executive vice president, he even refused to participate in various executive committee sessions, pretending that his scientific experiments did not permit him to spend time on administrative issues. As a result the executive committee was confronted with serious personnel problems throughout the research department as well as with an increasing deficit. What appeared on the surface to be an economic problem was actually a character problem in one man who was performing a secondary "alpha function." The struggle continued as long as the organization permitted him to act out and let his character structure take precedence over organizational necessities.

One of the most difficult problems in organizations is the tendency to force individuals into specific roles. Scapegoating in groups is a well-known phenomenon. More specific is the risk of being forced into a certain role that enables other team or group members to avoid burdensome tasks or personal exposure. The same applies to intergroup relations in organizations, as the Ahmedabad, Glacier Company, Unilever, and Findus experiments have proven. The relationship between work assignment, individual capacity, and compensation has been described by Jaques (1961) as the most valid factor for diagnosing and evaluating individual function or dysfunction in an appropriate way as well as diagnosing intergroup prejudice. Most of these research experiences published by the Tavistock Institute of London are based on psychoanalytic concepts. Unfortunately, in some countries psychoanalysis has taken a one-sided direction of dealing mainly with individual psychopathology and technical problems of treatment. We can only regret this loss, although many Europeans have begun to rediscover some of the earlier directions of applied psychoanalysis. The terminology has slightly changed but what is now encompassed by the term "psychosocial factor" was known but abandoned during the 1920s because of unsolved intragroup conflicts within the psychoanalytic organization. However, it has always been part of psychoanalytic theory. It is comforting to recognize that psychoanalysis as an organizational structure can suffer from the same symptoms as other organizations when the human factor is temporarily neglected.

The intraorganizational dynamics of interrelated functions are not abstractions, and none of these functions can be performed by other than human beings. Whatever automated programs may achieve, they cannot work without human beings—human beings who are motivated by psychological needs such as well-being, the

search for a stable environment, reduction of fear through pre-
dictability, recognition, satisfaction, communication, and trust.
Since each individual has to perform organizational functions in
the interest of his defined primary tasks, the interrelatedness of
these various functions determines the specific problems of organizational diagnosis. The psychiatrist must avoid the trap of
accepting the irrational group assumption that one group or one
individual is to blame for dysfunctional symptoms. Our recent
experience during the worldwide monetary crisis has again confirmed the fact that the individual executive suffers from increasing anxiety and fear because the changing circumstances deprive
him of his main virtue, to arrive at rationally based predictions.
The symptomatology shows all variations of illnesses, described
by Selye (1956) as an accumulation of stress through intrapsychic
conflict between ego ideal and social reality.

The description of interrelated functions within organizational
systems and subsystems forms a highly abstract and complex theoretical level of organizational theory. However, before any descriptive phenomenology can become the basis for an organizational
theory or philosophy, it must be recognized that organizational
functions are predominantly determined by people who continuously negotiate their personal needs for satisfaction and well-
being on various levels and under varying conditions besides their
technical or operational task assignments.

"Benedict pointed out that societies that had social orders in
which the individual by the same act and at the same time served
his own advantage and that of the group were characterized by
a low incidence of aggressive behavior" (Marmor, 1974, p. 422).
The reason was not that people were entirely unselfish but merely
that societal institutions provided enough flexibility for personal
desires to coincide with social obligations. Therefore, aggressive
behavior was not provoked by societal tasks because it was unnecessary. Benedict (1934) distinguished between "high synergy"
and "low synergy" cultures, defining the latter as societies where
"the advantage of one individual was generally at the expense of
another and thus intrasocial competitiveness was fostered" (Mar-

mor, 1974, p. 422). From these studies she found that emotional security appeared to be more important than the distribution of wealth.

Part of this concept can be applied to organizations if it is kept in mind that the synergy level depends on different variables. Dealing with organizations never becomes a depersonalized abstract pattern for the psychiatrist. By contrast, however, economic and sociological approaches have become more mechanical and less personal. Approaches based on abstract research, economic data, statistical surveys, and structural analysis by management consultants have not only failed to recognize human needs but in some cases have led to serious distress and more disorganization. The human capacity to adapt to rapid changes, the unconscious resistances to change, the deterioration of informal communication, the tolerance for tension, and the unconscious need for security were underestimated, resulting in more organizational dysfunction.

The search for remedies and the uncritical application of various encounter group methods have created a phony atmosphere of pseudo-instant intimacy. The often desperate need for unreflected action without diagnosis has contributed to many symptoms of organizational dysfunction such as high turnover rates (especially among the younger generation), increasing absenteeism, illness, alcoholism, and inappropriate social behavior, as well as costly production failure rates, recalls, or decreases in quality. These functional or dysfunctional results can be left to neighboring disciplines as long as they are willing to recognize that the neglected human factor, the psychology of well-being, and the need for effective methods of mental health maintenance are at the bottom of these symptoms of organizational dysfunction. It is necessary to stress the importance of human factors which are often considered the unwanted byproduct of successful operations in business, government, and community institutions.

The increasing divorce rate among police officers, the escalating political violence, the struggle to control school systems, the growing alcoholism in industry and business, more frequent coronary attacks and psychosomatic illness among top executives can no longer be ascribed exclusively to individual intrapsychic conflict. The impact of organizational conditions and structures that might cause a high percentage of these allegedly individual symptoms are also connected with changing societal values and attitudes as well as with increasing collective fears.

The challenge of these problems to the psychiatrist has its counterpart in the law. The law enforcement officer must wait until a criminal act has been committed although he might have foreknowledge that a crime will be committed. No law permits interference with personal rights. This example is a striking instance of an institutionalized ideology that has developed an independent autonomy because the formal organizational conditions are perceived as representing a higher value than human needs. The law becomes an abstract pattern which the individual automatically follows regardless of the destructive results.

Psychiatry is in danger of restricting itself in a similar way to an erroneous medical model which fails to interfere and apply its knowledge as long as no illness can be defined. Scheff (1966) describes the physician's dilemma by distinguishing two alternatives: (1) Nobody should be treated who is not sick; (2) no illness should be overlooked. Both contradicting principles are applied differently depending upon conditions. During a war or emergency, illness is not defined the same way as it is during better times. In the affluent society diagnostic methods are intensified because no illness is overlooked as long as costs permit extensive diagnosis. The process reverses itself during wars or catastrophies when even sick people are used for emergency, maintenance, or defense services. Thus, we can observe the impact of changing value systems on diagnostic criteria. These standards depend upon the environmental circumstances and human needs as well as on the autonomy of institutions which develop a life of their own once they have been formed. The autonomous institution can force the individual professional to become a servant of institutional maintenance.

Most organizations know that some important factors are lacking within their conventional economic and technical structures. Many organizations have begun to recognize the serious complaints of their leading executives who claimed that the traditional annual health checkup never solved their problem of critically assessing their lives and family situations as well as their personal future. The medical model rarely recognizes psychological problems as signs of real beginning illness. However, we know from Menninger et al. (1963) as well as from Selye's (1956) research on stress that illness as defined in medicine has various premorbid stages. One of the first stages is psychological stress which leads to functional symptoms and finally to organic illness if the internal psychological conflicts are not solved. The diagnostic question to be answered in the future deals with the crucial problem of the extent to which organizations impose conditions on individuals which lead to psychological stress and consequently to vital decompensations, dysfunctions, or illnesses.

Returning to the question about the adequacy of the traditional medical model, I want to point out the importance of developing new methods for organizational diagnosis through a multidisciplinary approach. The organizational climate is only one variable in determining the chances for the maintenance of mental health or destructive decompensation and illness. In the past there have been various psychiatric efforts to apply to organizations untenable generalizations from individual psychiatry or personality theory. These trial and error periods have made it more difficult to arrive at a different approach safeguarded from such oversimplifications. The whole scientific theory of organizations is full of traps and pitfalls as long as we assume one discipline can solve all the existing problems. In a multidisciplinary group approach, sociological, economic, psychological, and psychosocial data would be cross-examined by various disciplines, each dealing with specific problems of individual relationships within organizations. The psychiatrist in such a multidisciplinary team would be forced to know more about sociology, anthropology, psychology, and applied psychoanalysis as well as about technical, economic, and structural management conditions. Knowledge from a variety of disciplines enables the psychiatrist to tailor his diagnosis to help the organization's leaders who are often without appropriate knowledge of how to implement those changes that are highly dependent on the human factor.

A short but rather typical example may demonstrate the necessity of having a psychiatrist on the team making the diagnosis and suggestions for resolving existing organizational problems. A well-known management consultant firm completed a major survey of a large business and advised the organization to change its basic structure from being headed by an executive committee to being headed by two elected individuals—a chairman of the board and a president. This new leadership structure was announced to the organization's top executives in a forty-five minute session without any further comment; the meeting was concluded with, "That's it—any questions?" Although there was an increasing level of anxiety, no questions were asked. This change put the majority of vice presidents on a lower level and required them to deal individually with either one of the leaders, who were rarely present at the same time but substituted for each other. Within a few months serious infighting, dysfunctioning, uncertainty, and depression developed within the group of vice presidents. Their reactions had dysfunctional repercussions throughout the organization. The negative consequences of this recommended structural change are apparent. The organizational diagnosis oriented primarily toward evaluating economic and management data failed because the importance of human psychological needs was completely overlooked.

Space does not permit other examples, but additional evidence would only strengthen the conclusion that the most important factor in organizational diagnosis is the exploration of relationships within organizations and the discovery of hidden agendas among top-level managers. The hierarchy and the relationship between vice presidents, department heads, or various secondary "alpha functions" determine the basic organizational climate and create within the majority of "gamma functions" either trust and willingness to follow, or develop instead distrust, opposition, and the use of "omega functions" by "gamma functions" as destructive weapons against "alpha functions." The voice of the "beta function" within organizations is usually ignored until the "omega" parts of the organization are presented as more and more dangerous symptoms threatening to destroy or paralyze the leading "alphas," who then tend to scapegoat the "omega function." Once we have identified the units or subunits of a larger system, we can return to the question of whether there are any coping mechanisms of organizations analogous to those of persons.

It must be kept in mind that any analogy between an abstract organization and an individual will fail because an organization as an entity per se would not or could not exist without persons who, by their individual actions and decisions determine the organization's goals and directions. It is the individual motivation for implementing, avoiding, procrastinating, or delegating decisions within the organization's hierarchy of families that determines organizational functioning. These individual factors are necessary basic information for organizational diagnosis. The various individual defense mechanisms and object relations of persons in "alpha" positions also determine whether the organization is perceived as an autonomous entity, demanding each individual to serve a maintenance function, or as an interchangeable wheel, or whether the organization can create a high synergy level by providing the individual functions that benefit the person as well as the group or organization in the same act. Job satisfaction, group solidarity, feelings of well-being and belonging, and the development of a genuine identity depend on this primary choice. This goal involves not only the work satisfaction of employees but also their family relations and their private lives.

We are entering the terra incognita of psychiatry and psychology. The natural reaction is to stay out of this dangerous new territory which seems full of traps and pitfalls. However, we must explore new diagnostic frontiers because neither the sociological nor the economic approaches have penetrated the darkness of this unknown territory. Psychiatry and psychoanalysis are under attack because they withdrew from the main societal and social problems and instead focused on individual treatment. The psychiatrist claims to be the advocate of reality for his patient who tries to escape into a private world of delusions or infantile dreams. However, since more than sixty percent of the people in Western civilizations spend a minimum of eight hours per day working for some kind of organization, we cannot retreat into a professional dream world where psychiatrists only diagnose the solitary patient. We must face the real problems of organizations and answer some basic questions such as: What are organizations doing to people? Can we prevent the autonomous organization from usurping the individual? Can we stop organizational autonomy? But before answering these questions, we must decide how much of our own professional intention is biased by organizational prejudice. Martin Buber (1949) reminds us of the first step to knowledge when he considers the reaction of the first man to the voice of God calling, "Adam, where are you?" We cannot attempt a single solution to the problems of organizational diagnosis if, like Adam, we are found hiding.

REFERENCES

Asch, S. E. (1940), Studies in the Principles of Judgments and Attitudes. II. Determination of Judgments by Group and by Ego Standards. *J. Soc. Psychol.*, 12:431-65.
——— (1951), Effects of Group Pressure upon the Modification and Distortion of Judgments. In: *Groups, Leadership and Men: Research in Human Relations*, ed. H. S. Guetzkow. Pittsburgh: Carnegie Press.
——— (1952), *Social Psychology*. New York: Prentice-Hall.
Benedict, R. (1934), *Patterns of Culture*. Boston: Houghton Mifflin.
Bion, W. R. (1948a), Experiences in Groups. I. *Human Relations*, 1:314-320.
——— (1948b), Experiences in Groups. II. *Human Relations*, (1):487-496.
——— (1949a), Experiences in Groups. III. *Human Relations*, 2:13-22.
——— (1949b), Experiences in Groups. IV. *Human Relations*, 2:295-303.
——— (1950a), Experiences in Groups. V. *Human Relations*, 3:3-14.
——— (1950b), Experiences in Groups. VI. *Human Relations*, 3:395-402.
——— (1952), Group Dynamics: A Re-View, *Internat. J. Psycho-Anal.*, 33:235-347.
Brocher, T., et al. (1975), *Study of Private Business Sector Involvement in Community Intervention*. Topeka, Kan.: Center for Applied Behavioral Sciences, The Menninger Foundation. Unpublished.
Buber, M. (1949), *Die Erzaehlugen Der Chassidim*. Zurich: Manesse Verlag.
Cartwright, D. P., & Zander, A., Eds. (1960), *Group Dynamics: Research & Theory*. Evanston, Ill.: Row, Peterson.
Freud, S. (1921), Group Psychology and the Analysis of the Ego. *Standard Edition*, 18:65-143. London: Hogarth Press, 1955.

Gouldner, A. W. (1965), Explorations in Applied Social Science. In: *Applied Sociology: Opportunities and Problems*, ed. A. W. Gouldner & S. M. Miller. New York: Free Press.

Green, A., et al. (1972), *Study of Community Intervention*. Topeka, Kan.: Department of Preventive Psychiatry, The Menninger Foundation. Unpublished.

Janis, I. L. (1958), *Psychological Stress: Psychoanalytic and Behavioral Studies of Surgical Patients*. New York: Wiley.

Jaques, E. (1961), *Equitable Payment*. New York: Wiley.

Kuhn, A. (1974), *The Logic of Social Systems: A Unified, Deductive, System-Based Approach to Social Science*. San Francisco: Jossey-Bass.

Lewin, K. (1951), Field Theory. In: *Social Science: Selected Theoretical Papers*, ed. D. P. Cartwright. New York: Harper.

——— et al. (1939), Patterns of Aggressive Behavior in Experimentally Created Social Climates. *J. Soc. Psychol.*, 10:271-299.

Marmor, J. (1974), *Psychiatry in Transition: Selected Papers*. New York: Brunner/Mazel.

Menninger, K., et al. (1963), *The Vital Balance*. New York: Viking.

Menninger, W. C. (1947), Psychiatric Experiences in the War, 1941-1946. *Amer. J. Psychiat.*, 103:577-586.

Milgram, S. (1965), Some Conditions of Obedience and Disobedience to Authority. *Human Relations*, 18:57-76.

Neff, F. W. (1965), Survey Research: A Tool for Problem Diagnosis and Improvement in Organizations. In: *Applied Sociology: Opportunities and Problems*, ed. A. W. Gouldner & S. M. Miller. New York: Free Press.

Satten, J., et al. (1970-1971), *Study of Community Intervention*. Topeka, Kan.: Department of Preventive Psychiatry, The Menninger Foundation. Unpublished.

Scheff, T. (1966), *Being Mentally Ill: A Sociological Theory*. Chicago: Aldine.

Selye, H. (1956), *The Stress of Life*. New York: McGraw-Hill.

Sherif, M. (1966), *The Psychology of Social Norms*. New York: Harper & Row.

——— & Sherif, C. (1953), *Groups in Harmony and Tension: An Integration of Studies of Intergroup Relations*. New York: Harper.

——— et al. (1955), Status in Experimentally Produced Groups. *Amer. J. Sociol.*, 60:370-379.

This chapter presents a detailed and comprehensive diagnosis of an orga-
nization. Using a Kleinian frame of reference, Menzies analyzes the problems
of the nursing staff of a general teaching hospital in London. She examines the
causes and effects of anxiety on the nursing service, and explores the defensive
techniques which are used to diffuse these anxieties, showing the consequences
of such techniques both for the individual and the institution.

19

A Case-Study in the Functioning of Social Systems as a Defense Against Anxiety: A Report on a Study of the Nursing Service of a General Hospital

ISABEL E. P. MENZIES

This study was initiated by a hospital which sought help in developing new methods of carrying out a task in nursing organization. The research data were, therefore, collected within a socio-therapeutic relationship in which the aim was to facilitate desired social change.

The hospital is a general teaching hospital in London. That is, in addition to the normal task of patient care, the hospital teaches undergraduate medical students. Like all British hospitals of its type, it is also a nurse-training school. The hospital has about 700 beds for inpatients and provides a number of outpatient services. Although referred to as "the hospital," it is, in fact, a group of hospitals, which at the time of the study, included a general

This chapter originally appeared in *Human Relations*, 13:95-121, 1960. By permission of Plenum Publishing Corporation.

hospital of 500 beds, three small specialist hospitals, and a convalescent home. The group of hospitals has an integrated nursing service run by a matron located in the main hospital. Nursing staff and students are interchangeable between hospitals.

The nursing personnel of the hospital number about 700. Of these, about 150 are fully trained staff and the remainder are students. The nurse-training course lasts four years. For the first three years, the student nurse is an "undergraduate." At the end of the third year she takes the examination which leads to "state registration," in effect, her nursing qualification and license to practice. In the fourth year, she is a postgraduate student.

The trained nursing staff are entirely deployed in administrative, teaching, and supervisory roles, although those who are deployed in operational units working with patients also carry out a certain amount of direct patient care. Student nurses are, in effect, the nursing staff of the hospital at the operational level with patients, and carry out most of the relevant tasks. From this point of view, it is necessary that student nurses be deployed so as to meet the nurse staffing requirements of the hospital. The student nurse spends comparatively little time undergoing formal instruction. She spends three months in the Preliminary Training School before she starts nursing practice, and six weeks in the nursing school in each of the second and third years of training. For the rest of the time, she is in "practical training," acquiring and practicing nursing skills by carrying out full-time nursing duties within the limits of her competence. The practical training must be so arranged that the student has the minimal experience of different types of nursing prescribed by the General Nursing Council.[1] The hospital offers, and likes nurses to have, certain additional experience available in specialist units in the hospital. The hospital's training policy is that the student nurse has approximately three months continuous duty in each of the different types of nursing. Each student nurse must be deployed in a way that fulfils these training requirements.

[1] The nursing body that controls nurse-training.

The possibilities of conflict in this situation are many. The nursing establishment of the hospital is not primarily determined by training needs, which take second place to patient-centered needs and the needs of the medical school. For some considerable time before the start of this study, the senior nursing staff had been finding it increasingly difficult to reconcile effectively staffing needs and training needs. Pressures from patient care demanded that priority be given to staffing, and constant training crises developed. The policy of three-month training tours had in effect been abandoned and many tours were very short,[2] some nurses came almost to the end of their training without having had all the necessary experience, and others had a serious imbalance owing to too much of the same kind of practice. These crises created the more acute distress because senior staff wished to give increasing priority to training and to raise the status of the nurse as a student.

The senior staff began to feel that there was a danger of complete breakdown in the system of allocation to practical work and sought our help in revising their methods. My purpose in writing this paper is not, however, to follow the ramifications of the problem. I will make some reference to it at relevant points, and will consider later why the existing method persisted so long without effective modification in spite of its inefficiency.

The therapeutic relationship with the hospital was to some extent based on the belief that we would be wise to regard the problem of student-nurse allocation as a "presenting symptom" and to reserve judgment on the real nature of the difficulties and the best form of treatment until we had done further diagnostic work. We began, therefore, with a fairly intensive interviewing program. We held formal interviews with about seventy nurses, individually and in small groups, and with senior medical and lay staff; we carried out some observational studies of operational units; and we had many informal contacts with nurses and other

---

[2]A sample check of actual duration showed that thirty percent of student moves took place less than three weeks after the previous move and forty-four percent less than seven weeks.

staff. Respondents knew the problem we were formally studying, but were invited to raise in interview any other issue that they considered central to their occupational experience. Much further research material was collected in the later meetings with senior staff as we worked together on the findings from the interviewing program.[3]

As our diagnostic work went on, our attention was repeatedly drawn to the high level of tension, distress, and anxiety among the nurses. We found it hard to understand how nurses could tolerate so much anxiety, and, indeed, we found much evidence that they could not. In one form or another, withdrawal from duty was common. About one-third of student nurses did not complete their training. The majority of these left at their own request, and not because of failure in examinations or practical training. Senior staff changed their jobs appreciably more frequently than workers at similar levels in other professions and were unusually prone to seek postgraduate training. Sickness rates were high, especially for minor illnesses requiring only a few days' absence from duty.[4]

As the study proceeded we came to attach increasing importance to understanding the nature of the anxiety and the reasons for its intensity. The relief of the anxiety seemed to us an important therapeutic task and, moreover, proved to have a close connection with the development of more effective techniques of student-nurse allocation. The remainder of this paper is concerned with considering the causes and the effects of the anxiety level in the hospital.

[3]It is a feature of therapeutic study of this kind that much of the most significant research material emerges in its later stages when the emphasis of work shifts from diagnosis to therapy. Presentation and interpretation of data, and work done on resistances to their acceptance, facilitate the growth of insight into the nature of the problem. This extends the range of information seen to be relevant to its solution, and helps overcome personal resistances to the disclosure of information. An impressive feature of the study here reported was the way in which, after a spell of working on the data, the senior nursing staff themselves were able to produce and execute plans directed toward dealing with their problems.

[4]There is much evidence from other fields that such phenomena express a disturbed relation with the work situation and are connected with a high level of tension. See, for example, Hill and Trist (1953).

NATURE OF THE ANXIETY

A hospital accepts and cares for ill people who cannot be cared for in their own homes. This is the task the hospital is created to perform, its "primary task." The major responsibility for the performance of that primary task lies with the nursing service, which must provide continuous care for patients, day and night, all the year round.[5] The nursing service, therefore, bears the full, immediate, and concentrated impact of stresses arising from patient-care.

The situations likely to evoke stress in nurses are familiar. Nurses are in constant contact with people who are physically ill or injured, often seriously. The recovery of patients is not certain and will not always be complete. The nursing of patients who have incurable diseases is one of the nurse's most distressing tasks. Nurses are confronted with the threat and the reality of suffering and death as few lay people are. Their work involves carrying out tasks which, by ordinary standards, are distasteful, disgusting, and frightening. Intimate physical contact with patients arouses strong libidinal and erotic wishes and impulses that may be difficult to control. The work situation arouses very strong, mixed feelings in the nurse: pity, compassion, and love; guilt and anxiety; hatred and resentment of the patients who arouse these strong feelings; envy of the care given the patient.

The objective situation confronting the nurse bears a striking resemblance to the phantasy[6] situations that exist in every individual in the deepest and most primitive levels of the mind. The intensity and complexity of the nurse's anxieties are to be attributed primarily to the peculiar capacity of the objective features

---

[5]My colleague, G. F. Hutton, in analyzing the data from another hospital study, as yet unpublished, drew attention to the descent of modern hospitals from their original management by orders of nursing sisters. These early hospitals were entirely administered by nurses. Doctors and priests were necessary and important visitors, but visitors only. They met special needs of patients but had no administrative responsibility. The tradition of what Hutton called "nurse-directed communities" remains strong, in spite of the complexity of organization of modern hospitals and the number and diversity of patient-centered staff.

[6]Throughout this paper I follow the convention of using "fantasy" to mean conscious fantasy, and "phantasy" to mean unconscious phantasy.

of her work situation to stimulate afresh these early situations and their accompanying emotions. I will comment briefly on the main relevant features of these phantasy situations.[7]

The elements of these phantasies may be traced back to earliest infancy. The infant experiences two opposing sets of feelings and impulses, libidinal and aggressive. These stem from instinctual sources and are described by the constructs of the life instinct and the death instinct. The infant feels omnipotent and attributes dynamic reality to these feelings and impulses. He believes that the libidinal impulses are literally life-giving and the aggressive impulses death-dealing. The infant attributes similar feelings, impulses, and powers to other people and to important parts of people. The objects and the instruments of the libidinal and aggressive impulses are felt to be the infant's own and other people's bodies and bodily products. Physical and psychic experiences are very intimately interwoven at this time. The infant's psychic experience of objective reality is greatly influenced by his own feelings and phantasies, moods and wishes.

Through his psychic experience the infant builds up an inner world peopled by himself and the objects of his feelings and impulses (Klein, 1952a, 1959). In the inner world, they exist in a form and condition largely determined by his phantasies. Because of the operation of aggressive forces, the inner world contains many damaged, injured, or dead objects. The atmosphere is charged with death and destruction. This gives rise to great anxiety. The infant fears for the effect of aggressive forces on the people he loves and on himself. He grieves and mourns over their suffering and experiences depression and despair about his inadequate ability to put right their wrongs. He fears the demands that will be made on him for reparation and the punishment and revenge that may fall on him. He fears that his libidinal impulses and those of other people cannot control the aggressive impulses sufficiently to prevent utter chaos and destruction. The poignancy of the situation is increased because love and longing themselves

[7]In my description of infantile psychic life, I follow the work of Freud, particularly as developed and elaborated by Melanie Klein (1952a, 1959).

are felt to be so close to aggression. Greed, frustration, and envy so easily replace a loving relationship. The phantasy world is characterized by a violence and intensity of feeling quite foreign to the emotional life of the normal adult.

The direct impact on the nurse of physical illness is intensified by her task of meeting and dealing with psychological stress in other people, including her own colleagues. It is by no means easy to tolerate such stress even if one is not under similar stress oneself. Quite short conversations with patients or relatives showed that their conscious concept of illness and treatment is a rich intermixture of objective knowledge, logical deduction, and fantasy (Janis, 1958). The degree of stress is heavily conditioned by the fantasy, which is, in turn, conditioned, as in nurses, by the early phantasy situations. Unconsciously, the nurse associates the patients' and relatives' distress with that experienced by the people in her phantasy world, which increases her own anxiety and difficulty in handling it.

Patients and relatives have very complicated feelings towards the hospital, which are expressed particularly and most directly to nurses, and which often puzzle and distress them. Patients and relatives show appreciation, gratitude, affection, respect; a touching relief that the hospital copes; helpfulness and concern for nurses in their difficult task. But patients often resent their dependence; accept grudgingly the discipline imposed by treatment and hospital routine; envy nurses their health and skills; are demanding, possessive, and jealous. Patients, like nurses, find strong libidinal and erotic feelings stimulated by nursing care, and sometimes behave in ways that increase the nurses' difficulties, for example, unnecessary physical exposure. Relatives may also be demanding and critical, the more so because they resent the feeling that hospitalization implies inadequacies in themselves. They envy nurses their skill and jealously resent the nurse's intimate contact with "their" patient.

In a more subtle way, both patients and relatives make psychological demands on nurses which increase their experience of stress. The hospital is expected to do more than accept the ill patient, care for his physical needs, and help realistically with his psychological stress. The hospital is implicitly expected to accept and, by so doing, free patients and relatives from certain aspects of the emotional problems aroused by the patient and his illness. The hospital, particularly the nurses, must allow the projection into them of such feelings as depression and anxiety, fear of the patient and his illness, disgust at the illness and at necessary nursing tasks. Patients and relatives treat the staff in such a way as to ensure that the nurses experience these feelings instead of, or partly instead of, they themselves, e.g., by refusing or trying to refuse to participate in important decisions about the patient and so forcing responsibility and anxiety back on the hospital. Thus, to the nurses' own deep and intense anxieties are psychically added those of the other people concerned. As we became familiar with the work of the hospital, we were struck by the number of patients whose physical condition alone did not warrant hospitalization. In some cases, it was clear that they had been hospitalized because they and their relatives could not tolerate the stress of their being ill at home.

The nurse projects infantile phantasy situations into current work situations and experiences the objective situations as a mixture of objective reality and phantasy. She then reexperiences painfully and vividly in relation to current objective reality many of the feelings appropriate to the phantasies. In thus projecting her phantasy situations into objective reality, the nurse is using an important and universal technique for mastering anxiety and modifying the phantasy situations. Through the projection, the individual sees elements of the phantasy situations in the objective situations that come to symbolize the phantasy situations.[8] Successful mastery of the objective situations gives reassurance about the mastery of the phantasy situations. To be effective, such symbolization requires that the symbol *represents* the phantasy object, but *is not equated* with it. Its own distinctive, objective characteristics must also be recognized and used. If, for any rea-

---

[8]Klein (1948a) stresses the importance of anxiety in leading to the development of symbol formation and sublimation.

son, the symbol and the phantasy object become almost or completely equated, the anxieties aroused by the phantasy object are aroused in full intensity by the symbolic object. The symbol then ceases to perform its function in containing and modifying anxiety.[9] The close resemblance of the phantasy and objective situations in nursing constitutes a threat that symbolic representation will degenerate into symbolic equation and that nurses will consequently experience the full force of their primitive infantile anxieties in consciousness. Modified examples of this phenomenon were not uncommon in the hospital. For example, a nurse whose mother had had several gynecological operations broke down and had to give up nursing shortly after beginning her tour of duty on the gynecological ward.

By the nature of her profession the nurse is at considerable risk of being flooded by intense and unmanageable anxiety. That factor alone, however, cannot account for the high level of anxiety so apparent in nurses. It becomes necessary to direct attention to the other facet of the problem, that is to the techniques used in the nursing service to contain and modify anxiety.

Defensive Techniques in the Nursing Service

In developing a structure, culture, and mode of functioning, a social organization is influenced by a number of interacting factors, crucial among which are its primary task, including such environmental relationships and pressures as that task involves; the technologies available for performing the task; and the needs of the members of the organization for social and psychological satisfaction, and, above all, for support in the problem of dealing with anxiety (Breuer and Freud, 1893-1895; Freud, 1926; Klein,

[9]Segal (1957) uses the terms symbolic representation and symbolic equation. In developing this distinction, she stresses the acute anxieties experienced by patients in whom the symbol does not merely represent the phantasy object but is equated with it. She illustrates from the material two patients for both of whom a violin was a phallic symbol. For one patient the violin *represented* the phallus and violin playing was an important sublimation through which he could master anxiety. For the other more deeply disturbed patient, the violin was *felt to be* the phallus and he had had to stop playing because he could not touch a violin in public.

1948b, 1952; Rice 1958).[10] In my opinion, the influence of the primary task and the technology for performing it can easily be exaggerated. Indeed, I would prefer to regard them as limiting factors, i.e., the need to ensure viability through the efficient performance of the primary task and the types of technology available to do this set limits to possible organization. Within these limits, the culture, structure, and mode of functioning are determined by the psychological needs of the members.[11]

The needs of the members of the organization to use it in the struggle against anxiety leads to the development of socially structured defense mechanisms, which appear as elements in the structure, culture, and mode of functioning of the organization (Jaques, 1955). An important aspect of such socially structured defense mechanisms is an attempt by individuals to externalize and give substance in objective reality to their characteristic psychic defense mechanisms. A social defense system develops over time as the result of collusive interaction and agreement, often unconscious, between members of the organization as to what form it shall take. The socially structured defense mechanisms then tend to become an aspect of external reality with which old and new members of the institution must come to terms.

In what follows I shall discuss some of the social defenses that the nursing service has developed in the long course of the hospital's history and which it still uses. It is impossible here to describe the social system fully, so I shall illustrate only a few of the more striking and typical examples of the operation of the service as a social defense. I shall confine myself mainly to techniques used within the nursing service and refer minimally to ways in which the nursing service makes use of other people, notably patients and doctors, in operating socially structured

---

[10]Bion (1955) has put forward a similar concept in distinguishing between the sophisticated or work group concerned with a realistic task and the basic-assumption group dominated by primitive psychological phenomena; the two "groups" being simultaneously operative aspects of the same aggregation of people.

[11]The different social systems that have developed under long-wall coal-mining conditions, using the same basic technology, are a good example of how the same primary task may be performed differently using the same technology when social and psychological conditions are different. They have been discussed by Trist and Bamforth (1951).

mechanisms of defense. For convenience of exposition, I shall list the defenses as if they are separate, although, in operation, they function simultaneously and interact with and support each other.

Splitting Up the Nurse-Patient Relationship

The core of the anxiety situation for the nurse lies in her relation with the patient. The closer and more concentrated this relationship, the more the nurse is likely to experience the impact of anxiety. The nursing service attempts to protect her from the anxiety by splitting up her contact with patients. It is hardly too much to say that the nurse does not nurse patients. The total workload of a ward or department is broken down into lists of tasks, each of which is allocated to a particular nurse. She performs her patient-centered tasks for a large number of patients, perhaps as many as all the patients in the ward, often thirty or more in number. As a corollary, she performs only a few tasks for, and has restricted contact with, any one patient. This prevents her from coming effectively into contact with the totality of any one patient and his illness and offers some protection from the anxiety this arouses.

Depersonalization, Categorization, and Denial of the Significance of the Individual

The protection afforded by the task-list system is reinforced by a number of other devices that inhibit the development of a full person-to-person relationship between nurse and patient, with its consequent anxiety. The implicit aim of such devices, which operate both structurally and culturally, may be described as a kind of depersonalization or elimination of individual distinctiveness in both nurse and patient. For example, nurses often talk about patients, not by name, but by bed numbers or by their diseases or a diseased organ, "the liver in bed 10" or "the pneumonia in bed 15." Nurses themselves deprecate this practice, but it persists. Nor should one underestimate the difficulties of re-

membering the names of say thirty patients on a ward, especially
the high-turnover wards. There is an almost explicit "ethic" that
any patient must be the same as any other patient. It must not
matter to the nurse whom she nurses or what illness. Nurses find
it extraordinarily difficult to express preferences even for types
of patients or for men or women patients. If pressed to do so,
they tend to add rather guiltily some remark like "You can't help
it." Conversely, it should not matter to the patient which nurse
attends him or, indeed, how many different nurses do. By implication it is the duty as well as the need and privilege of the
patient to be nursed and of the nurse to nurse, regardless of the
fact that a patient may greatly need to "nurse" a distressed nurse
and nurses may sometimes need to be "nursed." Outside the
specific requirements of his physical illness and treatment, the
way a patient is nursed is determined largely by his membership
in the category of patient and minimally by his idiosyncratic wants
and needs. For example, there is one way of bedmaking, except
when the physical illness requires another; only one time to wash
all patients—in the morning.

The nurses' uniforms are a symbol of an expected inner and
behavioral uniformity; a nurse becomes a kind of agglomeration
of nursing skills, without individuality; each is thus perfectly interchangeable with another of the same skill level. Socially permitted differences between nurses tend to be restricted to a few
major categories, outwardly differentiated by minor differences
in insignia on the same basic uniform, an arm strip for a second-
year nurse, a slightly different cap for a third-year nurse. This
attempts to create an operational identity between all nurses in
the same category.[12] To an extent indicating clearly the need for
"blanket" decisions, duties and privileges are accorded to categories of people and not to individuals according to their personal
capacities and needs. This also helps to eliminate painful and
difficult decisions, e.g., about which duties and privileges should

[12]In practice it is not possible to carry out these prescriptions literally, since a whole
category of nurses may temporarily be absent from practical duties on formal instruction
in the nursing school or on leave.

fall to each individual. Something of the same reduction of individual distinctiveness exists between operational subunits. Attempts are made to standardize all equipment and layout to the limits allowed by their different nursing tasks, but disregarding the idiosyncratic social and psychological resources and needs of each unit.

Detachment and Denial of Feelings

A necessary psychological task for the entrant into any profession that works with people is the development of adequate professional detachment. He must learn, for example, to control his feelings, refrain from excessive involvement, avoid disturbing identifications, maintain his professional independence against manipulation and demands for unprofessional behavior. To some extent the reduction of individual distinctiveness aids detachment by minimizing the mutual interaction of personalities, which might lead to "attachment." It is reinforced by an implicit operational policy of "detachment." "A good nurse doesn't mind moving." A "good nurse" is willing and able without disturbance to move from ward to ward or even hospital to hospital at a moment's notice. Such moves are frequent and often sudden, particularly for student nurses. The implicit rationale appears to be that a student nurse will learn to be detached psychologically if she has sufficient experience of being detached literally and physically. Most senior nurses do not subscribe personally to this implicit rationale. They are aware of the personal distress as well as the operational disturbance caused by overly frequent moves. Indeed, this was a major factor in the decision to initiate our study. However, in their formal roles in the hierarchy they continue to initiate frequent moves and make little other training provision for developing genuine professional detachment. The pain and distress of breaking relationships and the importance of stable and continuing relationships are implicitly denied by the system, although they are often stressed personally, i.e., nonprofessionally, by people in the system.

This implicit denial is reinforced by the denial of the disturbing feelings that arise within relationships. Interpersonal repressive techniques are culturally required and typically used to deal with emotional stress. Both student nurses and staff show panic about emotional outbursts. Brisk, reassuring behavior and advice of the "stiff upper lip," "pull yourself together" variety are characteristic. Student nurses suffer most severely from emotional strain and habitually complain that the senior staff do not understand and make no effort to help them. Indeed, when the emotional stress arises from the nurse's having made a mistake, she is usually reprimanded instead of being helped. A student nurse told me that she had made a mistake that hastened the death of a dying patient. She was reprimanded separately by four senior nurses. Only the headmistress of her former school tried to help her as a person who was severely distressed, guilty, and frightened. However, students are wrong when they say that senior nurses do not understand or feel for their distress. In personal conversation with us, seniors showed considerable understanding and sympathy and often remembered surprisingly vividly some of the agonies of their own training. But they lacked confidence in their ability to handle emotional stress in any way other than by repressive techniques, and often said, "In any case, the students won't come and talk to us." Kindly, sympathetic handling of emotional stress between staff and student nurses is, in any case, inconsistent with traditional nursing roles and relationships, which require repression, discipline, and reprimand from senior to junior.

The Attempt to Eliminate Decisions by Ritual Task Performance

Making a decision implies making a choice between different possible courses of action and committing oneself to one of them; the choice being made in the absence of full factual information about the effects of the choice. If the facts were fully known, no decision need be made; the proper course of action would be self-

evident. All decisions are thus necessarily attended by some uncertainty about their outcome and consequently by some conflict
and anxiety, which will last until the outcome is known. The
anxiety consequent on decision making is likely to be acute if a
decision affects the treatment and welfare of patients. To spare
staff this anxiety, the nursing service attempts to minimize the
number and variety of decisions that must be made. For example,
the student nurse is instructed to perform her task list in a way
reminiscent of performing a ritual. Precise instructions are given
about the way each task must be performed, the order of the
tasks, and the time for their performance, although such precise
instructions are not objectively necessary, or even wholly desirable.[13]

If several efficient methods of performing a task exist, e.g.,
for bedmaking or lifting a patient, one is selected and exclusively
used. Much time and effort are expended in standardizing nursing
procedures in cases where there are a number of effective alternatives. Both teachers and practical-work supervisors impress on
the student nurse from the beginning of her training the importance of carrying out the "ritual." They reinforce this by fostering
an attitude toward work that regards every task as almost a matter
of life and death, to be treated with appropriate seriousness. This
applies even to those tasks that could be effectively performed
by an unskilled lay person. As a corollary, the student nurse is
actively discouraged from using her own discretion and initiative
to plan her work realistically in relation to the objective situation,
e.g., at times of crisis to discriminate between tasks on the grounds
of urgency or relative importance and to act accordingly. Student
nurses are the "staff" most affected by the "rituals," since ritual-
ization is easy to apply to their roles and tasks, but attempts are
also made to ritualize the task structure of the more complex
senior staff roles and to standardize the task performance.

---

[13]Bion (1955), in describing the behavior of groups where the need to be dependent
is dominant, has commented on the group's need for what he calls a "bible." It is not
perhaps surprising to find that, in the hospital, whose primary task is to meet the dependency needs of patients, there should be a marked need for just such a definitive
prescription of behavior.

Reducing the Weight of Responsibility in Decision Making by Checks and Counterchecks

The psychological burden of anxiety arising from a final, committing decision by a single person is dissipated in a number of ways, so that its impact is reduced. The final act of commitment is postponed by a common practice of checking and rechecking decisions for validity and postponing action as long as possible. Executive action following decisions is also habitually checked and rechecked at intervening stages. Individuals spend much time in private rumination over decisions and actions. Wherever possible, they involve other nurses in decision making and in reviewing actions. The nursing procedures prescribe considerable checking between individuals, but it is also a strongly developed habit among nurses outside areas of prescribed behavior. The practice of checking and counterchecking is applied not only to situations where mistakes may have serious consequences, such as in giving dangerous drugs, but to many situations where the implications of a decision are of only the slightest consequence, e.g., on one occasion a decision about which of several rooms, all equally available, should be used for a research interview. Nurses consult not only their immediate seniors but also their juniors and nurses or other staff with whom they have no functional relationship but who just happen to be available.

Collusive Social Redistribution of Responsibility and Irresponsibility

Each nurse must face and, in some way, resolve a painful conflict over accepting the responsibilities of her role. The nursing task tends to evoke a strong sense of responsibility in nurses, and nurses often discharge their duties at considerable personal cost. On the other hand, the heavy burden of responsibility is difficult to bear consistently, and nurses are tempted to give it up. In addition, each nurse has wishes and impulses that would lead to irresponsible action, e.g., to scamp boring, repetitive tasks or to become libidinally or emotionally attached to patients. The balance of opposing forces in the conflict varies between individuals, that is, some are naturally "more responsible" than others, but the conflict is always present. To experience this conflict fully and intrapsychically would be extremely stressful. The intrapsychic conflict is alleviated, at least as far as the conscious experiences of nurses are concerned, by a technique that partly converts it into an interpersonal conflict. People in certain roles tend to be described as "responsible" by themselves and to some extent by others, and in other roles people are described as "irresponsible." Nurses habitually complain that other nurses are irresponsible, behave carelessly and impulsively, and in consequence must be ceaselessly supervised and disciplined. The complaints commonly refer not to individuals or to specific incidents but to whole categories of nurses, usually a category junior to the speaker. The implication is that the juniors are not only less responsible now than the speaker, but also less responsible than she was in the same junior position. Few nurses recognize or admit such tendencies. Only the most junior nurses are likely to admit these tendencies in themselves and they then justify them on the grounds that everybody treats them as though they were irresponsible. On the other hand, many people complain that their seniors as a category impose unnecessarily strict and repressive discipline, and treat them as though they have no sense of responsibility.[14] Few senior staff seem able to recognize such features in their own behavior to subordinates. Those "juniors" and "seniors" are, with few exceptions, the same people viewed from above or below, as the case may be.

We came to realize that the complaints stem from a collusive system of denial, splitting, and projection that is culturally acceptable to, indeed culturally required of, nurses. Each nurse tends to split off aspects of herself from her conscious personality and to project them into other nurses. Her irresponsible impulses, which she fears she cannot control, are attributed to her juniors. Her painfully severe attitude toward these impulses and her bur-

---

[14]This has long been a familiar complaint in British hospitals and emerged as a central finding in a number of nursing studies.

densome sense of responsibility are attributed to her seniors. Consequently, she identifies juniors with her irresponsible self and treats them with the severity which that self is felt to deserve. Similarly, she identifies seniors with her own harsh disciplinary attitude to her irresponsible self and expects harsh discipline. There is psychic truth in the assertion that juniors are irresponsible and seniors harsh disciplinarians. These are the roles assigned to them. There is also objective truth, since people act objectively on the psychic roles assigned to them. Discipline is often harsh and sometimes unfair, since multiple projection also leads the senior to identify all juniors with her irresponsible self and so with each other. Thus, she fails to discriminate between them sufficiently. Nurses complain about being reprimanded for other people's mistakes while no serious effort is made to find the real culprit. A staff nurse[15] said, "If a mistake has been made, you must reprimand someone, even if you don't know who really did it." Irresponsible behavior was also quite common, mainly in tasks remote from direct patient care. The interpersonal conflict is painful, as the complaints show, but is less so than experiencing the conflict fully intrapsychically, and it can more easily be evaded. The disciplining eye of seniors cannot follow juniors all the time, nor does the junior confront her senior with irresponsibility all the time.

Purposeful Obscurity in the Formal Distribution of Responsibility

Additional protection from the impact of specific responsibility for specific tasks is given by the fact that the formal structure and role system fail to define fully who is responsible for what and to whom. This matches and objectifies the obscurity about the location of psychic responsibility that inevitably arises from the massive system of projection described above. The content of roles and the boundaries of roles are very obscure, especially at

---

[15]A staff nurse if a fully qualified nurse who is the sister's deputy.

senior levels, where the responsibilities are more onerous so that protection is felt as very necessary. Also the more complex roles and role relationships make it easier to evade definition. As described, the content of the role of the student nurse is rigidly prescribed by her task list. However, in practice, she is unlikely to have the same task list for any length of time. She may, and frequently does, have two completely different task lists in a single day.[16] There is therefore a lack of stable person-role constellations, and it becomes very difficult to assign responsibility finally to a person, a role, or a person-role constellation. We experienced this obscurity frequently in our work in the hospital, finding great difficulty, for example, in learning who should make arrangements or give permission for nurses to participate in various research activities.

Responsibility and authority on wards are generalized in a way that makes them non-specific and prevents them from falling firmly on one person, even the sister. Each nurse is held to be responsible for the work of every nurse junior to her. Junior, in this context, implies no hierarchial relationship, and is determined only by the length of time a student nurse has been in training, and all students are "junior" to trained staff. A student nurse in the fourth quarter of her fourth year is by implication responsible for all other student nurses on the ward; a student nurse in the third quarter of her fourth year for all student nurses except the previous one, and so on. Every nurse is expected to initiate disciplinary action in relation to any failure by any junior nurse. Such diffused responsibility means, of course, that responsibility is not generally experienced specifically or seriously.

The Reduction of the Impact of Responsibility by Delegation to Superiors

The ordinary usage of the word "delegation" in relation to tasks implies that a superior hands over a task and the direct

---

[16]There are usually three different lists of tasks in a ward, numbered 1, 2, and 3, and a student nurse may well be Number 1 in the morning and Number 2 in the afternoon, e.g., if the Number 2 of the morning goes off duty in the afternoon.

responsibility for its detailed performance to subordinates, while he retains a general, supervisory responsibility. In the hospital, almost the opposite seems to happen, i.e., tasks are frequently forced upward in the hierarchy, so that all responsibility for their performance can be disclaimed. Insofar as this happens, the heavy burden of responsibility on the individual is reduced.

The results of many years of this practice are visible in the nursing service. We were struck repeatedly by the low level of tasks carried out by nursing staff and students in relation to their personal ability, skill, and position in the hierarchy. Formally and informally, tasks are assigned to staff at a level well above that at which one finds comparable tasks in other institutions, while the tasks are organized so as effectively to prevent their delegation to an appropriate lower level, e.g., by clarifying policy. The task of allocating student nurses to practical duties was a case in point; it was carried out by the first and second assistant matrons[17] and took up a considerable proportion of their working time. In our opinion, the task is, in fact, such that, if policy were clearly defined and the task appropriately organized, it could be efficiently performed by a competent clerk part-time under the supervision of a senior nurse, who need spend little time on it.[18] We were able to watch this "delegation upward" in operation a number of times as new tasks developed for nurses out of changes resulting from our study. For example, the senior staff decided to change the practical training for fourth-year nurses so that they might have better training than formerly in administration and supervision. This implied, among other things, that they should spend six months continuously in one operational unit during which time they would act as understudy-cum-shadow to the sister or the staff nurse. In the circumstances, personal compatibility was felt to be very important, and it was suggested that the sisters take part in the selection of the fourth-year students for their own wards. At first, there was enthusiasm for the proposal, but as definite plans were made and the intermediate staff began to feel

---

[17] The nurses third and fourth in seniority in administration.
[18] Arrangements are almost complete for the restructuring of the task along such lines.

that they had no developed skill for selection, they requested that, after all, senior staff should continue to select for them as they had always done. The senior staff, although already over-burdened, willingly accepted the task.

The repeated occurrence of such incidents by mutual collusive agreement between superiors and subordinates is hardly surprising considering the mutual projection system described before. Nurses as subordinates tend to feel very dependent on their su-periors in whom they psychically vest by projection some of the best and most competent parts of themselves. They feel that their projections give them the right to expect their superiors to un-dertake their tasks and make decisions for them. On the other hand, nurses, as superiors, do not feel they can fully trust their subordinates in whom they psychically vest the irresponsible and incompetent parts of themselves. Their acceptance of their sub-ordinates' projections also conveys a sense of duty to accept their subordinates' responsibilities.

Idealization and Underestimation of Personal Development Possibilities

In order to reduce anxiety about the continuous efficient per-formance of nursing tasks, nurses seek assurance that the nursing service is staffed with responsible, competent people. To a con-siderable extent, the hospital deals with this problem by an at-tempt to recruit and select "staff," that is, student nurses, who are already highly mature and responsible people. This is reflected in phrases like "nurses are born, not made" or "nursing is a vocation." This amounts to a kind of idealization of the potential nursing recruit, and implies a belief that responsibility and per-sonal maturity cannot be "taught" or even greatly developed. As a corollary, the training system is mainly oriented to the com-munication of essential facts and techniques, and pays minimal attention to teaching events oriented to personal maturation within the professional setting.[19] There is no individual supervi-

[19]This is connected also with the attempt to eliminate decision making as far as possible. If there are no decisions to be made, the worker simply needs to know what to do and how to do it.

sion of student nurses, and no small-group teaching event concerned specifically to help student nurses work over the impact of their first essays in nursing practice and handle more effectively their relations with patients and their own emotional reactions. The nursing service must face the dilemma that, while a strong sense of responsibility and discipline are felt to be necessary for the welfare of patients, a considerable proportion of actual nursing tasks are extremely simple. This hospital, in common with most similar British hospitals, has attempted to solve this dilemma by the recruitment of large numbers of high-level student nurses who, it is hoped, are prepared to accept the temporary lowering of their operational level because they are in training.

This throws new light on the problem of the 30 percent to 50 percent wastage of student nurses in this and other British hospitals. It has long been treated as a serious problem and much effort has been expended on trying to solve it. In fact, it can be seen as an essential element in the social defense system. The need for responsible semi-skilled staff greatly exceeds the need for fully trained staff, e.g., by almost four-to-one in this hopsital. If large numbers of student nurses do not fail to finish their training, the nursing profession risks being flooded with trained staff for whom there are no jobs. The wastage is, therefore, an unconscious device to maintain the balance between staff of different levels of skill while all are at a high personal level. It is understandable that apparently determined efforts to reduce wastage have so far failed, except in one or two hospitals.

Avoidance of Change

Change is inevitably to some extent an excursion into the unknown. It implies a commitment to future events that are not entirely predictable and to their consequences, and inevitably provokes doubt and anxiety. Any significant change within a social system implies changes in existing social relationship and in social structure. It follows that any significant social change implies a change in the operation of the social system as a defense system.

While this change is proceeding, i.e., while social defenses are being restructured, anxiety is likely to be more open and intense.[20] Jaques (1955) has stressed that resistance to social change can be better understood if it is seen as the resistance of groups of people unconsciously clinging to existing institutions because changes threaten existing social defenses against deep and intense anxieties.

It is understandable that the nursing service, whose tasks stimulate such primitive and intense anxieties, should anticipate change with unusually severe anxiety. In order to avoid this anxiety, the service tries to avoid change whenever possible, almost, one might say, at all cost, and tends to cling to the familiar even when the familiar has obviously ceased to be appropriate or relevant. Changes tend to be initiated only at the point of crisis. The presenting problem was a good example of this difficulty in initiating and carrying through change. Staff and student nurses had for long felt that the methods in operation were unsatisfactory and had wanted to change them. They had, however, been unable to do so. The anxieties and uncertainties about possible changes and their consequences inhibited constructive and realistic planning and decision. At least, the present difficulties were familiar and they had some ability to handle them. The problem was approaching the point of breakdown and the limits of the capacities of the people concerned when we were called in.

Many other examples of this clinging to the inappropriate familiar could be observed. For example, changes in medical practice and the initiation of the National Health Service have led to more rapid patient turnover, an increase in the proportion of acutely ill patients, a wider range of illness to be nursed in each ward, and greater variation in the workload of a ward from day to day. These changes all point to the need for increasing flexibility in the work organization of nurses in wards, but no such increase in flexibility has taken place in this hospital. Indeed, the difficulty inherent in trying to deal with a fluctuating workload by the rather

[20]This is a familiar experience while the individual's defenses are being restructured in the course of psychoanalytic therapy.

rigid system described above has tended to be handled by increased prescription and rigidity and by reiteration of the familiar. As far as one could gather, the greater the anxiety, the greater the need for such reassurance in rather compulsive repetition.

The changing demands on nurses described above call for nursing care that is ever more technically skilled. This has not, however, led to an examination of the implicit policy that nursing can be carried out largely by semi-qualified student nurses.

Commentary on the Social Defense System

The characteristic feature of the social defense system, as we have described it, is its orientation toward helping the individual avoid the experience of anxiety, guilt, doubt, and uncertainty. As far as possible, this is done by eliminating situations, events, tasks, activities, and relationships that cause anxiety or, more correctly, evoke anxieties connected with primitive psychological remnants in the personality. Little attempt is made positively to help the individual confront the anxiety-evoking experiences and, by so doing, develop her capacity to tolerate and deal more effectively with the anxiety. Basically, the potential anxieties in the nursing situation are felt to be too deep and dangerous for full confrontation, and to threaten personal disruption and social chaos. In fact, of course, the attempt to avoid such confrontation can never be completely successful. A compromise is inevitable between the implicit aims of the social defense system and the demands of reality as expressed in the need to pursue the primary task.

It follows that the psychic defense mechanisms that have, over time, been built into the socially structured defense system of the nursing service are, in the main, those which protect nurses by permitting them to evade the full experience of anxiety. These are derived from the most primitive psychic defense mechanisms. Those mechanisms are typical of the young infant's attempts to deal, mainly by evasion, with the severe anxieties aroused by the interplay of his own instincts that are intolerable at his immature age.[21]

Individuals vary in the extent to which they are able, as they grow older, to modify or abandon their early defense mechanisms and develop other methods of dealing with their anxieties. Notably, these other methods include the ability to confront the anxiety situations in their original or symbolic forms and to work them over, to approach and tolerate psychic and objective reality, to differentiate between them and to perform constructive and objectively successful activities in relation to them.[22] Every individual is at risk that objective or psychic events stimulating acute anxiety will lead to partial or complete abandonment of the more mature methods of dealing with anxiety and to regression to the more primitive methods of defense. In our opinion, the intense anxiety evoked by the nursing task has precipitated just such individual regression to primitive types of defense. These have been projected and given new objective existence in the social structure and culture of the nursing service, with the result that anxiety is to some extent contained, but that true mastery of anxiety by deep working through and modification is seriously inhibited. Thus, it is to be expected that nurses will persistently experience a higher degree of anxiety than is justified by the objective situation alone. Consideration in more detail of how the socially structured defense system fails to support the individual in the struggle towards more effective mastery of anxiety may be approached from two different but related points of view.

I will first consider how far the present functioning of the nursing service gives rise to experiences that in themselves either reassure nurses or arouse anxiety. In fact, as a direct consequence of the social organization, many situations and incidents arise that

[21]I will enumerate briefly here some of the most important of these defenses. In doing so, I follow the work of Freud as developed by Melanie Klein (1952a, 1959). The infant makes much use of splitting and projection, denial, idealization, and rigid, omnipotent control of himself and others. These defenses are, at first, massive and violent. Later, as the infant becomes more able to tolerate his anxiety, the same defenses continue to be used but are less violent. They begin to appear also in what are perhaps more familiar forms, e.g., as repression, obsessional rituals, and repetition of the familiar.

[22]Or, expressed otherwise, the capacity to undertake sublimatory activities.

clearly arouse anxiety. On the other hand, the social system frequently functions in such a way as to deprive nurses of necessary reassurance and satisfactions. In other words, the social defense system itself arouses a good deal of secondary anxiety as well as failing to alleviate primary anxiety. I shall illustrate these points with some typical examples.

Threat of Crisis and Operational Breakdown

From the operational point of view, the nursing service is cumbersome and inflexible. It cannot easily adapt to short- or long-term changes in conditions. For example, the task-list system and minutely prescribed task performance make it difficult to adjust workloads when necessary by postponing or omitting less urgent or important tasks. The total demands on a ward vary considerably and at short notice according to such factors as the types and numbers of patients and of operating days. The numbers and categories of student nurses also vary considerably and at short notice. Recurrent shortages of second-year or third-year nurses occur while they spend six weeks in the school; sickness or leave frequently reduce numbers. The work/staff ratio, therefore, varies considerably and often suddenly. Since work cannot easily be reduced, this generates considerable pressure, tension, and uncertainty among staff and students. Even when the work/staff ratio is satisfactory, the threat of a sudden increase is always present. The nurses seem to have a constant sense of impending crisis. They are haunted by fear of failing to carry out their duties adequately as pressure of work increases. Conversely, they rarely experience the satisfaction and lessening of anxiety that come from knowing they have the ability to carry out their work realistically and efficiently.

The nursing service is organized in a way that makes it difficult for one person, or even a close group of people, to make a rapid and effective decision. Diffusion of responsibility prevents adequate and specific concentration of authority for making and implementing decisions. The organization of working groups makes it difficult to achieve adequate concentration of necessary knowledge. For example, the task-list system prevents the breakdown of a ward into units of a size that allows one person to be fully acquainted with what is going on in them, and of a number that allows adequate communication between them and to the person responsible for coordinating them. In a ward, only the sister and the staff nurse are in a position to collect and coordinate knowledge. However, they must do this for a unit of such size and complexity that it is impossible to do it effectively. They are, inevitably, badly briefed. For example, we came across many cases where the sister did not remember how many nurses were on duty or what each was supposed to do, and had to have recourse to a written list. Such instances cannot be attributed primarily to individual inadequacy. Decisions tend to be made, therefore, by people who feel that they lack adequate knowledge of relevant and ascertainable facts. This leads to both anxiety and anger. To this anxiety is added the anxiety that decisions will not be taken in time, since decision making is made so slow and cumbersome by the system of checking and counterchecking and by the obscurity surrounding the localization of responsibility.

Excessive Movement of Student Nurses

The fact that a rise in work/staff ratios can be met only within very narrow limits by a reduction in the workload means that it is often necessary to have staff reinforcements, usually, to move student nurses. The defense of rigid work organization thus appears as a contributory factor to the presenting problem of student allocation. The unduly frequent moves cause considerable distress and anxiety. Denial of the importance of relationships and feelings does not adequately protect the nurses, especially since the moves most directly affect student nurses, who have not yet fully developed these defenses. Nurses grieve and mourn over broken relationships with patients and other nurses; they feel they are failing their patients. One nurse felt compelled to return to her previous ward to visit a patient who, she felt, had depended a great deal on her. The nurse feels strange in her new surroundings. She has to learn some new duties and make relationships with new patients and staff. She probably has to nurse types of illness she has never nursed before. Until she gets to know more about the new situation she suffers anxiety, uncertainties, and doubts. Senior staff estimate that it takes a student two weeks to settle down in a new ward. We regard this as an underestimate. The suddenness of many moves increases the difficulty. It does not allow adequate time for preparing for parting and makes the parting more traumatic. Patients cannot be handed over properly to other nurses. Sudden transfers to a different ward allow little opportunity for psychological preparation for what is to come. Nurses tend to feel acutely deprived by this lack of preparation. As one girl said, "If only I had known a bit sooner that I was going to the diabetic ward, I would have read up about diabetics and that would have helped a lot." Janis (1958) has described how the effects of anticipated traumatic events can be alleviated if an advance opportunity is provided to work over anxieties. He has described this as the "work of worrying," a parellel concept to Freud's concept of the "work of mourning" (Freud, 1917). The opportunity to work over the anticipated traumata of separation is, in the present circumstances, denied to nurses. This adds greatly to stress and anxiety.

This situation does indeed help to produce a defensive psychological detachment. Students protect themselves against the pain and anxiety of transfers, or the threat of transfers, by limiting their psychological involvement in any situation, with patients or other staff. This reduces their interest and sense of responsibility and fosters a "don't care" attitude of which nurses and patients complain bitterly. Nurses feel anxious and guilty when they detect such feelings in themselves, and angry, hurt, and disappointed when they find them in others: "Nobody cares how we are getting on, there is no team spirit, no one helps us." The resulting detachment also reduces the possibility of satisfaction from work well done in a job one deeply cares about.

Underemployment of Student Nurses

Understandably, since workloads are so variable and it is difficult to adjust tasks, the nursing service tries to plan its establishments to meet peak rather than average loads. As a result, student nurses quite often have too little work. They hardly ever complain of overwork and a number complained of not having enough work, although they still complained of stress. We observed obvious underemployment as we moved about the wards, in spite of the fact that student nurses are apt to make themselves look busy doing something and talk of having to look busy to avoid censure from the sister. Senior staff often seemed to feel it necessary to explain why their students were not busier, and would say they were "having a slack day" or they "had an extra nurse today."

Student nurses are also chronically underemployed in terms of level of work. A number of elements in the defense system contribute to this. Consider, for example, the assignment of duties to whole categories of student nurses. Since nurses find it so difficult to tolerate inefficiency and mistakes, the level of duties for each category is pitched low, i.e., near to the expected level of the least competent nurse in the category. In addition, the policy that makes student nurses the effective nursing staff of the hospital condemns them to the repetitive performance of simple tasks to an extent far beyond that necessary for their training. The performance of simple tasks need not of itself imply that the student nurse's role is at a low level. The level depends also on how much opportunity is given for the use of discretion and judgment in the organization of the tasks—which, when, and how. It is theoretically possible to have a role in which a high level of discretion is required to organize tasks that are in themselves quite simple. In fact, the social defense system specifically minimizes the exercise of discretion and judgment in the student nurse's organization of her tasks, e.g., through the task-list system. This ultimately determines the underemployment of many student nurses who are capable of exercising a good deal of judgment and could quickly be trained to use it effectively in their work. Similar underemployment is obvious in senior staff connected, for example, with the practice of delegating upwards.

Underemployment of this kind stimulates anxiety and guilt, which are particularly acute when underemployment implies failing to use one's capacities fully in the service of other people in need. Nurses find the limitations on their performance very frustrating. They often experience a painful sense of failure when they have faithfully performed their prescribed tasks and express guilt and concern about incidents in which they have carried out instructions to the letter, but, in so doing, have practiced what they consider to be bad nursing. For example, a nurse had been told to give a patient who had been sleeping badly a sleeping draught at a certain time. In the interval he had fallen into a deep natural sleep. Obeying her orders, she woke him up to give him the medicine. Her common sense and judgment told her to let him sleep and she felt very guilty that she had disturbed him. One frequently hears nurses complain that they "have" to waken patients early in the morning to have their faces washed when they feel that the patients would benefit more by being left asleep. Patients also make strong complaints. But "all faces must be washed" before the consultant medical staff arrive in the wards in the morning. The nurses feel they are being forced to abandon common-sense principles of good nursing, and they resent it.

Jaques (1956) has discussed the use of discretion and has come to the conclusion that the level of responsibility experienced in a job is related solely to the exercise of discretion and not to carrying out the prescribed elements. Following that statement, we may say that the level of responsibility in the nurse's job is minimized by the attempt to eliminate the use of discretion. Many student nurses complain bitterly that, while ostensibly in a very responsible job, they have less responsibility than they had as senior schoolgirls. They feel insulted, indeed, almost assaulted, by being deprived of the opportunity to be more responsible. They feel, and are, devalued by the social system. They are intuitively aware that the further development of their capacity for responsibility is being inhibited by the work and training situation and they greatly resent this. The bitterness of the experience is intensified because they are constantly being exhorted to behave responsibly, which, in the ordinary usage of the word in a work situation, they can hardly do. In fact, we came to the conclusion that senior staff tend to use the word "responsibility" differently from ordinary usage. For them, a "responsible" nurse is one who carried out prescriptions to the letter. There is an essential conflict between staff and students that greatly adds to stress and bitterness on both sides. Jaques (1956) has stated that workers in industry cannot rest content until they have reached a level of work that deploys to the full their capacity for discretionary responsibility. Student nurses, who are, in effect, "workers" in the hospital for most of their time, are certainly not content.

Deprivation of Personal Satisfactions

The nursing service seems to provide unusually little in the way of direct satisfaction for staff and students. Although the dictum "nursing should be a vocation" implies that nurses should not expect ordinary job satisfaction, its absence adds to stress. Mention has already been made of a number of ways in which nurses are deprived of positive satisfactions potentially existent in the profession, e.g., the satisfaction and reassurance that come from confidence in nursing skill. Satisfaction is also reduced by the attempt to evade anxiety by splitting up the nurse-patient relationship and converting patients who need nursing into tasks that must be performed. Although the nursing service has considerable success in nursing patients, the individual nurse has little direct experience of success. Success and satisfaction are dissipated in much the same way as the anxiety. The nurse misses the reassurance of seeing a patient get better in a way she can easily connect with her own efforts. The nurse's longing for this kind of experience is shown in the excitement and pleasure felt by a nurse who is chosen to "special" a patient, i.e., to give special, individual care to a very ill patient in a crisis situation. The gratitude of patients, an important reward for nurses, is also dissipated. Patients are grateful to the hospital or to "the nurses" for their treatment and recovery, but they cannot easily express gratitude in any direct way to individual nurses. There are too many and they are too mobile. The poignancy of the situation is increased by the expressed aims of nursing at the present time: to nurse the whole patient as a person. The nurse is instructed to do that and it is usually what she wants to do, but the functioning of the nursing service makes it impossible.

Sisters, too, are deprived of potential satisfactions in their roles. Many of them would like closer contact with patients and more opportunity to use their nursing skills directly. Much of their time is spent in initiating and training student nurses who come to their wards. The excessive movement of students means that sisters are frequently deprived of the return on that training time and the reward of seeing the nurse develop under their supervision. The reward of their work, like the nurse's, is dissipated and impersonal.

The nursing service inhibits in a number of ways the realization of satisfactions in relationships with colleagues. For example, the traditional relationship between staff and students is such that students are singled out by staff almost solely for reprimand or criticism. Good work is taken for granted and little praise given. Students complain that no one notices when they work well, when they stay late on duty, or when they do some extra task for a patient's comfort. Work teams are notably impermanent. Even three-monthly moves of student nurses would make it difficult to weld together a strong, cohesive work team. The more frequent moves, and the threats of moves, make it almost impossible. In such circumstances, it is difficult to build a team that functions effectively on the basis of real knowledge of the strengths and weaknesses of each member, her needs as well as her contribution, and adapts to the way of working and type of relationship each person prefers. Nurses feel hurt and resentful about the lack of importance attached to their personal contribution to the work, and the work itself is less satisfying when it must be done not only in accordance with the task-list system but also with an informal, but rigid, organization. A nurse misses the satisfaction of investing her own personality thoroughly in her work and making a highly personal contribution. The "depersonalization" used as a defense makes matters worse. The implied disregard of her own needs and capacities is distressing to the nurse, she feels she does not matter and no one cares what happens to her. This is particularly distressing when she is in a situation fraught with risks and difficulty and knows that sooner or later she will have great need of help and support.

Such support for the individual is notably lacking throughout the whole nursing service within working relationships. Compensation is sought in intense relationships with other nurses off-duty.[23] Working groups are characterized by great isolation of their members. Nurses frequently do not know what other members of their team are doing or even what their formal duties are; indeed, they often do not know whether other members of their team are on duty or not. They pursue their own tasks with minimal regard to colleagues. This leads to frequent difficulties between nurses. For example, one nurse, in carrying out her own tasks correctly by the prescription, may undo work done by another nurse also carrying out her tasks correctly by the prescription because they do not plan their work together and coordinate it. Bad feeling usually follows. One nurse may be extremely busy while another has not enough to do. Sharing of work is rare. Nurses complain bitterly about this situation. They say "there is no team spirit, no one helps you, no one cares." They feel guilty about not helping and angry about not being helped. They feel deprived by the lack of close, responsible, friendly relations with colleagues. The training system, orientated as it is to information giving, also deprives the student nurse of support and help. She feels driven to acquire knowledge and pass examinations, to become "a good nurse," while at the same time she feels few people show real concern for her personal development and her future.

---

[23]By tradition a nurse finds her closest nurse friends in her "set", i.e., the group with which she started nursing. Friendship between nurses in different sets is culturally unacceptable. But nurses in the same set spend little working time together except in their short spells in formal instruction.

The lack of personal support and help is particularly painful for the student nurse as she watches the care and attention given to patients. It is our impression that a significant number of nurses enter the profession under a certain confusion about their future roles and functions. They perceive the hospital as an organization particularly well equipped to deal with dependency needs, kind and supportive, and they expect to have the privilege of being very dependent themselves. However, because of categorization, they find that they are denied the privilege except on very rare occasions, notably when they get sick themselves and are nursed in the hospital.

I go on now to consider the second general approach to the failure of the social defenses to alleviate anxiety. This arises from the direct impact of the social defense system on the individual, regardless of specific experiences, i.e., from the more directly psychological interaction between the social defense system and the individual nurse.

Although, following Jaques, I have used the term "social defense system" as a construct to describe certain features of the nursing service as a continuing social institution, I wish to make it clear that I do not imply that the nursing service as an institution operates the defenses. Defenses are, and can be, operated only by individuals. Their behavior is the link between their psychic defenses and the institution. Membership necessitates an adequate degree of matching between individual and social defense systems. I will not attempt to define the degree but state simply that if the discrepancy between social and individual defense systems is too great, some breakdown in the individual's relation with the institution is inevitable. The form of breakdown varies, but, in our society, it commonly takes the form of a temporary or permanent break in the individual's membership. For example, if the individual continues to use his own defenses and follows his own idiosyncratic behavior patterns, he may become intolerable to other members of the institution who are more adapted to the social defense system. They may then reject him. If he tries to behave in a way consistent with the social defense system rather than his individual defenses, his anxiety will increase and he may find it impossible to continue his membership. Theoretically, matching between social and individual defenses can be achieved by a restructuring of the social defense system to match the individual, by a restructuring of the individual defense system to match the social, or by a combination of the two. The processes by which an adequate degree of matching is achieved are too complicated to describe here in detail. It must suffice to say that they depend heavily on repeated projection of the psychic defense system into the social defense system and repeated introjection of the social defense system into the psychic defense system. This allows continuous testing of match and fit as the individual experiences his own and other people's reactions (Heimann, 1952).

The social defense system of the nursing service has been described as an historical development through collusive interaction between individuals to project and reify relevant elements of their psychic defense systems. However, from the point of view of the new entrant to the nursing service, the social defense system at the time of entry is a datum, an aspect of external reality to which she must react and adapt. Fenichel makes a similar point (1946). He states that social institutions arise through the efforts of human beings to satisfy their needs, but that social institutions then become external realities comparatively independent of individuals which affect the structure of the individual. The student nurse is faced with a particularly difficult task in adapting to the nursing service and developing an adequate match between the social defense system and her psychic defense system. It will have been made clear that the nursing service is very resistant to change, especially change in the functioning of its defense system. For the student nurse, this means that the social defense system is to an unusual extent immutable. In the process of matching between the psychic and social defense systems, the emphasis is heavily on the modification of the individual's psychic defenses. This means in practice that she must incorporate and operate the social defense system more or less as she finds it, restructuring her psychic defenses as necessary to match it.

An earlier section described how the social defense system of the hospital was built of primitive psychic defenses, those characteristic of the earliest phases of infancy. It follows that student nurses, by becoming members of the nursing service, are required to incorporate and use primitive psychic defenses, at least in those areas of their life space which directly concern their work. The use of such defenses has certain intrapsychic consequences. These are consistent with the social phenomena already referred to in other contexts in this paper. I will describe them briefly to complete the account. These defenses are oriented to the violent, terrifying situations of infancy, and rely heavily on violent splitting which dissipates the anxiety. By permitting the individual to avoid the experience of anxiety, they effectively prevent the individual from confronting it. Thus, the individual cannot bring the content of the phantasy anxiety situations into contact with reality. Unrealistic or pathological anxiety cannot then be differentiated from realistic anxiety arising from real dangers. Therefore, anxiety tends to remain permanently at a level determined more by the phantasies than by the reality. The forced introjection of the hospital defense system, therefore, perpetuates in the individual a considerable degree of pathological anxiety.

The enforced introjection and use of such defenses also interferes with the capacity for symbol formation. The defenses inhibit the capacity for creative symbolic thought, for abstract thought, and for conceptualization. They inhibit the full development of the individual's understanding, knowledge, and skills that enable reality to be handled effectively and pathological anxiety to be mastered. Thus the individual feels helpless in the face of new or strange tasks or problems. The development of such capacities presupposes considerable psychic integration, which the social defense system inhibits. It also inhibits self-knowledge and understanding and with them realistic assessment of performance. The deficient reality sense that follows from the defense system also interferes with judgment and provokes mistakes. The individual is confronted with them when it is too late and a sense of failure, increased self-distrust, and anxiety ensue. For example, mistakes, guilt, and anxiety arise from following out the prescriptions rather than applying the principles of good nursing. This situation particularly affects belief and trust in positive impulses and their effectiveness to control and modify aggression. Anxiety about positive aspects of the personality is very marked in nurses, e.g., fear of doing the wrong thing, expectation of mistakes, fear of not being truly responsible. The social defenses prevent the individual from realizing to the full her capacity for concern, compassion, and sympathy, and for action based on these feelings which would strengthen her belief in the good aspects of herself and her capacity to use them. The defense system strikes directly, therefore, at the roots of sublimatory activities in which infantile anxieties are reworked in symbolic form and modified.

In general, one may say that forced introjection of the defense system prevents the personal defensive maturation that alone allows for the modification of the remnants of infantile anxiety and diminishes the extent to which early anxieties may be evoked again and projected into current real situations. Indeed, in many cases, it forces the individual to regress to a maturational level below that which she had achieved before she entered the hospital. In this, the nursing service fails its individual members desperately. It seems clear that a major motivational factor in the choice of nursing as a career is the wish to have the opportunity to develop the capacity for sublimatory activities in the nursing of the sick, and through that to achieve better mastery of infantile anxiety situations, modification of pathological anxiety, and personal maturation.

It may be interesting, in view of this, to add one further comment on wastage. It seems more serious than number alone suggests. It appears to be the more mature students who find the conflict between their own and the hospital defense system most acute and are most likely to give up training. Although the research objectives did not permit us to collect statistics, it is our distinct impression that among the students who do not complete training are a significant number of the better students, i.e., those who are personally most mature and most capable of intellectual, professional, and personal development with appropriate training. Nurses often talked of students who had left as "very good nurses." No one could understand why they had not wanted to finish their training. We had the opportunity to discuss the matter with some students who were seriously considering leaving. Many said they still wanted to nurse and found it difficult to formulate why they wanted to leave. They suffered from a vague sense of dissatisfaction with their training and the work they were doing and a sense of hopelessness about the future. The general content of the interviews left little doubt that they were distressed about the inhibition of their personal development. There is also a striking difference in the personalities of groups of students at different stages of training. Some of the differences appear to arise from self-selection of students to give up training. If we are correct in this impression, the social defense system impoverishes the nursing service for the future, since it tends to drive away those potential senior staff whose contribution to the development of nursing theory and practice would be greatest. Thus the wheel turns full circle and the difficulty in changing the system is reinforced. It is the tragedy of the system that its inadequacies drive away the very people who might remedy them.

SUMMARY AND CONCLUDING COMMENTS

This paper has presented some data from a study of the nursing service of a general teaching hospital. Its specific purpose was to consider and, if possible, account for the high level of stress and anxiety chronic among nurses. In following through the data, it was suggested that the nature of the nurse's task, in spite of its obvious difficulties, was not enough to account for the level of anxiety and stress. Consequently, an attempt was made to understand and illustrate the nature of the methods the nursing service provided for the alleviation of anxiety, i.e., its social defense system, and to consider in what respects it failed to function adequately. The conclusion reached was that the social defense system represented the institutionalization of very primitive psychic defense mechanisms, a main characteristic of which is that they facilitate the evasion of anxiety, but contribute little to its true modification and reduction.

In concluding, I wish to touch briefly on a few points that space does not permit me to elaborate. I have considered only incidentally the effect of the defense system on the efficiency of task performance, apart from stating that it does permit the continuing performance of the primary task of the service. It will have been apparent, however, that the nursing service carries out its task inefficiently in many respects, e.g., it keeps the staff/patient ratio unduly high, it leads to a significant amount of bad nursing practice, it leads to excessive staff turnover, and it fails to train students adequately for their real future roles. There are many other examples. Further, the high level of anxiety in nurses adds to the stress of illness and hospitalization for patients and has adverse effects on such factors as recovery rates. An investigation by Revans (1959) has connected recovery rates of patients quite directly with the morale of nursing staff. Thus the social structure of the nursing service is defective not only as a means of handling anxiety, but also as a method of organizing its tasks. These two aspects cannot be regarded as separate. The inefficiency is an inevitable consequence of the chosen defense system.

This leads me to put forward the proposition that the success and viability of a social institution are intimately connected with the techniques it uses to contain anxiety. Analogous hypotheses about the individual have long been widely accepted. Freud put forward such ideas increasingly as his work developed (1926). The work of Melanie Klein and her colleagues has given a central position to anxiety and the defenses in personality development and ego functioning (1948a). I put forward a second proposition, which is linked with the first, namely, that an understanding of this aspect of the functioning of a social institution is an important diagnostic and therapeutic tool in facilitating social change. Bion (1955) and Jaques (1955) stress the importance of understanding these phenomena and relate difficulties in achieving social change to difficulty in tolerating the anxieties that are released as social defenses are restructured. This appears closely connected with the experiences of people, including many social scientists, who have tried to initiate or facilitate social change. Recommendations or plans for change that seem highly appropriate from a rational point of view are ignored, or do not work in practice. One difficulty seems to be that they do not sufficiently take into account the common anxieties and the social defenses in the institution concerned, nor provide for the therapeutic handling of the situation as change takes place. Jaques (1955, p. 498), states that "effective social change is likely to require analysis of common anxieties and unconscious collusions underlying the social defenses determining phantasy social relationships."

The nursing service presents these difficulties to a high degree, since the anxieties are already very acute and the defense system both primitive and ineffectual. Efforts to initiate serious change were often met with acute anxiety and hostility, which conveyed the idea that the people concerned felt very threatened, the threat being of nothing less than social chaos and individual breakdown. To give up known ways of behavior and embark on the unknown were felt to be intolerable. In general, it may be postulated that resistance to social change is likely to be greatest in institutions whose social defense systems are dominated by primitive psychic defense mechanisms, those which have been collectively described by Melanie Klein as the paranoid-schizoid defenses (Klein, 1952, 1959). One may compare this socio-therapeutic experience with the common experience in psychoanalytic therapy, that the most difficult work is with patients whose defenses are mainly of this kind, or in phases of the analysis when such defenses predominate.

Some therapeutic results were achieved in the hospital, notably in relation to the presenting symptom. A planned set of courses has been prepared for student nurses, which jointly ensures that the student nurses have adequate training and that the hospital is adequately staffed. Interestingly, it was in preparing these courses that objective data were calculated for the first time about discrepancies between training and staffing needs. For example, to give adequate gynecological training the gynecological wards would have to carry four times too many staff; to keep the operating theatres staffed, the nurses would have to have one and a half times too much theatre experience for training. Before this time, the existence of such discrepancies was known, but no one had collected reliable statistical data, a simple matter, and no realistic plans had been made to deal with them. To prevent emergencies from interfering with the implementation of the planned courses, a reserve pool of nurses was created whose special duty was to be mobile and deal with them. A number of other similar changes were instituted dealing with other problems that emerged in the course of the investigation.[24] The common features of the changes, however, were that they involved minimal disturbance of the existing defense system. Indeed, it would be more correct to say that they involved reinforcing and strengthening the existing type of defense. Proposals were made for more far-reaching change, involving a restructuring of the social defense system. For example, one suggestion was that a limited experiment be done in ward organization, eliminating the task-list system and substituting some form of patient assignment. However, although the senior staff discussed such proposals with courage and seriousness, they did not feel able to proceed with the plans. This happened in spite of our clearly expressed views that, unless there were some fairly radical changes in the system, the problems of the nursing service might well become extremely serious. The decision seemed to us quite comprehensible, however, in view of the anxiety and the defense system. These would have made the therapeutic task of accomplishing change very difficult for both the nursing service and the therapist.

The full seriousness of the situation is not perhaps clear without considering this hospital in the context of the general nursing services in the country as a whole. The description of the hospital makes it seem a somewhat serious example of social pathology,

---

[24]For example, the revised training program for fourth-year students.

but within the context of other general hospital nurse-training schools is fairly typical. Nothing in our general experience of hospitals and nursing leads us to believe otherwise (Skellern, 1953; Sofer, 1955; Wilson, 1950). There are differences in detail, but the main features of the structure and culture are common to British hospitals of this type and are carried in the general culture and ethic of the nursing profession. The hospital studied has, in fact, high status. It is accepted as being one of the better hospitals of its type.

The nursing services in general have shown a similar resistance to change in the face of the greatly altered demands made on them. There can be few professions that have been more studied than nursing, or institutions more studied than hospitals. Nurses have played an active part in initiating and carrying out these studies. Many nurses have an acute and painful awareness that their profession is in a serious state. They eagerly seek solutions, and there have been many changes in the expressed aims and policy of the profession. There have also been many changes in the peripheral areas of nursing, i.e., those which do not impinge very directly or seriously on the essential features of the social defense system. Against that background, one is astonished to find how little basic and dynamic change has taken place. Nurses have tended to receive reports and recommendations with a sense of outrage and to react to them by intensifying current attitudes and reinforcing existing practice.

An example of a general nursing problem that threatens crisis is the recruitment of nurses. Changes in medical practice have increased the number of highly technical tasks for nurses. Consequently, the level of intelligence and competence necessary for a fully trained and efficient nurse is rising. The National Health Service has improved the hospital service and made it necessary to have more nurses. On the other hand, professional opportunities for women are expanding rapidly and the other professions are generally more rewarding than nursing in terms of the opportunity to develop and exercise personal and professional capacities as well as in financial terms. The increasing demand for

high-level student nurses is therefore meeting increasing competition from other sources. In fact, recruiting standards are being
forced down in order to keep up numbers. This is no real solution,
for too many of the recruits will have difficulty in passing the
examinations and be unable to deal with the level of the work.
Many of them, on the other hand, would make excellent practical
nurses on simpler nursing duties. So far, no successful attempt
has been made in the general hospitals to deal with this problem,
e.g., by splitting the role of nurse into different levels with different training and different professional destinations.

It is unfortunately true of the paranoid-schizoid defense system
that they prevent true insight into the nature of problems and
realistic appreciation of their seriousness. Thus, only too often,
no action can be taken until a crisis is very near or has actually
occurred. This is the eventuality we fear in the British general
hospital nursing services. Even if there is no acute crisis, there
is undoubtedly a chronic state of reduced effectiveness, which in
itself is serious enough.

References

Bion, W. R. (1955), Group Dynamics: A Review. In: *New Directions in Psycho-Analysis,*
    ed. M. Klein, P. Heimann, & R. E. Money-Kyrle. New York: Basic Books.
Breuer, J., & Freud, S. (1893-1895), *Studies on Hysteria. Standard Edition,* 2. London:
    Hogarth Press, 1955.
Fenichel, O. (1946), *The Psychoanalytic Theory of the Neuroses.* New York: Norton.
Freud, S. (1917), Mourning and Melancholia. *Standard Edition,* 14:237-258. London:
    Hogarth Press, 1957.
———— (1926), *Inhibitions, Symptoms and Anxiety. Standard Edition,* 20:75-175. London:
    Hogarth Press, 1959.
Heimann, P. (1952), Certain Functions of Introjection and Projection in Earliest Infancy.
    In: *Developments in Psycho-Analysis.* London: Hogarth Press.
Hill, J. M. M., & Trist, E. L. (1953), A Consideration of Industrial Accidents as a Means
    of Withdrawal from the Work Situation. *Human Relations,* 6:357-380.
Janis, I. L. (1958), *Psychological Stress: Psycho-Analytic and Behavioral Studies of Surgical
    Patients.* London: Chapman & Hall.
Jaques, E. (1955), Social Systems as a Defence against Persecutory and Depressive Anx-
    iety. In: *New Directions in Psycho-Analysis,* ed. M. Klein, P. Heimann, & R. E.
    Money-Kyrle. New York: Basic Books.
———— (1956), *Measurement of Responsibility: A Study of Work, Payment, and Individual
    Capacity.* Cambridge, Mass.: Harvard University Press.
Klein, M. (1948a), The Psychogenesis of Manic-Depressive States. In: *Contributions to
    Psycho-Analysis.* London: Hogarth Press.

———— (1948b), The Importance of Symbol Formation in the Development of the Ego. In: *Contributions to Psycho-Analysis*. London: Hogarth Press.

———— (1952), Some Theoretical Conclusions Regarding the Emotional Life of the Infant. In: *Developments in Psycho-Analysis*. London: Hogarth Press.

———— (1959), Our Adult World and Its Roots in Infancy. *Human Relations*, 12:291-303.

Revans, R. W. (1959), The Hospital as an Organism: A Study in Communications and Morale. Preprint No. 7 of a paper presented at the 6th Annual International Meeting of the Institute of Management Sciences, September, Paris. New York: Pergamon.

Rice, A. K. (1958), *Productivity and Social Organization: The Ahmedabad Experiment*. London: Tavistock.

Segal, H. (1957), Notes on Symbol Formation. *Internat. J. Psycho-Anal.*, 38:391-397.

Skellern, E. (1953), *Report on the Practical Application to Ward Administration of Modern Methods in the Instruction and Handling of Staff and Student Nurses*. London: Royal College of Nursing.

Sofer, C. (1955), Reactions to Administrative Change: A Study of Staff Relations in Three British Hospitals. *Human Relations*, 8:291-316.

Trist, E. L., & Bamforth, K. W. (1951), Some Social and Psychological Consequences of the Longwall Method of Coal-Getting. *Human Relations*, 4:3-38.

Wilson, A. T. M. (1950), Hospital Nursing Auxiliaries. *Human Relations*, 3:1-32.

Maccoby discusses the relationship between diagnosis and those projects designed to bring about change in which the individuals concerned participate in a study of the problem. In his view, psychoanalysis is a form of participant study, and the concept of resistance is essential to all forms of participant study. The interest in change, the desire for self-exploration, and the role of the researcher are further elements of participant study projects.

20

Participant Study at Work

MICHAEL MACCOBY

PARTICIPANT STUDY

Participant study involves people in the critical examination of themselves and their own situation. Unlike methods in which people are studied by an outsider, participant study can be a process of learning and self-discovery for those involved. However, this process does not always run smoothly. Making use of experience from both psychoanalysis and participant studies in the workplace, this paper is a commentary on the motivation for and resistance to participant study and the role of the researcher.

Psychoanalysis is a form of participant study. Two people try to study one of them. Although it has been said that psychoanalysis is more successful as a research method than a therapy, the purpose of this study is not pure knowledge, but to help at least one of them improve his life. Psychoanalysis is a change project. The psychoanalyst as the professional researcher-educator brings to this project two types of knowledge. One type has to do with

This chapter was originally presented at the Annual Meeting of the American Anthropological Association, December, 1980. By permission of the author.

content: symbolism, quality of feeling, the nature of developmental stages. The other type has to do with process, including a method of study (free association) and the interpretation of resistance.

The content of resistances turn out to be unconscious attitudes and memories that may be acted out in psychoanalysis. The concept of resistance is essential not only to psychoanalysis but to all forms of participant study.

Like psychoanalysis, participant study requires a project for change and a spirit of hope. The individual or group is moved to self study and to the analysis of resistance because of a combination of discomfort with things as they are and hope of improvement. It is in the workplace that participant study has proved most useful, in cases where technology and organizational purpose allow possibilities for higher levels of cooperation and participation in management, and leadership sees benefits in sharing power.

My first experience with participant study outside of psychoanalysis was in a Mexican village where Erich Fromm, I, and other collaborators were exploring a basic question about economic and human development (Fromm and Maccoby, 1970). Taking note of the high incidence of violence, the prevalence of alcoholism, the poverty and absence of productive activity, we asked: Would these people act in a different, healthier way if they had better economic opportunities, or is the pathology rooted in character? Interviews and participant observations led to interpretations about social character as a determining factor, but these could be tested only by offering opportunities for change and observing the results. A project was organized with a group of boys between the ages of twelve and eighteen, who were given chickens, pigs, a cow, and a plot of land to farm. It soon became clear that their cooperation depended totally on receiving orders from the researchers who were treated as the authorities. The boys were unwilling to accept responsibility; they helped each other only when commanded by adult authority. I began to meet once a week with the boys to talk about their attitudes and behavior. They agreed, intellectually, that it was irrational for them to act so egocentrically. Here was a chance to learn new skills and make money if they could cooperate, and if they could not, they would lose it all after the researchers left.

To make a long story short, we began to explore their attitudes. The first breakthrough came one day when everyone said nothing or spoke without interest, until I challenged them to say what was really on their minds. I learned that the resistance was their fear of telling me they all wished our meeting was over so that they could be at a fiesta, the birthday of a fifteen-year-old girl, taking place nearby. The fear of authority became the theme for subsequent meetings, and they described memories of their upbringing, based on punishment, never praise or appreciation. They agreed that in the village, when authorities were involved, one acted to avoid punishment, get the task over with, rather than to achieve positive satisfaction. Furthermore, they had been taught a sense that their wishes for pleasure were evil, that they could be good only by submitting to authority. A new awareness allowed them to confront their fear and fatalism and begin to learn and cooperate. Twenty years later when I returned to the village, one of the boys from the poorest families was running a prosperous chicken and egg business, with his own son behind the counter of his store. I asked him if our training in caring for chickens and marketing eggs had been the key to his success. "Not so much that," he answered. "It was learning that we were just as good as any authority, that we had no reason to be afraid to try something new."

Back in the U.S., I applied the methods of studying social character—by interviews and participant observations—to managers and executives of corporations creating advanced technology (Maccoby, 1976). This study raised the question with participants of how their work affected their intellectual and emotional development. Although some managers participated in the design of the study, it was not until later that these findings proved useful for participant studies of work. One corporate chief executive, Sidney Harman, offered to sponsor a study in collaboration with the United Auto Workers in a Bolivar, Tennessee factory (Maccoby, 1975). That study, using a combination of survey methods, participant observation, and interviews explored culture, statements about work and social character—the emotionally charged values and attitudes shared by groups of people. Here, as in the Mexican village, methods of anthropology combined with survey research provided material to make interpretations about the relationships between work and social character which could be tested only in a participative project to improve work. Based on the interviews, interpretations were made of different social character types and how they reacted to work.

The researchers, Robert and Margaret Duckles, engaged groups of factory workers in experiments to restructure work, using methods developed by Einar Thorsrud and his Norwegian collaborators (Thorsrud, 1966, 1976). In some instances, the limits to change were in the production, technology, and power relationships. In others, where technology and authority were more flexible, resistance was rooted in values and attitudes toward work which contradicted assumptions made by some theorists of job enrichment that everyone would welcome more challenging work. For example, some workers did not want to enlarge their jobs, because they preferred simple tasks that allowed time for sociability. This did not imply fear or lack of ability, since these same people welcomed complexity and innovation in work carried out at home or on small farms.

In fact, by taking seriously the resistance to change, not as something to be overcome by "education" but rather to be understood by exploration, we discover the changing social character moving from a traditional farming to modern industrial context.

Regrettably, I have no time to explore the findings from these projects. As you will hear, the project in the Bolivar factory became a model which was then applied to work-improvement projects in the federal government. Participant study has been employed to explore alternative ways of organizing work, and values and behavior of employees and managers in the Departments of Commerce and State, and ACTION (Maccoby, Duckles, and Duckles, 1980; Lenkerd, 1979).

At the State Department, a group of some fifteen foreign service officers and civil servants, under the leadership of the Director General of the Foreign Service who is responsible for personnel policy and administration, have participated in a study of management within the State Department. Their goal is to establish practices which will support the development of the capabilities and character of the foreign service officers, and to this end the group selected examples of managers they considered closest to the ideal. With my help, they constructed a question-naire concerning managerial philosophy and practice and its re-lationship to the goals of foreign policy. Each member of the group participated with me in interviews of the managers, and some also interviewed subordinates to check out the manager's description of his practices. The group has participated in the analysis of data and the formulation of conclusions. They have discussed two causes of resistance. One is a sense of powerlessness to affect positive change. The other is the fear of being punished for telling unpleasant truths. The question remains to be answered of how much these resistances are rational responses to bureau-cratic pressures, and how much they are rooted in the character of the cautious careerist. The participants see the process as val-uable not only in the content or substance of its findings and in the training for self-study, but also in developing a more coop-erative approach to solving problems.

The Role of the Researcher

Projects for change and studies that further change are gen-erally funded by someone with an idea of the kind of change desired. In psychoanalysis, the patient wants more control over himself and his life. In bureaucracies, managers typically want to increase their power, and they pay consultants for studies that justify their aims or show them how to carry them out.

For participant study to succeed, the participants must agree on goals and values which generally combine organizational ef-fectiveness and the well-being of the participants themselves.

Those who control the funds will sponsor a participant study, only if convinced that by sharing power and concerning themselves with the well-being of employees, the organization will function better and their own position will be enhanced. Their subordinates will participate only because there is hope of making work more satisfying. Today, as the social character of more educated employees becomes more self-affirmative, and work requires more responsibility and care, increasingly it is in the interest of authority to gain greater involvement of the employees in decision-making and the design of work. Participant study is a method toward this end.

The role of the professional researcher-educator in participant research includes two main functions. One is as a resource in offering a methodology or alternative methodological tools for the participants to employ. The other is the role of interpreting resistances.

Once in process, participant study may bump into resistance. Participants may be unwilling to admit to feelings and thoughts which make them uncomfortable, for example, forcing them to criticize authorities. Or they may resist taking responsibility because they lose the right to object to decisions. As in psychoanalysis, the resistance may be expressed in the transference toward the researcher. Here the participant researcher can find himself in a tight situation. Unlike the participant observer who can remain relatively independent and retreat to his tent when confused by events, the participant researcher must interpret the resistance, or the process may grind to a halt.

One form of transference resistance commonly encountered in participant study is the attempt to make the researcher into an all-knowing guru, thereby putting all the responsibility on him. As in psychoanalysis, failure to analyze the transference resistance transforms study into collusion.

In the workplace, the researcher who colludes with the need for an all-knowing authority merely steps into a bureaucratic authority role and thereby short-circuits the process. It may be the case that the resistance expresses such fear or hopelessness that the change project is unrealistic and should be abandoned. But we cannot reach that conclusion without analyzing the resistance and allowing the group an opportunity to understand and overcome it. If either the internal resistance or external forces are indeed too powerful to overcome, participant study will come to an end, and the researcher can then become a participant observer able to contribute, at least, to understanding the limits to change.

REFERENCES

Fromm, E., & Maccoby, M. (1970), *Social Character in a Mexican Village*. Englewood Cliffs, N.J.: Prentice-Hall.

Lenkerd, B. (1979), *Study-Project to Improve the Quality of Working Life at ACTION*. Unpublished report.

Maccoby, M. (1975), Changing Work: The Bolivar Project, *Working Papers*. Summer, pp. 43-55.

———— (1976), *The Gamesman: The New Corporate Leaders*. New York: Simon & Schuster.

———— Duckles, M. M., & Duckles, R. (1980), *Bringing Out the Best*. Discussion Paper Series, John F. Kennedy School of Government, Harvard University, No. 91D, June.

Thorsrud, E. (1966), *Industrial Democracy: Involvement, Commitment, Action: Some Observations During Field Research*. Institute for Human Relations, Doc. T., 886, October.

———— (1976), *Democracy at Work and Perspectives on the Quality of Working Life in Scandinavia*. International Institute for Labour Studies, Research Series #8.

Elaborating on the theme of participant study, Maccoby illustrates the points made in the preceding chapter by presenting a socio-psychoanalytic study of change among workers in a factory in Tennessee—the Bolivar project—the goal of which was to create an American model of industrial democracy that would be acceptable to unions and that might stimulate further union efforts in this direction. The author demonstrates how a typology of predominant character types in the factory helped to explain differences in attitudes toward work, and he illustrates how this understanding led to self-exploration, reduced conflict, and a better working environment.

21

Changing Work: The Bolivar Project

MICHAEL MACCOBY

Attempts to reorganize industrial work are not new. Particularly in recent years, numerous experiments involving job enrichment, "work humanization," and even some measure of worker self-management on the job have been carried out. The Bolivar project, which involves workers at an automobile mirror factory in southwest Tennessee, is an experiment in this tradition.

But the outcome of Bolivar may be more significant than the results of most such projects. The goal of the Bolivar project is to create an American model of industrial democracy: a model that is acceptable to unions and that might stimulate further union efforts. The project is based on the view that a national movement to improve the quality of work is unlikely to succeed without union support—and that union leaders are practical people who

This chapter originally appeared in *Working Papers*, Summer, 1975, pp. 43-55. By permission of the author.

can't be expected to struggle for abstract concepts like "humanized work" or self-management without something concrete to point to. If the project is successful, the workers and managers at Harman International Industries in Bolivar, Tennessee, will develop practices that not only change the character of their work but that also can be adopted by unions as goals for collective bargaining.

It's unusual for a work-reorganization experiment to have such far-reaching objectives, but—in the case of the Bolivar project—it's not accidental. The project originated in 1973-1974 with officials of the United Auto Workers, notably Vice-President Irving Bluestone, who were interested in relating the humanization of work to union concerns. For his part, the idealistic president of Harman International Industries, Sidney Harman, wanted to create a progressive example for businessmen. Like the Norwegian Industrial Democracy Project, but unlike most American attempts to improve work, the Bolivar project thus began with the active involvement of the union as well as management. Our staff of social scientists was invited in jointly by the union and management as an independent third party, and we accepted because we shared the project's goals.

Some aspects of the project that distinguish it from others naturally flowed from this fact of joint sponsorship. For one thing, the project includes the whole Harman auto mirror factory at Bolivar, Tennessee, rather than a single department, as is often the case with projects to restructure work (e.g., Corning Glass, Motorola, and Texas Instruments). (The plant, and the project, includes industrial processes such as die cast, polishing, painting, plating, assembly, and packing; and indirect departments such as data processing, inspection, and so forth.) Also, Harman is an established factory with an existing unionized workforce. It's not a plant designed from scratch and manned with carefully selected nonunion workers, like the General Foods plant in Topeka (where another well-known work reorganization experiment was carried out).

The project's goals for changing the working environment are similarly ambitious. Often, quality of work experiments attempt simply to enlarge jobs, raise employee morale, decrease turnover or absenteeism, or increase productivity. With the Bolivar project, the objective has been to reorganize the way the company itself operates. To this end, we began by spelling out the principles that everyone agreed should govern the worklife of hourly employees and managers alike.

Every organization, of course, is based on principles; they may either be stated explicitly as corporate ideology or remain hidden. Principles determine the practices of both individuals and organizations. Where the main principles are maximum profit and corporate growth, changes in the technology of production are likely to serve the goal of increasing productivity by strengthening centralized control over the worker. The worker becomes a standardized replaceable part of the process, and anger, hostility, depression, and stifled creativity are often the result. This was the case at the factory in Bolivar, where the economics of the auto parts industry, fierce competition and fluctuating demand, intensified insecurity and the dehumanizing conditions of work.

When they first pledged to support the project, both Harman's managers and the UAW officials understood that new principles would be needed to reconstruct the system in a more humane way. New principles would be a yardstick to measure new programs, a basis for making critical decisions, and an impetus to developing a new spirit.

Four principles were agreed on: security, equity, democracy, and an objective we termed "individuation." How are these principles defined and how do they determine practice?

Security refers to job security, health, and safety. Working for an auto parts manufacturer is not the most secure job, especially right now. Sudden upturns in auto sales require more workers, and downturns produce layoffs. The company cannot change the market. But it is now pursuing a policy that maximizes worker security, both by providing as many jobs as possible and by offering an educational program that prepares workers for other employment.

During the past year, for example, workers in experimental

programs began to meet standards established by time study according to the contract in less than the full eight hours. The Working Committee, composed of five representatives from management and five from the union, decided not to allow them to produce more for extra pay, because in the present economic situation this would have meant loss of jobs. Instead, the workers could use the time to go home early, for meetings, or for classes at the new school that has developed from the program. Many workers are farmers or mothers, for whom time may be more important than money. In making this decision, some members of the committee also argued that if they had allowed workers to increase production and earnings, they would have been stimulating the kind of materialistic attitude that contrasts to the principle of individuation.[1]

Equity refers to fair rules, regulations, and compensation—and to overcoming discrimination because of race, sex, or age. Equity means fair pay differentials. If changes in the workplace lead to higher productivity, the workers and managers contributing to these profits should share them equitably.

At Bolivar, the agreement signed by the plant management and union in 1974 begins by emphasizing the goal of the project and affirming the principle of equity in relation to any gains in productivity that might result:

> The purpose of the joint management-labor Work Improvement Program is to make work better and more satisfying for all employees, salaried and hourly, while maintaining the necessary productivity for job security.
> The purpose is not to increase productivity. If increased

---

[1]Before the experiments, many workers considered the standards unfair, and worked on the average at about 85 percent of standard. The only penalty received by failure to meet standards was a reprimand. Some of the first meetings with workers in polish and buff, brought out the fact that there were many variables affecting standards. When they felt the standard was unfair, workers often spent time arguing with the foreman, or their anger led to a slowdown. On their own, they came up with the idea of forming groups with a joint standard, and they developed a process for reevaluating the fairness of the standard of any part. Now, by allowing them use of time remaining after the standard is reached, the company also benefits. Other company benefits may be in quality, less absenteeism, turnover, and above all, a more cooperative environment.

productivity is a by-product of the program, ways of rewarding the employees for increased productivity will become legitimate matters for inclusion in the program.

The ideal of fairness is deeply rooted in the character of the Bolivar workers, most of whom come from farm backgrounds. As in most rural farming societies, independence, self-reliance, frugality, and hard work are all valued highly. With these values goes the belief that each person should receive a just reward for his or her efforts, and that no one is entitled to a free ride in life.

A survey carried out by the staff at the start of the project showed that many workers at the factory resented unfairness in a number of areas. A majority stated that the employees' share of earnings was not fair, that the method of promotion was not fair, and that workers were not rewarded equitably for doing their jobs well. Almost half felt the grievance procedure was not used sufficiently. And a significant number of black and women workers complained about discrimination against them.

As the project developed, some of these fairness issues were faced and steps taken toward greater equity. In February, 1974, for example, just as the first seminar on methods of developing workshop democracy was beginning, workers rejected a contract after management and the union had shaken hands on it, claiming that the contract did not protect them adequately from the rising cost of living. Management and union leaders were astonished by the rejection. But all parties decided to proceed with the seminar while continuing to bargain over the contract.

The demand for equity also forced the program to expand—from volunteer experiments in three departments to the whole plant—more quickly than planned. Once the experiments proved rewarding for the participants, the majority of workers demanded to be let in, threatening to end the project if they weren't. (In contrast to Bolivar, workers at Hunsfos Fabrikker in Norway have for ten years maintained an industrial democracy project that involves no more than forty percent of the workers in restructuring their work.)

CHANGING THE HIERARCHY

Principles of security and equity can be viewed as traditional union goals that compensate the worker for submitting to the industrial system and that protect him from extreme exploitation. Principles of democracy and individuation go beyond this. Here the objective is transforming the hierarchical organization to one based on concern for human development and mutual support.

Democracy in the project has been defined by the participants as "giving each worker more opportunities to have a say in the decisions that affect his life, including his work life." While the union has maintained democratic procedures in the election of stewards and officers, for the most part workers had no say about methods of production and the organization of work. The development of new democratic practices at the plant began, in a way, with the initial interview-survey of 300 workers and 50 managers. The survey stimulated people to think critically in a new way about their jobs, supervision, working conditions, fairness, and so forth. Until then, management and workers had freely criticized each other, but neither questioned the work structure and the roles that put both sides at each other's throats. Managers were policemen, and the main creative outlet for many workers was to figure out how to avoid work or how to infuriate the foreman. But in the survey, 70 percent of the workers told us they had ideas on how to improve work that they had never told to anyone, either because no one would listen or because others would take the credit. The process of thinking critically about work began to spark hope that it might be possible to improve conditions.

The survey showed that the most pressing issues were working conditions such as heat, cold, and poor ventilation. However, a majority of workers also wanted a greater say in deciding matters such as how fast the work should be done, setting pay standards, taking breaks, job assignments, promotions, work methods, selection of supervisors, discipline, and deciding when the work day begins and ends. At that time there was no mechanism for instituting new democratic procedures.

In the fall of 1973, the project's staff—an independent group invited in by management and the union—suggested the formation of an ad hoc management-union committee. The committee would try to resolve the problems of improving the working environment by exploring alternative solutions. The staff suggested this might develop a relationship and a process for deciding how to solve problems. The idea was accepted, and the new Working Committee was formed, composed of five management representatives and five union members (the local president and four members appointed by him subject to review by the bargaining committee).[2] For the first few months, the Working Committee dealt with ventilation and other problems such as parking, traffic jams at the change of shift, congestion in punching the time clock, and keeping bill collectors out of the factory. The group then organized a credit union. But a process for creating democracy on the shop floor was still lacking.

At this point, we invited Einar Thorsrud, director of the Norwegian Industrial Democracy Project, to conduct a seminar on ways of democratically analyzing and changing work. He came for three days, and together with the project staff and Working Committee developed a methodology and strategy of inviting volunteer groups to experiment with changes in the assembly and buff-and-polish departments. The method begins by bringing a work group together (including the supervisor) to analyze work processes according to human and social criteria (e.g., work satisfaction, chances for learning, fairness in assignments) as well as technical and economic criteria. Possible variations are discussed, and the group can propose to experiment with changes. This process is quite different from job enrichment, in which experts may enlarge a job for workers. The workers at Harman may decide to make changes similar to job enrichment (e.g., job rotation or a longer work cycle), but *they* have made the changes and reserve the

---

[2]We originally suggested that the union members should be the elected bargaining committee, but some of them refused to join the Working Committee. This resulted in the problem that some of the elected union officials feel threatened by the program as it has gained support. On the other hand, the program has allowed the development of new leaders who are interested in cooperative rather than adversary relationships.

right to modify them. The goal is to institute a *process* of democratic decision making and evaluation rather than any specific changes in tasks.

The right to experiment and the evaluation of results are determined by the Working Committee, under the guidelines established by collective bargaining. The success of the first experiments (involving sixty people in four departments over a period of nine months) led the Working Committee to decide to expand the project to include all workers in this democratic process.

Early on, too, Sidney Harman concluded that the growth of democratic process on the shop floor could not proceed without a change in the hierarchical relationship among managers at all levels, and he instituted a company-wide process aimed at this goal. Sanford Berlin, executive vice-president of Harman, took the lead in developing a new collegial managerial decision-making process at the plant, and both he and Harman maintain that if the project has done nothing else for the company, it has resulted in much more effective management.

Einar Thorsrud's role, like that of other project members (such as Robert and Margaret M. Duckles, who have lived in Bolivar for over a year) was as an educator and researcher, not a decision maker. From the start, the project staff established itself as an independent third party invited in by management and the union to serve an educational function but not to take orders or make decisions. (Whenever a project member has pushed an idea, forgetting who is supposed to make decisions, the result has been trouble.) The project's independence is buttressed by its academic affiliation (to the Harvard Seminar on Science, Technology, and Public Policy) and its success in supplementing funds from the company and union with support from other organizations.

As project director, my role was to bring together the participants at the top, and with them to clarify the principles in relationship to key decisions and potential conflicts. Often, at the start, we had to affirm the project's independent role. We were not consultants to either side, not arbitrators, and not detached observers. We did provide new channels of communication at all levels, between workers and managers, between executives and union officials, and between the project and the local community. From such communication and the experience of joint problem solving, trust developed and new roles emerged. Beyond this, it was my task to watch out for and warn against directions taken by participants and staff members that threatened the project, to call attention to them and, in Paolo Freire's term, to "problematize" them, forcing the participants to analyze alternatives and make decisions.

The project has served two educational functions. The first, through the survey and study, was to help people learn about themselves and to stimulate critical, independent thinking about alternatives. The second was to provide models for improving work that the participants could use and develop, including decision-making structures like the Working Committee, and methods of analyzing and evaluating work. One result of the first experiments was that workers asked for training in how standards are set, and in other industrial engineering subjects; they have begun to request classes in business subjects such as pricing and accounting. In 1974, a group of workers and managers traveled to Sweden and Norway, visiting Volvo's Kalmar plant and Hunsfos. The main value of the trip to many people was their conclusion that they had to develop their own model, different from any they had seen in Scandinavia.

The full development of democracy, of course, depends not just on education and the development of independent, critical thinking, but also on cooperative attitudes. Otherwise, the traditional individualistic attitude tends to limit democracy to mutual self-protectiveness and defense of shared interests. A spirit of "what's mine is mine and yours is yours" or "don't tread on me" can control exploitation, but it can't develop community. If people are to go beyond self-protectiveness to a spirit of mutuality, they need to develop a concern for others' needs. The principle of individuation expresses the goal of stimulating the fullest possible development of each individual's creative potential.

In the simplest sense, individuation means that no one should be treated as a standardized machine part, and that work should not rob people of the opportunity to perfect their skills, use their minds, and participate in decisions. It implies, furthermore, that different people have legitimate needs which must be met if they are to develop their creative potential.

For some people, this seems utopian. "Of course everyone is different," they say, "but how can any organization support a separate program for everyone?" The answer is that while individual programs may not be possible, to say "everyone is different" is to conclude that everyone is the same as far as the organization is concerned, and that there can be but one program for all. In fact, there is a middle ground. The staff began to discover this ground by identifying significant numbers of workers who share particular needs and goals.

In describing different types of workers, we focus on the human reality of the factory, which is what is missing in so many standard sociological accounts. From our point of view, the ultimate evaluation of the project must be in terms of its success in stimulating the human development of the different types of people involved. The original attitudes of the workers and managers can be seen as the baseline measure of the project, and we are continuing to study its development in a sample of individuals.

The knowledge of different types also has served practical purposes, besides helping to make sense of the various attitudes and feelings expressed in the survey. Above all, it cut off the kind of fruitless debate so common among managers where each speaks in terms of his personal needs, experiences, and prejudices about what the workers "really" want ("to get away with little or no work," "a chance to make more money," "opportunity for advancement," and so on). From the start we could show that everyone didn't have the same goals or want exactly the same kind of program. When some workers stood back from beginning experiments, our reaction was not to consider them as "negative" or "uncooperative," but to try to understand why their needs were not being met. As we shall see, understanding of character types

also provided knowledge for developing different kinds of educational programs that moved beyond improving the work environment to a concern with stimulating human development.

SIX CHARACTERS

What Are the Various Groups?

Most workers know intuitively that while all of them share
certain traits such as respect for work, some workers are more
militant unionists, others are more resigned, dutiful, and opposed
to rocking the boat, while still others are oriented toward getting
ahead in their careers, and so on. To go beyond these intuitive
judgments, we employed socio-psychoanalytic methods to discover the predominant character types in the factory.[3]

In the first stage of our study, we interviewed a sample of
sixty workers using a questionnaire with both open-ended and
multiple choice questions. Each interview lasted four hours, and
asked about work, values, life goals, physical and emotional problems. It also included asking for material that could be used for
the psychoanalytic interpretation of character, such as dreams and
family relationships, as well as questions relating to feelings about
authority. These interviews were subsequently analyzed for the
respondents' character traits, leading first to a summary of traits
shared by the majority of the factory workers (the "social char-

[3]The socio-psychoanalytic approach was based on that used by Erich Fromm and
Michael Maccoby (1970).

Our approach to character type was also determined by two criteria: (1) The essential
aspect we were studying was orientation to work, rather than to love. (2) We were looking
at character from the individual's point of view, and not as in the approach of many social
scientists, from the organizational point of view (e.g., intrinsically interested in work vs.
extrinsic interest in rewards).

In developing our methods, we tried to use words that describe what we had learned
in a way that could be understood by everyone. We tried to build on and systematically
develop the intuitions which the people themselves had about different types.

This attempt to make social psychology useful to those who are studied seems to us
a needed step in social change projects. We hope that these descriptions of types based
on people's own view of their reality and expressed in their language can show how human
needs and strivings can be taken into account concretely in the process of progressive
social change.

acter") and second, to subgroups representing different character types.

The social character of the workers includes traits common to most people in rural west Tennessee or Mississippi. The workers, like others, are emotionally controlled and self-reliant, hard working, family oriented, and cautiously conservative. Their values and attitudes are those of traditional craftsmen. They believe in fair play and the kind of democracy based on "each to his own." Although the hard-crusted, self-contained character is dominant, the majority of workers also express more receptive and sociable traits, and tend to be submissive to traditional authorities (parents, preachers, benevolent bosses, and political leaders).

This character is better adapted to a disappearing rural society than to a modern organizational life dominated by regimentation and by demands for constant performance according to machine-set standards. Not surprisingly, a majority of the workers we interviewed agreed with the statement, "It's hardly fair to bring children into the world with the way things look for the future."

Our intensive analysis of the sixty cases led to the discovery of six character subtypes among Bolivar workers. The subtypes emphasize different orientations to work. We termed them the unionists, the dutiful craftsmen, the receptive craftsmen, the sociables, the farmer-workers (or housewife-workers), and the ambitious.

In the larger survey of 300 workers, we lacked time to give four-hour interviews and to spend further hours on character interpretation. As a substitute, we constructed brief statements representing each of the character types and asked the workers to choose the statement that best described them. (People were also asked to select a second statement, if they felt that it would contribute to their self-description). Although we thus depend mainly on the workers to select their own character typing, a check between our interpretative scoring of the survey and their self-selection shows high enough agreement (in about 70 percent of cases) to consider these types a good approximation of the more time-consuming interpretative method.

These six types help to explain key differences in attitudes and reactions to work and in goals. Concepts such as work satisfaction and dissatisfaction are not absolutes; they vary with the different social and emotional attitudes of people's characters. Furthermore, both physical and emotional symptoms of dissatisfaction seem in part determined by character.

In the following discussion, each of the six types is headed by the brief description checked by workers and managers. Common traits (derived from the sixty in-depth interviews) are described, followed by an analysis based on how people of each type responded to the survey questions. In trying to put together each character type, we interpret the pattern of responses. No individual fits any of these descriptions perfectly. The descriptions are general approximations based as much as possible on the way different people see themselves. Of course, many people are a mixture of traits and might fit into more than one type. It is noteworthy that race, sex, and age make a difference only in the sociable type, which is composed of more white women than the average, and the receptive craftsman, a category that includes more men. The other types have representative percentages of white and black, male and female, younger and older workers. However, the ambitious type has traits that are generally more common to younger than older workers, and the dutiful craftsman represents attitudes more generally common to older workers.

The Unionist

"You like skilled work and you stand for what you believe. You support the union when it works for greater justice. You believe in helping those less fortunate than you."

The unionists include 29 percent of the workers. As a group, they are less educated (fewer high school graduates) and less well off financially than the others. However, they are most like the average in terms of social character, except they are more concerned with social justice and with helping others. They are hard working and reliable, and their goal is to enjoy the work they are doing and to be able to do a good job of it. In a rapidly changing society, where workers in general suffer from feelings of powerlessness, they find support and a sense of identity through their membership in the United Automobile Workers. When surveyed, their goals were those that would strengthen the union and increase fairness in rules and pay and the grievance system.

The Dutiful Craftsman

"You are skilled and competent. You do your duty and work hard. You like strong people who do their job well and don't complain."

The dutiful craftsmen include 14 percent of the workers (but over 50 percent of the foremen). On the average, they are the best off economically of any of the workers. This is partly due to the fact that their character helps them to get the best jobs. They are the most self-controlled, frugal, and self-driving, and they show a craftsmanlike concern for work. They are more likely to hoard than spend their money. They tend to be the most conservative of the workers, with a lower than average union membership, and a stronger tendency to defer to authorities they consider legitimate. They think that young people should not question traditional ways of doing things, and they are strong believers in strict discipline for children. On the other hand, they believe that everyone deserves respect, and they are angered by authorities who play favorites.

The dutiful craftsmen believe that "willpower" is crucial for getting ahead. Their self-control makes them hard workers, but it has its cost in emotional currency. Such people feel they constantly blame themselves, that they keep their feelings bottled up (most admit they are often "boiling inside"), that they plan too carefully, and that they give in too easily to authority.

Yet despite these symptoms, they are among the most satisfied in the plant. Not only do they complain less, but they also feel on top of their jobs; they report that they get along very well with their spouses at home, and they live comfortably. Their goals in life are being able to afford the things they want, doing what's expected of them (duty), and having other people think highly of them and appreciating what they do. The dutiful craftsmen are less concerned than the average with helping people. They believe in fair play, but they are contemptuous of fellow workers who sometimes limit production and do not appreciate those, like themselves, who work the hardest. They are opposed to the seniority system and favor promotion by merit. Survey findings indicated that the dutiful were one of the groups most satisfied with their work. They considered the pay and amount of work fair (but not the workers' share of company earnings, which, considering how hard they work, they did not consider fair). Although satisfied, they were critical of poor supervision and lack of fairness and respect on the part of supervisors. They also complained about a number of working conditions, including poor ventilation, too much noise, too much dust, leaks in the roof, oil on the floor, and dirty toilets. As they themselves tend to be neat and orderly, they are particularly sensitive to lack of order and cleanliness around them.

The Receptive Craftsman

"You enjoy skilled work and you also like socializing. You don't get too heated up by problems. You tend to believe in 'live and let live.' "

The 19 percent who described themselves in this way tend to worry less and enjoy life more than the average. They are the least up-tight group. They enjoy work, but they also like shooting the breeze. Their orientation to enjoyment means they are less concerned with saving money and getting ahead. They are adaptable and optimistic.

In their responses to questions having to do with feelings about work, they were much more likely to say they often look forward to work in the morning, enjoy the work, and feel on top of their jobs. That they experience pleasure in the work activity itself seems to be their most outstanding characteristic. The receptive craftsmen checked fewer emotional and physical symptoms than the average. Significantly, they suffer less self-blame and worry less than most workers. However, they admitted to being too easily influenced by others.

Workers of this type feel positively toward both fellow workers and top management, but they are critical of supervisors who play favorites and make decisions without consulting those affected. They are also positive toward the union and attend meetings more than the average, but they have avoided running for office because they do not enjoy taking on the adversary role. They like cooperation, and the work improvement program has given some of them the opportunity to exercise a new type of leadership. Survey results indicated that although they had adapted to their role in the hierarchy they preferred a more democratic workplace. They were critical of the work pace, repetitiveness, and lack of freedom in determining how one does the job. Indeed, for receptive craftsmen, the new program has been an opportunity for them to realize deeply felt goals and develop new skills of self-management.

The Sociables

"What you like most about work is being with and talking to people. You are basically sociable."

The sociables included 7 percent, mainly older white women. Many of these people seek a sense of belonging and self-worth from their jobs, or better yet, from other people at work. They are very talkative, inclined to be gossipy, and they want more contact, reassurance, and emotional give-and-take than most people. They are less concerned than other types with making factory work itself more craftsmanlike; more than most groups, their goals at work are extrinsic to the task itself.

At the start of the project, some of these women appeared the most troubled of the workers. More than others, they reported that they were extremely nervous and worried much of the time, and they blamed themselves for real or imagined things. They smoked much more than the others, and they reported more physical or psychosomatic symptoms (aches and pains) than any other group. But they did not blame their troubles mainly on the work.

If we did not understand their character, their attitude to the work would seem highly contradictory. On the one hand, they reported they were very satisfied with work and enjoyed it. On the other hand, there were many signs of deep dissatisfaction. They considered they did not have enough freedom in their jobs, and wanted a say in determining the pace of work. They complained that their equipment was outdated, that housekeeping was poor in the factory, and that the factory was not a good place to work. Most significant, they reported they were depressed and unhappy.

How can this contradiction be understood? The answer, we believe, is that the sociables are dependent and conventional, with an extremely strong need for approval. Like the dutiful craftsmen, they say their main goal in life is "to have people think highly of you and appreciate what you do." But unlike the craftsmen, they are not inner-directed, but dependent on others (especially mother figures) to approve them. Like many such people who conform in order to be praised as "good children," the result is likely to be anger and resentment at giving up one's freedom. This anger is not always conscious, since the individual tries to repress it. To experience the anger would force him or her to wake up to feelings of oppression and might lead to a confrontation with those he or she "needs" so deeply. Lacking hope and courage, such a person continues to conform and seek approval, but the cost is increasing depression, bitterness, or even hardening of the heart. Instead of facing the causes of misery, sociables try to alleviate the symptoms—the "bad thoughts," headaches, insomnia, and nervousness.

In the interviews, some of these workers expressed their wish for totally different kinds of work. Many enjoy crafts work, gardening, canning, etc. Some would enjoy work that would be more humanly satisfying, such as nursing. At the start of experiments, some of these women stood back from attempts to restructure the work. They resisted taking on any more responsibility or demand. What has made the difference for them is the chance to gain free time to use either at home or for classes in nurse's aid training, sewing, and typing. Some would like classes in painting and country music. A result of this training may be that these women leave the factory for other work. But in the meantime, they are happier, more effective, and cooperative in their work than before. Above all, they are more hopeful that their talents and true interests can be developed.

The Farmer-Workers

"You work here to make a living, but you would rather be back on the farm or at home. You do your duty at work, but you are more interested in what goes on at home than what goes on at the factory."

The 18 percent who characterized themselves this way included men and women who work in the factory only because they can no longer support themselves by farming. One-third still work part-time on farms. The others have left farms recently, and almost all would prefer working on a farm to industry, if the income were the same.

The farmer-workers are the group most dissatisfied with factory work. In a sense the farmer-worker is an independent and democratic character who has to fit into a mechanistic and hierarchical structure where he or she is not respected as an equal. Supervisors sometimes consider such people disgruntled and lazy, because they resist adaptation to a system they detest. But once they got a chance to participate in democratic work groups, their whole attitude has changed.

When we first interviewed the farmer-workers, they complained more than others about being worn out at the end of the day and having trouble getting up in the morning. Many worked hard at two jobs, and more than the others they felt beaten down on the job. Since they dislike the work and prefer to be home, they are particularly opposed to forced overtime. Yet they have little time for leisure, and watch TV less than others. (They also dislike the values expressed on TV.) They are confused by rapid social change going on around them, fearful of the future, and uncertain of their own goals, other than the fact that they seek a satisfying home life and the chance to feel needed and useful. They complain that they have little say either in government or at work. Feeling that no one listens to them, they are silent and resentful.

In other words, the farmer-workers feel alienated from society and work. They have been made powerless and have been denied the chance to make a living at work that allows them self-respect. But, they are less alienated from themselves than many others who are resigned to a constricting work role and tell interviewers they are satisfied with work and society. They are cooperative and friendly with their co-workers. They all, including the whites, believe that special efforts should be made to promote blacks.

The farmer-workers' main complaints about the factory work were: The work does not allow them autonomy. They do not have enough time to do a good job, and they are not required to think. The work is too repetitious and too fast-paced. Finally, the farmer-workers complained that there is too much work required and not enough time to talk with others. After all, they say, they are human beings and not machines. The farmer-workers also were the group most dissatisfied with the union, because the union has not done enough to make work more interesting.

The Ambitious

"You are interested in challenging work and you are ambitious. You believe that those who are smarter and have more ability should move ahead rapidly."

This 13 percent of the factory population represents the character type most different from the social character described above. But despite their small numbers, the ambitious play a key role in the factory. Half the foremen are in this group, and most of the top management share many traits with the ambitious hourly workers. Since those with ambitious characters have the most schooling of any group, they may represent the social character of the future. They are the most "modern" group in aspirations and style, more like urban workers than any of the other types.

The hourly workers who are ambitious craftsmen are among the most dissatisfied in the factory, but the nature of their dissatisfaction is different from that of the more democratic farmer-workers. The ambitious are oriented to hierarchical organizations and they want their work to be a means for their career advancement. For them equity has a low priority and social justice is equated with meritocracy.

The ambitious workers are, on the whole, an efficient and competent group of people. They are more articulate and less reserved than the average. Paradoxically, they communicate more easily, but they are angrier and less friendly than most workers. Many express symptoms of being cut off from themselves just as they are detached from the traditional society. The one strong feeling they most reported was their anger. More than other groups, they often felt like hitting people and smashing things and they admitted getting very angry about little things. This anger and resentment is fed by frustration at work.

The ambitious group sets itself the goal of getting ahead, but their schooling and work experience have alienated them from their own creative interests. They are the one group with a high percentage of answering "no" to the question, "If you were to get enough money without having to work, to live as comfortably as you'd like for the rest of your life, would you continue to work anyway?" They also complained of a number of symptoms that they blamed on the work. They reported that they suffered from headaches and colds, that they had trouble breathing, and that they became very tired in a short time.

To compensate for the drudgery of work, many find their main satisfaction in consumer activities and exciting competition. They spend more time watching TV and attending spectator sports than the average, and they are also more likely to play team sports such as football and basketball. It is not surprising that the ambitious group is least likely to attend church, since the church is so much a part of the traditional society and expresses values they have begun to reject. Some belong to secular clubs like the Masons or the Elks, or, in the case of the blacks, to groups like the NAACP.

Politically, the ambitious presented a complex pattern in terms of attitudes and issues. They supported welfare measures such as early retirement and a guaranteed income. More exposed to the media than the others, they were the first to be aware of the newer issues, such as air and water pollution, Watergate, and governmental corruption. Like everyone else in the plant, they were concerned with rising prices and too-low wages. Yet, their concern with these issues did not imply across-the-board liberalism. The whites in this group were Wallace supporters and male chauvinists (they would prefer a black male to a white female supervisor). The group in general supported fighting Communism, and favored the death penalty.

In the factory, the ambitious are more likely to be on the side of management than the side of the union (though those in the union tend to gain official posts). They have little trust or confidence in fellow workers, and tend to be competitive with them, and don't look forward to being with them. On the other hand, this group is more positive than the average toward their supervisors and to top management. Although critical of the work, they do not knock the company; they want to get ahead.

What was the nature of their dissatisfaction with work? They complained first of all that the work did not give them the opportunity to develop their special abilities, nor were they given a chance to do the things they do best. They felt that given the chance for career development, they would work harder. They did not consider job assignments fair, and they favored getting rid of the seniority system, substituting tests. They favored incentive plans. Second, they complained that the work was uninteresting and monotonous. There was not enough learning or variety. Third, the work allowed no autonomy. They wanted more say in deciding "how the job will actually be carried out, the methods used," and in how work tasks should be divided up. They were least critical about health and safety conditions, housekeeping, and equipment in the factory.

A new democratic system without the principle of individuation could easily become dominated by ambitious workers. More articulate and self-confident than the others, and more oriented to management, they would sway the program in a direction that supported increased productivity and gain for those who work better. Many "quality of work" programs in other factories seek to hire such individuals and provide them with the kind of system they find most satisfying.

But most of us are a mixture of sometimes conflicting attitudes. Which attitudes are dominant depends on how we lead our lives. Probably some Bolivar managers figured that if cooperation was the way to please Sidney Harman, then ambition required a democratic attitude. However, others welcomed the chance to be less ambitious and more helpful to other people. One manager who had left the company a few years earlier returned because the program allowed him to act in a way that made him happy with himself. The new knowledge about different kinds of people and their needs helped these managers to greater compassion in relation to those they had previously characterized as lazy or hostile.

The Bolivar project has offered both workers and managers an alternative, where they can become less alienated from themselves and from others. The newest development in the program has been the establishment of a school at the factory. This grew out of experimental groups where workers asked for courses in subjects ranging from industrial engineering to first aid and typing. These courses were originally held at the factory during time gained by workers due to experimental improvements in work methods. The courses given now are also those requested by workers and range from welding, sewing, and crafts to courses on black studies and how the business is run. In some cases, workers and managers are the teachers. The school has the cooperation of the Hardeman County vocational education program, which pays some of the teachers. A new, full-time school coordinator has been approved by the Education Committee, which is composed of representatives of management, the union, and the project staff.

Ambitious workers were among the first volunteers in an experiment in which a group agreed to pool their work and were able to leave the factory if they finished early. One woman in the group, a farmer-worker, was slower than the others and, sensing their annoyance that they had to help her out in order to finish, she asked to withdraw from the experiment. The others met and decided to ask her to stay. In acting out of character, they were demonstrating that character can change for the better, if a democratic workplace supports cooperation and stimulates the development of the individual's talents, compassion, and capacity for reasoning.

REFERENCE

Fromm, E., & Maccoby, M. (1970), *Social Character in a Mexican Village*. Englewood Cliffs, N.J.: Prentice-Hall.

In "The Glacier Project," Jaques describes the changes which took place in the relationships between management and workers in one department of an engineering factory in England. Using the Kleinian perspective (see also Chapters 10 and 19), the author shows how defenses against paranoid and depressive anxiety operate at the phantasy social level when changes are made. He advances the view that one of the primary forces pulling individuals into institutionalized human association is that of defense against paranoid and depressive anxiety, and conversely, that all institutions are unconsciously used by their members as mechanisms against these forms of anxiety.

22

The Glacier Project

ELLIOTT JAQUES

The case to be presented is one part of a larger study carried out in a light engineering factory, the Glacier Metal Company, between June, 1948, and the present time. The relationship with the firm is a therapeutic one; work is done only on request from groups or individuals within the firm, for assistance in working through intragroup stresses, or in dealing with organizational problems. The relationship between the social consultant (or therapist) and the people with whom he works is a confidential one; and the only reports published are those which have been worked through with the people concerned and agreed by them for publication. Within these terms of reference, I have published a detailed report on the first three years of the project (1951).

The illustration I shall use is taken from work done with one

This chapter originally appeared in longer form as "Social Systems as Defence against Persecutory and Depressive Anxiety" in *New Directions in Psychoanalysis*. London: Tavistock, 1955. By permission of the Melanie Klein Trust.

department in the factory (1950, 1951). The department employs roughly sixty people. It was organized with a departmental manager as head. Under him was a superintendent, who was in turn responsible for four foremen, each of whom had a working group of ten to sixteen operatives. The operatives had elected five representatives, two of whom were shop stewards, to negotiate with the departmental manager on matters affecting the department. One such matter had to do with a change in methods of wages payment. The shop had been on piece rates (i.e., the operatives were paid a basic wage, plus a bonus dependent on their output). This method of payment had, for a number of years, been felt to be unsatisfactory. From the workers' point of view it meant uncertainty about the amount of their weekly wage, and for the management it meant complicated rate-fixing, and administrative arrangements. For all concerned, the not infrequent wrangling about rates that took place was felt to be unnecessarily disturbing. The possibility of changing over to a flat rate method of payment had been discussed for over a year before the project began. In spite of the fact that the change was commonly desired they had not been able to come to a decision.

A Period of Negotiation

Work with the department began in January, 1949, by attendance at discussions of a subcommittee composed of the departmental manager, the superintendent, and three workers' representatives. The general tone of the discussions was friendly. The committee members laid stress upon the fact that good relationships existed in the department and that they all wanted to strive for further improvement. From time to time, however, there was sharp disagreement over specific points, and these disagreements led the workers' representatives to state that there were many matters on which they felt they could not trust the management. This statement of suspicion was answered by the management members, who emphasized that they for their part had great trust in the workers' sense of responsibility.

The workers' suspicion of management also revealed itself in discussions held at shop-floor level between the elected representatives and their worker constituents. The purpose of these discussions was to elicit in a detailed and concrete manner the views of the workers about the proposed changeover, but they had some doubt as to whether they could trust the management to implement and to administer the changeover in a fair manner. What guarantees did they have, they asked, that management had nothing up its sleeve? At the same time, the workers showed an ambivalent attitude towards their own representatives. They urged and trusted them to carry on negotiations with management, but at the same time suspected that the representatives were management "stooges" and did not take the workers' views sufficiently into account. This negative attitude towards their representatives came out more clearly in interviews with the workers alone, in which opinions were expressed that although the elected representatives were known as militant trade unionists, nevertheless they were seen as liable to be outwitted by the management and as not carrying their representative role as effectively as they might.

The day-to-day working relationships between supervisors and workers were quite different from what would be expected as the consequence of these views. Work in the shop was carried out with good morale, and the supervisors were felt to do their best for the workers. A high proportion of the shop had been employed in the company for five years or more, and genuinely good personal relationships had been established.

The discussions in the committee composed of the managers and elected representatives went on for seven months, between January and July, 1949. They had a great deal of difficulty in working towards a decision, becoming embroiled in arguments that were sometimes quite heated and had no obvious cause—other than the workers' suspicion of the management, counterbalanced by the management's idealization of the workers. Much of the suspicion and idealization, however, was autistic, in the sense that although consciously experienced, it was not expressed openly as between managers and workers. These attitudes came out much more sharply when the elected representatives and the managers were meeting separately. The workers expressed deep suspicion and mistrust, while the managers expressed some of their anxieties about how responsible the workers could be—anxieties which existed alongside their strong sense of the workers' responsibility and of their faith in them.

ANALYSIS OF THE NEGOTIATION PHASE

I now wish to apply certain of our theoretical formulations to the above data. This is in no sense intended to be a complete analysis of the material. Many important factors, such as changes in the executive organization of the shop, personal attitudes, changes in personnel, and variations in the economic and production situation all played a part in determining the changes which occurred. I do wish, however, to demonstrate how, if we assume the operation of defenses against paranoid and depressive anxiety at the phantasy social level, we may be able to explain some of the very great difficulties encountered by the members of the department.[1] And I would emphasize here that these difficulties were encountered in spite of the high morale implied in the willingness of those concerned to face, and to work through in a serious manner, the group stresses they experienced in trying to arrive at a commonly desired goal.

The degree of inhibition of the autistic suspicion and idealization becomes understandable, I think, if we make the following assumptions about unconscious attitudes at the phantasy level. The workers in the shop had split the managers into good and bad—the good managers being the ones with whom they worked, and the bad being the same managers but in the negotiation situation. They had unconsciously projected their hostile destructive impulses into their elected representatives so that the rep-

---

[1]Editor's note: See Chapter 10, footnote 1, for an explanation of the paranoid and the depressive position. Note, too, that Jaques follows the convention of using "phantasy" to refer to unconscious fantasies.

resentatives could deflect, or redirect, these impulses against the bad "management" with whom negotiations were carried on, while the good objects and impulses could be put into individual real managers in the day-to-day work situation. This splitting of the management into good and bad, and the projective identification with the elected representatives against the bad management served two purposes.[2] At the reality level it allowed the good relations necessary to the work task of the department to be maintained; at the phantasy level it provided a system of social relationships reinforcing individual defenses against paranoid and depressive anxiety.

Putting their good impulses into managers in the work situation allowed the workers to reintroject the good relations with management, and hence to preserve an undamaged good object and alleviate depressive anxiety. This depressive anxiety was further avoided by reversion to the paranoid position in the negotiating situation.[3] During the negotiations paranoid anxiety was partially avoided by the workers by putting their bad impulses into their elected representatives. The representatives, while consciously the negotiating representatives of the workers, became unconsciously the representatives of their bad impulses. These split-off bad impulses were partially dealt with and avoided because they were directed against the bad objects put into management in the negotiation situation by the workers and their representatives.

Another mechanism for dealing with the workers' own projected bad objects and impulses was to attack their representatives, with an accompanying despair that not much good would come of the negotiations. These feelings tended to be expressed privately by individuals. The workers who felt like this had introjected their representatives as bad objects and maintained them as a segregated part of the ego. Intrapsychic projection and

[2]Editor's note: See Chapter 10, footnote 2, for an explanation of projective and introjective identification.

[3]M. Klein (1948) has described how paranoid fears and suspicions are often used as a defense against the depressive position.

aggression against these internal bad objects were supported by introjective identification with other workers, who held that the representatives were not doing their job properly. That is to say, other members of the department were introjected to reinforce the intrapsychic projection, and as protection against the internal bad representatives attacking back. In addition to defense against internal persecution, the introjection of the other workers provided social sanction for considering the internalized representatives as bad, offsetting the harshness of superego recrimination for attacking objects containing a good as well as a persecuting component.

From the point of view of the elected representatives, anxiety about bad impulses was diminished by unconsciously accepting the bad impulses and objects of all the workers they represented. They could feel that their own hostile and aggressive impulses did not belong to them but belonged to the people on whose behalf they were acting. They were thus able to derive external social sanction for their aggression and hostile suspicion. But the mechanism did not operate with complete success, for there still remained their own unconscious suspicion and hostility to be dealt with, and the reality of what they considered to be the good external management. Hence, there was some anxiety and guilt about damaging the good managers. The primary defense mechanism against the onset of depressive anxiety was that of retreat to the paranoid position. This came out as a rigid clinging to attitudes of suspicion and hostility even in circumstances where they consciously felt that some of this suspicion was not justified by the situation they were actually experiencing.

From the management side, the paranoid attitude of the elected representatives was countered by the reiteration of the view that the workers could be trusted to do their part. This positive attitude unconsciously contained both idealization of the workers and placation of the hostile representatives. The idealization can be understood as an unconscious mechanism for diminishing guilt, stimulated by fears of injuring or destroying workers in the day-to-day work situation through the exercise of managerial authority—an authority which there is good reason to believe is, at least to some extent, felt unconsciously to be uncontrolled and omnipotent. To the extent that managers unconsciously felt their authority to be bad, they feared retaliation by the operatives. This in turn led to a reinforcement of the idealization of the elected worker representatives as a defense against paranoid anxiety; that is to say, as a means of placating the hostility of the workers, and hence of placating internal persecutors. These idealizing and placatory mechanisms were employed in the meetings with the elected representatives, so that reality mechanisms could operate in the relationships with workers in the work situation, less encumbered with the content of uncontrolled phantasy.

It can thus be seen that the unconscious use of paranoid attitudes by the workers and idealizing and placatory attitudes by the management were complementary, and reinforced each other. A circular process was set in motion. The more the workers' representatives attacked the managers, the more the managers idealized them in order to placate them. The greater the concessions given by management to the workers, the greater was the guilt and fear of depressive anxiety in the workers, and hence the greater the retreat to paranoid attitudes as a means of avoiding depressive anxiety.

DESCRIPTION AND ANALYSIS OF THE POST-NEGOTIATION PHASE

In June, six months after the discussions began, these attitudes, rather than the wages problem, were for a time taken as the main focus of consideration. A partial resolution occurred, and the workers decided, after a ballot in the whole department, to try out a flat-rate method of payment. The condition for the change-over, however, was the setting up of a council, composed of managers and elected worker representatives, which would have the authority to determine departmental policy—a procedure for which the principles had already been established in the company. The prime principle was that of unanimous agreement on all decisions, and the agreement to work through all obstacles to unanimous decision by discovering sources of disagreement so that they could be resolved.

It appeared as though the open discussion of autistic attitudes facilitated a restructuring of the phantasy social relations in the department—a restructuring which brought with it a greater degree of conscious or ego control over their relationships. The fact, however, that there was only a partial restructuring of social relations at the phantasy level showed itself in the subsequent history of the shop council. For, following the changeover to a flat-rate method of payment, the council came up against the major question of reassessing the times in which given jobs ought to be done.

Under piece rates, such assessment of times was necessary, both for calculation of the bonus to operatives and for giving estimated prices to customers. On flat rates, it was required only for estimating to customers; but the times thus set inevitably constituted targets for the workers. Under piece rates, if a worker did not achieve the target, it meant that he lost his bonus; in other words, he himself paid for any drop in effort. Under flat rates, however, a drop below the target meant that the worker was getting paid for work that he was not doing. A detailed exploration of workers' attitudes showed that the changeover from piece rates to flat rates had in no way altered their personal targets and personal rate of work (Jaques, 1951). They felt guilty whenever they fell below their estimated targets, because they were no longer paying for the difference. In order to avoid this guilt, the workers applied strong pressure to keep the estimated times on jobs as high as possible, as well as pressure to get the so-called tight times (times on jobs that were difficult to achieve), reassessed. There were strong resistances to any changes in job assessment methods which the workers suspected might set difficult targets for them.

On the management side, the changeover to flat rates inevitably stirred whatever unconscious anxieties they might have about authority. For under piece rates, the bonus payment itself acted as an impersonal and independent disciplinarian, ensuring that workers put in the necessary effort. Under flat rates it was up to managers to see that a reasonable rate of work was carried on. This forced upon them more direct responsibility for the supervision of their subordinates, and brought them more directly into contact with the authority they held.

The newly constituted council, with its managers and elected representatives, had great difficulty in coping with the more manifest depressive anxiety both in the managers and in the workers. This showed in managers' views that the council might possibly turn out to be a bad thing because it slowed down administrative developments in the department. Similar opinions that the council would not work and might not prove worthwhile played some part in the decision of five out of six of the elected worker representatives not to stand for reelection in the shop elections which occurred sixteen months after the setting up of the council. These five were replaced by five newly elected representatives, who in turn brought with them a considerable amount of suspicion. That is, there was again a retreat to the paranoid position while the managers' depressive anxiety continued to show to some extent in the form of depressive feelings that the council would not work. It has only been slowly, over a period of two years, that the council has been able to operate in the new situation as a constitutional mechanism for getting agreement on policy and at the same time intuitively to be used for the containment of the phantasy social relationships. An exploration of the re-rating problem has been agreed upon and is being carried on with the assistance of an outside industrial consultant.

This case study, then, illustrates the development of an explicit social institution, that of meetings between management and elected worker representatives, which allowed for the establishment of unconscious mechanisms at the phantasy level for dealing with paranoid and depressive anxieties. The main mechanisms were those of management idealizing the hostile workers, and the workers maintaining an attitude of suspicion towards the idealizing management. To the extent that splitting and projective identification operated successfully, these unconscious mechanisms helped individuals to deal with anxiety, by getting their anxieties into the phantasy social relations structured in the management-elected-representative group. In this way the anxieties were eliminated from the day-to-day work situation, and allowed for the efficient operation of the sophisticated work task and the achievement of good working relationships.

However, it will be noted that the elected representative-management group was also charged with a sophisticated work task—that of negotiating new methods of wages payment. They found it difficult to get on with the sophisticated task itself. In terms of the theory here propounded, these difficulties have been explained as arising from the manner in which the predominant unconscious phantasy relations in the negotiating group ran counter to the requirements of the sophisticated task. In other words, an essentially constitutional procedure, that of elected worker representatives meeting with an executive body, was difficult to operate because it was being used in an unrecognized fashion at the phantasy level to help deal with the depressive and paranoid anxieties of the members of the department as a whole.

SOME OBSERVATIONS ON SOCIAL CHANGE

In the above case study, it might be said that social change was sought when the structure and culture no longer met the requirements of the individual members of the department, and in particular of the managers and the elected worker representatives. Manifest changes were brought about, and in turn appeared to lead to a considerable restructuring of the phantasy social form and content of the institution. Change having taken place, however, the individual members found themselves in the grip of new relationships, to which they had to conform because they were self-made. But they had brought about more than they had bargained for, in the sense that the new relationships under flat rates and the policy-making council had to be experienced before their implications could be fully appreciated.

The effects of the change on individuals were different according to the roles they occupied. The elected representatives were able to change roles by the simple expedient of not standing for reelection. And this expedient, it will be noted, was resorted to by five of the six representatives. The managers, however, were in a very different position. They could not relinquish or change their roles without in a major sense changing their positions, and possibly status, in the organization as a whole. They had, therefore, individually to bear considerable personal stress in adjusting themselves to the new situation.

It is unlikely that members of an institution can ever bring about social changes that suit perfectly the needs of each individual. Once change is undertaken, it is more than likely that individuals will have to adjust and change personally in order to catch up with the changes they have produced. And until some readjustment is made at the phantasy level, the individual's social defenses against psychotic anxiety are likely to be weakened. It may well be because of the effects on the unconscious defense systems of individuals against psychotic anxiety, that social change is resisted—and in particular, imposed social change. For it is one thing to readjust to changes that the individual has himself helped to bring about; it is quite another to be required to adjust one's internal defense systems in order to conform to changes brought about by some outside agency.

Summary and Conclusions

Freud has argued that two main processes operate in the formation of what he calls artificial groups, like the army and the church; one is identification by introjection, and the other is replacement of the ego ideal by an object. I have suggested that this latter process implicitly contains the concept, formulated by Melanie Klein, of identification by projection. Further, Melanie Klein states explicitly that in the interaction between introjective and projective identification lies the basis of the infant's earliest relations with its objects. The character of these early relations is determined by the way in which the infant attempts to deal with its paranoid and depressive anxieties, and by the intensity of these anxieties.

Taking these conceptions of Freud and Melanie Klein, the view has here been advanced that one of the primary dynamic forces pulling individuals into institutionalized human association is that of defense against paranoid and depressive anxiety; and, conversely, that all institutions are unconsciously used by their members as mechanisms of defense against these psychotic anxieties. Individuals may put their internal conflicts into persons in the external world, unconsciously follow the course of the conflict by means of projective identification, and re-internalize the course and outcome of the externally perceived conflict by means of introjective identification. Societies provide institutionalized roles whose occupants are sanctioned, or required to take into themselves the projected objects or impulses of other members. The occupants of such roles may absorb the objects and impulses—take them into themselves and become either the good or bad object with corresponding impulses; or, they may deflect the objects and impulses—put them into an externally perceived ally, or enemy, who is then loved, or attacked. The gain for the individual in projecting objects and impulses and introjecting their careers in the external world, lies in the unconscious co-operation with other members of the institution or group who are using similar projection mechanisms. Introjective identification then allows more than the return of the projected objects and impulses. The other members are also taken inside, and legitimize and reinforce attacks upon internal persecutors, or support manic idealization of loved objects, thereby reinforcing the denial of destructive impulses against them.

The unconscious cooperation at the phantasy level among members of an institution is structured in terms of what is here called the phantasy social form and content of institutions. The form and content of institutions may thus be considered from two distinct levels: that of the manifest and consciously agreed upon form and content (including structure and function, which, al-

though possibly unrecognized, are nevertheless in the preconscious of members of the institution, and hence are relatively
accessible to identification by means of conscious study); and that
of the phantasy form and content, which are unconsciously
avoided and denied, and, because they are totally unconscious,
remain unidentified by members of the institution.

A case study is presented to illustrate how, within one department in a factory, a sub-institution (a committee of managers
and elected workers' representatives), was used at the phantasy
level for segregating hostile relations from good relations, which
were maintained in the day-to-day production work of the department. When, however, the committee was charged with a
serious and conscious negotiating task, its members encountered
great difficulties because of the socially sanctioned phantasy content of their relationships with each other.

Some observations are made on the dynamics of social change.
Change occurs where the phantasy social relations with an institution no longer serve to reinforce individual defenses against
psychotic anxiety. The institution may be restructured at the
manifest and phantasy level; or the manifest structure may be
maintained, but the phantasy structure modified. Individuals may
change roles or leave the institution altogether. Or, apparent
change at the manifest level may often conceal the fact that no
real change has taken place, the phantasy social form and content
of the institution being left untouched. Imposed social change
which does not take into account the use of institutions by individuals to cope with unconscious psychotic anxieties, is likely to
be resisted.

Finally, if the mechanisms herein described have any validity,
then at least two consequences may follow: First, observation of
social processes may provide one means of studying, as through
a magnifying glass, the operation of paranoid and depressive anxieties and the defenses built up against them. Unlike the psychoanalytic situation, such observations can be made by more
than one person at the same time. And second, it may become
more clear why social change is so difficult to achieve, and why

many social problems are so intractable. For from the point of view here elaborated, changes in social relationships and procedures call for a restructuring of relationships at the phantasy level, with a consequent demand upon individuals to accept and tolerate changes in their existing pattern of defenses against psychotic anxiety. Effective social change is likely to require analysis of the common anxieties and unconscious collusions underlying the social defenses determining phantasy social relationships.

REFERENCES

Jaques, E. (1950), Collaborative Group Methods in a Wage Negotiation Situation. *Human Relations*, 3:223-229.
———— (1951), *The Changing Culture of a Factory*. London: Tavistock.
Klein, M. (1948), *Contributions to Psycho-Analysis*. London: Hogarth Press.

Name Index

481

Subject Index